Behind the Development Banks

Behind the Development Banks

Washington Politics, World Poverty, and the Wealth of Nations

SARAH BABB

THE UNIVERSITY OF CHICAGO PRESS   CHICAGO AND LONDON

SARAH BABB is associate professor of sociology at Boston College. She is the author of *Managing Mexico: Economists from Nationalism to Neoliberalism* and the coauthor, with Bruce Carruthers, of *Economy/Society: Markets, Meanings, and Social Structure.*

The University of Chicago Press, Chicago 60637
The University of Chicago Press, Ltd., London
© 2009 by The University of Chicago
All rights reserved. Published 2009
Printed in the United States of America
18 17 16 15 14 13 12 11 10 09   1 2 3 4 5

ISBN-13: 978-0-226-03364-8 (cloth)
ISBN-13: 978-0-226-03365-5 (paper)
ISBN-10: 0-226-03364-3 (cloth)
ISBN-10: 0-226-03365-1 (paper)

Library of Congress Cataloging-in-Publication Data
Babb, Sarah L.
    Beyond the development banks : Washington politics, world poverty, and the wealth of nations / Sarah Babb.
        p.   cm.
    Includes bibliographical references and index.
    ISBN-13: 978-0-226-03364-8 (hardcover : alk. paper)
    ISBN-13: 978-0-226-03365-5 (pbk. : alk. paper)
    ISBN-10: 0-226-03364-3 (hardcover : alk. paper)
    ISBN-10: 0-226-03365-1 (pbk. : alk. paper) 1. Development banks—Government policy—United States   2. Development economics—Government policy—United States.   I. Title.
HG1975.B33   2009
332.1'53—dc22

                                                    2008040620

♾ The paper used in this publication meets the minimum requirements of the American National Standard for Information Sciences—Permanence of Paper for Printed Library Materials, ANSI Z39.48-1992.

FOR EDDY AND ELENA

Contents

Preface

About two decades ago, a participant at a conference on the Latin American debt crisis observed that economists and policymakers in and around Washington, DC, had converged on a common set of prescriptions for developing countries. "The economic policies that Washington urges on the rest of the world," he observed, "may be summarized as prudent macroeconomic policies, outward orientation, and free-market capitalism."[1]

These were not mere scholarly abstractions: they were the basis of the policies of international financial institutions (IFIs) such as the World Bank and the International Monetary Fund (IMF) that, in turn, influenced the economic policies of developing-country governments around the world. Yet, only a decade later, the prescriptions emanating from Washington had already evolved considerably. The new conventional wisdom was that developing countries needed to supplement open markets with strong institutions, such as protections for the poor and banking regulations. The emergence of this new "post-Washington Consensus," or "augmented Washington Consensus" led another observer to remark wryly that the ideas guiding economic policy reforms had become "as faddish as skirt lengths and tie widths."[2]

Where did the Washington Consensus come from, and why did it change? It was my interest in answering these questions that led me to this project. Many observers attributed these changes to shifts in the "marketplace for development ideas," focusing on the accumulation of evidence and changing intellectual currents among economists. However, I strongly suspected that this "idealist" story was incomplete. After all, the Consensus was not just a description of the world; it was a blueprint for the policies of IFIs. And, although IFIs have hundreds of economists on their staffs and respond to trends within the academy, their activities also respond to the policy initiatives of the powerful governments that own them. The most influential government shaping the policies of IFIs is, as the term *Washington Consensus* implies, that of the United States. Yet almost nothing had been written on how Washington policies and politics shaped the trajectory of the Washington Consensus.

One obvious reason for the lack of literature on the role of Washington in the Washington Consensus is, undoubtedly, the paucity of reliable sources of information. Although the World Bank and the IMF have made many official documents available to the public in recent years, those pertaining to Executive Board meetings (i.e., meetings among the representatives of member governments) are still mostly classified. I had a relatively favorable experience with getting some older Executive Board documents through the IMF archive. At the World Bank, however, a request I made in 2006 to look at two-decade-old Executive Board archival documents languished in process for more than a year before being rejected without explanation. Equally frustrating, from a researcher's point of view, is the fact that much of what goes on between the IFIs and their most important shareholders does not occur in formal, documented Executive Board meetings. For example, it is commonly observed that loans opposed by powerful governments, such as the United States, are usually kept from coming to a vote through quiet, behind-the-scenes discussions with management. Large-scale policy disagreements among shareholders are hammered out in meetings for which no transcripts are available, such as the periodic meetings among the Group of Eight (G8) finance ministers or the International Development Association (IDA) deputies. We the public may be able to see the final output, in such forms as the annual "G8 communiqué." But, as with sausage, we do not get to observe the original positions, debates, and compromises that went into it. In short, donor politics affect the policies of IFIs inside a "black box" to which outside observers lack the key.

I was, therefore, extremely fortunate to have the opportunity to spend nine months as a research fellow at the Woodrow Wilson International Center for Scholars in Washington, DC. This gave me time to poke around Washington-area archives and government documents, to talk to people who knew about my object of study firsthand, and to generally explore the world in which Washington politics and development policy collide.

What I soon discovered was that U.S. policy toward the World Bank and the regional development banks was forged through a very interesting procedure—a procedure that shed light into the "black box" of donor politics. Unlike the IMF, which is largely self-financing, the multilateral development banks (MDBs) are highly dependent on shareholder contributions, particularly to finance the operations of their "soft loan windows," which provide grants and very low-interest loans to very poor countries. This means that shareholder governments are frequently called on to provide money for the banks—and are frequently in a position to make policy demands on the banks' management. Consequently, every year, the U.S. Treasury has to explain U.S. policy toward the MDBs to Congress and to convince Congress to provide funding for ongoing U.S. participation.

In these annual hearings before congressional subcommittees, members of Congress ask questions, criticize, and demand further information; outside groups, such as nongovernmental organizations (NGOs), also testify on past and potential policies. These hearings provide a rich source of policy discourse and rationalizations for why the United States should support the MDBs. Moreover, because Congress demands accountability from the Treasury, and because members of Congress have the means to investigate the validity of the Treasury's claims, these hearings in aggregate provide us with information about the origins, nature, and consequences of U.S. policies. Most important, unlike internal MDB documents or the proceedings of G8 meetings, these congressional hearings are available to the public.

A Note on Research Methods

To construct the story told in this book, I engaged in a kind of scavenger historical sociology, bringing in all the primary and secondary sources I could find—including MDB publications and databases, official histories, media accounts, and personal interviews. At the core of my story, however, are the annual congressional subcommittee hearings in which the Treasury Department and Congress discuss U.S. policy toward the MDBs.

The U.S. Treasury Department is the agency officially in charge of the administration's policy toward the banks. However, all U.S. foreign aid legislation must also pass through Congress, and, every year, the Treasury must convince the relevant congressional subcommittees to authorize and appropriate funds. These subcommittees "mark up" the Treasury's "international programs" legislation, vote on it, and send it to the floor, where it is amended and voted on by the full House or Senate. Then a joint House-Senate committee is created to negotiate the differences so that a final bill can be voted on once again by both chambers and signed into law by the president.[3]

To convince the congressional subcommittees to authorize and appropriate the money, the Treasury testifies about how the banks serve the American national interest and provides information on the banks' recent activities and the administration's recent reform initiatives. Prior to the 1970s, the informational content of these Treasury testimonies was quite thin. After 1970, however, Congress began to demand, with escalating stridency, to have a larger voice in U.S. MDB policy and to know more about what both the banks and the administration were doing. This meant that records from the congressional subcommittee hearings provided an increasingly detailed public documentation of U.S. policies and their evolution over time.

I have drawn on these documents to construct a story about the origins, nature, and consequences of U.S. policy toward the MDBs during the past three decades. However, while these documents are very effective indicators of some things, they are less effective indicators of others. Below, I elaborate on the strengths and liabilities of using these hearings as a source of factual information and outline how I have attempted to compensate for problems of missing or potentially unreliable information.

U.S. Policy Discourses

The congressional hearings are direct indicators of the policy discourses used by Congress and the U.S. executive. I trace the evolution of these policy discourses over time, paying particular attention to Treasury "framing" of U.S. interests in the banks. Originally developed by Irving Goffman, the concept of frames is used by political sociologists to refer to interpretive devices that "function to organize experience and guide action," thus "rendering events or occurrences meaningful."[4]

Frames do not necessarily tell us anything about the deeply held beliefs of the framers. They are used by political actors to mobilize political support—in the case at hand, by administration representatives who want to mobilize congressional support for MDB financing. Thus, in some cases, the words of a framer may constitute a cynical marketing ploy. Yet, in the political arena, frames cannot be replaced as easily as they can in advertising campaigns. Political actors are constrained in the frames that they can apply to a particular issue by real-world evidence, the beliefs and political biases of their audience, and their own ideology and political platform. When the Nixon administration attempted to sell the MDBs to Congress, it had to do so in a way that was commensurate with its economic and foreign policy agenda; the result was a different frame from that developed by the Reagan or the Clinton administrations. Frames are derived from, and, hence, tell us something about, the political positions of the actors who produce them as well as the political context in which they are produced.

U.S. Reform Initiatives and Their Success

The Treasury regularly tells the congressional subcommittees about the policies it plans to promote within the banks, particularly through multilateral shareholder negotiations over replenishing or increasing the banks' resources (for a more detailed explanation, see chapter 1). The Treasury also discusses its success in promoting past initiatives.

As a record of evolving administration policies and the relative success of administration initiatives in affecting the banks' activities, the annual hearings are relatively reliable. Official statements of the Treasury to Congress are a matter of public record; inaccuracies, if discovered, can be potentially embarrassing. Members of Congress have a strong interest in getting accurate information from the Treasury and have a number of ways to investigate the validity of statements that they believe to be false or misleading, including the research of their own staff, the Congressional Research Service, and the Government Accountability Office. Although the Treasury may fudge or dissemble in the interest of getting its MDB budget passed in any given year, these inaccuracies are likely to be revealed in subsequent years (a good example of this is the so-called 10 percent limit on structural adjustment lending discussed in chapter 4). Therefore, whereas testimony may be factually questionable in one particular year, overall it provides a reasonably accurate record.

These hearings also provide relatively reliable information about the policies the congressional subcommittees are promoting in the banks. Because the views of subcommittee members do not necessarily reflect those of congressional Democrats and Republicans overall, I also use accounts of the policy discussions on the floor of the House and Senate provided by the *Congressional Quarterly Almanac*. Included with the congressional subcommittee hearings are also statements—either written or oral—from interested parties, such as interest groups, NGOs, church groups, and think tanks. These statements provide us with a snapshot of the range of civil society and other groups that are trying to influence Congress in the area of MDB policy at any given time. Whenever the positions and rhetoric of these groups are echoed by a legislator, it provides evidence that he or she is drawing on the policy positions developed by these outside groups.

These hearings thus provide a rich source of information about U.S. policies and their proximate political causes. By *proximate political causes*, I mean the most visible and immediate factors shaping U.S. policy toward the banks—in particular, the policy agenda of the U.S. executive, the shifting positions of political parties in Congress, and the positions of outside groups attempting to shape U.S. policy. Some readers will want to know more about the deeper causes behind these political factors and their origin in a single underlying dynamic or motivating cause, such as the shifting preferences of the ruling class or the changing role of the United States in the world system. Unfortunately, the congressional hearings shed little light on these kinds of underlying causes, and I have mostly refrained from speculating on them; I leave such interpretations to future researchers.

The Role of Other Shareholders and MDB Management

The interactions of donor governments with the IFIs and with one another occur in a "black box" to which outsiders have little access. There is no public record of negotiations among G7 or G8 finance ministers, of negotiations among MDB donors, or even of the official meetings of the MDBs' boards of directors. Nor do we have access to the discussions— often informal—that occur between MDB management and the U.S. Treasury. This absence of documentation poses methodological problems reminiscent of the dilemmas of cold war "Kremlinologists."

The U.S. congressional approval process provides a window into the black box of donor politics—but, unfortunately, an imperfect window. In testifying to Congress, the U.S. Treasury has a strong interest in creating the impression that it is getting things done in the banks and, thereby, effectively serving U.S. interests. Throughout this book, there are a number of examples of the Treasury testifying to Congress that it is promoting a particular policy in the MDBs, followed by testimonies from subsequent years that the United States was successful in persuading other shareholders and pressing MDB management to adopt the policy in question. We cannot necessarily take these statements at face value, and their validity is difficult to verify. Because disagreements among major shareholders, or between the United States and MDB management, are hammered out in nonpublic forums, Congress is in a poor position to confirm or disconfirm such Treasury claims.

At the same time, the logic of the MDBs' governance, discussed at greater length in chapter 1, allows us to establish some guiding assumptions for making better guesses about what is going on behind the scenes. For example, we can assume that no MDB can implement a major policy initiative without the support, or at least the acquiescence, of its major shareholders. Although the United States cannot unilaterally impose its agenda on the banks, it is uniquely well positioned to block shareholder and MDB initiatives of which it does not approve, both through its formal voting share on the banks' boards of directors and through its leverage in periodic donor negotiations. Thus, we can also assume that, although U.S. backing is not sufficient for the implementation of an MDB policy initiative, it is always necessary.

Although we can assume that policy initiatives need U.S. acquiescence to succeed, this does not necessarily mean that the United States has taken the lead in these initiatives—even when the Treasury claims to Congress, as it frequently does, that it is the primary author of MDB policies. Some plausible alternative possibilities are that the policy in question was generated by general consensus among shareholder governments, agreement between the United States and MDB management, or both. To shed light into the black boxes of the politics of intrashareholder and U.S.-management interactions, I have drawn on secondary literature and media accounts, particularly those from the English-language business press and the *Washington Post*. In the era of Lexis-Nexis and other online databases, it is easy to scour these sources for evidence of public disagreements among shareholders and between shareholders and MDB management.

I have also triangulated my educated guesses with the many interviews and informal conversations I had with individuals in and around Washington, DC. These informants provided me firsthand perspectives on events and read chapters to provide feedback on the accuracy of my interpretations. I have respected my informants' confidentiality and have made reference to individuals by name only when they explicitly gave their permission to do so.

Finally, I have attempted to compensate for the lack of information on intrashareholder and shareholder-MDB interactions through strategic comparative analysis *among* the MDBs' policies. As we will see in the introduction, governance varies from bank to bank and has changed over time. Consequently, the United States is in a better position to promote its policy preferences in certain banks at certain times—depending on the ability of MDB management, borrowing governments, and other shareholders to block U.S.-led initiatives. In recent years, for example, the Asian Development Bank (AsDB) has been slower to adopt the "measurable-results" agenda than other banks have been, suggesting that the Japanese—who have the same voting share in the AsDB as the United States—are somewhat less enthusiastic about this agenda than are policymakers in Washington.

*   *   *

This book tells a story about how U.S. policy toward the MDBs has evolved over the past three decades, how U.S. politics has shaped this policy, and how U.S. initiatives have shaped the MDBs' policies. The final product owes a very large debt to many individuals who helped guide my way through the streets of Washington and who provided feedback on drafts of chapters. Thanks to the team of librarians at the Woodrow Wilson Center—particularly Janet Spikes, through whose wisdom I was able to stumble on the documents that make up the core of my story. Many thanks also to Nitsan Chorev, Carmen Diana Deere, Frank Dobbin, Catherine Gwin, Bruce Kutnick, Tom Melito, Tom Medvetz, Jonathan Sanford, Jordan Siegel, Mark Weisbrot, and Martin Weiss. I am especially indebted to Matt McHugh, John Sewell, and Donald Sherk, all of whom took the time to read drafts of multiple chapters and provide extensive and thoughtful comments.

Introduction

On a wall inside the lobby of the World Bank's headquarters is the motto "Our dream is a world free of poverty." The World Bank is the leading member of a group of organizations that are officially in the business of realizing this mission. Collectively known as *the multilateral development banks* (MDBs, or *the banks* for short), they also include four regional banks: the Inter-American Development Bank, the Asian Development Bank (AsDB), the African Development Bank, and the European Bank for Reconstruction and Development.

In theory, the MDBs' actions are guided by their mission to promote economic development in poor and medium-income countries—to create "a world free of poverty." This development mandate distinguishes the MDBs from the International Monetary Fund (IMF), another international financial institution (IFI) with a somewhat different mission. In practice, however, the banks' official mandate provides remarkably little guidance for their actions—and room for a wide range of possible activities. *Development* is a complicated concept with multiple possible definitions, and, even among experts sharing a common definition, there have always been major disagreements about the best means to pursue this end. Is the best way to cure world poverty through building infrastructure or funding education? Should development be promoted through financing projects or through providing advice? Should development assistance go to governments, to nongovernmental organizations (NGOs), or directly to the poor through microcredit loans? Should it be provided as grants or as loans? Should it emphasize government intervention or free markets?

During their half century of existence, the MDBs have answered these questions in varying ways, and their ideas and activities have varied accordingly. In part, their development prescriptions have responded to their own internal dynamics. Like all complex organizations, the MDBs have an overriding interest in keeping themselves in business. This survival imperative necessarily favors some development visions over others—for example, they are more likely to favor development programs that involve their own expansion over those that involve their downsizing. Moreover, like all such organizations, the banks have unique bureaucratic cultures and structures that influence the kinds of answers they provide to development dilemmas.

However, the banks do not bear sole responsibility for their ideas and actions: like all complex organizations, they respond to forces in their environment. One set of environmental forces comes out of systems of expert knowledge. The banks adjust their views and development prescriptions in line with intellectual trends among economists and other development experts as well as with emerging real-world evidence about the impact of their policies.

A second set of environmental factors is political and emanates from the governments that officially own and control the banks. The MDBs' member governments are conventionally known as *shareholders* because members are the ultimate source of the banks' capital stock. Because in all the MDBs voting share is allocated according to capital contribution, major shareholders control a very large bloc of votes as well as a number of other levers for wielding influence. The most important MDB shareholders are the United States, Japan, Great Britain, Germany, and France.

The U.S. government is the banks' most important shareholder and has consistently been at the lead of shareholder initiatives to reform the banks over the past several decades. This is not only because the United States possesses the largest voting share overall but also because of its uniquely strong bargaining position. In part because of the unusual structure of the American political system, the United States is unusually reluctant to support the banks. This often gives MDB management and other shareholders little choice but to follow the American lead in initiatives for reform. These U.S.-led reform initiatives, in turn, are forged through a domestic political process that includes input not only from academic experts but also from government technocrats, members of Congress, think tanks, interest groups, and social movements.

This book is about the role of Washington politics in forging U.S. policies toward the MDBs over the past several decades and the role of U.S. policies in shaping the banks' ideas and activities. American policies toward the banks, which are shaped by Washington politics, have considerable influence over the banks' organizational trajectories: Washington politics matters for what the banks say and do. What the banks say and do, in turn, helps set the agenda for debates among development experts. The banks thus bridge two very different worlds: Washington politics, on the one hand, and scholarly ideas about economic development, on the other.

Economic Development in Perspective

Economic development is controversial. Nobody questions the fact that large inequalities exist among the nations of the world—disparities in power, resources, and standards of living. But, over the course of the past century, there have been significant disagreements over how to characterize these inequalities and even more controversy over how to ameliorate them.

The definition of *economic development* has shifted considerably over time. When development experts speak about *economic development* (or *development* for short) today, they are referring generally to economic progress that improves the lives of people in poor countries. An implicit assumption of the term is that development is an object of government policy—that actions by national governments can either help or hinder the development process. This contemporary meaning of the term did not acquire widespread currency until after the Second World War. During the nineteenth century, many governments engaged in actions that today would be considered to be economic development projects, but these policies were referred to under the rubric of *modernization* or *Westernization*. In the mid-nineteenth century, Marx referred to the "development" of capitalism, and, toward the beginning of the twentieth, Schumpeter published his famous *Theory of Economic Development* (1911). But neither of these thinkers viewed development primarily as an object of government policies; rather, they saw it as a naturally occurring process.[1]

With the end of the Second World War, something much more like *development* in the contemporary sense began to emerge. For postwar economists and other development experts, the hallmarks of successful development were signs that backward countries were making progress— for example, building roads, dams, and smoke-belching factories—along the Western trajectory. In economics, this was the era of Rostow's famous "stages of economic development" and Rosenstein-Rodan's "big push."[2] Although these ideas may seem naive or even offensive to contemporary observers, they were not all that different from the model of development being promoted by the Soviet bloc or by nonaligned Third World nationalist leaders, from Jawaharlal Nehru in India to Juscelino Kubitschek in Brazil. *Development*, as it was widely understood in the 1950s and 1960s, was based on an unadulterated modernism that had yet to encounter any significant challenge.

By the 1970s, however, the dominant definition of *development* began to change. Development specialists increasingly observed that the benefits of economic growth were not necessarily trickling down to the impoverished masses. Consequently, growth in national income lost its status as the sole indicator of economic progress, and various social indicators— such as literacy and infant mortality—were added to the concept. With the establishment of the UN's Human Development Index in the 1990s, this expanded notion of development became permanently institutionalized. Meanwhile, a large and vocal environmental movement had been calling into question whether it was acceptable to increase GNP at the cost of gross and even irreversible ecological damage, leading to the invention of the term *sustainable development*. With the end of the cold war, the definition of *development* expanded further to include institutions associated with political freedom known under the broad rubric of *governance*.[3]

Today, *development* has acquired a much more nuanced and complicated meaning than the early postwar concept. In the words of two seasoned Washington development experts: "Most policymakers and practitioners would [when defining *economic development*] probably emphasize three things: increases in per capita incomes that lead to a sustained reduction in poverty; an expansion in the physical infrastructure and public services (such as education and health) that are both the means and ends of social and economic progress; and increasingly capable and effective governments that provide for security, the rule of law, responsible economic management, social inclusion, and political freedoms that are also means as well as the ends to improving the human condition."[4] This multifaceted definition leaves considerable room for prioritizing some aspects of development over others—for example, poverty reduction over growth or security over democracy. In contrast to the early postwar concept of development, the current one provides much more ambiguous guidelines for action.

Yet, even among experts who agree on a common definition, economic development continues to be a controversial topic. There are a number of reasons for the persistence of debate. One is simply that underdevelopment persists. No matter how we measure development—in terms of infant mortality, literacy, political freedoms, or economic growth—there continue to be large disparities among nations in spite of many decades of development projects of various sorts.

A second reason is that national economies are complicated. This makes it impossible to come up with definitive explanations for economic success or failure that will satisfy all observers. Development facts do not speak for themselves: they are subject to interpretation. For example, during the early 1980s, it was common to attribute the success of the East Asian "miracle" economies to their market-friendly policies. But a subsequent wave of scholarly literature pointed out that countries such as Korea, Taiwan, and Singapore also benefited from large amounts of judicious government intervention.[5] Or, to take another example, today sub-Saharan Africa is universally recognized as a development failure, but experts disagree about the reasons for this failure and, therefore, arrive at different conclusions. For Jeffrey Sachs, the region's problems can be traced mostly to crushing debt burdens and a lack of capital; more generous foreign aid from wealthy countries is the key to solving the problem. But, for William Easterly, aid is the problem, not the solution: the citizens of poor African countries are the victims of aid donors in cahoots with bad governments that squander foreign aid on ill-conceived projects and Swiss bank accounts.[6]

A third reason for the ongoing controversy is that scholars who do research on economic development and publish on the topic are almost all social scientists—and social scientists are a notoriously contentious lot. Practitioners of the "hard sciences," such as biology or physics, tend to share an enormous body of common assumptions about how to do research and basic facts; the historian of science Thomas Kuhn referred to these assumptions as "paradigms." But, among social scientists, there tends to be considerable disagreement about which findings constitute facts as well as about the best way to go about establishing them. This is particularly true of scholarship on economic development. As one development economist recently observed of the subfield: "Instead of a handful of simple and clear-cut laws that tell us what to do and what to expect, we have a hundred competing tendencies and possibilities, of uncertain strength and, quite often, direction, with little guidance as to how to add them up. . . . Indeed, the only theories that we hold onto with some confidence are disaster warnings—banning all trade is bad, as is banning all private enterprise and printing money to pay everyone. With anything more nuanced, or less negative, there are too many doubts and differences."[7]

At any given moment in history, scholarly experts are generating many different ideas about the best way to improve the human condition. Yet not all these ideas are put into practice as policy—and even fewer are applied by governments around the globe. Many are called, but only a few are chosen—and it is with these chosen few that this book is concerned.

Why the Banks Are Important

The MDBs are major players in the controversial field of economic development. In the midst of the debates that continue to rage about development, the banks devise straightforward policy prescriptions that are adopted by the governments of scores of developing countries. The biggest, oldest, and best known of the MDBs is the World Bank, which provides financing for development projects and programs around the globe (see table I.1).[8]

The MDBs' mandates and activities overlap with those of other organizations. To understand what makes the MDBs different, it is helpful to refer back to the term *multilateral development bank*: they are *multilateral* organizations, in the business of economic *development*, and behave primarily as *banks*. Because they are multilateral, they are distinct from bilateral aid agencies, such as the U.S. Agency for International Development (USAID) in the United States, which are directly controlled by individual donor governments. Instead, they are financed and controlled by many governments. All these banks share a common purpose, laid out in their formal charters: namely, to provide financing for economic development in poor countries. Because their mandate specifically concerns development, they differ from another well-known IFI, the IMF, which has a different mandate. At the same time, unlike other multilateral organizations concerned with development, such as the World Health Association

TABLE I.1. **The Multilateral Development Banks (MDBs)**

Multilateral Development Bank	Year Founded	Total Loans and Grants, 2006 (US$ billions)
World Bank	1944	$23
Inter-American Development Bank (IDB)	1959	$6.4
Asian Development Bank (AsDB)	1964	$7.9
African Development Bank (AfDB)	1964	$2.6
European Bank for Reconstruction and Development (EBRD)	1991	$6.1

or the UN Children's Fund, the MDBs are banks: they are in the business of moving large amounts of money.

The banks influence policies in developing countries and ideas about economic development. They do this primarily by engaging in three kinds of activities. The first (and most traditional) activity is providing financing for investment projects—tangible things that are seen as important to economic progress, such as highways to connect different regions or schools to educate people to be economically productive citizens. The kinds of projects that the MDBs are willing to finance influence the kinds of policies poor countries pursue—but also shape overall thinking about economic development. For example, early in its history, the World Bank focused on lending for infrastructure projects, such as highways and dams. In the 1970s, however, it began to provide financing for different kinds of projects, such as loans to benefit small- and medium-sized farmers and for education; this encouraged both governments to engage in different kinds of activities and policymakers and development experts to conceive of economic development in a different way.

The second type of MDB activity is providing loans for policy reforms. In contrast to project loans, which are earmarked for the purchase of goods and services, *program loans*—also known as *nonproject* or *policy-based loans*—provide governments with financing in return for particular government policies, such as the privatization of state-owned industries or education reform. To ensure that governments are holding up their end of the bargain, these loans are disbursed in installments and suspended if governments fall out of compliance. The practice of tying loans to policy reforms is known as *conditionality*. Before 1980, it was extremely rare for the MDBs to engage in these kinds of loans. Since the 1980s, however, nonproject lending has become a major component of the banks' activities. The most famous nonproject lending program is the World Bank's

Structural Adjustment Facility, which encouraged borrowers to implement market-liberalizing policy reforms in the 1980s and 1990s and was
associated with the rise of the Washington Consensus.[9]

The third way in which the MDBs exert influence over development
policies is through conducting and disseminating development research.
This is most true of the World Bank, which since the 1970s has built up
a reputation for being a leader in the development field. Every year the
Bank publishes hundreds of studies and reports on various topics in the
area of economic development—from trade to infant mortality—and also
selectively disseminates the work of external scholars. Research occurs
throughout the Bank, but the most important site is the Development
Economics Vice Presidency.[10]

The World Bank's research output is highly influential. Tens of thousands of copies of the Bank's annual publication, the *World Development Report*, are distributed around the globe every year. World Bank
research informs the policies of bilateral development agencies in wealthy
industrialized countries as well as those of the World Bank itself and
other MDBs.[11] It also shapes scholarly debates about economic development. For example, an internal World Bank study found that, in a collection of university course syllabi on the topic of economic development,
one-sixth of the entries were by World Bank authors.[12] As one prominent World Bank observer put it, the *World Development Report* shapes
"accepted wisdom among development thinkers. Commentators outside
the Bank spen[d] much of their time reacting to World Bank ideas and
citing World Bank data."[13]

Development ideas that are propagated through the World Bank
receive a far wider audience and application than ideas that are confined
to the pages of scholarly publications. This allows the Bank to help set the
terms of professional debates over economic development and to be at
the center of these debates. For example, during the 1980s, World Bank
research publications, such as the *World Development Report*, focused on
the issue of how to change national economic policies to liberate market
forces—an emphasis that encouraged development scholars to focus on
the issue of the relative benefits of states versus markets.[14] At that time,
the Bank was widely viewed as the headquarters of the new orthodoxy
in development thinking, also known as the *Washington Consensus*.[15] The
Bank was also at the vanguard of subsequent efforts to reform the Washington Consensus through protecting the poor and introducing "governance" reforms. Whenever the World Bank chooses to adopt, research,
and disseminate any given theme—whether it is market liberalization

or governance—this theme is echoed in the debates among development professionals around the world, including debates among academic economists.

The leading voice of the World Bank shows that not all MDBs have equal weight in discussions of economic policies and economic development. Arguably, the least policy-influential of the banks is the European Bank for Reconstruction and Development, which is much more like a commercial bank than a development bank: the majority of its funds go to private enterprise rather than to governments, and it is not known as a center for thinking about economic development.[16] The other three regional banks—the Inter-American Development Bank, the African Development Bank, and the AsDB—are somewhat more influential since all three focus more on lending to national governments and engage in policy-based lending. As the oldest and most policy-influential of the MDBs, the World Bank will play the largest role in the story told in this book.

Expert Ideas and Policy Programs

If the MDBs are influential disseminators of ideas and policies, then where do these ideas and policies come from in the first place? Throughout this book, I argue that the banks' ideas and activities are generated at the intersection of two very different social systems: national politics and expert knowledge.

The connection between these two social systems is not immediately obvious. Experts, particularly academic experts working at universities, are supposed to form their opinions based on objective evidence, untainted by political interests or ideologies. Conversely, politicians are often observed to ignore expert advice—for example, to flout scientists' warnings about global warming. Politicians cannot afford to consistently follow expert advice because such advice may conflict with the interests or political ideologies of their economic or political supporters.

Nevertheless, sometimes politicians may draw selectively on the ideas of experts to help generate political support or to devise policies in areas where they have little knowledge or experience. For example, the economic policies of the Reagan administration borrowed from conservative economic ideas coming out of academic institutions such as the University of Chicago.[17] These were not the only ideas to be coming out of American economics departments at that time: Republicans selected *among* expert ideas for those that were most in line with their own political goals.[18] Yet the Republican Party also benefited from the overall state of the economics discipline, which had, in the United States in the 1980s, moved away from postwar Keynesianism and in a more conservative, market-friendly direction. This trend in economic expertise benefited the Republicans because it helped them construct a conservative economic policy platform that had scholarly legitimacy.

The ideas associated with "Reaganomics" exemplify what the political sociologist John Campbell terms a "policy program"—a collection of concepts, theories, and strategies for policy.[19] By providing the inspiration for policy programs, scholars can influence policy outcomes in both the short term and the long. In the short term, they can help inform broader societal debates about what is to be done and, thereby, determine the outcomes of political contests. Social issues do not usually speak for themselves; they are interpreted and packaged in particular ways, a process sociologists refer to as "framing."[20] Political actors can use the legitimacy of scholarly ideas to persuade the public to adopt a particular interpretation of events, thereby helping them get elected.

In the long term, scholarly ideas can achieve durable policy influence by becoming institutionalized and taken for granted. For example, during the decades following the Second World War, economic policies in the United States and other industrialized democracies were informed by the ideas of the British economist John Maynard Keynes, who thought that governments needed to play an active role in stimulating the economy and preventing recessions. Keynes's ideas were initially adopted by governments in response to the Great Depression. Once adopted, Keynesian ideas routinely informed the practices of government technocrats insulated from the world of politics. The political scientist Peter Hall refers to such sets of taken-for-granted ideas and practices as "policy paradigms." Like Kuhn's scientific paradigms, policy paradigms are durable: they make up a background of shared assumptions among policymakers that persists over time.[21] In short, a policy paradigm is an institutionalized policy program with lasting impact.

Policy programs draw on expert ideas because scientific knowledge has legitimacy in modern societies.[22] A politician trying to sell a policy, such as a hike in taxes, is more likely to convince a skeptical public if she can find Nobel Prize–winning economists to publicly agree with her proposal. However, the fate of this policy depends on politics as well as expertise. There may simultaneously be another group of economists whose ideas support the platform of a rival politician who wants to reduce taxes. Even if the experts all agree on the desirability of higher taxes, whether the policy gets implemented depends on any of a number of political factors, including the support or opposition of organized interest groups, the decisions of national voters, and the need to compromise with other politicians.

Thus, policy programs that draw on expert knowledge belong neither purely to the world of scholarship nor purely to the world of politics. In the language of the French sociologist Pierre Bourdieu, they occupy the intersection of different "fields." For Bourdieu, a *field* is an arena of social action occupied by individuals and organizations competing for authority or power. Different fields have different rules of competition and distinct rewards for those who succeed. Politicians occupy the political field; they struggle over political power according to the formal and informal rules of national political systems.

Academics occupy the intellectual field, a world whose the rules and the stakes are distinct from those of the worlds of politics and business. If you are an academic, you compete with your peers for a range of resources— a good salary, a light teaching load, job security, grants, awards, the respect of your colleagues, or a position at a prestigious university, just to name the most important items. Your ability to obtain these resources depends on how well you play the academic game. The rules of this game vary from discipline to discipline but always involve submitting your research findings to the evaluation of experts in the field—through the peer review processes of journals, dissertation and tenure review committees, and so on. The rules of politics or of the market do not, at least in theory, apply. For example, your tenure decision is not supposed to have anything to do whether you have been called to testify on Capitol Hill.

Bourdieu's theory of how the different forms of capital interact is extremely nuanced and complicated, and I am only scratching the surface here. Fields, for Bourdieu, are not independent. Individuals can occupy distinct fields, and the fields themselves interact with one another through the "conversion" of different resources or "forms of capital."[23] For example, to scholars with policy-relevant ideas, the political field can offer prestigious positions and the ability to put their ideas into action. Conversely, to politicians interested in selling their ideas, scholars can offer ideas that have scholarly legitimacy. This does not mean that scholars are objective: academics from Milton Friedman to Paul Krugman are famous for taking controversial positions on the political issues of the day. However, the *output* of such scholars has public legitimacy to the extent that it is perceived as being produced through a rigorous process that makes it more credible than pure political ideology—through a game that is distinct from the game of politics. This makes it possible for scholars to convert their intellectual capital into political capital and for politicians to gain legitimacy by using scholarly ideas. Policy programs that draw on expert ideas are hybrid products, manufactured in a social space in which politics and scholarship collide. They select among scholarly ideas to promote those that mesh with political ideologies; they are put into place by political processes but benefit from the legitimacy of the world of scholarship.

We can similarly describe different organizations in terms of their location in political and intellectual fields. For example, the Democratic Party is situated rather obviously in the political field and the Harvard University Philosophy Department in the intellectual field. However, some organizations are situated somewhere in between. For example, Thomas Medvetz argues that American think tanks occupy an "interstitial" field between the intellectual and the political worlds.[24]

The MDBs are also examples of organizations that straddle political and intellectual worlds. Their substantial influence stems in part from the fact that they have considerable endowments of resources—and countries that want access to these resources are usually asked, to a greater or lesser extent, to take their advice. At the same time, the banks' influence also stems from their considerable intellectual legitimacy—a legitimacy that sets them apart from bilateral aid sources, such as USAID, an affiliate of the U.S. State Department. In part because they are viewed as tinged by political partisanship, the publications of USAID are rarely cited as authoritative sources on economic development topics.

In contrast, because they are multilateral organizations and staffed by highly trained professionals, the MDBs are perceived as being purveyors of advice that is more neutral and less politicized, which is partly why their ideas and publications weigh so heavily in development debates. The banks draw heavily on the ideas of scholarly professionals, particularly those of economists. During the 1970s, the World Bank began to bring more economists onto its staff and to assume its current role as a leader in development thinking. Since that time, economists with advanced degrees from American and British universities have overwhelmingly come to dominate the Bank's management and staff.[25]

Yet the MDBs are not organizations of professors working for tenure, promotion, and peer-reviewed publications. They overlap with the intellectual field, but they also overlap with the political field: they are resource-dependent organizations that need to attend closely to the demands of the governments that finance them. These shareholder demands, in turn, are forged out of a complex process that includes both political and intellectual factors. Shareholder policies toward the MDBs may be shaped directly by input from economic interest groups or civil society actors, such as NGOs and social movements. At the same time, shareholder demands are shaped by policy programs in several areas, including economic policy programs (e.g., Reaganomics) and foreign policy programs (e.g., neoconservatism). These policy programs often have input from social science experts (e.g., supply-side economists or neoconservative scholars) but also respond to political interests and ideologies. Thus, in responding to shareholder demands, the MDBs are indirectly responding to input from both the intellectual and the political fields.

The Role of Congressional Politics

What the MDBs say and do is influenced by political processes within donor countries—the countries whose governments provide the banks with the bulk of their resources. Yet not all donors are equally influential. The United States is the donor that controls the largest bloc of votes in the World Bank and the largest share in the banks overall. Other sources of U.S. influence in the MDBs are discussed at greater length in chapter 1.

Among the most important sources of American influence is a dynamic that is not captured by voting share: the reluctance of the United States to support the banks. Periodically, donor governments meet to negotiate financial contributions and MDB policies. In these negotiations, the United States is notorious for being the squeaky wheel—the shareholder with the most demands and complaints and the one least willing to compromise. It is also famous for later reneging on intershareholder agreements and failing to contribute the resources to which it originally agreed. It is the only shareholder that consistently fails to deliver the promised financing and that remains in arrears year after year.

The reluctance of the U.S. government to support the MDBs, in turn, can be traced to both cultural and structural factors. On the cultural side, the American tradition of economic libertarianism provides policymakers with a ready set of arguments against spending on foreign aid.[26] Foreign aid that is provided through *multilateral* vehicles such as the World Bank is even more likely to be criticized since it violates the principles of

American exceptionalism: multilateral organizations seem to inhibit the actions of a special nation that should be allowed to forge its own destiny.[27] This attitude may prevent U.S. policymakers from distinguishing between multilateral organizations run on a one-country, one-vote basis, such as the United Nations, and those in which the United States has a leading influence, such as the World Bank and the IMF.

However, an even more important reason for American ambivalence toward the MDBs originates in the structure of the American political system. The United States is the only major donor nation that has a fully presidential system, with relatively clearly separated branches of power. With the exception of France (which has a semipresidential system), all other major donors (Japan, Great Britain, Germany, and Canada) have parliamentary systems.[28] In a parliamentary democracy, the government is beholden to the parliament for its ongoing tenure in office. Its head (the prime minister) appoints the heads of cabinet positions—the secretary of the treasury, the secretary of state, and so on—who are also answerable to the parliament. In this system, the legislative and the executive are necessarily of one mind, and foreign aid policy is informed by a relatively uniform and consistent set of policies—at least until the executive loses the parliament's confidence and is forced to resign.

In contrast, the American president and his cabinet do not depend on Congress for remaining in office, and a majority in Congress may disagree with the president's policies. The American electoral system makes members of Congress more beholden to local constituents than to either national parties or the broad coalitions that bring the president to power. The congressional policy agenda tends to be based on local concerns, and weak party discipline means that neither the president nor the party can consistently bring unruly legislators into line with a national platform.[29] To thwart the policy agendas of the executive, Congress possesses a range of powers, including the power to make laws and to appropriate funds, that it uses to exert influence in all areas of policy—including U.S. policy toward the MDBs.[30]

The American political system tends to generate very weak political support for foreign aid and even weaker support for the MDBs.[31] When the executive branch proposes spending on foreign aid, Congress almost always resists. Congress often makes foreign aid policy with the reactions of local constituents in mind, often assuming that local constituents would rather spend taxpayer dollars at home.[32] Pressure for cutbacks is heightened when there is an influx of new, inexperienced members of Congress who have little knowledge of, or support for, such programs.

In 2003, the United States spent only 0.15 percent of its gross national income on foreign aid, the lowest percentage among all wealthy industrialized nations.[33]

Congress is even more resistant where foreign aid spending is going to support *multilateral* organizations. The MDBs provide foreign aid collectively, through jointly governed multilateral organizations that the United States does not entirely control. American legislators may be averse to such organizations for the cultural reasons mentioned above. Yet, even more important, the *structure* of the American polity is highly prone to generating congressional opposition to multilateralism in all its forms. Multilateral agreements—including agreements for funding and shaping the policies of the MDBs—are produced through negotiations among sovereign executive branches: they are based on what Walter Russell Mead dubs a "Continentalist" model of negotiation and agreement among sovereign, unitary states.[34] Such negotiations necessarily exclude the U.S. Congress. When called on to ratify multilateral agreements or finance multilateral organizations, Congress will often express its displeasure at the process by refusing to go along.

This dynamic imposes considerable constraints on the U.S. executive, which, unlike other governments, is not free to make multilateral agreements as it chooses. In this book, however, I demonstrate that U.S. administrations have also learned to use the uncertainties of the congressional approval process to their advantage. The administration can wield Congress as an implicit threat or bargaining chip in its negotiations with MDB shareholders (and with the management of the MDBs)—in effect, telling these parties that, if the U.S. position is not adopted, Congress will fail to ratify the agreement and appropriate the requisite funds. As one World Bank history suggests: "By being the reluctant, retreating, partner, the United States has had even greater leverage than its sheer size would suggest. Having the Congress as a constraint has further strengthened the hand of the U.S. administrations in bargaining with other members."[35] And as another author observes of U.S. participation in the AsDB: "The U.S. budgetary process, which requires that individual installments to the capital increases and AsDF [Asian Development Fund] replenishments be subject to annual approval by Congress, has given the United States considerable leverage."[36]

In the language of game theory, the case of the United States and the MDBs provides us with an example of how states engage in "two-level games," simultaneously manipulating domestic and diplomatic politics. Because Congress is likely to ratify only a limited number of possible multilateral agreements, the U.S. executive enters negotiations with a small "win set," a fact that it can use to exact concessions from other states with which it is negotiating.[37]

Of course, to use this tactic effectively, the executive needs to have previously consulted with Congress and tailor its bargaining position to match congressional preferences. Congressional preferences are shaped by a number of factors, including policy programs, input from interest groups, and the perceived preferences of constituents. They are also shaped by input from civil society actors, including think tanks, NGOs, and church groups.[38]

Congress is able to assert and maintain its role in MDB policy by refusing to go along with the administration's proposals. However, as will be seen in the chapters to come, not all members of Congress are equally intransigent: although resistance has come from both sides of the aisle, since the 1970s Republicans in Congress have been more resistant, overall, than Democrats—with the bulk of the resistance coming from right-wing (rather than moderate) Republicans.

How can we explain this overarching partisan difference? One possible explanation lies in the underlying political economy of the two parties; for example, perhaps the economic interest groups backing Democrats are more internationalist than those backing Republicans. A second possibility is that Democratic and Republican voters have distinct policy preferences, with more support for multilateral institutions among the constituents of the former than among those of the latter.

My own view, however, is that neither of these two explanations sheds much light on partisan differences surrounding the MDBs. Within the world of congressional politics, the MDBs constitute an arcane policy area, one of relatively little interest to either constituents or major lobbyists. The local constituents to whom legislators are beholden are notoriously uninterested in foreign policy (except insofar as it affects voters directly), and the banks are a lesser-known issue within the general field of foreign policy.[39] The annual budget for the MDBs is a tiny fraction of overall U.S. government spending and the impact of MDB policies on major economic interests complex and uncertain: for big-money lobbyists, there are many more obvious issues, with much more money at stake.[40] It is true that Congress is routinely lobbied by firms that bid for MDB procurement contracts—firms that have an interest in increased U.S. funding. Yet this interest group apparently wields little influence in Congress, which cuts U.S. contributions to these organizations year after year. Because members of Congress are unlikely to receive any clear policy direction on the MDBs, either from major economic backers or from voters back home, many of them are quite uninformed about the nature of these organizations. This is particularly apparent in the House of Representatives, where there is a higher turnover than in the Senate and more new, inexperienced members.

I believe that partisan differences in congressional support for the banks are best explained, not by the interests of rent-seeking lobbyists or the preferences of political constituencies, but by differences in policy programs. Because the MDBs constitute a policy area in which legislators often lack a clear set of predefined preferences, they turn to policy programs to guide their positions. The menu of available policy programs, in turn, is different for right-wing Republicans than it is for Democrats or more moderate Republicans, and this fact has consequences for their respective positions toward the banks. For example, right-wing Republicans tend to be guided by a hawkish foreign policy program—one that tends to imply a greater role for military force and a diminished role for economic diplomacy and multilateralism. Particularly since the 1970s, most Republicans have endorsed a small-government economic policy program, one that implies less government spending in nonpriority areas. Perhaps most important of all, since the 1970s, conservative Republican legislators have drawn on the ideas of influential right-wing think tanks (such as the Heritage Foundation and the Cato Institute), which have developed a menu of policy programs in a range of specific areas.[41] As we will see in future chapters, the anti-MDB positions of these think tanks have often been echoed by Republican members of Congress.

Congressional Democrats, along with moderate Republicans, draw on a different menu of economic and foreign policy programs and tend to derive their specific positions toward the MDBs from more mainstream sources, including the research output of the MDBs themselves. This is not to say that all Democratic legislators have endorsed the status quo at all times—indeed, we will see that Democrats have often been strong advocates for MDB reforms in areas ranging from the environment to poverty. However, would-be Democratic reformers of the MDBs are handicapped by the fact that—unlike many of their Republican colleagues—they tend to be unwilling to threaten to defund the banks to leverage reforms, precisely because they tend to be more committed to these institutions. Thus, just as the MDBs' least-committed shareholder, the United States, is able to wield disproportionate influence among the other shareholders because of its lack of commitment, so too are conservative congressional Republicans within the domestic policymaking process.

Significantly, however, this partisan difference in Congress largely dis-appears at the executive level. Once in the White House, even right-wing Republican policymakers tend to moderate their anti-MDB populism and to become pragmatists, recognizing that the banks serve a host of useful purposes—from procurement contracts for U.S. firms to the promotion of long-term American economic interests. This pattern is, perhaps, evoca-tive of a Marxian (rather than a rent-seeking) political economy interpre-tation, one in which "the executive of the modern state is but a committee for managing the common affairs of the whole bourgeoisie."[42] Put some-what differently, once they are in the executive office, officially in charge of U.S. policy toward the banks, and beholden to national interest groups and constituencies, Republican policymakers recognize that they cannot allow their policies to be governed by parochial or radical ideologies: the banks are simply too useful.

The Plan of the Book

The organization of this book is chronological, with the exception of the topical chapters 1 and 7. Chapter 1 reviews the MDBs' histories and governance and argues that the banks can be usefully conceptualized as resource-dependent organizations that serve an ambiguous array of pur-poses for donor governments. Chapter 7 looks at how increased congres-sional activism in the banks created an opening for civil society groups to shape U.S. policy toward them, with a particular focus on three issue areas: human rights in the 1970s, the environment in the 1980s and 1990s, and HIPC (heavily indebted poor country) debt relief in the 1990s and into the twenty-first century.

Chapters 2, 3, 4, 6, and 8 tell the chronological story of the evolution of U.S. policy toward the MDBs since 1970. Chapter 2 introduces the esca-lating congressional controversies over the MDBs during the course of the 1970s—controversies that ended with Congress slashing most of the proposed U.S. budget for the MDBs in the last year of the Carter adminis-tration. This paved the way for a new approach to U.S. MDB policy dur-ing the administration of Ronald Reagan. Chapters 3, 4, and 5 examine the consequences of the Reagan revolution for the MDBs and the rise of a new U.S. policy program toward the banks in the 1980s and 1990s. Soon known as the *Washington Consensus*, this policy program conceptualized the banks as serving long-term American economic interests through the promotion of market-liberalizing reforms in the developing world. Chap-

ter 6 examines the political and intellectual trends in the 1990s that contributed to the erosion of the original Washington Consensus and the
expansion of policy-based lending into new areas, such as building sound
institutions and protecting the poor. Finally, Chapter 8 looks at developments in U.S. MDB policy during the George W. Bush administration and
argues that, the spectacular rise and fall of Paul Wolfowitz at the World
Bank aside, the Bush team's policies were mostly quite continuous with
the past. Chapter 8 also reviews the main arguments of the book and their
implications for the future of the MDBs.

CHAPTER ONE

The Banks and Their Shareholders

The U.S. government does not always get exactly what it wants in the multilateral development banks (MDBs). As Treasury Secretary Lloyd Bentsen put it in to Congress in 1993: "We pay a price for the cost-sharing benefits we get from the banks. The price is, we must also share the influence that we exercise over bank activities with the other member countries. . . . We do not always get our way, or get our way as quickly as we would like. By and large ours is the predominant voice in oversight of the banks and other members are often able to accept our views. But [as in] Congress, sometimes there is gridlock."[1]

Nevertheless, the United States is able to exert strong leadership in the banks, for at least two reasons. The first is that the banks are designed to be responsive to the demands of their donors. In the early postwar period, developing countries pushed for development financing to be delivered through the United Nations, a multilateral organization run on a one-country, one-vote basis. Yet wealthy donor countries—particularly the United States—were unwilling to make a significant capital investment in an organization in which they were not awarded significant control. Consequently, the best-funded and most influential multilateral development agencies to emerge after the Second World War were the MDBs—organizations that awarded donors considerable influence in their policies and operations. As the largest donor to the MDBs overall, the United States has a range of formal and informal means through which to exert influence in these donor-dominated organizations. The second reason that the United States is able to exert strong leadership—already discussed in the introduction—is that it is uniquely willing to abandon the banks, which means that other shareholders and the MDB management must placate it to avoid conflict and financing problems.

This chapter describes the history, governance, and financing of the MDBs and argues that it is useful to think of them as resource-dependent organizations. Like private corporations, they rely on external resources and award influence to external actors—their shareholders—to secure access to financing. Yet, unlike private corporations, which can measure shareholder return in dollars and cents, the MDBs are seen by their owners as means to pursue a shifting array of heterogeneous ends—from procurement contracts to poverty alleviation. Which conception of shareholder value prevails at any given time depends heavily on political dynamics in donor countries. As the banks' leading and most ambivalent donor, the United States has often been able to function as an activist shareholder.

The Third World and the Rise of the MDBs

In the decades following the Second World War, it seemed for a time that the United Nations might emerge as a leading source of financing for economic development. Such financing was one of the principal demands of an emerging group of poor countries making their voices heard on the floor of the General Assembly. Some observers claimed that these nations, many of them freshly decolonized, fit into neither the capitalist nor the Communist bloc and made up a "Third World" with its own problems and nationalist aspirations.[2]

This emergent Third Word bloc was particularly interested in development financing provided through multilateral agencies, such as the United Nations and the World Bank.[3] By the 1950s, the United Nations was clearly the preferred organization. It was a logical choice because it had a clear mandate for economic development and had considerable expertise in this new field. Leading economists from around the world worked for the United Nations and its specialized agencies, and a special subcommission of the UN Economic and Social Council was issuing recommendations for how to solve problems of economic backwardness.[4]

The United Nations was also a logical choice because the World Bank seemed neither willing nor able to meet the Third World's development demands. The Bank had been founded primarily to help reconstruct war-torn European economies, and the issues of developing countries were hardly discussed at the 1944 Bretton Woods meetings that led to the Bank's creation.[5] The World Bank of the 1950s was quite modest in size, and its economic research department was "small and underfunded."[6] Even worse, it lent at market interest rates that few Third World clients could afford: more than half of all Bank loans between 1946 and 1952 went to Europe and Australia.[7] Nor did it show any signs of becoming larger or more heavily subsidized; at the time, the United States, which dominated the Bank, was promoting the idea that the financing needs of developing countries should be met through private foreign investment— not through multilateral organizations, and certainly not on concessional terms.[8]

Perhaps the biggest advantage of the United Nations, from a Third World point of view, was that it gave every national member a single vote. Although the World Bank was technically part of the UN system, it had been founded with a very different governing structure.[9] The Bank allocated decisionmaking power according to how much capital each government contributed, with a dominant role for the United States; it thus gave little representation to developing countries. In contrast, as more developing countries became independent nations, the Third World acquired an increasingly strong voice within the United Nations.

In 1953, the UN Economic and Social Council had drawn up a detailed plan for the Special United Nations Fund for Economic Development (SUNFED), which would provide low-interest-rate loans and grants for developing countries.[10] The SUNFED proposal was enthusiastically supported by many Third World governments but opposed by the leading donor countries that would need to provide the bulk of its financing. The most strident opposition came from the United States, the wealthiest and most powerful country to emerge from the Second World War.

American opposition to the proposed UN development fund seems to have resulted from a combination of ideological and geopolitical factors. On the ideological side, the United Nations had already staked out a position on economic development that was noticeably to the left of mainstream opinion in U.S. policy circles.[11] At that time, American politics was caught in a whirlwind of anti-Communist sentiments, and some UN economists were even victims of Senator Joseph McCarthy's purges. SUNFED was also seen as geopolitically problematic at a time when it seemed as if the United Nations was increasingly being used by the Communist bloc to manipulate the Third World against the United States and its allies. Given this perception, it would have been difficult, if not impossible, to get financing for SUNFED through Congress. In the face of steady U.S. opposition, the United Nations had, by 1950, dropped its original proposal, instead establishing its Special Fund, which would not engage in lending operations.[12]

Although Washington opposed SUNFED, it soon relented in its opposition to concessional aid to the Third World. By the beginning of the 1960s, the United States had increased its bilateral aid program significantly and also supported the establishment of two development-financing organizations within the World Bank: the International Finance Corporation (IFC), which provided loans for private investment in developing countries, and the International Development Association (IDA), which provided low-interest loans to Third World governments. Both the IFC and IDA represented attempts to defuse Third World demands for development financing through the United Nations. In the words of the World Bank historians Edward Mason and Robert Asher, SUNFED was a proposal "so repugnant to conservative secretaries of the U.S. Treasury that, by comparison, the notion of an IFC came in time to seem to them positively attractive."[13] World Bank President George Woods later admitted in an interview that IDA "was really an idea to offset the urge for SUNFED."[14]

The United States and other wealthy governments also responded to Third World demands by allowing the World Bank to expand in size, and providing resources for the establishment of the Inter-American Development Bank (IDB) and the Asian Development Bank (AsDB). Like the World Bank, these regional development banks had governance structures that awarded participation according to capital contribution, with a leading role for the United States. As the MDBs expanded and multiplied in the decades that followed, the United Nations continued to issue statements, provide technical support, and generate an array of suborganizations dealing with development issues. It did so, however, with limited resources.[15]

The Banks in Brief

The MDBs are members of a common family and share family traits. All have formal charters, or "articles of agreement," laying out the general rules for the organization. All have boards of governors made up mostly of the finance ministers (or the structural equivalents) of member governments. All also have boards of directors made up of executive directors appointed by member governments. The executive directors are full-time employees of their respective governments who live in the cities where the MDBs are located. They are charged with policymaking responsibility and attend frequent meetings, at which they vote on behalf of their countries as their governments direct. Finally, in all the banks, there is a separation of ownership and management: although the banks are governed by their executive directors, they are run by professional management and staff—from their presidents on down.

All the MDBs derive their operating resources from three separate sources: member contributions, the interest on bonds that they issue on international capital markets, and loan "reflows" (i.e., repayments of principle, plus interest). All have a "hard loan," or "ordinary capital resources," facility that provides loans at market rates of interest but at much longer terms than commercial banks. To offer this service, they borrow funds on international capital markets and then relend them to member countries. The banks' creditworthiness is backed by wealthy member governments, which provide both seed money for the banks (known as *paid-in capital*) and a form of guarantee known as *callable capital*, discussed at greater length later in this chapter.

The MDBs' "soft loan," or concessional, facilities lend at heavily subsidized interest rates to the poorest countries. Unlike the banks' hard loan windows, the soft loan facilities are not profitable and, hence, require periodic replenishments from donor governments. These facilities include IDA (within the World Bank), the Fund for Special Operations (FSO) (within the Inter-American Development Bank), the African Development Fund (AfDF), and the Asian Development Fund (AsDF). The European Bank for Reconstruction and Development (EBRD) does not have a soft loan facility.[16]

Since all members contribute to the banks' capital stock, technically all members are shareholders. However, there are enormous disparities in capital contribution among them, with wealthy developed nations contributing the lion's share of the financing. In all the banks, member voting is weighted by capital contribution. Table 1.1 shows that, in all the banks but the African Development Bank (AfDB), more than 40 percent of the voting shares are controlled by the G7—a group of leading industrialized countries (the United States, the United Kingdom, France, Germany, Japan, Canada, and Italy) whose finance ministers have met annually since the 1970s.[17] The wealthiest shareholders in the MDBs have the privilege of selecting their own directors, who are answerable only to them. For ex-

TABLE 1.1. **The Governance of the Multilateral Development Banks, 2006**

	G7 Voting Share (%)	U.S. Voting Share (%)	Location of Headquarters	U.S. Largest Shareholder?	U.S. "Veto"?	U.S. Selects President?
World Bank	42.9	16.4	Washington	Yes	Yes	Yes
IDB	45.7	30	Washington	Yes	Yes	No
AsDB	40.4	12.9	Manila	Yes (with Japan)	No	No
AfDB	27.5	6.5	Tunis	No (second after Nigeria)	No	No
EBRD	62.6	10	London	Yes	No	No

Source: Annual Reports, World Bank, IDB, AsDB, AfDB, and EBRD.

ample, in the World Bank, the United States, the United Kingdom, Germany, and France have their own executive directors; in contrast, Mexico, Venezuela, Spain, and the nations of Central America share a single director who controls only 4.5 percent of the votes. A similar situation holds true on the executive boards of the IDB, the AfDB, the AsDB, and the EBRD. In short, in the MDBs, the shareholders that donate a lot but do not borrow are far better represented than those that borrow from the banks but donate little.

These family resemblances among the banks are not coincidental. All the banks face a similar set of organizational incentives, trading influence within the organization for access to external financial resources. Moreover, all the regional banks were to a greater or lesser extent deliberately modeled on their organizational forerunner: the World Bank.[18] Nevertheless, despite these overall similarities, the banks are not identical. The following sections outline the history and organizational structure of each bank in turn, with a particular focus on how each manages two potential lines of cleavage: the division between management and the Executive Board; and the division on the Executive Board between major shareholder and borrowing governments.

The World Bank

The World Bank was founded along with the International Monetary Fund (IMF) in 1944 at a famous conference of policymakers in Bretton Woods, New Hampshire. The two organizations had complementary goals: the mission of the IMF was to promote international economic stability by helping countries manage their exchange rates; that of the Inter-

national Bank for Reconstruction and Development (IBRD), soon to
be known simply as the World Bank, was to help rebuild the economies
destroyed by the Second World War and to foster the economic advancement of poor countries. Both were heavily financed by the United States
and deliberately designed to give it a leading voice in their activities.

The organizational structure of the World Bank was closely modeled
on that of the IMF.[19] The initial voting shares in both the Bank and the
IMF were negotiated directly among the great powers present at the Bretton Woods meetings.[20] When the Bank opened for business, the United
States controlled 37.2 percent of the votes, giving it control over changes
to the Bank's articles of agreement (but not over decisions on individual
loans), modification of which required an 80 percent majority vote.[21]

Over more than half a century, the World Bank evolved in a number of
important ways. One important change was that, from the late 1960s on,
the United States steadily reduced its financial share in the Bank, from
more than 37 percent in 1946 to just over 16 percent today. To preserve
the U.S. veto, the rules concerning the Bank's constitutional majority were
changed in 1989 so that an 85 percent rather than an 80 percent majority was needed to modify the articles of agreement.[22] A second important
change was the proliferation of suborganizations within the "World Bank
Group," which increased the number and complexity of the Bank's activities. The first additions to the World Bank Group were the IFC in 1956 and
IDA in 1960. Thereafter, the original facility was referred to as the IBRD
(the original name of the World Bank), to distinguish it from the more
recent lending windows. In 1988, the Bank inaugurated its Multilateral
Investment Guarantee Agency, which provided political risk insurance for
foreign investors in developing countries as well as technical assistance
and dispute mediation. And, in 1990, the Bank also became a joint admin-
istrator (along with two specialized agencies of the United Nations) of the
Global Environment Facility, which funded environmental projects and
programs in developing countries.

A third aspect of the Bank that varied over time was the level of delegation of authority from shareholders to professional managers. The
World Bank's Executive Board was historically relatively weak with
respect to management.[23] There has always been a notable exception to
this tilt in favor of management: the United States has possessed a range
of channels of influence, such as management's practice of consulting with
the U.S. executive director on loans and all major issues to be brought to
the board.[24] The United States also has the traditional privilege of selecting the Bank's president, who has always been an American citizen.

The balance of power between management and shareholders has also fluctuated over time. During the 1950s, the Bank successfully raised money on international capital markets, money that it used to make prudent and profitable investments. The establishment of IDA, however, shifted the balance of power between management and shareholders by bringing the Bank regularly, hat in hand, to the donors who filled the till. This meant, as two World Bank historians put it, that "the Executive directors for Part I [i.e., donor] countries could, in effect, say to the president, 'This is our money. You can't do as you please with it . . . and you will need our full cooperation to replenish the coffers when they become empty.'"[25] Although the founding of IDA increased the leverage of the World Bank's largest shareholders, during the presidency of Robert McNamara (1968–81), they were, apparently, willing to delegate significant authority to management. After McNamara's resignation in 1982, this era of relative autonomy came to an end, for reasons that are explored in chapters 3 and 4.

The Inter-American Development Bank

The IDB was founded in 1959 as an answer to Latin American demands for greater economic development financing. Because it was also founded to respond to U.S. concerns about the spread of communism in its regional backyard, the IDB had a more socially conscious organizational character than the World Bank and was granted a soft loan window (the FSO) at its founding. From the very beginning, the IDB possessed a clear mandate to lend for social purposes, and it was active much earlier than the World Bank in funding poverty-oriented projects, such as loans for peasant farmers.[26] It was only in the 1970s that it began to emphasize lending for traditional, World Bank–style projects, such as dams and power plants, and only in 1986 that it acquired a private-sector lending facility analogous to the World Bank's IFC. Known as the Inter-American Investment Corporation, this lending facility financed private-sector investment projects, with a focus on small and medium-sized enterprises.[27]

The United States is the shareholder in greatest proximity to IDB borrowers and has always been in a strong leadership position. The IDB's headquarters are in Washington, DC. At the bank's foundation, the United States controlled 42 percent of its voting shares, and membership was restricted to regional (including North American) governments; it was not until the 1970s that first Canada and then nonregional large donors were brought into the bank.[28] Between 1980 and 1994, nonregional donors increased their voting share from 5.51 to 15.95 percent, with a corresponding decline in the voting shares of borrowing members. Because modification of the IDB's charter requires a two-thirds majority of regional members, the United States possesses a veto analogous to its veto in the World Bank. In the IDB, as in the World Bank, the United States cannot veto individual loans. However, it *can* veto individual loans in the FSO (the IDB's soft loan window), the only lending facility in any of the MDBs in which this is the case. The United States does not appoint the IDB's president, who is always from the region and is elected by a simple majority of the Board of Governors. However, it does appoint the IDB's vice president, who is traditionally a U.S. citizen.[29]

Like the World Bank, the IDB historically awarded a strong role to management. Unlike, the World Bank, however, it also gave a relatively strong voice to borrowing members and had a voting structure that granted borrowing governments more than half the voting shares. Armed with this majority share, Latin American board members were active participants in forging IDB policy and sometimes even successfully opposed the United States. For example, over U.S. objections, the IDB provided a loan to Chile under the Marxist government of Salvador Allende in the early 1970s.[30] In contrast, the World Bank discreetly stopped lending to Chile during this period.[31]

Remarkably, in spite of such defiance, the United States continued to be an extremely generous patron of the IDB for some time.[32] However, this combination of generous financing and minimal control was not destined to last. During the Reagan presidency, the United States demanded increased control over the organization, along with a number of policy changes. This led to a crisis in U.S.-IDB relations, a drastic decline in IDB financing, and, ultimately, the IDB's acquiescence to the substance of U.S. demands (described at length in chapter 5). Since the late 1980s, there have been no major public disagreements either between the United States and borrowing members or between the United States and IDB members.

The Asian Development Bank

The AsDB was founded in 1965, after originally being proposed at a UN-sponsored meeting in Bangkok. Although the United States was slow to support the initiative, the Johnson administration eventually decided that a regional bank might help forestall conflicts of the sort the United States was trying to quell in Indochina.[33] Unlike the IDB, but like the World

Bank, the AsDB began its existence with an explicit mandate to build infrastructure rather than to tackle poverty; its concessional lending facility was not established until 1973, and it has only been in more recent decades that the bank has incorporated fighting poverty as a central component of its organizational mission. The AsDB does not have a facility dedicated to private-sector financing, but, after 1983, it engaged in lending to private-sector projects through its regular lending window.[34]

The most obvious factor distinguishing the AsDB from the other banks is its strong Japanese influence. It is the only MDB in which the United States has always been codominant with another shareholder government: at its founding, the United States and Japan each had 17.2 percent of the votes within the bank; since then, their shares have been reduced to 12.9 percent each. To preserve its claim to being an Asian institution, the AsDB is required to have at least 60 percent of its subscribed capital held by countries in the region. However, regional countries have included Australia and New Zealand, which tend to side with the United States.[35] Currently, nonregional members (the United States plus Canada and the European countries), combined with Australia and New Zealand, control just over 41 percent of the votes. The AsDB president is traditionally a Japanese national, selected by the Japanese government from a list drawn up by the U.S. Treasury.

Compared to both the World Bank and IDB, the AsDB is structured so that the president plays a more passive role—and the Executive Board a more active role—in guiding the organization.[36] Also in contrast to the IDB, with its history of independent-minded borrowers, the AsDB is a donor-dominated bank, in which borrowing countries have little voting share and little voice.[37] However, because it is jointly dominated by the United States and Japan, the nature of this donor dominance is somewhat peculiar. Relations between the president of the bank, who is always Japanese, and the U.S. executive director have sometimes been difficult and are even rumored to have been the cause of the resignation of one president, Kimimasa Tarumizu, in 1993.[38]

Nevertheless, there have been few recorded instances of friction between the bank's two leading shareholders. In part, this can be attributed to the congruence of U.S. and Japanese interests; in 1972, one author of a book on the regional MDBs referred half jokingly to the bank an "agency for the promotion of a US-backed Japanese hegemony."[39] However, a more recent analysis of the AsDB by Nihal Kappagoda has suggested that another reason is that Japan and other donor governments have always made a great effort to accommodate U.S. demands. For example, despite the misgivings of other leading shareholders, the AsDB refrained from lending to Vietnam for many years after the humiliating U.S. withdrawal.[40] The Japanese have also shown forbearance in the face of diminishing American contributions. The U.S. voting share on the AsDB's Executive Board exceeds its capital contributions: although Japan and the United States contribute equivalent amounts to the bank's ordinary capital resources, the United States contributes considerably less than Japan to the AsDF, which shares the AsDB's voting structure.[41] That Japan is, in effect, subsidizing American influence within the bank is strong evidence of the lengths to which it is willing to go to keep the peace with its codominant partner.

The African Development Bank

In contrast to the three banks discussed above, the AfDB was founded, in 1964, entirely at the initiative of countries from the region—not by wealthy donor governments. Inspired by the ideals of pan-Africanism, the bank originally limited its membership to African governments. As a consequence of this limited membership, soon after its founding the AfDB ran into considerable financial difficulties, particularly stemming from the absence of callable capital pledges from wealthy donors. The consequent inability to secure the confidence of international capital markets restricted the bank to lending only out of its paid-in capital—the limited funds that it had at hand from member contributions.[42]

Over time, the AfDB's members came to the conclusion that it was better to sacrifice some measure of autonomy in order to build a bigger and more influential bank. In 1973, the AfDF was inaugurated with $82.6 million in grants from thirteen nonregional governments, who would be members of the soft but not the hard lending window. On the bank's reaching the limits of its lending capacity in the late 1970s, African members approved the entry of nonregional members into its hard loan window. However, donors and regional members disagreed on the terms of this arrangement, and it was not until 1982 that nonregional governments officially became members of the AfDB.[43]

The 1982 agreement had a number of stipulations designed to maintain the African character of the bank. Its headquarters would always be located on the continent (currently temporarily in Tunisia), and its president, to be elected by a majority of both the overall membership and the African members, would always be African. Nonregional members—the donor governments—would be limited to one-third of the votes within the AfDB and half the votes within the AfDF. The United States was the only nonregional government that had its own executive director.[44]

The AfDB's unusually independent history has shaped relationships between borrowing and donating members and between management and shareholders. Until relatively recently, regional governments had a majority of voting shares on the bank's Board of Directors. Major donors have often been challenged by regional representatives, and even the objections of the U.S. executive director could (at least at one time) be described as "easily overruled."[45] This borrower-dominated board has always been an unusually active and vocal body and has the right to suspend the president; even the position of the AfDB's vice president is filled by the Board of Directors, albeit at the president's recommendation.[46]

In spite of its notoriously feisty regional members, for approximately a decade following the 1982 agreement the African bank was remarkably successful at mobilizing resources: whereas total AfDB and AfDF loan approvals between 1979 and 1981 were only about $1.7 billion, in the period 1991–93 they had risen to $8.9 billion—roughly a threefold increase, in inflation-adjusted terms.[47] The regional members of the AfDB during this period were, like those of the IDB in the 1960s and 1970s, granted considerable leeway by leading shareholders to run the bank as they saw fit.

In the 1990s, however, a long-brewing crisis nudged the AfDB toward a closer resemblance to its fellow MDBs. By that time, the bank was in grave financial trouble. The Third World debt crisis had hit Africa hard, and the bank's ratio of debt to usable capital had risen precipitously, leading to a downgrading of its ratings in international bond markets.[48] Ultimately, donor governments bailed out the AfDB, but they conditioned their assistance on major reforms. As a result, nonregional members collectively raised their voting share from one-third to 40 percent, and voting rules for modifying the articles of agreement were changed to require a 70 percent majority—effectively giving nonregional members a veto.[49]

The European Bank for Reconstruction and Development

Established in 1991 to assist in the post-Communist transitions of Eastern European states, the EBRD is the MDB with the most undifferentiated structure. Unlike the banks mentioned above, it does not have a soft loan facility. Indeed, because it lends heavily to private investors, in many respects it looks more like the World Bank's IFC, or even a private bank, than it does a development bank.[50]

To establish the EBRD, leading donors first needed to resolve a number of outstanding disagreements between the United States and European donors. One dispute concerned the bank's mandate: whereas the Bush administration wanted the EBRD to lend exclusively to the private sector, European shareholders envisioned something more like the IBRD within the World Bank, funneling money to infrastructure and other state-provided projects. The compromise solution was a bank that emphasized private-sector lending but in which up to 40 percent of loans could go to support public infrastructure.[51] A second set of disagreements, concerning voting shares, was resolved by agreeing that European Community (later European Union) donors would control 51 percent of the bank but that the United States would have the single largest voting share: 10 percent. As in the other banks, loans would be approved by simple majority. Revising the articles of agreement, however, would require an 85 percent majority, which meant that, in coalition with another member, the United States would possess a veto.[52]

Like the AsDB, but unlike the IDB and the AfDB, the EBRD has always been a donor-dominated bank, in which borrowers have little say in the overall direction of the organization.[53] Uniquely among the MDBs, the EBRD is controlled by European donors, who have the biggest bloc of voting shares, and the bank's headquarters are neither in Eastern Europe nor in Washington but in London.

The EBRD will play only a minor part in this book. In part, this is because the U.S. role in the EBRD is minor compared to its role in the other banks, but there are two other important reasons. First, because it lends mostly to the private sector and does not engage in lending for economic policy reforms, the EBRD has played little role in either debates over economic development or the dispensing of policy advice to borrowing governments. Second, its lack of a concessional lending facility has exempted it from participation in the increasingly important debates over how to tackle the issue of poverty. This lack of a concessional lending facility also insulates the EBRD from the shareholder pressures that are exerted during the periodic replenishments of other MDBs' soft loan windows.

The MDBs and Resource Dependence

International financial institutions—the IMF and the MDBs—are complex organizations that can be described in dramatically different ways depending on observers' theoretical perspectives. For some, they represent multilateral solutions to collective-action problems that individual states would be unable to address on their own.[54] For others, they are tools for the promotion of the domination of poor countries by the developed world.[55] And, for still another group of observers, they are viewed primarily as bureaucracies, with all the accompanying virtues and pathologies of bureaucratic organizations.[56]

For the purposes of this book, however, I propose a somewhat different view of the banks—one broadly inspired by the institutionalist tradition within the sociology of organizations.[57] Institutionalists often observe that organizations are not isolated organisms and seek to understand the ways in which they interact with forces in their environment. Irrespective of their formal missions, complex organizations share a fundamental interest in their own survival and flourishing, which occurs to the extent that they are successful in securing external resources. This resource dependence, in turn, influences organizational behavior. For example, private corporations need large injections of capital to fulfill their purpose as profit-making institutions. Consequently, the behavior of corporations is influenced by the preferences and behavior of their shareholders—the external actors that provide corporations with the resources they need to survive.

Because private corporations are analogous in structure to the MDBs—with boards of directors, shareholders, and so on—and because so much has been written on corporate governance, it is worth exploring the corporate management of resource dependence in greater detail. Investors in corporations want to ensure that they will receive a return. To attract investors, corporations set up governance structures that give shareholders a say in how the organization is run, awarding a greater say to investors who contribute more. However, shareholders do not have the time to oversee the details of how their companies are run and, therefore, delegate authority to management—well-paid professionals whose job it is to run the company and maximize its financial return.[58] Beyond such general characteristics, corporate governance structures can vary considerably, particularly by geographic region—for example, French companies tend to be structured differently from U.S. companies—as well as over time.[59] A particularly relevant change in U.S. corporate governance over the past several decades has been the rise of shareholder activism, the phenomenon of shareholders taking a much more active role in governing the corporation than they did in previous decades, when most decisions were delegated to management.[60]

Viewing corporations as resource-dependent organizations in no way implies that they are passive tools. Corporate managers have their own interests—job security, high salaries, a tidy share of the profits, and so on—that may not necessarily align with the interests of leading shareholders. Managers always seek to maximize autonomy, although their success in doing so varies. Because they control the proximate levers of organizational control, managers can buffer themselves from external pressures using various strategies. For example, they can use conciliatory language and make symbolic gestures without actually complying with shareholder demands. Organizational insiders pursue these strategies of "ceremonial conformity," in part, because they control the flow of information to the outside, which makes it possible for them to substitute ceremonial for substantive conformity. One specific means of achieving ceremonial conformity, identified in the institutionalist literature, is "loose coupling," or the delinking of organizational subunits to protect the core from substantive compliance.[61] One illustrative study found that, rather than complying with affirmative action legislation by fully integrating management, U.S. companies introduced equal employment opportunity offices, giving the impression that they were serious about ending discrimination.[62]

Moreover, like other resource-dependent organizations, corporations are resistant to external pressures for the simple reason that they are bureaucracies, with their own internal dynamics. These include red tape, resistance to change, and the preferential treatment of easy and clear over difficult and ambiguous tasks. Corporations are also influenced by the powerful professions that staff them and by fads and fashions among similar organizations in their environments.[63]

The MDBs' management of external resource dependence resembles that of private corporations in a number of respects. Like corporations, the MDBs are organizations that are heavily dependent on *financial* resources: they cannot operate on a shoestring but, rather, need large amounts of capital to carry out their organizational mandates. Like corporations, the MDBs secure control over external financial resources by granting influence over their activities to external actors: namely, the governments that finance them. The logic of the banks' weighted voting systems can be seen as analogous to that of private corporate governance. That is, if investors (governments) are to be persuaded to part with their resources, they must be given a say in how the organization is run—as a form of insurance that they will get a return on their investment.

Because the MDBs' financial resources also come from international capital markets, the role of private investors in determining the MDBs' behavior requires further explanation. The MDBs raise money on international capital markets by issuing bonds, which consistently receive very high ratings from international bond-rating agencies such as Moody's and Standard and Poor's. A very important reason for these high ratings is that, in addition to providing liquid resources, leading shareholder, or donor, governments provide the banks with callable capital—pledges to back up the banks in case of financial distress. Thus backed by the full faith and credit of the world's wealthiest governments, the MDBs represent a sound investment indeed.[64] In the history of the MDBs, there has never been recourse to the callable resources of shareholder governments.

Unlike shareholding governments, private bondholders are not awarded a vote on the MDBs' boards of directors. By expressing reluctance to purchase the banks' bonds, and by downgrading their bond ratings, the international financial community can, in a sense, vote on the banks' policies. Yet, in the history of the banks over more than half a century, such interventions have been extremely rare because bondholders are interested in financial return and MDB bonds have almost always been an extremely sound investment. While the bond markets may, in rare cases, react to the banks' efficacy as money managers, they are agnostic on the issue of more specific MDB policies, such as whether the banks' resources are directed to finance projects versus policy reforms.

Another aspect of the MDBs that resembles private corporate governance is the delegation of authority to management. The president and top management of each bank are selected by shareholder governments. As in private corporations, the willingness of shareholders to delegate authority to management is a variable, rather than a constant: sometimes shareholders are active, and sometimes they are more passive. Also as in private corporations, MDB managers may have their own agendas that conflict with that of the shareholders that put them there.[65] The fundamental interest of all bureaucracies is in surviving, and this goal may put MDB management at odds with shareholder governments attempting to maximize other goals.[66] As complex organizations staffed by professionals—most notably, economists—the MDBs may develop in ways that respond to professional, rather than shareholder, pressures.[67] Finally, the MDBs may be resistant to shareholder pressures for change owing to the simple fact that they are bureaucracies possessing a range of tactics for actively resisting change, from controlling the flow of information to the outside to the loose coupling of organizational subunits.

Yet, in spite of all the fundamental similarities between the MDBs and private corporations, there are also some significant differences. Most important, whereas in private firms shareholder return is easily measured in dollars and cents, in the MDBs return on investment is much more difficult to quantify. All the MDBs are expected to be profitable, but leading shareholder governments do not receive a portion of these profits. Nor do they borrow from the banks (some wealthy industrialized countries did borrow from the World Bank in the postwar period, but they have not done so for decades). The ostensible justification for wealthy governments' financing of the MDBs is that they promote the economic development of poor countries. Yet, as we saw in the introduction, *development* is a complex idea that has been defined in different ways at different points in history, and this mandate provides little insight into why donor governments provide the banks with their financing.

In reality, leading shareholders invest in the MDBs in order to pursue a host of heterogeneous goals, goals linked to policy programs in a variety of areas. Historically, these goals have included the promotion of national security, the promotion of economic growth in developing countries, the opening of Third World markets to serve as sources of raw materials and markets for shareholder exports, the generation of procurement contracts for shareholder firms, and the combating of poverty. More recently, the MDBs have been viewed by leading shareholders as tools for promoting economic and social transitions in formerly Communist countries, managing postconflict transitions, and addressing global issues, such as climate change and AIDS.[68]

The ambiguous and heterogeneous nature of shareholder return in the MDBs has important consequences for the dynamics of shareholder demands within the banks. One consequence is that different shareholders can have very different ideas about what the MDBs are for and, hence, different ideas about what should be done with them. These shareholder goals and priorities may also change over time, transforming the policies and ideas promoted by the banks themselves. For example, during the 1980s, leading donors began to view liberalizing policy reform in developing countries as a top priority. The MDBs changed along with this focus—both increasing the proportion of their resources that went to supporting such reforms and producing a higher volume of research dedicated to market-liberalizing themes.

What determines which conception of shareholder value prevails at any given moment? Politics. Major shareholders develop their goals and priorities for the MDBs through a political process—one that includes a host of domestic political actors, from political parties to organized interest groups to social movements. Because the United States is the leading shareholder in the MDBs, Washington politics are of particular consequence for the activities they pursue and the ideas they promote.

The United States as Activist Shareholder

The United States has a number of rationales for supporting the MDBs and a range of vehicles for advancing U.S. goals. Which among many possible conceptions of shareholder value predominates at any given time is determined through a political process involving the policy programs of both the executive and the legislative branches as well as political input from constituents, interest groups, and civil society. The U.S. Treasury has several means through which to exert influence in the MDBs and, thereby, to pursue the current conception of U.S. interests. Perhaps the most important of these mechanisms is what I refer to as *donor leverage*, whereby the United States withholds (or threatens to withhold) resources from the banks unless its policy agenda is followed. Overall, the United States is uniquely positioned among major donors to behave as an activist shareholder.

Framing U.S. Interests

If we survey the annual U.S. Treasury testimonies to Congress from the early 1970s through the present, we find a range of rationales for supporting the MDBs, rationales based on different conceptions of U.S. interests in the banks. I say *rationales* rather than *purposes* because such public statements cannot necessarily be taken at face value—they are interpretive frames designed to garner support from a particular audience. Nevertheless, as perennially useful interpretive frames designed to resonate with Congress and to reflect the administrations' overall agendas, these rationales provide us with insight into underlying policy goals and purposes.

The three most important policy objectives mentioned over this three-decade span can be categorized as *strategic, economic,* and *humanitarian*.[69] Strategic rationales focus on the utility of foreign aid in promoting U.S. security. Sometimes security interests have been framed as advanced through the support of friendly regimes; for example, the George W. Bush administration strongly emphasized the MDBs' role in supporting "key

U.S. foreign policy priorities," such as reconstruction in Iraq and Afghanistan.[70] More generally, financing for the MDBs is sometimes justified on the grounds that it serves as a symbol of the commitment of wealthy countries to the problems of the developing world.[71] As Treasury Secretary William Miller put it in 1980: "IDA is … the centerpiece of U.S. North/South strategy, and the symbol of our commitment to Third World Development. It serves to undermine those in the developing world who favor confrontation with the United States."[72]

Among economic rationales, one of the most common has always been that the MDBs promote economic growth in developing countries—thereby making them "more productive and self-reliant."[73] This goal is framed sometimes as an end in itself and sometimes as a means for promoting U.S. interests. As Treasury Secretary Lloyd Bentsen told Congress in 1993: "We have a strong interest in encouraging greater economic growth in developing countries [which are] the most rapidly growing market for a broad range of U.S. goods and services."[74] The banks are also frequently portrayed as serving U.S. interests by helping open foreign markets to U.S. exports and investment and generating new sources of raw materials.

The humanitarian rationale is based on a purely moral appeal. Under this rationale, the banks serve U.S. interests by improving the lives of the poor, eliminating contagious diseases, and so on. As Assistant Treasury Secretary Fred Bergsten put it to Congress in 1977: "Poverty and misery remain endemic in many parts of the world. Our very spirit as a nation requires that we do our part toward alleviating those conditions."[75]

In addition to these metapolicy goals, the annual Treasury testimonies to Congress also commonly invoke two sets of secondary objectives (referred to as "operational" objectives in an important 1982 Treasury report on U.S. policy toward the MDBs).[76] One set concerns U.S. commercial interests. Procurement contracts for MDB projects (e.g., to build roads or dams) can be quite lucrative for the companies awarded them. As Treasury Secretary Donald Regan told Congress in 1983: "Procurement of American goods and services for projects assisted by the MDBs has been running at approximately $1.2 billion per year, benefiting virtually all regions of the United States."[77] The second set of operational rationales concerns cost-effectiveness: as multilateral institutions, the MDBs allow the United States to share the burden of economic development financing with other wealthy nations.

Although the major justifications for the MDBs can be categorized as strategic, economic, or humanitarian in theory, in practice the three goals have always been inextricably intertwined. Very frequently, the Treasury will construe the prosperity of poor countries (an economic goal) as being essential for quelling social discontent and, thereby, promoting international security. For example, in 1977, Congress was told by the U.S. Treasury: "International instability in [developing] countries ... can often be fostered—or even produced—by lack of economic progress, [and] can create international tension and conflict which in turn can draw the United States into dangerous international situations."[78] Humanitarian goals, such as improving the lot of the poor, were similarly often portrayed as means to U.S. security goals. This was particularly clear in Bush administration testimonies after the September 11, 2001, attacks on the World Trade Center: "When governments fail to meet the most basic needs of their people, these failed states can become havens for terror."[79]

As this long list of objectives implies, there is no such thing as a single U.S. policy toward the MDBs. Members of Congress often advance their own priorities among the above-mentioned objectives as well as means to achieving these ends. Meanwhile, outside actors—from private firms interested in procurement contracts to church groups concerned with poverty—bring ideas about U.S. interests into the congressional approval process. Which conceptions of U.S. interests predominate at any given time depends on the economic and foreign policy programs of both the administration and members of Congress and how willing Congress is to go along with the administration's proposal. Eventually, out of this complex political process emerge the policies that are pursued by the U.S. Treasury.

Advancing U.S. Interests

The U.S. Treasury has a number of tools at its disposal for advancing U.S. interests in the MDBs. The most obvious of these is its formal voting share. As table 1.1 above illustrates, the United States has the largest share of votes in three of the five banks and is codominant with Japan in the AsDB. It possesses a formal veto in the World Bank and the IDB. This veto applies, not to individual loans, but to more major proposals to modify the organizations' charters; it is only in the IDB's FSO that the United States can veto individual loans. Over time, the U.S. voting share in the IBRD, IDA, and the IDB/FSO has decreased significantly, as the U.S. gov-

TABLE I.2. **U.S. Percentage Voting Share in the MDBs, 1970–2006**

	IBRD	IDA	IDB/FSO	AsDB/AsDF	AfDB	AfDF	EBRD
1970	24	25.2	42.47	16.5	0	0	N.A.
1980	20.84	21.35	34.9	11.19	0	4	N.A.
1982	22.4	18.97	35.17	13.57	0	6.19	N.A.
1984	19.36	19.63	34.54	13.88	5.83	6.81	N.A.
1986	19.88	18.61	34.51	14.91	5.61	6.54	N.A.
1988	18.72	18.11	34.5	12.36	5.8	7.36	N.A.
1990	15.12	17.22	34.63	12.39	5.93	6.86	N.A.
1992	17.37	16.22	34.66	13.1	6.5	8.5	10
1994	17.42	15.67	34.7	13.37	5.9	6.8	10
1996	17.43	15.08	31.78	13.2	5.64	6.5	10
1998	16.68	14.93	31	13	5.7	5.8	10
2000	16.5	14.86	31	13.1	5.6	6.075	10
2002	16.45	14.52	30.01	13	6.57	6.35	10
2004	16.39	14.28	30.01	12.9	6.6	6.2	10
2006	16.39	13.39	30.01	12.8	6.5	6.1	10

Source: Annual Reports, World Bank, IDB, AsDB, AfDB, and EBRD.

ernment has worked to reduce the costs of its participation in the MDBs (see table 1.2).

However, the distribution of voting shares in the MDBs provides a very incomplete picture of U.S. influence in the banks. A number of informal practices enhance U.S. influence far beyond what its voting share would suggest. One is the practice of bringing votes to the boards of the various banks only after an extensive consultation with the major shareholder governments and especially with the U.S. executive director.[80] This effect is enhanced by the fact that two of the MDBs, including the World Bank, are located in the U.S. capital. Such behind-the-scenes U.S. influence explains, for example, why the World Bank made no new loans to Chile under during the Allende government from 1970–73—not because the United States opposed such loans through a formal vote, but because informal U.S. opposition meant that they were never brought to the Executive Board in the first place.[81]

Another influence-enhancing practice is the traditional U.S. privilege of filling key positions in the MDBs' top management. In the IDB, the United States always gets to select the executive vice president (the president is always a Latin American); in the AsDB, a U.S.-nominated American citizen holds one of the three vice presidencies; and, in the EBRD, the United States gets to nominate the vice president. Most important, the United States always gets to nominate the president of the World Bank, who is always a U.S. citizen.[82]

However, perhaps the most critical informal vehicle for U.S. influence is the U.S. role in periodic financial contributions to the banks and their soft loan windows. These contributions provide the opportunity for the United States to exert what I refer to as *donor leverage*.

Donors make two main kinds of contributions to the MDBs: capital increases for their hard loan windows and replenishment of the banks' soft loan windows. Periodically, donors agree that there needs to be an increase in the capital stock of MDBs' hard loan windows (e.g., because of the growth in the size of the global economy). These resources are provided in the form of general capital increases.[83] In contrast, because they are not profitable, the banks' soft loan or concessional windows are dependent on frequent replenishments from donor governments. Soft loan replenishments are much more frequent than general capital increases, as table 1.3 shows. For example, the World Bank has had three general capital increases in its history, while IDA, the Bank's soft loan window, has had fourteen replenishments. Sometimes banks use the hard loan windows as cash cows through which to subsidize the soft loan windows; for example, since 1964, the original lending wing of the World Bank, IDA, has transferred a portion of its net annual income to IDA, the Bank's soft loan facility.[84] For the most part, however, the concessional lending facilities still rely on financing from donor governments.

Replenishments and general capital increases occur through a complex process with multiple stages. First, representatives of the donor governments must reach agreement among themselves about the size of the resources to be given, how much money each government will contribute, and the kinds of bank policies on which the replenishment is to be conditioned. These negotiations lead to the production of a document laying out the terms to which the donors agree, a document that is then presented to the Board of Directors on a take-it-or-leave-it basis. Then the Board of Directors presents a report to management containing the donors' decisions for the bank's policy direction. For example, the negotiations for the fourteenth replenishment of IDA, known to the development policy community simply as *IDA14*, were completed in March 2005, and the resulting document, nearly one hundred pages long, contains six pages of summarized policy recommendations. Increasingly, donor governments have been observed to use replenishments for the concessional wing of a bank (e.g., IDA) as an occasion to make demands of the bank as a whole (e.g., the World Bank Group, including IDA, the IBRD, and the IFC).[85]

TABLE 1.3. **MDBs, General Capital Increases (GCI), and Concessional Facility Replenishments (Repl.)**

	World Bank		IDB		AsDB		AfDB		EBRD	
	GCI	Repl.	GCI	Repl.	GCI	Repl.	GCI	Repl.	GCI	Repl.
1959	GCI-1									
1960										
1961										
1962										
1963										
1964		IDA-1		FSO-1						
1965										
1966										
1967				FSO-2						
1968										
1969		IDA-2								
1970										
1971			IDB-3	IDB-3	GCI-1					
1972		IDA-3								
1973										
1974						AsDF-1				
1975		IDA-4	IDB-4	IDB-4						
1976					GCI-2	AsDF-2	GCI-1	AfDF-1		
1977		IDA-5								
1978										
1979			IDB-5	IDB-5		AsDF-3	GCI-2	AfDF-2		
1980	GCI-2									
1981										
1982		IDA-6	IDB-6	IDB-6		AsDF-4		AfDF3		
1983					GCI-3		GCI3			
1984										
1985		IDA-7						AfDF-4		

Year								
1986								
1987								
1988	GCI-3	IDA-8			AsDF-5	GCI-4	AfDF-5	
1989								
1990			IDB-7					
1991		IDA-9		IDB-7				
1992					AsDF-6		AfDF-6	
1993		IDA-10	IDB-8					
1994				IDB-8				
1995								
1996				GCI-4			AfDF-7	GCI-1
1997		IDA-11			AsDF-7			
1998						GCI-5		
1999								
2000		IDA-12			AsDF-8		AfDF8	
2001								
2002							AfDF9	
2003		IDA-13						
2004								
2005		IDA-14			AsDF-9		AfDF10	
2006								
2007								

Sources: English and Mule, *African Development Bank*; Kappagoda, *Asian Development Bank*; World Bank, "Chronology"; World Bank, *Annual Report* (various years); IDB, *Annual Report* (various years); U.S. Treasury Department, *Treasury International Programs* (various years).

Note: Years indicate the year an agreement took effect. Shaded areas indicate that facility was/is not in existence.

Periodic contributions provide donors with the opportunity to push forward particular policy initiatives in the banks. U.S. leadership in these initiatives derives in part from the sheer size of its contributions to replenishments and general capital increases: the United States has the largest economy, is the largest overall contributor to the MDBs, and naturally has the greatest voice in the policies on which replenishments and general capital increases are conditioned.

Yet the weight of U.S. influence cannot be completely explained by the size of its contributions. Indeed, there are several outstanding examples of other major shareholders allowing the United States to maintain its formal influence in the banks even though its proportional contribution has declined. Although Japan is now the most generous donor to IDA, it is still the United States that maintains the largest voting share; a similar discrepancy between the United States and Japan can be seen in the governing structure of the AsDF.[86] There is evidence suggesting that other MDB donors would be willing to be much more generous in financing the banks but deliberately hold down their contributions to preserve the U.S. voting share.[87] In 1989, in deference to the United States, other donors allowed the rules for changing the World Bank's constitutional majority to be changed such that an 85 percent rather than an 80 percent majority was needed to modify the articles of agreement. The reason for the change was to preserve the U.S. veto in the face of declining U.S. contributions.[88]

Perhaps most tellingly, although the U.S. financial share in all the MDBs but the AfDB and the EBRD has steadily decreased since the 1970s, U.S. leadership in these banks seems to have increased.[89] As we will see in the chapters that follow, from the 1980s on, the United States has often behaved like an activist shareholder, leading other donors in major reform initiatives, and withholding contributions if American initiatives were not followed.

The United States has been able to play this role because it has been unique among leading shareholders in its willingness to abandon the banks. Most donor governments see the MDBs as a relatively cheap means of achieving a host of desirable objectives—from private-sector procurement opportunities to addressing the AIDS crisis in Africa. In contrast, within the U.S. Congress, the benefits of these organizations are not universally acknowledged or understood. Consequently, U.S. government support is always more insecure than is the support of Japan, the United Kingdom, France, Germany, or Canada. The insecurity of U.S. support, in turn, enhances American influence in replenishments and general capital increases.

Conclusion

The MDBs are not designed to be democracies of development ideas: they are organizations beholden to donor governments for their financial resources and designed to respond to their shareholders' policy initiatives. The MDBs are not passive tools of their shareholders—they possess their own organizational interests and a range of tactics to buffer themselves from shareholder demands. In the end, however, the shareholders own the banks and can use their formal representation on the banks' boards of directors and their financial leverage to determine the banks' overall trajectories. In contrast to private corporations, the MDBs' shareholder return cannot be measured in dollars and cents but, rather, corresponds to a shifting list of goals that are prioritized through domestic political processes. In the United States, this political process is unusually acrimonious and contested. Therefore, U.S. support for the banks is more insecure, a fact that enhances American leadership.

Yet the United States was not always the activist shareholder that it is today. Once upon a time, American policy toward the MDBs was expressed through a process of quiet agreements among shareholding governments and MDB management, with little or no input from Congress. In the chapters that follow, we will see that the rise of congressional controversies in the banks began in the 1970s, fueled by economic crisis and the breakdown of bipartisan consensus over U.S. foreign policy. Over the long term, the rise of congressional interest in the MDBs would contribute to a wave of U.S. shareholder activism that continues to the present day.

CHAPTER TWO

The Congressional Revolt

In the spring of 1980, the U.S. Treasury set out on its annual mission to convince Congress to fund the multilateral development banks (MDBs)—and failed miserably. As a result, the banks had to be financed through an emergency stopgap measure that cut the requested appropriation by two-thirds—the largest such cut in the history of U.S. participation in the MDBs.[1]

This chapter examines the historical origins of this 1980 congressional revolt. The Nixon, Ford, and Carter administrations were all firm supporters of the banks, which they portrayed as both beneficial to American economic interests and as bulwarks in the worldwide struggle against communism. Yet, during the 1970s, congressional support for this framing of U.S. interests was dwindling. Members of Congress—particularly in the House, and particularly on the Appropriations Committee—increasingly questioned the wisdom of spending taxpayer dollars on international programs at a time when the United States was suffering from economic problems at home. They questioned the economic efficacy of the banks' loans and criticized the banks' lack of accountability to the U.S. government and American voters. Perhaps most devastatingly of all, many were skeptical of the claim that the MDBs were effective guarantors of American national security. These various complaints would set the stage for a new rationale for supporting the MDBs under the presidential administration of Ronald Wilson Reagan.

U.S. Foreign Aid in the Postwar Period

The United States had entered the era of post–World War II development-financing with little real conviction. In his 1949 inaugural speech, Truman waxed eloquent about the obligation of the world's great democratic-capitalist power to help underdeveloped countries achieve higher standards of living. However, the speech emphasized forms of aid that were easy on U.S. taxpayers' checkbooks, such as technical assistance and increased foreign direct investment. Truman's original "Point Four" foreign aid program was designed to be small and temporary.[2]

Nevertheless, soon thereafter, the U.S. government was forced to re-examine this ambivalent approach and to build a larger and more permanent foreign aid program. Two key events leading to this outcome were the revolution in China in 1949 and the invasion of South Korea by the North in 1950. National security and stemming the spread of communism became the definitive argument for foreign aid, both military and economic. Although foreign economic aid was first envisioned as a means of providing short-term support to friendly governments—supplementing guns with butter—over the following years many U.S. policymakers became convinced that long-term economic development was the only way to keep Third World countries from joining the Communist bloc.[3]

No U.S. political leader better exemplified this tendency than John F. Kennedy, who expressed greater enthusiasm for economic development than any president before or since. Kennedy declared the 1960s to be the "decade of development."[4] Among his many contributions to the U.S. foreign aid program were the launching of the Alliance for Progress (an ambitious plan of economic development for Latin America), the founding of the Peace Corps, the consolidation of U.S. foreign aid programs under the umbrella of the U.S. Agency for International Development (USAID), and a fivefold increase in funding for the International Development Association (IDA).[5]

During these years, developing countries—many of them freshly decolonized—were experimenting with various kinds of state-led economic development schemes. Third World statism was most apparent in countries like China and Cuba, which emulated the Soviet model of state ownership of productive resources. Yet, even outside the socialist bloc, most Third World countries adopted illiberal economic regimes of one sort or another. Third World governments found intellectual and political support for these policies from various organizations in and around the

United Nations, such as the UN Economic Commission for Latin America (ECLA), the UN Council on Trade and Development (UNCTAD), and the Group of 77 (G77), an UNCTAD-sponsored political forum for developing countries. Intellectuals associated with these organizations, such as the famous Argentine economist Raul Prebisch, developed and disseminated the view that markets in developing countries did not function as well as they did in the wealthy North and that large-scale state interventions on behalf of industrial development were needed to compensate.

Throughout the postwar decades, the U.S. government periodically met Third World nationalism with violent opposition. In some cases, such as that of the Castro government in Cuba, the governments opposed were aligned with the Soviet bloc. Others, such as the Mossadegh government in Iran or that of Arbenz in Guatemala—both toppled by CIA-supported coups—espoused more moderate nationalistic ideologies. Nevertheless, as the cold war deepened and the foreign aid program expanded, the U.S. executive also developed considerable tolerance for Third World economic nationalism, accepting the idea that reformist national economic development projects—from state-owned industries in Venezuela to import substitution in India—needed to be accepted as part of the U.S. global strategy. Governments that adopted these strategies received large amounts of U.S. foreign aid. The thinking was that reformist nationalism offered Third World countries the alternative of satisfying demands for higher standards of living through capitalist economic development, rather than through socialist revolution.[6] As Walden Bello has observed of the postwar development regime: "While the U.S. upheld private enterprise and demanded access for its corporations, it was more tolerant when it came to protectionism, investment controls, and a strong role for government in managing the economy."[7]

The cold war thus created an opening for political liberals to help shape a new kind of U.S. policy toward developing countries. John Kenneth Galbraith recalled of this era: "In what was otherwise no springtime for liberals ... one could be for help to the poor of the world and explain that it was not suspect compassion but hard-boiled anti-Communism."[8] This allowed for the flourishing of the new subfield of development economics, which was sympathetic to Third World programs of national economic planning and import substitution and tended to call for large amounts of foreign economic aid. Development economists became increasingly visible in prestigious universities and the U.S. foreign aid bureaucracy; by the 1970s, they had become a major intellectual force within the World Bank.

Galbraith argued that the transformation of economic development into a respectable cold war doctrine lent the subfield both intellectual legitimacy and material support, in the form of jobs and grants.[9]

At the same time, development economics was the beneficiary of wider trends in the mainstream of the discipline—in particular, the dominance of Keynesianism. Development economics was not precisely Keynesian—it prescribed varieties of state intervention that went far beyond Keynes's "macroeconomic management." However, as Albert Hirshman famously argued, Keynesianism created an opening for development economics because it established that there were at least two kinds of economic laws—orthodox neoclassical laws, which applied only to economies that were at full employment, and another set of laws that applied when there was substantial unemployment. By "breaking the ice of neoclassical monoeconomics," as Hirshman put it, Keynesianism created the intellectual space for heterodox approaches to the problem of economic development.[10]

Nevertheless, both the ideal and the political foundations of postwar U.S. foreign aid policy were fragile and became more so over time. In the world of ideas, development economics was increasingly besieged by neoclassical economists and other critics who questioned its assumptions and disqualified its conclusions. In the world of politics, Congress became increasingly skeptical that foreign aid was helping achieve American goals abroad. Thus, in spite of ongoing support from the U.S. executive, foreign aid began to lose legitimacy.

The Rise and Partial Decline of Development Economics

Development economics was never based on a unitary theory but was rather a collection of ideas aimed at providing practical advice to Third World governments and foreign aid agencies. Over time, the World Bank became a major source of support for the subfield. For more than a decade after its founding, the Bank was a notoriously conservative institution, dominated by engineers and private bankers.[11] Following the arrival of Robert McNamara as the Bank's president in 1968, however, there was a major increase in internal resources for its research, and economists became increasingly prominent. Hollis Chenery, a well-known development economist, was hired to be director of research in 1970.[12] By the mid-1970s, the Bank had become "the preeminent player in development-related research" and a bastion of support for development economics.[13]

There were considerable intellectual disagreements among development economists, and it is impossible to do justice here to the subfield's various tendencies. However, it is important to mention a few of its most important characteristics since they will reappear in future chapters. One was its rejection of the monoeconomic claim that economic laws worked the same everywhere: most development economists maintained that, because of their unique structural features, developing economies could stagnate if they played by classical economic rules, such as indiscriminate opening to free trade. A related feature of development economics was its support for a variety of state interventions in developing countries, from import substitution to national economic planning. Within the subfield, Third World statism was not just tolerated but often enthusiastically advocated: as Gunnar Myrdal put it, the Third World economies were plagued by "vicious circles which can only be broken by large-scale state planning and state intervention."[14]

Third, many development economists also emphasized that Third World development was being blocked by shortages of capital. This idea was based on the Harrod-Domar model of economic growth, further developed by Hollis Chenery in his famous "two-gap" model. The two-gap model assumed that developing countries could not increase their foreign exchange earnings from exports enough to satisfy their development needs. Foreign exchange was essential for these countries to purchase capital and intermediate goods and, thereby, increase production. The main implication was that developing countries needed both to ration foreign exchange and to acquire investment capital from outside its borders. This provided a theoretical rationale for increasing concessional foreign aid.[15]

Over time, thinking among development economists evolved. The most important shift occurred in the late 1960s, when the subfield began to rethink its earlier emphasis on urban-industrial development and GNP growth. New data showed that the benefits of economic growth in developing countries had so far been extremely unequal. Launched by researchers at the International Labour Organization, the World Bank, and the Institute for Development Studies at the University of Sussex, the "basic needs" strategy focused more on social indicators (e.g., literacy and infant mortality) and put more emphasis on rural development and projects that directly benefited the poor (such as nutrition and education).[16] Hollis Chenery, who was by then the World Bank's research director, made a major contribution to this new philosophy with his book *Redistribution with Growth* (1974).

Yet development economics was never hegemonic. The rise of the subfield was accompanied, at all times, by strong criticisms from neoclassical and other economists who objected to its methods and conclusions. One of the most infamous critics was P. T. Bauer, an economist at the London School of Economics, but there were many others: Jacob Viner, Harry Johnson, Gottfried Haberler, and Herbert Frenkel are some prominent examples.[17]

The precariousness of the subfield's position within the economics discipline worsened in the 1960s and 1970s—just as it was achieving its zenith of popularity in the world of policy. The increased use of formal mathematical modeling by economists in the United States and the United Kingdom posed one set of problems for the subfield: many development economists resisted mathematical formalization.[18] Even worse, by the end of the 1970s, Keynesianism was going out of fashion, and more conservative macroeconomic ideas were becoming more influential in the United States and the United Kingdom. For these and other reasons, by the end of the 1970s, development economics appeared to be a subfield in crisis.[19] Meanwhile, congressional support for foreign aid was declining, for a very different set of reasons.

The Foreign Aid Revolt in Congress

During the 1950s and 1960s, the imminent threat of Communist expansion allowed for a tremendous expansion in U.S. foreign aid. This aid was overwhelmingly channeled through bilateral agencies, although these years also saw the founding of IDA and the Inter-American Development Bank (IDB).[20] Yet, just as the postwar U.S. foreign aid program was reaching its peak under the Kennedy administration, countervailing forces were gathering in Congress. Increasingly, Congress suffered from "aid fatigue"—the growing sense that the United States had been spending a lot on foreign aid but had little to show for it.[21]

Congressional quarrels with U.S. foreign policy came from two very different directions. On the one hand, some legislators on the left were concerned about Third World poverty and U.S. aid to right-wing military dictatorships. It was under the influence of this group that the so-called New Directions foreign aid legislation was passed in 1973. This modified the basic legal framework of U.S. foreign aid, bilateral and multilateral alike, restructuring it around "sectoral" activities, and mandating a reorientation toward the needs of the poor.[22] On the other hand, a very different set of concerns about foreign aid came mainly from con-

servative Democrats and Republicans, who questioned whether development financing was an effective use of taxpayer dollars.[23] Such legislators
began to assert that U.S. foreign policy toward the Third World was failing to enhance U.S. geopolitical objectives—a failure that was particularly
apparent in the case of U.S. involvement in Vietnam.

The congressional body that became notorious for blocking administration requests for foreign aid was the Subcommittee on Foreign
Operations of the House Committee on Appropriations. The culture of
the Appropriations Committee had always been fiscally conservative, a
by-product of its role as congressional guardian of the public purse as
well as the recruitment and self-selection of members.[24] New members of
the subcommittee in charge of foreign aid, the Foreign Operations Subcommittee, tended to have little knowledge of the programs being funded
and, hence, little interest in supporting them. In contrast, the subcommittees in charge of *authorizing* foreign aid legislation tended to contain
foreign policy establishment figures, such as Senator Hubert Humphrey,
formerly vice president under the Johnson administration, or Representative Henry Reuss of Wisconsin, a former deputy general counsel for the
Marshall Plan.[25] These policymakers tended to have a prior commitment
to foreign aid programs and were less predisposed toward cutting them.
Moreover, where cutting foreign aid was concerned, the Senate tended
to have a more moderate approach than the House—a trend that can be
attributed partly to its more accommodating legislative style and also to
longer terms in office, which undoubtedly made senators less prone to
populist grandstanding against government waste and more prone to taking the "long view."[26]

A key leader of the foreign aid revolt of the 1960s was the Foreign
Operations Subcommittee's chair, Otto Passman, a conservative Democrat from Louisiana. Passman was a colorful figure representing a folksy,
populist approach to foreign policy that had little in common with the
elite, cold war liberalism of such figures as Senator William Fulbright. A
fourth-grade dropout who had completed his high school degree in night
school and who had worked as an appliance salesman before entering
politics, Passman was once quoted as saying to an Eisenhower administration official: "Son, I don't smoke; I don't drink; my only pleasure in life
is to kick the shit out of the foreign aid program of the United States."[27]
Guided by this mission, Passman used his position on the Appropriations
Committee to regularly secure a 20–25 percent reduction in the foreign
aid amount requested by the administration.[28] In addition to reducing ap-

propriations, Congress began to attach legislative conditions to foreign aid bills to ensure that the money was spent wisely—from clauses guaranteeing that U.S. properties would not be expropriated to language prohibiting financing to governments that violated human rights.

The MDBs Become a Political Issue

From the founding of the World Bank on, the MDBs were considered by the United States to be instruments of American foreign policy and subjected to pressures from Washington to ensure that they "promoted development in ways that complemented U.S. long-term goals and short-term political and economic interests."[29] Yet, until the 1970s, the MDBs appeared to be immune to the congressional activism that was raging in other areas of foreign aid. In the postwar decades, U.S. policies toward the banks were negotiated through "quiet agreement between bank authorities and the U.S. executive," a process that excluded the legislative branch.[30] Nor did the legislative branch seem to mind being excluded. The size of U.S. contributions to the banks was extremely small compared to U.S. bilateral aid programs. Within the U.S. government, policy toward the banks was, in the words of one observer, "the minor concern of a handful of low-level executive officials," and few members of Congress bothered to learn the arcane details of the banks' governance and functioning.[31]

This did not mean that disagreements among donors, or between the United States and the banks, did not arise. For example, the second IDA replenishment (1965–69) took nearly four years to complete because of disagreements between the Johnson administration and World Bank management over funding levels.[32] Significantly, however, once the Bank and the administration arrived at an agreement, Congress appropriated funds for IDA with little comment. Figure 2.1 shows that, from fiscal year 1964 through fiscal year 1971, Congress appropriated all the funds that the administration requested for the MDBs.

Subsequently, however, Congress suddenly began to show an interest in the MDB program and to cut the administration's budget requests on a regular basis. The proximate cause of this increased congressional interest was the growing importance of the MDBs within the executive's foreign aid budget. By increasingly emphasizing multilateral foreign assistance, presidential administrations of the 1970s hoped to reconcile two conflicting objectives. The first was to address growing Third World militancy

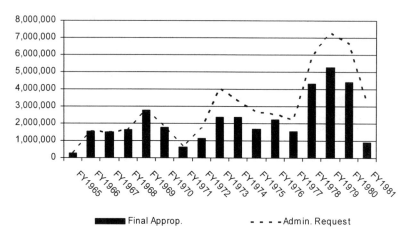

FIGURE 2.1. U.S. administration requests and final appropriations for the MDBs in thousands of U.S. dollars (2000), fiscal year 1965–fiscal year 1981. *Source: Congressional Quarterly Almanac* (various years).

through increased foreign aid. The second was to pacify the foreign aid rebellion in Congress by emphasizing foreign assistance that was funded multilaterally—and that therefore allowed the United States to share the financial burden with other donors. In the end, neither of these two objectives was achieved, and the MDB program was permanently transformed into a perennial bone of congressional contention.

One of the greatest strategic challenges faced by U.S. policymakers of the 1970s was the flourishing of Third World nationalism, in all its various forms. The national liberation forces in Vietnam triumphed against the most powerful nation in the world, and the producers of the world's most important commodity successfully organized into OPEC, bringing the U.S. economy to its knees. The decade's end was punctuated by two revolutions: a socialist revolution in Nicaragua, a country in the backyard of the United States, and an Islamic revolution in Iran, an oil-exporting country that had formerly been a key U.S. ally.

Even among more moderate governments, Third World demands had become more radical and insistent. By the 1970s, the general feeling within the ECLA and UNCTAD was that national development programs had not yielded the hoped-for results: they had helped economies grow, but the growth that was produced was both geographically and socially uneven, benefiting Third World elites and multinational corporations, and leaving the masses impoverished. Increasingly, the United Nations and its agencies proposed that ongoing dilemmas of development could be solved only through a redistribution of resources from North to South. Beginning in the 1960s, and increasingly in the 1970s, UNCTAD pressed wealthy countries to give the Third World a better deal through commodity price stabilization and preferential trade arrangements. These measures were meant to address Third World concerns about the declining terms of trade—the fact that they had to purchase goods from industrialized countries at stable or rising prices while selling raw materials and agricultural goods, such as sugar and coffee, at prices that were constantly being pushed downward. Commodity price stabilization essentially meant that wealthy countries would guarantee a floor price for Third World exports; preferential trade agreements meant that wealthy countries would open their markets to Third World imports without requiring reciprocal concessions. Another key UNCTAD demand was for greater financial assistance from the North, on more concessional terms.[33]

In line with this thinking, in 1974 UN General Assembly 3201 proposed the establishment of a "new international economic order," which included demands for increased Third World sovereignty over natural resources, Third World control over foreign investment, commodity price stabilization, increased development assistance and debt relief, and enhanced developing-country influence in both the World Bank and the International Monetary Fund.[34] Policymakers came to refer to these sorts of demands as part of the *NIEO* (new international economic order) and referred to negotiations between the Third World and the First on these issues as the *North-South dialogue.*

Different U.S. government agencies undoubtedly had different attitudes toward the North-South dialogue. Staffed by civil servants with a background in economics and finance, the U.S. Treasury tended to be less concerned with issues of economic development and more worried about macroeconomic issues (such as rates of return and interest rates), fiscal responsibility, and eliminating market distortions.[35] An anonymous Treasury official interviewed at the end of the 1970s suggested that negotiations among finance ministers tended to be more pragmatic than those among foreign ministries. The reason? "You can deal straightforwardly with issues ... and don't have to wade through hours of that new economic order crap. Finance ministers are more realistic—they understand how things really work."[36] In contrast, the State Department, which was in charge of managing U.S. relations with foreign governments, was more concerned with foreign aid as an instrument of cold war diplomacy and, hence, had reasons to encourage the North-South dialogue.[37]

During the 1970s, State Department–type concerns evidently predominated in U.S. foreign aid policy. Many development policy luminaries at the time—including Robert McNamara and Roger Hansen—charged that the United States was not serious about the North-South dialogue, as evidenced by declining foreign aid budgets.[38] Even the Republican U.S. presidencies of the 1970s were tolerant of the North-South dialogue, regularly expressed concern at Third World poverty, and regularly pledged their support for economic development and foreign aid. Nixon's policy of détente involved both negotiating with the Soviet Union and pulling the United States out of costly and ineffective military engagements in the Third World, such as Vietnam.[39] Good diplomatic relations with the non-Communist Third World was an important element in détente, and expressing openness to Third World demands was part of this strategy. As the Treasury representative testifying to Congress in 1973 put it: "A new international economic order—based on updated rules, international cooperation and a stronger institutional framework—is a basic part of creating a secure structure of peace."[40] This conciliatory attitude toward the North-South dialogue was even more pronounced under the Carter administration.

Yet U.S. executive support for the North-South dialogue was also problematic at a time when Congress was increasingly skeptical of the utility of foreign aid. From 1968 through 1970, three foreign aid task forces (the alliteratively named Perkins, Pearson, and Peterson commissions) recommended that the United States address the issue of aid fatigue by enlarging the multilateral aid program. Financing U.S. international programs multilaterally allowed for burden sharing with other donor governments: because U.S. contributions were increasingly being complemented by those of other donors, the total amount of development financing available could be vastly increased, with only a small increase in U.S. contributions.[41] Hoping thereby to rescue U.S. foreign economic aid, in a 1970 speech to Congress Nixon proposed: "The U.S. should channel an increasing share of its development assistance through the multilateral institutions as rapidly as practicable."[42]

Where cost cutting was concerned, Nixon's strategy was successful. As figure 2.2 shows, spending on multilateral development institutions remained quite modest and never came close to compensating for declining spending on bilateral economic aid: overall, foreign aid was costing

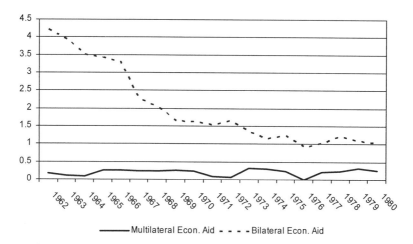

FIGURE 2.2. Spending on bilateral and multilateral economic aid as a percentage of U.S. government outlays, 1962–80. *Sources*: USAID, *U.S. Overseas Loans and Grants* (various years); and U.S. Bureau of the Census, "Statistical Abstract" (various years).

the U.S. taxpayer less. As a strategy for depoliticizing foreign aid, however, the switch from bilateral to multilateral aid was a failure. Many of the same congressional controversies that had developed around bilateral aid quickly spread like a contagious virus to the multilateral aid program. Members of Congress began to discuss the banks at greater length and to attempt to influence their activities in various ways. Moreover, as figure 2.1 illustrates, starting in 1971 (for fiscal year 1972), Congress began to make significant cuts in the administration's budget request for the MDBs.

Although spending on foreign aid was decreasing overall, Congress continued to be unhappy about spending tax dollars on a foreign aid program that did not seem to be providing the promised results, particularly at a time when the U.S. domestic economy was facing significant problems. Moreover, although the *amount* of U.S. spending on the MDBs had not increased significantly, the *proportion* of aid spending going to multilateral institutions became more important, making it a magnet for criticism. As members of Congress learned more about the MDBs, they became increasingly aware of Congress's limited influence on multilateral institutions, and this growing realization fanned the flames of congressional discontent. For all these reasons, the Nixon, Ford, and Carter administrations found themselves in the position of having to market the MDBs ever more aggressively to Congress in order to win the appropriations to finance them.

Framing the Banks to Congress

From the early 1970s through the last year of the Carter administration, the U.S. Treasury attempted to sell the MDBs to Congress using a variety of arguments—from the lure of procurement contracts to the emotional appeal of humanitarian concerns. The most frequent argument used during these years, however, was one emphasizing that the banks were indispensable both to U.S. security and to long-term U.S. economic interests. This rhetoric was remarkably similar across the presidential administrations of the 1970s, irrespective of political party. This suggests that, in spite of partisan differences, there was a relatively unified policy paradigm guiding U.S. policy toward the MDBs over the course of that decade.

In making these arguments for the banks, the Treasury was constructing frames, or interpretive schemes, designed to "organize experience and guide action."[43] As we have seen, frames are designed to resonate with their audiences and, thereby, mobilize support—but they do not always succeed in this mission. Such was the case with administration framing of U.S. interests in the MDBs during the 1970s. Over the course of the decade, Congress became harder to convince, raised many objections to U.S. spending on the MDBs, and began to attempt to change U.S. policy through passing laws and cutting financing.

The Banks as Guarantors of Security and Prosperity

Throughout the 1970s, the Treasury's annual testimony to the congressional subcommittees on behalf of the banks was heavily laced with geopolitical themes. The banks, Congress was told, were critical to maintaining U.S. security. As Ford's deputy assistant secretary of state for economic affairs, Paul Boeker, told the House Foreign Operations Subcommittee in 1976: "Our support for these institutions is an extremely important element in our relations with developing countries and in the overall north/south dialog. Our relations with these countries in turn are a major element of U.S. foreign policy."[44] And, as Carter's treasury secretary, Michael Blumenthal, asserted two years later: "The most likely areas of future conflict lie in the Third and Fourth Worlds. Success in our efforts to help avoid conflict within the Third and Fourth Worlds, and to slow down the growth of armaments, hinges critically on the quality of our economic and political relations with the developing countries, both individually and as a group."[45] The banks' soft loan windows were particularly important in this regard since they channeled resources to the poorest countries, where the potential for social unrest was the greatest. As Blumenthal explained in 1980: "IDA is ... the centerpiece of U.S. North/South strategy, and the symbol of our commitment to Third World Development. It serves to undermine those in the developing world who favor confrontation with the United States, to bolster U.S. economic and political interests in North/South fora, and to improve prospects for multilateral cooperation on issues of primary importance to the United States."[46]

Although strategic interests were a major element in the administration testimonies of the 1970s, economic interests were an equally important justification. For example, in 1972, appropriations for the IDB were justified as promoting important economic ties with Latin America "as Latin America's demand rises for U.S. exports and as the area becomes an increasingly important supplier for the United States, particularly of materials vital to our own industrial growth and economic health."[47] These themes—the banks' role in creating markets for U.S. exports and supplying raw materials for American industries—were repeated in 1973 and in 1976, 1977, 1978, and 1980. During most of the years of the Carter administration, an additional justification was that the banks provided lucrative procurement contracts for American firms and, hence, created American jobs.

One theme that emerged over the course of the 1970s was that the banks had a comparative advantage over bilateral aid in promoting economic reforms. During the 1960s, USAID had attempted to condition resources on such policies as administrative reform, agricultural modernization, land reform, export expansion, and increased foreign private investment. However, this effort was soon recognized as a failure.[48] In contrast, because they had a more neutral, less politicized reputation, the MDBs were seen as potentially more successful in this area. As Fred Bergsten of the Carter Treasury put it in 1978: "Bilateral efforts to force particular policies on aid recipients were counterproductive because of the appearance of imperialism or hegemony, or whatever you want to call it. . . . [But] an international institution of which these recipient countries are themselves members, when they have a voice in the policies themselves, doesn't carry any of the stigma of the bilateral donor dictating terms to the recipient."[49] Or, as Assistant Treasury Secretary for International Affairs John Hennesey put it in 1972: "Often [the multilateral institutions] can achieve with those countries what we can't achieve ourselves. They can be helpful in solving an expropriation problem, or in getting defaulted debts brought up to date. Without having their motives suspected they can emphasize to developing countries the value of open economies and the kind of private enterprise thinking that is most compatible with our own."[50]

Nevertheless, the benefits of lending for the specific purpose of policy reform were mentioned relatively infrequently, for the simple reason that such lending was relatively rare in the MDBs of the 1970s. Instead, the Treasury mostly cited economic benefits that did not involve ambitious plans for reworking national institutions, such as expanding access to raw materials, creating markets for U.S. exporters, and fostering procurement contracts for U.S. firms.

Whereas security and economic justifications for the MDBs were central to the discourse of the 1970s, humanitarian interests were mentioned less frequently. And, when mentioned, they were often framed as a means to achieving security goals, rather than as ends in themselves. In his question-and-answer session with the House Foreign Operations Subcommittee, Treasury Secretary Blumenthal explained: "If you are helpful in raising people from a level of misery to certain minimum standards in life, you reduce their frustrations, and quite apart from the humanitarian and basic American values that are involved in doing so, that you lessen their feeling of frustration as they look at other rich countries and see a widening income gap."[51] Federal Reserve Chairman Paul Volcker, who testified on behalf of the MDBs to the House Authorizations Committee in 1980, put it similarly:

When one looks at the disparities of wealth in the world and, at this moment in time, the particular pressure on some of the poorest countries from the increases in oil prices and indeed other prices of vital raw materials, and when one considers the kind of pressures that that creates in a country like ours, one has to conclude that that can be even more explosive in the poorest counties in the world. . . . When we look at the interest of the United States in the political stability and economic stability and economic development around the world, and, in a crude sense, the chances these countries are going to be on "our side," as opposed to the other side—"our side" meaning a basic orientation toward our kind of economic system, our kind of values—I would conclude [that supporting the banks] is in our interest.[52]

With Third World poverty thus linked to the spread of communism, U.S. humanitarian goals in the banks could be framed as means to an even more persuasive end: namely, fighting communism and promoting U.S. security.

Congress Responds

Over the course of the 1970s, Congress raised many concerns over U.S. participation in the MDBs and increasingly used its ability to pass authorizing legislation and withhold appropriations to attempt to change U.S. policy. At the heart of the rebellion against the banks was a single body: the House Foreign Operations Subcommittee of the Committee on Appropriations, the same subcommittee that had been instrumental in slashing bilateral aid budgets in the 1960s. After the unforgettable Otto Passman lost his seat in the House in 1976, the chairship of this subcommittee passed to Clarence Long, a Maryland Democrat with a long career in the House. Long was more liberal and far better educated than Passman had been: he had a Ph.D. in economics from Princeton University, a credential that won him the nickname "Doc Long."[53] This impressive background notwithstanding, Long was no technocrat, but rather a quirky populist with his own personal agenda for foreign aid and the development banks.

CONGRESSIONAL COMPLAINTS. The complaints raised by Congress during this period over U.S. participation in the MDBs can be categorized as broadly corresponding to the three major justifications for foreign aid: strategic, economic, and humanitarian. Where American security interests were concerned, members of Congress were increasingly unconvinced by the cold war argument that economic development aid was critical to the struggle against communism. After more than a decade of generous U.S. spending on foreign economic aid, the Third World seemed as rebellious, ungrateful, and uncompliant as ever. Developing countries in which U.S. property had been expropriated came to the U.S.-financed MDBs for loans. Many countries that received large loans from the MDBs, such as India, were openly criticizing the United States in the United Nations. As Charles Wilson, a Texas Democrat on the House Foreign Operations Subcommittee, noted in 1977: "The degree of hostility exhibited toward us by India is total. I know of no Communist country that talks about us the way India does, and indeed preaches to us."[54] These rhetorical insults were particularly stinging in the wake of the U.S. defeat in Vietnam—a country that continued to receive loans from the World Bank.

In short, the idea that the banks promoted American security by winning the Third World over to our side was wearing thin. As Long remarked at a hearing on financing for the Asian Development Bank (AsDB): "I don't know what security interests we are talking about, unless we are talking about [military] bases."[55] The economic justification for foreign aid was also losing its power. Members of Congress found it difficult to understand why, after so many years of development financing, poor countries remained underdeveloped. In 1973, Passman objected to financing for IDA, recalling: "People who appeared before this committee 20 years ago painted a very rosy picture that they were making great progress and every year now they would see improvement, by creating better family living, better education, and more schools ... but it would appear now at this late day after $250 billion of our resources have gone down the drain we have people now actually saying that poor people are poorer and we have 100 million more adult illiterate people today than 20 years ago." He then made a remark that would resonate over the course of the following decade: "[U.S. foreign aid] has taken money from the poor people in rich countries and given it to rich people in poor countries."[56]

The idea that foreign economic aid in general, and multilateral aid in particular, took money from beleaguered American taxpayers to subsidize elites in developing countries was a theme that would subsequently be taken up with great passion by Clarence Long, both before and during his term as subcommittee chair. As Long complained to Assistant Treasury Secretary Fred Bergsten in 1977: "I am not sure that I have ever been able to get the message over to you folks, and the State Department, that lending money to poor countries does not necessarily mean that you are lending money to help poor people. Some of the richest people you can find anywhere are living in poor countries."[57]

During the foreign operations hearings of the 1970s, Long would plague Treasury representatives with long lists of questions about the banks' efficacy. He repeatedly cited instances of loans for projects, such as tube wells in Bangladesh, that ostensibly targeted the poor but actually benefited the elites. He and others also complained that the primary beneficiaries of money appropriated for the banks were the banks themselves. Many scandalous instances of bureaucratic waste were brought to light, including bloated salaries and inflated travel expenses. Employees of the banks were also criticized for taking advantage of lavish perks, such as low-interest loans and (in the banks located in the United States) exemption from U.S. income taxes. By the end of the 1970s, some subcommittee members were also concerned that the MDBs were getting Third World governments increasingly mired in debts that they could not possibly repay. "Why," Long demanded in 1976, "do people like you continue to defend pouring more money down this gigantic rathole?"[58]

Another powerful set of arguments questioned the beneficial impact of the MDBs on the U.S. economy. The 1970s were a time of great economic difficulty for the United States, with skyrocketing oil prices, high inflation, and stagnant growth. They were also a time when many policymakers were concerned about persistent current account deficits (i.e., the United States was importing more than it was exporting) and mounting public debt. Subcommittee members began to ask the Treasury about how spending on the MDBs would affect the U.S. balance of payments. They also asked repeatedly why foreign aid spending should receive priority at a time of heightened budget austerity. As Long asked the Treasury representative in 1973: "Can you explain why your International Development Association should be asking for a big increase when we are actually cutting back on so many important domestic programs?"[59] And as the Nebraska Republican Virginia Smith complained in 1979: "If you were to go to the people of the United States, they would vote against these programs. The people in my district in a questionnaire last year in which I said, Shall we increase the international aid program, leave it as it is, or cut it? Fully 93 per cent of the people said, Cut it! And when we discussed it on the floor of Congress, other members of Congress said that the people of their district felt the same way."[60]

Whereas some economic arguments against the banks were based on lofty ideals—the stewardship of the public purse, the interests of the American people, and the efficacy of development programs—others were more particularistic. Many members of Congress wanted to know why U.S. companies were not receiving a higher share of the procurement contracts for bank-financed projects. Increasingly, they also complained that the banks were financing projects that led to the production of goods that directly competed with U.S. producers, such as citrus, sugar, aluminum, and steel.

Where humanitarian issues were concerned, it became increasingly common, as mentioned above, to complain that the banks were not really improving the lot of the poor in the Third World, that they simply had "taken money from the poor people in rich countries and given it to rich people in poor countries." Another humanitarian complaint was that the programs were subsidizing dictators who routinely abused the human rights of their people. Some of these human rights complaints came from Democrats, such as Clarence Long and David Obey on the House Foreign Operations Subcommittee, Daniel Inouye on the Senate Foreign Operations Subcommittee, and members of the authorizations subcommittees such as Senator Frank Church. Others came from conservative Republicans, such as Bill Young, who deplored MDB loans to left-wing dictatorships, particularly World Bank loans to Vietnam.

Finally, there was a group of congressional complaints that did not fit into either strategic, economic, or humanitarian categories and that can be described only as "procedural" quarrels about the functioning of multilateral organizations. Congress did not like the fact that U.S. contributions and policies were negotiated among donor governments and between the United States and the banks—a process that excluded the legislative branch. This procedure was particularly irksome to House Foreign Operations Subcommittee Chairman Otto Passman. Nearly every year, Passman demanded that the Treasury inform him whether other donors knew that the U.S. contribution to the banks had to be approved by Congress. Consider the following example from 1972:

MR. PASSMAN: Do these people [other donors] understand that the Committees on Appropriations have a right to make adjustments on these requests?

MR. STERNFELD: Mr. Chairman, it has been explained to them a number of times about our constitutional process.

MR. PASSMAN: Do they understand that when these authorizations pass the Congress that the Appropriations committee then must look over the amount of the authorization, and the amount of the request, if the Committee on Appropriations in its wisdom feels this level should be cut down, do they understand that we have that authority?

MR. STERNFELD: Mr. Chairman, it has been explained to them that we do not agree to subscribe until we have the appropriation for the first year.

MR. PASSMAN: I am not talking about the first, second, third, fourth, or fifth year. Do they understand the right to reduce the requests?

MR. STERNFELD: They understand the process.

MR. PASSMAN: I am going to get an answer even if I have to get Secretary Connally down here.[61]

Another frequent complaint was that the banks' policies and procedures were too opaque for Congress to provide the same degree of oversight as in bilateral aid programs. For example, in a 1979 House Foreign

Operations Subcommittee hearing, on being informed by Deputy Treasury Secretary Fred Bergsten that a majority of the World Bank's Executive Board supported lending to Vietnam, an exasperated Bill Young wanted to know: "How do we know it is a majority? Is there a record anyplace, is [sic] there minutes of a meeting, or is the dialogue transcribed? How do we know that that is the majority view?"[62]

To take policy action on its complaints about the banks, Congress had two major tools at its disposal: passing laws and withholding appropriations. Both tools had been used since the 1960s to shape the U.S. bilateral aid program; beginning in the 1970s, both were employed to influence U.S. policy toward the MDBs. Yet Congress soon discovered that, unlike bilateral aid agencies, multilateral organizations were difficult to influence through the passage of U.S. laws. Consequently, it increasingly used the withholding of appropriations to manifest its displeasure and press for policy changes.

PASSING LEGISLATION.   During the 1970s, Congress passed a number of laws aimed at reforming the U.S. foreign aid program, such as the New Directions legislation of 1973, which mandated a heightened focus on poverty alleviation. It was relatively straightforward to influence bilateral aid in this way: a new law would state that the United States should pursue a particular policy, and the administration had to abide by it. However, the MDBs were international organizations to which U.S. law did not apply.

To get around the fact that the MDBs did not respond directly to U.S. legislation, Congress passed a number of "legislative initiatives"—clauses in the authorizing or appropriating legislation requiring the administration to pursue particular kinds of policies, from poverty alleviation to nuclear nonproliferation. Typically, legislative initiatives would direct the U.S. executive directors at the MDBs to vote in a particular way regarding certain types of issues. Some of the most famous legislative initiatives directed U.S. executive directors to oppose loans to governments practicing gross violations of human rights (discussed at greater length in chapter 7). Other examples were the González Amendment of 1972, which required the U.S. executive director in the World Bank to vote against loans to countries where U.S. properties had been expropriated without compensation, the 1974 Percy Amendment on women in development, and the 1974 Long Amendment on nuclear nonproliferation.[63] As these legislative initiatives multiplied, it became increasingly common for U.S.

executive directors to cast negative votes or abstentions in response to particular congressional directives.[64]

However, it appears that the impact of these legislative initiatives on MDB policies was limited. In many cases, loans went forward in spite of a U.S. vote or abstention because the U.S. executive director did not have a majority vote in any of the banks and could veto specific loans only in the Fund for Special Operations of the IDB. A 1977 Congressional Research Service report on the effectiveness of U.S. policy toward the MDBs concluded that legislative initiatives were not a particularly effective vehicle for reform: "The United States must [instead] persuade other governments and not just rely on its voting strength if it is to affect bank operations."[65] Yet such persuasion of other donor governments—along with the persuasion of the banks themselves—was an executive prerogative. As Congress attempted to influence U.S. policy toward the banks through directing U.S. votes, it increasingly discovered that much of the real U.S. influence was wielded behind the scenes, through informal channels to which Congress had no access.

Congress also attempted to exert influence on the banks by placing limitations on how U.S. dollars in the MDBs should be spent. Such earmarking of funds was often applied to bilateral U.S. aid programs: for example, the Foreign Assistance Act of 1973 (the New Directions legislation) authorized the spending at particular levels for population planning and education, required that a certain amount be spent on cooperatives, mandated that no part of U.S. foreign assistance be used to pay for abortions, and so on.[66] Yet, with the MDBs, earmarking funds was much more complicated. This first became an issue in 1975, when Congress tried to force the IDB to spend specific amounts on cooperatives, credit unions, and savings and loans. To secure congressional appropriations, Ford signed the appropriations bill, thus amended, into law. However, the IDB's highly independent president, Antonio Ortíz Mena, objected to the earmarked funds and refused to accept them. Indeed, to avoid opening a Pandora's box of specific donor demands, all the MDBs' charters specified that their assets had to be free of such restrictions.[67] All the U.S. presidential administrations of the 1970s opposed earmarking as antithetical to the principles of multilateralism, as did most liberal Democrats. The most energetic proponents of earmarking, therefore, tended to be conservative House Republicans, who were more skeptical of multilateralism in general and the MDBs in particular.

A much larger and more fateful earmarking imbroglio erupted in 1977 when the Republican Bill Young of the House Foreign Operations Sub-committee tried to insert an amendment to prevent MDB lending to Communist countries, such as Cambodia, Laos, Uganda, and—most especially—Vietnam. Although the Carter administration attempted to placate Young by agreeing to vote against loans to those four countries, and although Young initially was unable to win enough support in Congress, the Republican legislator was as relentless as a pit bull on the issue of bank loans to Communists and proposed similar legislation in 1978 and 1979. To break the stalemate over earmarking in 1979, the Treasury negotiated an agreement in which World Bank President Robert McNamara promised in writing that, owing to "very serious questions about Vietnam's commitment to a rational development policy," there would be no new World Bank loans to the country in 1980.[68]

TIGHTENING THE PURSE STRINGS. Congress also expressed its disagreement with U.S. MDB policy through cutting appropriations. In 1971, the House Appropriations Committee denied the entire budget request for the IDB and the World Bank because of concerns about the procedural costs of redirecting U.S. financing from bilateral to multilateral aid.[69] In 1972, the House committee cut the entire $100 million requested for the AsDB and half of the amount requested for the IDB, in part to protest the fact that "the same degree of detailed examination which is possible in the bilateral assistance programs is not possible in the multilateral assistance programs which makes it more difficult to exercise the same degree of control."[70] In 1974, the annual foreign aid appropriations bill failed to pass until three months into fiscal year 1975 because of concerns about spending on foreign aid, including multilateral aid, at a time of economic suffering at home.[71] The fiscal year 1977 foreign aid appropriations bill contained a clause that required withholding funds from international financial institutions if U.S. representatives were denied access to information on employee salaries because, according to the Senate Appropriations committee, "the personnel management practices of the banks are suggestive of an institutionalized granting of lifetime sinecures where extraordinarily high salaries are commonplace and the pursuit of fringe benefits has been raised to an art form."[72]

Although these cuts in MDB budget requests posed a problem for all the presidential administrations of the 1970s, they were most problematic for the Carter administration. Even more than its predecessors, the Carter team was strongly committed to channeling foreign aid through multilateral institutions and negotiated agreements with other donors that committed the United States to large MDB contributions. As figure 2.1 above illustrates, the Carter administration made requests for MDB appropriations that were unprecedented in size.

Yet the timing could not have been worse: the Carter years coincided with a period of widespread economic problems, skyrocketing gasoline prices, and budget austerity in the United States. Thus, the administration was asking for more money precisely at a moment when many members of Congress found it particularly difficult to justify high levels of spending on foreign aid. As Clarence Long remarked irritably to Treasury Secretary Blumenthal in 1979: "You try to sell the argument that you have to give money abroad in order to stimulate the U.S. economy on your local constituents, and see how far you get with it."[73]

Conclusion

Once upon a time, the MDBs rested in comfortable obscurity, dealing directly with the executive branches of donor governments, which, in turn, made confidential agreements among themselves about the policies they should pursue. The congressional controversies of the 1970s over MDB financing permanently changed the character of both the relationship between the United States and the banks and the relationship between the United States and other major donors. Since 1972, there has not been a *single year* that Congress has appropriated all the funds for the MDBs that the administration requested. This is not because the United States spends an extraordinary amount on the banks: indeed, since 1981, such spending has fluctuated between only 0.06 and 0.18 percent of total U.S. government outlays and has consistently been dwarfed by spending on bilateral economic aid.[74] Rather, the annual discrepancy between administration requests and final appropriations reflects a permanent disjuncture between what the executive negotiates multilaterally and what Congress will deliver.

As a result of awakened congressional interest, the U.S. executive was forced to listen more closely to congressional concerns and to market them ever more forcefully. Over the course of the 1970s, Treasury testimony to the appropriations subcommittees became increasingly elaborate, and Congress was provided with much more information on the policy initiatives the United States was carrying out in the banks and what policy initiatives it had successfully pursued in the recent past. At the same time, it became more common for higher-level Treasury officials to testify to the appropriations subcommittees, to provide extra gravitas to the request; and, by decade's end, it was the Treasury secretary himself who came and spoke for the banks. Meanwhile, both the management of the banks and other donors came to recognize the importance of satisfying both the legislative and the executive branches of the U.S. government. For example, since the McNamara years, all World Bank presidents have employed former members of Congress as special advisers, as a way of helping them manage congressional demands.[75]

Because of such demands, by the final year of the Carter administration, the very future of U.S. participation in the MDBs seemed in doubt. It would take the new approach of a very different presidential administration to overcome the congressional stalemate, as we will see in the following chapter.

CHAPTER THREE

The Reagan Revolution

During the 1980s, the multilateral development banks (MDBs) began to change. There was a notable shift in ideas: in the 1970s, World Bank research had focused heavily on combating poverty; for much of the 1980s, however, it downplayed poverty and emphasized economic efficiency and the liberation of market forces. There was also a change in practice: most of the banks—but most especially the World Bank—began to devote an increased proportion of their resources to policy-based lending to promote market-liberalizing reforms.

There are at least two different kinds of stories we could tell about these trends. Some observers would conclude that these changes responded to changing intellectual fashions among economists and an accumulation of real-world evidence suggesting the need to rely more on market forces. Others would note that they fit well with the Reagan administration's economic policy agenda, which aimed at liberating the invisible hand of the marketplace from harmful government interventions.

Neither of these accounts alone is sufficient. The banks straddle both the intellectual and the political fields. Their ideas and activities are partly a function of intellectual fashions and accumulating evidence in the discipline of economics, but they also reflect the policy agendas of the donor states that control them. At the same time, like all complex organizations, the banks are entities with dynamics and interests of their own; in particular, they possess an overriding interest in perpetuating their own survival.

To this already complex analytic framework, we are forced to add a further complication: namely, that shareholder policies toward the banks also have heterogeneous origins. This is not only because shareholders are multiple and not necessarily of one mind but also because donor governments develop their policy agendas with input from both the intellectual and the political fields. Shareholder policies toward the banks grow out of economic policy programs that have both scholarly and political elements. The example most relevant for this chapter is Reaganomics, a policy program that was deeply partisan and political but that also reflected the movement of U.S. economics toward more conservative ideas.[1] Moreover, donors' policy agendas toward the MDBs have the potential to grow out of *different kinds* of policy programs, corresponding to different substantive policy areas. For example, we have seen that, in the 1970s, U.S. policy toward the MDBs was never purely a matter of economic policy but was also strongly shaped by a particular approach to national security. American policy toward the banks is also rendered heterogeneous by the simultaneous input of the executive and legislative branches, which often espouse different policy programs.

With these complexities in mind, this chapter sets out to explore the earliest consequences of the Reagan revolution for the MDBs. When Reagan was inaugurated as president, U.S. policies toward the MDBs were in a shambles: previously negotiated contributions to the banks had been slashed and those to the International Development Association (IDA) completely frozen, to the dismay of other donor countries. Into this chaotic U.S. policy arena stepped the Reagan administration, with few specific ideas about what to do with the banks, but with two policy programs that suggested a new approach. The first policy program was Reaganomics, the administration's folksy, popularized version of conservative economic theories. The second was Reagan's national security doctrine, which discarded the 1970s philosophies of détente and diplomacy in favor of a more militaristic approach.

The Reagan revolution would have two immediate consequences for the MDBs. The first was the selection of some forms of World Bank economic expertise over others, which contributed to a shift in the Bank's research output. The second was a new framing of U.S. interests in the MDBs, one in which American diplomatic interests in the banks were set aside. In this new view, the banks' greatest importance lay in their guarantee of long-term U.S. economic interests, which they could further by encouraging developing countries to rely on the magic of the marketplace. This new framing of the banks' purpose helped mollify congressional conservatives and made it possible for the Reagan administration to break the stalemate in Congress over MDB financing. Over the long term, it would pave the way for the transformation of the banks' activities to emphasize market-liberalizing policy reforms.

The Reagan Revolution and the MDBs

When the Reagan administration arrived in January 1981, all signs pointed toward a reorientation of American policy toward the MDBs. It seemed to many conservatives in Congress that, the more the United States conceded, the more the Third World demanded. Why were these countries not more grateful to the United States for its decades of commitment to the cause of economic development? Why were newly wealthy OPEC countries not providing more development financing at a time when the United States was suffering from an economic crisis induced by outrageous petroleum prices? And why were countries that benefited from U.S. development assistance, such as India, siding against the United States in the United Nations? Reagan's political coalition included members of Congress, such as Jack Kemp and Bill Young, who had been raising these kinds of questions for years on Capitol Hill and who were instrumental in creating the impasse over MDB financing in the last year of the Carter administration. Thus softened by political heat, American policy toward the banks was poised to be reshaped.

The new Reagan cabinet had little experience with international financial institutions (IFIs) and few specific ideas about what to do with them. Nevertheless, two features of Reagan's platform and coalition suggested that there would be a significant rethinking of U.S. policy toward the banks. The first was a new brand of conservative, market-liberating economics. The second was a new approach to U.S. foreign policy that emphasized military might over diplomacy and multilateralism. The combination of these economic and strategic visions implied a new policy toward the Third World.

The Rise of Reaganomics

During the 1970s, conservative economics began to become fashionable in the American academy. The validity of Keynesian macroeconomics was being challenged by real-world events; faith in the Phillips curve and the trade-off between inflation and unemployment was shaken by the experience of high inflation and low growth during the 1970s. Monetarists suggested that expanding the money supply could increase inflation without simultaneously increasing national output. Rational expectations theorists suggested that actors learned over time not to be fooled by expansionary monetary policies, rendering them impotent. And the academic exponents of supply-side theory suggested that expansionary fiscal policy might, under certain circumstances, merely create disincentives to work, save, and invest.[2]

These conservative trends in American economics were noted with interest by Republican strategists, who were searching for a new economic platform and a set of ideas to justify it. Over the course of the 1970s, Republicans increasingly drew on scholarly economic ideas to justify a political program of cutting taxes, deregulating, and generally downsizing government interference in the economy. Some of these ideas came directly from the ivory tower—for example, the well-known monetarist Milton Friedman served on Reagan's Economic Policy Advisory Board. However, Republicans also looked to the ideas of what Paul Krugman calls "policy entrepreneurs"—individuals who specialized in packaging abstruse economic ideas for political consumption. For example, Arthur Laffer popularized and simplified a scholarly economic theory called *supply-side economics* and boiled it down to a simple policy prescription: tax cuts would make everybody better off by stimulating economic growth and creating jobs. Another policy entrepreneur promoting supply-side economics was Jude Wanniski, a writer for the *Wall Street Journal* whose free market ideas reached thousands of readers across the country.[3] Republicans also drew heavily on the ideas of policy advocacy think tanks.[4] A particularly important source of ideas for the Republicans of the 1970s was the Heritage Foundation, founded in 1973 with money from the Coors Brewing Company. Termed affectionately by Reagan "that feisty new kid on the conservative block," the Heritage Foundation was (and still is) a strong proponent of supply-side economics.[5] Another was the Cato Institute, founded in 1977 to promote the principles of "limited government, free markets, individual liberty, and peace."[6]

These new ideas helped pave the road for Republican victory. The popularized version of supply-side economics espoused by Laffer, Wanniski, and the Heritage Foundation was quickly recognized as a far more politically palatable alternative to the "castor oil" economics of early-twentieth-century Republicans—the idea that the only way to long-term, sustainable growth lay through short-term suffering. Instead, the supply-side ideology suggested a happy win-win situation in which Americans could pay less in taxes, thereby liberating market forces and creating more jobs for everybody. This was a powerful idea at a time when the politicians in office were talking about making sacrifices, wearing sweaters indoors, and buying fuel-efficient cars. Early Republican converts to the supply-side doctrine included Jack Kemp, a representative from New York, and Senator William Roth of Delaware. Together, Kemp and Roth proposed a national, across-the-board tax cut that, in 1977, was endorsed by the Republican National Committee. In 1978, Reagan officially converted to the supply-side doctrine by also endorsing the Kemp-Roth bill. By this time, supply-side economics had inspired a far-reaching social movement that was pushing for property tax cuts across the nation and was widely supported on Wall Street. Midterm elections in 1978 reflected this movement's influence, bringing fifteen more Republicans into the House, and leading to the defeat of five prominent liberal Democrats in the Senate. In the 1980 election, the GOP gained twelve seats in the Senate and thirty-three seats in the House, putting the Republicans at the helm of both the Senate and the U.S. executive.[7] Thus, although many academic observers expressed skepticism at the theoretical soundness of Reaganomics, there was no denying its political appeal.[8]

The rise of Reaganomics was a worrisome development for supporters of U.S. participation in the MDBs. David Stockman, Reagan's director of the Office of Management and Budget, was a particularly devout believer in the power of cutting taxes and removing harmful government interventions as a way of stimulating growth and getting the U.S. economy back on track. Cutting taxes necessarily implied cutting government spending, and Stockman was very serious about axing government programs across the board. Even more specifically, he believed that "the organs of international aid . . . were infested with socialist error . . . turning Third World countries into quagmires of self-imposed inefficiency and burying them beneath mountainous external debts they would never be able to pay." In line with this view, in early 1981, Stockman proposed reducing both bilateral and multilateral aid by 45 percent and canceling Carter's previously negotiated commitment to IDA.[9]

Further weakening the banks' prospects was the fact that the U.S. Treasury—the branch of government in charge of designing U.S. policy toward the banks and shielding them from the congressional ax—was in the hands of a brand-new, inexperienced team. Its secretary, Donald Regan, had made a successful career in Merrill Lynch, a private brokerage company. According to Paul Krugman, who served on Reagan's Council of Economic Advisors, the first Reagan Treasury was notorious for its lack of expertise in international economic issues: the highest officials with any experience in international finance were only at the deputy assistant secretary level, and the department was looked on with scorn by the far better-qualified officials at the Federal Reserve.[10] The new undersecretary for monetary affairs, Beryl Sprinkel, was a Chicago-trained economist with a deep belief in the magic of the marketplace but little hands-on training in public finance.[11]

This inexperienced Treasury came into office without a clearly defined agenda for the MDBs. This is clearly evident in Treasury Secretary Regan's testimony to the appropriations subcommittees in 1982, in which he admitted: "The United States needs to develop a long term policy and planning perspective for the banks. It is our intention to establish an effective overall policy framework for future U.S. participation in the banks and to identify the major policy objectives which should be pursued in any future replenishment negotiation."[12]

Reagan's Approach to National Security

The second feature of Reagan's presidency with consequences for the MDBs was a new vision of how to promote U.S. national security. The Reagan administration revived the classic cold war doctrine of containment, according to which only military force could be relied on to stem the spread of communism. This philosophy was particularly appealing to the American public at a time when the United States was suffering from a perceived kicking around by Iran and other oil-exporting nations and still recovering from the humiliation of Vietnam. In line with this thinking, during the Reagan administration the United States stepped up military interventions to combat communism in the Third World and retreated from the diplomatic approach of the previous decade. In Reagan's first four years in office, there were no summit meetings between the United States and the Soviet leadership.[13]

In addition to this revival of cold war militarism, some within Reagan's political coalition endorsed radical right-wing critiques of multilateral institutions. The Heritage Foundation viewed the United Nations as compromising American sovereignty and getting fat off U.S. taxpayer dollars while pursuing policies that went contrary to American interests. Even though the voting structures of the World Bank and the International Monetary Fund (IMF) were far more amenable to U.S. influence than that of the United Nations, these institutions also became a target for the Heritage Foundation and other right-wing thinkers, such as P. T. Bauer.[14]

In its critique of multilateralism, the Heritage Foundation had gained the attention of key congressional Republicans. During the 1980 foreign aid hearings, which had led to the freezing of U.S. contributions to IDA, the Republican Bill Young of the House Foreign Operations Subcommittee had used some of the foundation's ideas to oppose Carter's budget request and had submitted a foundation report for the record. Entitled *The World Bank and the Future of U.S. Participation*, the report deplored the Bank's indulgence of Third World demands for a "new international economic order," in which "the industrialized West must exonerate itself for having exploited other nations for years while neglecting to 'enlighten' them," and suggested that recent increases in aid to developing nations were leading only to increased hostility and demands for further aid.[15] It noted that an increasing proportion of U.S. foreign aid was being channeled through multilateral development institutions and that the U.S. government could not directly control the destination of these funds—with the result that American dollars were going to finance enemy governments (such as that of Vietnam) as well as governments notable for criticizing the United States (such as that of India).

The Heritage Foundation report suggested that the MDBs were not a worthy destination for U.S. taxpayer dollars. To support its political allies, the United States was better off providing foreign aid through bilateral aid channels, which Americans could control directly. In contrast, the promotion of economic development in the Third World was best left to private investors. In line with these ideas, the 1980 Republican Party platform stated: "A Republican Administration will emphasize bilateral assistance programs whenever possible.... Bilateral programs provide the best assurance that aid programs will be fully accountable to the American taxpayer, and wholly consistent with our foreign policy interests."[16] The Reagan administration adopted a policy of restricting aid to Third World governments that routinely opposed the United States in the United Nations—a policy that was codified into laws that were enthusiastically supported by conservatives in Congress.[17]

Charting a New Course toward the Third World

Both the economic and the foreign policy dimensions of Reagan's policy platform were antithetical to demands for a new international economic order. It was, therefore, at a singularly inopportune moment that an independent commission chaired by the former German chancellor Willy Brandt published its recommendations for solving global poverty and inequality in 1980.

The idea for the Brandt Commission had originally come in 1977 from World Bank President Robert McNamara, who hoped that it would come up with a new agenda for the "North-South dialogue." The commission included representatives from both North and South and such international luminaries as Olof Palme and Edward Heath. Among the report's many suggestions were emergency poverty alleviation for the poorest countries, an end to mass hunger and malnutrition, population programs, international nuclear and conventional weapons disarmament, wider participation in the development process through "decentralized government administrative systems and support for relevant voluntary organizations," technology sharing by transnational corporations, the creation of a global energy research center, and regional and subregional economic integration.[18]

Most ambitiously, the report called for a sort of "global Keynesianism," with an international currency to settle accounts among central banks, and the greatly increased transfer of resources from the North to the South. Overseeing this transfer would be a new IFI—the World Development Fund—with decisionmaking powers shared evenly between developed and developing countries.[19] In essence, the Brandt Commission was reviving an expanded and enhanced version of the proposal for the Special United Nations Fund for Economic Development (SUNFED) that had perished in the 1950s. But, whereas the SUNFED proposal had come at a time when U.S. policy elites had been willing to propose a compromise with the Third World's proposals (albeit through different institutional channels), the Brandt Report came at a time when Americans were in a decidedly different mood.

The Reagan team's lack of sympathy for the North-South dialogue was motivated simultaneously by its economic and its foreign policy philosophies. The ideology of Reaganomics set the administration against anything that smacked of state interventionism—and the Brandt recommendations were interventionist in the extreme. At the same time, the

Reagan coalition's foreign policy philosophy was less sanguine about the benefits of multilateralism than previous administrations had been and less oriented toward diplomacy. Nixon, Ford, and Carter had all tolerated the North-South dialogue as a diplomatic front in the cold war. Although none of these U.S. administrations had been as forthcoming with resources as LDC leaders would have liked, they were willing to keep the dialogue alive.[20] This tolerance was premised on the notion that the Third World could be treated as a bloc that could be won over to side with the United States in the fight against communism. In contrast, the Reagan administration was skeptical of the notion of the Third World as a coherent bloc: Secretary of State Alexander Haig even spoke of the "so-called Third World ... a misleading term if there ever was one." Convinced that the North-South dialogue was an artifact of the excessively radical positions taken by Third World delegates to the United Nations, the administration sought to negotiate directly with developing country governments, which espoused more moderate positions.[21]

Although the Reagan team had little sympathy for the North-South dialogue, other industrialized countries were more supportive. An American participant in the meetings of the G7 in Ottawa in July 1981 recalls that the differences between the United States and other summit participants were "enormous," with other countries (particularly Canada) taking the position that the wealthy North needed to engage in constructive dialogue with the Third World and increase foreign aid levels substantially. The United States was the "skunk at the party" whenever North-South issues were discussed.[22] The text of the final Ottawa G7 communiqué had an entire section on "relations with developing countries," supporting their "stability, independence and genuine nonalignment," and affirming the G7's readiness to "support the developing countries in the efforts they make to promote their economic and social development within the framework of their own social values and traditions."[23]

Only a few months later, in October, Reagan had the opportunity to meet directly with heads of state of developing countries in a "North-South summit held in Cancún, Mexico. This meeting had been called by Willy Brandt, who wanted heads of state from North and South to discuss his report's findings face-to-face. According to one account, Reagan had to be persuaded to attend by British Prime Minister Margaret Thatcher, his like-minded colleague from across the Atlantic.[24] In Cancún, both Reagan and Thatcher politely expressed sympathy with Third World poverty and respect for Third World nationalist aspirations. However, it was clear that neither was even remotely willing to consider the Brandt Report's recommendations. Among the most forcefully rejected items was the proposal for development financing to be channeled through a World Development Fund in which poor developing countries would have the same voting power as the countries of the industrialized North. Thatcher later recalled: "I said that there was no way that I was going to put British deposits into a bank which was totally run by those on overdrafts."[25]

The Cancún summit did not pave the way for a new international economic order, as Brandt and others had hoped. Rather, it demonstrated that Third World demands would get little traction in the new era of Reagan and Thatcher. Reagan's position at Cancún, although delicately put, was that the first priority of the United States was to get its own economic house in order and that the restoration of economic growth in the United States would, ultimately, serve to benefit developing countries. Reagan also suggested that perhaps developing countries needed to start looking at how ill-conceived government interventions were preventing progress in their own economies. The Reagan team agreed to take the North-South negotiations a step further—but only provided that the existing structure of IFIs, including the U.S.-dominated World Bank and the IMF, were left intact. These provisions were unacceptable to a number of Third World delegates, and no resolution was reached. Over the following months, a series of fruitless proposals and counterproposals were floated as to where to go next, until the North-South negotiations finally died in the June 1982 G7 summit at Versailles.[26]

In lieu of the North-South dialogue, the Reagan administration proposed a new agenda for developing countries. In his speech at the annual meeting of the boards of governors of the World Bank and the IMF on September 29, 1981, Reagan expressed support for these institutions, which "contributed enormously to the spread of hope of a better life throughout the world community." However, he also hinted that they needed to be open to "constructive suggestions" for making themselves more efficient. More specifically, the speech suggested that these institutions needed to start solving their own problems: "The societies which have achieved the most spectacular broad-based economic progress in the shortest period of time are not the most tightly controlled, not necessarily the biggest in size, or the wealthiest in natural resources. No, what unites them all is their willingness to believe in the magic of the marketplace."[27] This line in Reagan's speech foreshadowed the essence of his administration's policies toward the MDBs.

The Transformation of World Bank Research

The Reagan team came into office with strong ideas about economic policy, but few that could be applied specifically to developing countries. Much of the intellectual inspiration for Reaganomics came from macroeconomists like Milton Friedman and policy entrepreneurs such as Arthur Laffer of "Laffer curve" fame, *Wall Street Journal* editorialists, and rightwing think tanks such as the Heritage Foundation and the Cato Institute. The resulting policy agenda, which focused on reforming fiscal, monetary, and regulatory policy, was appropriate to the U.S. brand of regulatory capitalism but had little application in the Third World, where national economies were governed by more direct government interventions, such as state-owned industries, currency rationing, and regimes of import protection.

Yet, although Reaganomics was not specifically designed for the situation of the Third World, it provided political inspiration for a new approach. During the Reagan administration, World Bank research and publications moved suddenly away from the dominant theme of the 1970s—the alleviation of poverty—and toward the theme of the benefits of markets. Intellectual trends within the economics discipline provided a background for these changes—for at least a decade, Keynesianism had been losing ground to more conservative macroeconomic theories, and development economists had been under attack from neoclassical thinkers. However, the sudden transformation of World Bank research in the 1980s would not have been possible without the Reagan revolution. It took a political change—and the consequent selection of some forms of economic expertise over others—to install a new policy paradigm within the World Bank.

Shifts in the Intellectual Field

As we saw in the previous chapter, the postwar period witnessed the rise of new ideas about developing countries within universities and foreign aid agencies. Development economists emphasized that things worked differently in developing countries, which could not, therefore, be expected to follow the same economic laws as the wealthy, industrialized North. Development economists were sympathetic to Third World experiments with state-led economies, such as regimes of protection from foreign imports and state-owned industries.

However, by the end of the 1970s, development economics was in a somewhat fragile state. At a conference in 1977, the development economist Paul Streeten noted the problems of developing countries and acknowledged that many of the subfield's early assumptions, such as "trade pessimism" and the emphasis on central government planning, were being discarded by development economists.[28] Some of the challenges to development economics came from empirical research showing that ill-conceived state interventions were having harmful effects. In the 1960s and 1970s, the World Bank economist Bela Balassa directed two major comparative studies that concluded that trade protection under import-substituting regimes was seriously hampering economic performance.[29] A research report published in 1970 out of the Development Centre of the Organisation for Economic Co-Operation and Development focused on the costs of excessive trade protection.[30] In 1981, shortly after Reagan's election, the World Bank published a report directed by Elliot Berg that found that state-owned industries in sub-Saharan Africa were extremely inefficient.[31]

These facts did not necessarily speak for themselves. For example, the superior economic performance of the East Asian "Tigers" (particularly South Korea and Taiwan) was subject to interpretation. It was clearly true that their success in producing for exports flew in the face of the trade pessimism that previously prevailed among development economists.[32] Yet a number of authors later persuasively argued that these economic miracles were actually premised on major state interventions.[33]

Although the facts of the East Asian cases did not speak for themselves, by the early 1980s, they were increasingly interpreted in light of economic theories that focused on the defects of states and the efficiency of markets. The erosion of Keynesianism had an impact on the overall intellectual climate concerning economic development; in the words of one firsthand observer, it contributed "to a generally more jaundiced view of the effects of government policy interventions."[34] Where issues of developing countries were specifically concerned, an influential theoretical approach was the "new political economy"—a microeconomic research agenda devoted to exposing the errors underlying state interventions. Two of the most famous proponents of this thinking were Jagdish Bhagwati and Anne Krueger, both of whom conducted early research on the perverse effects of state intervention in the Third World under the auspices of the National Bureau of Economic Research.[35] The term that would become famously associated with this school of thought was *rent seeking*—the engaging of states and private firms in mutually profitable yet unproductive activities. The quintessential example of such rent seeking occurred under regimes of trade protection, in which inefficient firms paid off government officials to protect them from foreign competition, thus enriching both firms and officials—at the expense of the ordinary consumer and of the economy as a whole.

However, in spite of these new intellectual currents both inside its halls and beyond, the World Bank remained, during the presidency of Robert McNamara and the research directorship of Hollis Chenery, a haven for economists of all theoretical stripes, including development economists. The emphasis of Bank research output during these years remained strongly on combating poverty, not on liberating market forces.[36] This changed with a new U.S. presidential administration and the selection of new leadership in the World Bank.

The Shift in the Bank's Research Department

Unlike lending policies, which are insulated from sudden changes by bureaucratic inertia and the need to mobilize majority support from major donors, World Bank research can be more responsive to U.S. pressures. The intellectual output of the World Bank's research department reflects both the intellectual agenda of the director and the general policy agenda of the top management. Since the directors of the World Bank's economic research department are appointed by the World Bank president, which the United States always selects, it is possible for a political change in the United States to have a relatively swift impact on the Bank's research output.

This was particularly clear after World Bank President Robert McNamara was replaced by A. W. (Tom) Clausen in 1981. The Carter administration had nominated Clausen in October 1980, after clearing the choice with the Reagan team. Clausen had been chosen specifically because of his acceptability to the Reagan team, which seemed likely to win the election. The former president of the Bank of America, he was sympathetic to Reagan's market-friendly agenda.[37] For reasons that are not entirely clear, his sympathetic views were not rewarded: relations between the Reagan team and Clausen were strained, and he was forced to resign in 1986.[38] Nevertheless, during Clausen's term, the Bank's research moved strongly in a Reaganomic direction, under the direction of Vice President for Research Anne Krueger, who replaced Hollis Chenery in 1982.

The top candidate for the position of vice president for research had previously been Albert Fishlow. An economic historian by training, Fishlow was best known for his research on income distribution in Brazil. His approach to development issues was perhaps best characterized as eclectic and empirically driven; he was neither an uncritical proponent of Third World statism nor a representative of the "neoclassical resurgence." Because he was a specialist on both Latin America and issues of Third World indebtedness, his candidacy was well-timed to occur just as the debt crisis was about to become an all-consuming policy issue in Washington.

However, Fishlow's chances for the job were spoiled by a *Wall Street Journal* editorial attacking his alleged statist propensities. A distinguished panel of outside economists was then enlisted to come up with a short list, from which Clausen selected Krueger.[39] In addition to being the first woman to occupy a World Bank vice presidency, Krueger was a representative of the "new political economy" and a long-standing critic of misguided Third World interventionism. Determined to work with a team that shared her point of view, she did a considerable amount of hiring and firing within her first years, thus gathering around her a team of like-minded economists who "regarded the former incumbents as deficient in appropriate technical economic skills and wedded to the 'statist' ways of the past."[40]

From 1982 until the late 1980s, World Bank publications shifted in focus away from poverty and toward macroeconomics and trade.[41] As one development economist observed critically in 1986: "In recent years, the Bank's research has ... gained a reputation for reduced diversity of approach and increased predictability of results. It has devoted quite disproportionate effort to the documentation of the errors of governments and the advantages of reliance upon markets."[42] The Bank's *World Development Report*, its most-read publication, focused on the correction of domestic policy errors through trade opening and other market-liberalizing measures.[43] While the emphasis on markets increased, the emphasis on poverty declined. According to one study, in 1985 only 1 percent of World Bank reports mentioned poverty in their titles and abstracts, compared to 6 percent in 1980.[44] A development economist conducting interviews within the World Bank in the mid-1980s discovered a new faith in the notion that a "rising tide lifts all boats" and a general sense that internal incentives did not reward staff who were "doing brilliant work on poverty alleviation."[45] Figure 3.1 shows the result of a simple content analysis of *World Development Report* mentions of the word *poverty* ver-

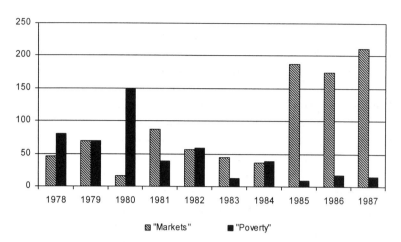

FIGURE 3.1. Mentions of the terms *poverty* and *markets/the market* in the *World Development Report*, 1978–87. *Source*: *World Development Report*, electronic version (various years).

sus mentions of *markets* or *the market* between 1978 and 1987. Although the frequency of terms used in the *World Development Report* depends partly on the thematic issues chosen for any particular year, the overall trend is clearly toward less discussion of poverty and greater discussion of markets.

Although these changes in the research output of the Bank were indirectly related to trends in the economics discipline, economics was not then, nor is it today, intellectually monolithic. Although the spectrum of views then in vogue had shifted to the right, considerable variety nevertheless remained—as the alternative candidacies of Krueger and Fishlow demonstrate. Instead, during the first Reagan administration, the World Bank selected *among* economic experts to construct a set of economic views that occupied the far end of two different spectrums: the "states versus markets" spectrum, for those who focused on the virtues of markets and the defects of states, and the "equity versus efficiency" spectrum, for those more concerned with the efficient use of resources and less concerned with poverty and social welfare.[46] Under a different administration—for example, a second Carter administration—the World Bank would almost certainly have had a different kind of leadership, and the Bank's research output would have followed a distinctly different trajectory.

By contributing to the reshaping of the content of World Bank research, the Reagan revolution indirectly shaped debates about economic development, both in Washington and around the world. Although many development specialists disagreed with the new emphasis, the Bank had the resources to disseminate its views widely and the legitimacy to weigh in heavily on development debates.[47]

Nevertheless, these changes initially occurred primarily in the realm of ideas and research output—not in the realm of World Bank lending operations, which were evolving according to a somewhat different logic. In 1980, McNamara's Bank had inaugurated its structural adjustment lending program, which was the Bank's first major foray into nonproject lending—that is to say, making loans that were not attached to particular projects. The rationale behind these loans was that Third World countries facing external shocks (e.g., high oil prices and interest rates) needed temporary resources to help them adapt their economies to changed international circumstances.[48] Although the program was extremely small, because structural adjustment loans were linked to policy reforms (such as trade liberalization), they had the potential to be harnessed to Reagan's market-friendly agenda for the developing world. However, before this could occur, a U.S. presidency with little experience with IFIs had to arrive at a new policy for the banks.

The 1982 Treasury Assessment

By the end of the Reagan team's first year in office, it was clear that the United States was not going to end, or even radically downsize, U.S. participation in the MDBs. One important player in rescuing the MDBs was Secretary of State Alexander Haig. Unlike Budget Director David Stockman, Haig believed that foreign aid was a worthy destination for U.S. taxpayer dollars; unlike the Heritage Foundation, he thought that the MDBs could be used to further U.S. government interests. According to one source, career civil service Treasury officials were also important internal advocates for the MDB program and played a key role in convincing high-level Reagan Treasury appointees of the banks' utility.[49] Consequently, first in the initial budget request, and later through supplemental appropriations, Stockman found his major cut in foreign aid whittled down to more modest proportions. The administration decided that there would be cuts in U.S. contributions, but not nearly as large as the banks' die-hard opponents would have liked; moreover, the United

States would continue to participate in the IDA replenishment negotiated during the Carter administration.[50]

To forge a new policy toward the banks, however, the Reagan administration needed to work with Congress. The administration entered office at a time when congressional objections to the banks had created a political impasse, and the political climate for the MDBs was getting worse. Liberal Democrats, who tended to be at the core of the banks' congressional support, had taken a drubbing in the 1978 and 1980 elections. Although there were still supporters of the banks in Congress, Reagan's ascendant Republican allies favored diverting government spending from foreign aid to military uses. Some, such as Jack Kemp and Bill Young, also viewed the MDBs as expensive boondoggles or even as bastions of socialism.

To answer these congressional criticisms, and to make up its own mind about what to do, in the spring of 1981 the administration launched an interagency review of U.S. policy toward the MDBs led by the U.S. Treasury. In charge of coordinating the study was James Conrow, a politician who had formerly worked on the House Foreign Operations Subcommittee as Bill Young's chief staff member; Conrow was hired by Treasury specifically to work on the report and specifically owing to the working knowledge of the banks he had acquired in his previous job.[51] Working under Conrow was a team of veteran civil service Treasury officials with long-standing MDB experience.

The results of the Treasury study were first disseminated in the fall of 1981 and then published in February 1982 in a report entitled *United States Participation in the Multilateral Development Banks in the 1980s.*[52] The report's introduction praised the legislative branch for bringing up "serious issues" with the banks and noted that the assessment had been conducted in consultation with Congress. To answer congressional concerns, the report systematically addressed a series of anti-MDB arguments recently promulgated by P. T. Bauer, the Heritage Foundation, *Forbes*, and the *Wall Street Journal.*

A common right-wing complaint about the banks was that they represented an excessive delegation of U.S. sovereignty to foreign governments. In response to this critique, the Treasury assessment argued that the United States had a commanding influence in the banks: "The magnitude of the U.S. financial participation in the MDBs and the central U.S. role as a founding member have assured us a major role in the MDB decision making process by tradition, law, and practice."[53] The level of influence varied somewhat across different banks: for example, the Asian Development Bank, in which Japanese influence was strong, followed policies "generally consistent with U.S. concerns," and, in the Inter-American Development Bank (IDB), U.S. influence was somewhat tempered by the substantial voting strength of Latin American members (at the time, the United States was not a member of the African Development Bank (AfDB), although it was a member of the African Development Fund, the AfDB's soft loan window). The report found that the MDB in which the United States had most effectively and consistently exercised influence was the World Bank—not only because of the U.S. voting share, but also because of the Bank's "location in Washington," which "permits U.S. policymakers to interact first hand with Bank management and other member countries."[54] The report surveyed a range of issue areas in the MDBs and found that the United States had been "completely or partially successful" in achieving its objectives in 85 percent of the cases. The report also noted that U.S. influence was heightened in replenishment negotiations, particularly when "Congress acted or threatened to act on funding requests to secure a specific MDB response."[55]

A related criticism was that the MDBs pursued policies that were contrary to U.S. interests. In answer to this charge, the Treasury assessment offered an extensive analysis of the ways in which the banks served U.S. policy goals, which it defined conventionally as strategic, economic, and humanitarian. It also pointed out that the banks pursued a host of secondary objectives, including burden sharing with other donors and the promotion of U.S. private commercial interests (e.g., through increasing U.S. exports to developing countries, access to raw materials, and procurement opportunities for American companies). The report had the least to say about humanitarian objectives, merely noting that the soft loan windows of the banks were most important where such interests were concerned.[56]

The report's findings regarding the banks' contribution to U.S. security interests were mixed. On the one hand, and in line with the views of many congressional Republicans, it argued that the MDBs were not as effective at promoting U.S. security interests as had previously been claimed. To this end, bilateral aid was a much more effective vehicle since it allowed the U.S. government to channel funds directly to friendly governments and to withhold financing from enemies. Rather, the banks' main contribution to U.S. security was indirect: they were "most effective in contributing to the achievement of our *global economic and financial objectives* and thereby also helping us in our long term political/strategic interests."[57]

In line with this view, the Treasury assessment found that the banks were most effective at serving U.S. economic objectives—particularly through their "cost-effective contribution to LDC economic growth and stability."[58] However, Third World countries could not grow and prosper through receiving handouts from international agencies. Rather: "If development is to succeed, the developing countries must mobilize their own resources to the maximum extent possible, and *adopt appropriate domestic policies* which are conducive to the *efficient allocation and utilization of these domestic resources* in conjunction with external assistance. *Unless a recipient country adopts such policies, no amount of external assistance is likely to produce sustained economic progress.*"[59] Therefore, the United States would reform the banks "to encourage adherence to free and open markets, emphasis on the private sector as a vehicle for growth, minimal government involvement, and assistance to the needy who are willing to help themselves."[60] "It is our judgment," the report contended, "that the United States does have sufficient influence in the institutions to work constructively with like-minded members and MDB management to secure such improvements."[61]

This market-friendly philosophy was then translated into a series of eight policy recommendations. First, U.S. policy toward the MDBs was to "emphasize attention to market signals and incentives, to private sector development and to greater financial participation by banks, private investors, and other sources of private financing." Second, the banks needed to emphasize promoting policy reform, both through "selectivity" (being choosier about their borrowers) and through "policy conditionality" (linking loans to economic policy reforms). Significantly, the report suggested that both the World Bank's structural adjustment lending program and the IDB's sectoral lending program "should be closely monitored to assess the potential for achieving policy reform." Third, the MDBs should allocate their resources with an eye toward projects with a reasonable rate of return, and more lending should be dedicated to reforming borrowers' economic policies.[62]

At the same time, the Treasury assessment proposed that both U.S. participation in the banks and the banks themselves be scaled back. Its fourth and fifth recommendations were that, wherever possible, borrowers should be "matured" from the soft loan to the hard loan windows and that the wealthiest borrowers should be "graduated" out of borrowing from the MDBs altogether. Sixth, the United States should lower its contribution to the paid-in capital of the banks and eventually phase it out entirely. Seventh, there should be a significant reduction, in real terms, of U.S. participation in the banks' soft loan windows. Finally, in such times of budget austerity, the United States should prioritize its contributions to the banks according to a number of criteria, including the principle that increased capital for hard loan windows was preferable to replenishing soft loan windows.[63]

Reframing U.S. Interests in the Banks

The 1982 Treasury assessment argued that the banks responded to U.S. leadership, promoted U.S. interests, and could be used even more effectively. At the same time, it advocated the reduction in U.S. expenditures, particularly on the banks' soft loan windows, and the eventual phasing out of U.S. financing altogether. This apparent mismatch between diagnosis and prescription was criticized by Fred Bergsten, Carter's assistant treasury secretary for international affairs, who testified to Congress that the report was "fatally flawed by internal contradictions."[64]

Yet, in spite of these logical inconsistencies, the Treasury assessment was important. It provided possible alternative directions for future U.S. policies and demonstrated the Reagan administration's commitment to continue supporting the banks, at least for the immediate future. Perhaps its greatest importance, however, lay in its construction of a new frame for understanding U.S. interests in the MDBs.

As we saw in the previous chapter, to market U.S. participation in the MDBs to Congress, the administrations of the 1970s became increasingly preoccupied with framing U.S. interests in the banks. The dominant interpretive frame of those years was that the banks were indispensable for both U.S. security and U.S. economic interests. While drawing on the same themes as previous administrations, the Reagan administration retooled this frame in ways that responded simultaneously to congressional concerns and to the administration's economic and geopolitical policy programs.

As had earlier administrations, the Reagan Treasury assessment framed the MDBs as tools for the promotion of U.S. and global security. However, the Reagan Treasury's report had a different interpretation of this security objective. According to the administrations of the 1970s, the MDBs had promoted security in two ways: first, by promoting economic growth, development, and higher standards of living in the developing world, and, second, by serving as "the symbol of [U.S.] commitment to Third World development."[65] Thus, the banks promoted U.S. security interests by serving not only an economic function (promoting development) but also a diplomatic one (serving as a symbol of U.S. commitment to helping developing nations). In contrast, for the 1982 Treasury assessment, the diplomatic function dropped out entirely: the banks fostered security exclusively to the extent that they promoted good economic, not diplomatic, outcomes. This was very much in keeping with the administration's foreign relations philosophy.

Also as earlier administrations did, the Reagan Treasury framed economic development as an important goal in itself. Yet, here too, the emphasis was subtly different. In previous Treasury budget justifications, the assumption had been that economic development could be attained through transferring a particular *level* of resources through multilateral aid. In contrast, the Reagan Treasury explicitly stated that the central issue was not the volume of resources but, rather, the quality of borrower policies. Of course, this can be read as a mere rationalization of objective circumstances: Congress was not willing to finance the banks at previous levels, so the Treasury had to come up with a theoretical reason for why decreased financing for the banks was appropriate. But it also reflected a significant rejection of previous conventional wisdoms: after all, one of the major messages of development economists had been that Third World countries needed large-scale transfers of concessional foreign aid. In short, the emphasis on the quality of borrower policies rather than quantity of financing suggested that the administration was listening to a different set of economists.

Both the administrations of the 1970s and the Reagan Treasury strongly focused on U.S. economic interests; however, the type of economic interest emphasized by the Reagan Treasury was different. The framing of the 1970s had emphasized the economic interests of creating markets for U.S. exports, sources of raw materials, and procurement contracts for U.S. firms. In contrast, the Reagan Treasury deemphasized these middle-range benefits—all three of which could arguably be provided even more reliably through bilateral aid programs. Instead, it proposed a much more ambitious, longer-term goal: the banks' most important role was to "encourage adherence to free and open markets," with an "emphasis on the private sector as a vehicle for growth, minimal government involvement, and assistance to the needy who are willing to help themselves." Or as Donald Regan told Congress in 1984: "The chief strength of the MDBs is not the financial resources which they provide, but the potential impact of their market-oriented policy advice."[66]

This focus on the banks as missionaries of the marketplace was not entirely new: it amplified and honed themes from earlier administrations. As we saw in the previous chapter, Democratic and Republican administrations alike recognized that it was difficult to use bilateral aid to change Third World policies (it created too much anti-imperialist resentment); multilateral institutions had greater potential for the promotion of policy reforms. This idea became particularly noticeable under the Ford administration, whose Treasury Secretary (William Simon) was both a notorious opponent of the North-South dialogue and a critic of the World Bank. As Deputy Assistant Treasury Secretary Bushnell, a top member of Simon's staff, put it in 1976: "The basic justification for the appropriations has to be that these banks do a good job in using the money to help the developing countries help themselves." He also noted the need to "stress the role of market forces in the allocation of resources and the development of outward-looking trading economies."[67] In contrast, the Nixon administration had less ambitious policy goals in mind. As Treasury Undersecretary Charles Walker put it in 1971: "The international lending agencies bring international influence on a collective basis to bear on recipient countries to maintain economic discipline and to follow *generally acceptable development policies*." An example was the World Bank's withholding of loans to countries that expropriated the property of foreign investors without proper compensation.[68] Encouraging "generally acceptable" policies meant upholding the property rights of U.S. citizens and keeping Third World governments from joining the Communist bloc.

In practice, the policies toward the banks followed by both Democratic and Republican administrations of the 1970s adhered more closely to the "generally acceptable" model than to the "market forces" vision. There is no evidence that the United States pushed the banks to push their borrowers in a more market-friendly direction during these years, and no such initiative was reported to Congress by the U.S. Treasury. There are many likely reasons for this, but at least one of them was that U.S. interests in the banks were largely viewed in terms of the MDB's diplomatic function as a "symbol of our commitment to Third World development."[69] This diplomatic framing of the banks' purpose reached its peak under the Carter administration. In that administration's first testimony to the congressional subcommittees, Assistant Treasury Secretary

Fred Bergsten explained that the developing countries were demanding many concessions (e.g., widespread debt relief, commodity price stabilization) that were not acceptable to the United States. In lieu of these diplomatic concessions, "a program of enthusiastic support for the international development lending institutions is of consummate importance to the United States across this entire range of North-South issues."[70] To aggressively press the banks to liberalize borrower policies would have made little sense at a time when the banks were seen as marketing a positive image of the United States to the Third World.

In contrast, the Reagan administration was not interested in using foreign aid to engage the Third World as a diplomatic bloc. Rather, foreign aid could support U.S. strategic objectives either through supporting key military allies in the fight against communism or through promoting long-term growth and market liberalization. The first of these two goals was best met through bilateral military and economic aid, with economic aid more specifically targeted toward military allies, such as the anti-Communist government of El Salvador. Although there was some move under the Reagan administration to tie bilateral economic aid to market-liberalizing policies, geopolitical objectives predominated.[71] The MDBs had a different function. Because the United States did not control them directly, they could not be used as a reliable means of supporting strategic allies. However, they could be used to further the long-term economic interests of the United States through spreading the magic of the marketplace.

Selling the New Frame to Congress

The Reagan administration was relatively successful in selling its new framing of U.S. interests in the MDBs to a recalcitrant Congress. During its first year, it waged a concerted campaign to convince congressional conservatives that the ideologues of the Heritage Foundation were wrong: the banks could, indeed, serve U.S. interests. In the Reagan Treasury's first testimony to the House Foreign Operations Subcommittee, John Porter, a Republican from Illinois, wanted to know how the administration was going to promote "supply-side economics" in its foreign policy. "I think the word 'incentive' has long been out of our lexicon," Regan replied. "I think that putting incentives back into these economies is the area in which we will be working. . . . Chile is the most recent example of where they changed the system and put incentives back in."[72] The sub-committee's response to this vision was quite enthusiastic. Clarence Long, the quirky Maryland Democrat who chaired the committee, sympathized with Regan's approach, remarking, "These developing countries are all flying under the banner of socialism. They think it is the great panacea. We are going along with them on it. . . . We are just asking them to fill up a bottomless pit, no matter how inefficiently they run their economies."[73] Jack Kemp, a recent recruit to the subcommittee (and a devoted supply-sider), was also enthusiastic: "Development is predictable, and it is not a question of anything other than democracy, and free markets, and free people, and incentives, and sound money, and sound trade policies, and sound regulatory policies."[74]

In addition to persuading Congress that the MDBs could be used to uproot erroneous statist policies, the administration worked hard to con-vince the legislative branch that they were not (as the Heritage Foun-dation claimed) examples of multilateralism run amok, immune to U.S. influence. As the Treasury official Marc Leland explained to the House Foreign Operations Subcommittee in 1981: "If I were convinced that these institutions were run on one-man, one-vote principles, I would be very skeptical about the idea of going along and supporting them. I am frank about that, but they are not run on that basis. . . . [I]f you just abstract the idea of creating an international institution situated in Wash-ington, D.C., in which we are the only ones with a veto and over which we together with our allies have the commanding influence and by work-ing together . . . we can get the objectives we want, I think you would still create that kind of institution."[75] But what of the banks' support for "socialist" (i.e., state-interventionist) economic policies in the Third World? In a particularly candid moment, Leland pointed out that the banks had previously supported these policies *because of*, rather than in spite of, U.S. influence: "I can't see how we can attack [the World Bank] for doing something that the United States has asked them and wanted them to do."[76]

Although the Treasury seems to have been relatively successful in con-vincing Congress that the banks could be used to promote U.S. interests, the fiscal environment of the early 1980s made matters more difficult. The Budget Reconciliation Act of 1981 forced the administration to pare its budget request down to only about $1.4 billion for the MDBs, less than half of what the Carter administration had requested the year before.[77] Even with reduced requests, passage of the foreign aid bill was delayed by deep differences between the House and Senate over how much to cut from military aid to U.S. allies (which the Republican-controlled Senate supported) and from foreign economic aid (which the Democrat-controlled House supported). On December 7, 1981, Reagan and Secretary of State Alexander Haig issued personal appeals to Republicans to work to get foreign aid legislation through Congress. Surprisingly, the administration was aided in this effort by Jack Kemp, who suddenly reversed his previous opposition to the banks and proposed an amendment to the House legislation that would bring it closer to a compromise with the Senate.[78] House supporters of foreign economic aid got behind the Kemp Amendment as a way of rescuing the program from another year of stopgap funding. On December 16, Congress cleared its first regular foreign aid spending bill since 1978.[79]

The final fiscal year 1982 appropriation for the MDBs was only about 9 percent less than Reagan's appropriation request. However, the amount that the administration had asked for in its revised request was very low— the lowest, in real terms, of any MDB budget request since 1972. In addition to stretching out appropriations to the general capital increase of the World Bank, the final bill also pushed U.S. installments to IDA replenishment from three to four years and sharply reduced the U.S. share within IDA from 31 to 23 percent.[80] Although those present did not know it at the time, this approximate level of administration request and appropriation would set a long-term trend. The boom years of U.S. financing for the MDBs had ended, and the real value of both administration requests and congressional appropriations would remain at or below their early-1980s level for the next two decades.[81]

The Reagan team's strategy was not only to hold down the requests to more modest levels but also to make Congress feel involved in the policy-development process by actively soliciting congressional feedback—a trend that had been initiated in the 1970s. The Reagan team also continued the earlier trend of providing Congress with more information about U.S. policy initiatives in the banks. In 1988, the last year of the Reagan administration, the U.S. Treasury began to supply the congressional subcommittees with an information-rich annual report on the MDBs and U.S. policies that resembled a marketing brochure, a document that continues to be presented annually to Congress today.

Of course, soliciting the feedback of Congress was a double-edged sword. On the one hand, it pacified members of Congress by making them feel consulted, but, on the other hand, it opened the door for Congress to make many more demands than it ever had previously. But never again would there be the level of congressional hostility toward the MDBs as there was at the end of the Carter years and never the same level of congressional cuts. From the Reagan years onward, U.S. policy toward the MDBs would be governed by a shaky, but nevertheless durable, modus vivendi between the executive and the legislative branches.

The Reagan administration's program for the MDBs was not only the basis for a new intragovernment consensus across the executive and the legislative branches; it also helped bridge differences between Democrats and Republicans. The Reagan program had something to offer both sides. For Republicans and conservative Democrats, the administration offered an implicit promise that the banks would no longer be supporting Third World socialism, along with the appealing feature of lowered administration budget requests. For liberal Democrats and the handful of pro-MDB Republicans, the new policy was appealing because it rescued the banks from abandonment and saved the programs dearest to their hearts, particularly the banks' soft loan windows that channeled resources on concessional terms to the poorest countries.

Moreover, at the core of the Reagan program for the banks was an initiative on which both sides in Congress apparently agreed: the promotion of liberalizing reforms in the Third World. In 1982, there was a review of the Treasury assessment conducted by the House Subcommittee on International Development Institutions and Finance, an authorizing body that had historically been supportive of the banks and that was led by a Democratic majority. Overall, the subcommittee agreed with the report, with two major points of concern: it felt that the banks needed more resources than the administration was giving them, and it hoped that the administration would be discreet in its promotion of liberalizing reforms through the banks. "It is potentially counterproductive," it concluded, "for the United States Government to publicly urge the MDBs to press countries to adopt particular economic policies, especially if such policies are seen as being strongly ideological. If the MDBs are viewed as politically biased and as merely an extension of U.S. foreign economic policy, their effectiveness will be diminished." In principle, however, the subcommittee concurred with the idea that the MDBs should "couple their lending activities with the extension of policy advice"; they merely needed to do so in a way that was sensitive and diplomatic.[82]

This does not mean that Reagan had quelled all major partisan dispute about the MDBs. Against both the Reagan administration and Republicans in Congress, congressional Democrats successfully pushed for U.S. contributions to the World Bank's Special Facility for Sub-Saharan Africa to help alleviate the region's humanitarian crisis. Democrats became increasingly concerned about the impact of policy-based lending on poverty and urged the World Bank to "focus more on projects directly benefiting poor people."[83] Moreover, throughout the Reagan years, MDB appropriations were pulled back and forth in a political tug-of-war between Democrats, who favored foreign economic aid, particularly multilateral aid, and Republicans, who wanted to prioritize bilateral military and economic aid to strategic allies. Thus, for example, in 1983, the Reagan Treasury requested $1.1 billion for the U.S. contribution to IDA; the Democratic-controlled House approved $945 million, the Republican-controlled Senate only $700 million. In 1984, the Senate refused to appropriate funds for a special economic policy initiative" for Africa. And, in 1985, all Republican members of the House Foreign Operations Subcommittee except Silvio Conte refused to sign the foreign aid section of the legislation in symbolic protest.[84]

Lack of discipline within the Republican Party put the Reagan administration in the awkward position of having to rely on Democratic votes to pass its budget request—and put the Democrats in the irritating position of carrying water for a Republican administration. In 1985 and 1986, House Foreign Operations Subcommittee Chair David Obey, a Democrat from Wisconsin, lambasted the Reagan administration for not mobilizing Republican votes for the MDBs, which allowed congressional Republicans to pose as opponents of foreign aid, which was politically unpopular, while scapegoating Democrats as liberal spendthrifts.[85] To resolve this untenable situation, in 1987 the administration held a budget summit with congressional leaders during which overall foreign aid spending levels were hammered out beforehand. Consequently, in the last year of the Reagan administration, Congress discussed foreign aid in friendly, bipartisan tones, and final appropriations for the MDBs (for fiscal year 1989) were only about 1 percent less than what the administration requested.[86]

Yet what was perhaps most notable about these partisan debates about the MDBs was what both sides of the aisle agreed on—and, therefore, did not bring into the debate. In the eight years of the Reagan administration, there was never a major initiative launched by either party against using the banks as a means of promoting market liberalization in developing countries. On this point, both Democrats and Republicans could agree. This attests to a strong bipartisan foundation for what would later be known as the *Washington Consensus*.

Conclusion

The inauguration of Ronald Wilson Reagan as president had two immediate consequences for the MDBs. One was an important shift in the research output of the World Bank. The other was a successful new framing of U.S. interests in the MDBs—one that allowed congressional appropriations to go through, albeit at diminished levels.

Although Reagan's election was an important precondition for both these trends, we have also seen that both responded to a complex amalgam of intellectual and political factors. It would have been impossible for World Bank research to evolve in the direction that it did without the presence of influential schools of thought within economics that endorsed market-liberalizing prescriptions. At the same time, Reagan's new framing of U.S. interests in the banks was partly built on the ideology of Reaganomics, which was itself a politicized version of the ideas of conservative economists. However, the new policy toward the banks responded at least as much to Reagan's foreign policy as to the agenda of Reaganomics. The administration's militaristic foreign policy vision successfully divorced U.S. MDB policy from the diplomatic concerns surrounding the North-South dialogue. The new plan for the banks reflected the commitment of Reagan Republicans to fighting communism through bilateral economic and military aid and to using the MDBs to spread the free market gospel around the world.

Using the banks to change the details of national economic governance—rather than encouraging "generally acceptable" policies—was a qualitatively different approach from that of the previous decade and one that implied driving much harder bargains with Third World governments. With historical hindsight, we might be tempted to attribute this new policy agenda to the decreased bargaining power of Third World countries that resulted from the outbreak of the debt crisis. However, we have seen that the administration began extinguishing the North-South dialogue and developing its plan for the banks very early on—well before the official outbreak of the Third World debt crisis on August 12, 1982. Moreover, as we will see in the following chapter, the evidence overwhelmingly suggests that the debt crisis took the Reagan team entirely by surprise. The administration's new plan for the banks seems to have grown entirely out of its long-standing ideological commitments to spreading markets and fighting communism—not out of a vision of how to take advantage of the plight of indebted countries.

Although the Treasury assessment was immediately successful as a *po-*

litical document—as a way of convincing Congress to finance the banks—
it was less so as a *policy* document. As former Assistant Treasury Secretary Fred Bergsten pointed out, there was a fault line running through
the middle of the Treasury assessment: on one side was the Heritage
Foundation–inspired idea that U.S. participation in the banks should be
scaled back, replaced by private financing, and eventually ended entirely;
on the other side was the idea that the United States should use the banks
to spread liberalizing reforms, with a particular eye toward the potential
of structural adjustment lending programs. The following chapter suggests
that, during the remainder of the first Reagan administration, the latter of
these two policy initiatives was largely set aside. It was not until the second Reagan administration, after 1985, that the U.S. government began to
wholeheartedly endorse and promote structural adjustment.

CHAPTER FOUR

Disciplining the Banks

In early 1982, as we have seen, the Reagan Treasury published an assessment of U.S. policy toward the multilateral development banks (MDBs). The banks, the assessment argued, had been used effectively to promote U.S. interests in the past—and could be used even more effectively in the future. "U.S. support for the MDBs," it concluded, "should be designed to encourage adherence to free and open markets, emphasis on the private sector as a vehicle for growth, minimal government involvement, and assistance to the needy who are willing to help themselves."[1]

With this statement as its battle cry, the administration seemed poised to export the Reagan revolution to developing countries around the world. However, for several years, nothing of the sort occurred. The most effective way to use the MDBs to promote the magic of the marketplace was through policy-based program lending, exemplified by the World Bank's newly minted structural adjustment program. Yet, during the first Reagan administration, structural adjustment seems mostly to have been ignored. This chapter draws on Treasury testimonies to Congress in the 1980s to examine the first Reagan administration's policies toward the MDBs. During this period, the Treasury's annual testimonies to Congress were characterized by a disciplinary tone toward the MDBs. The banks were expected to shape up by becoming leaner and more efficient and by getting more involved in cofinancing Third World projects with the private sector. At the same time, the administration successfully encour-

aged the MDBs to devote an increasing portion of their resources to supporting private enterprise rather than state-sponsored projects. Structural
adjustment, however, languished in obscurity. The first Reagan administration's relative quiescence on structural adjustment can be attributed
to ambivalence about this kind of lending, both within the administration
and among members of Congress.

The Early History of Policy-Based Lending

In contrast to the Heritage Foundation, which contended that bilateral
aid was the best vehicle for U.S. foreign policy, the Reagan administration recognized that multilateral institutions had a comparative advantage when it came to offering economic policy advice. Such advice, coming from an apparently neutral international organization, was more
likely to be accepted and less likely to generate resentment. As Treasury Secretary Regan testified in the spring of 1983: "By providing assistance through the MDBs we are in a much better position to encourage
economic policy reforms in developing countries than we are capable of
doing in the bilateral context."[2] At the time Regan made this statement,
however, the MDBs had little experience in this area. The MDB with the
most experience in changing borrower policies was the World Bank—but,
even there, policy-based lending made up only a small fraction of its activities. The International Monetary Fund (IMF) was the international organization that was most accustomed to getting borrowing governments to
change their policies. However, the kinds of policies that the IMF was
accustomed to reforming were short-term, macroeconomic ones, not the
long-term, structural ones that the Reagan administration envisioned.
Thus, both the IMF and the MDBs would need some changes if they were
to play a significant role as missionaries of the marketplace.

The Postwar IMF

The IMF had a long and controversial history of providing loans[3] that were
conditioned on policy reforms. The IMF had originally been conceived as
an organization that would help governments maintain exchange rates
pegged to the U.S. dollar by making emergency loans. It was envisioned as
a lender primarily for developed countries. However, by the mid-1950s—
only a decade after its founding—it was increasingly specializing in lend-

ing to developing countries and attaching policy conditions to its loans. This practice resulted from a combination of factors coming from both outside and inside the organization. On the external side, the United States— its most important shareholder—pressured the IMF to develop a policy of making conditional loans. On the internal side, early experiences with Latin American borrowers suggested to IMF management and staff the need to guarantee that the money was being used to encourage prudent macroeconomic policies.[4] As the decades passed, and as wealthy industrialized countries increasingly borrowed from international capital markets, the IMF found itself lending to an exclusively Third World clientele.

The IMF's postwar policy conditions were directly related to its role in helping governments manage their balance of payments—an accounting unit summarizing national revenues (e.g., exports, foreign investment, and external borrowing) and expenditures (e.g., imports and foreign debt payments). Under the Bretton Woods system of pegged exchange rates, a country with a balance-of-payments deficit would experience a loss of hard currency reserves in its central bank; this would lead to currency devaluation, which could contribute to domestic inflation; this, in turn, could create more pressure to devalue, and further inflation, and so on. The IMF's lending conditions were supposed to break this vicious cycle by stamping out inflation. Typically, governments would be required to cut spending and lower the money supply as a way of holding down inflationary pressures. These "stabilization" policies were intended to lead to "adjustment"—a new long-run equilibrium between domestic and international economies. The predictable short-term result was domestic recession and increased unemployment. To make sure that governments did not renege on their policy promises, the IMF began to disburse its loans in installments and to suspend loans midway in cases of noncompliance. Not surprisingly, the IMF's practice of "conditionality" soon generated bitter complaints from Third World leaders, who saw it as both excessively harsh and impinging on national sovereignty.

These complaints notwithstanding, what in retrospect seems most extraordinary about postwar IMF conditionality was its extremely limited nature. For the most part, IMF conditions aimed exclusively at fixing a country's macroeconomic variables, such as the exchange rate, money supply, and fiscal deficit. IMF officials almost never tinkered with the underlying structure of a borrower's economy—with its mix of private and public sectors, its level of trade protection, and so on. These issues were not considered to be directly relevant to a country's balance of payments and, hence, were not within the IMF's legitimate policy domain. Moreover, the changes mandated by the IMF were temporally limited: once the terms of the loan were over, it was very easy for the country in question to go back to whatever fiscal or monetary policies it wanted. The postwar IMF was a conservative institution; yet, it was not a purveyor of long-term liberalizing reforms.[5]

Nevertheless, the Reagan administration clearly wanted it to be both. In April 1981, only three months into the Reagan presidency, the IMF's Research Department prepared a research memo entitled "Supply-Oriented Adjustment Policies." Almost certainly put together at the behest of the United States, the memo discussed the benefits of "supply-side policies" at great length and proposed that IMF lending be used to promote "structural," rather than just macroeconomic, reforms. At that time, the proposal confronted considerable opposition on the IMF's Executive Board and failed to produce a major policy change.[6]

The Postwar MDBs

Compared to the IMF, the MDBs had relatively limited experience with policy-based lending. During the postwar decades, it was generally understood that the purpose of the MDBs was to make loans for projects— for dams, schools, highways, and so on—and this understanding was reflected in their articles of agreement. Project loans were conditional, in the sense that they were predicated on policies that were necessary for the financial viability of the project; for example, a loan for a power plant might be conditioned on raising electricity tariffs to make it profitable.[7] In the 1960s, some World Bank project loans were denied to countries with poor macroeconomic policies, such as overvalued exchange rates and excessive inflation. But project loans were not, as a rule, conditioned on overall economic policy changes.[8]

In addition to lending for projects, the postwar Bank made a limited number of "program" or "nonproject" loans, which were designed to help finance imports rather than pay for roads, dams, and other such development projects.[9] According to one internal World Bank report, as of the end of 1968, there had been twenty-two such loans in the Bank's history, out of six hundred International Development Association (IDA) and International Bank for Reconstruction and Development (IBRD) loans, or less than 4 percent of the total.[10] These rare nonproject loans were loosely connected to market-liberalizing policy reforms.[11] One particularly important case was the Bell mission to India in 1964, which represented a joint effort between the Bank and the United States to lend in exchange for liberalizing an economy that was extraordinarily regulated, even by the standards of the day. The most major and controversial of these reforms was the devaluation of India's overvalued exchange rate; other reforms included the limitation of military spending and the liberalization of agricultural prices.[12] During the 1970s, however, there were powerful forces that militated against the application of tougher conditionality. By this time, many Third World governments had greater access to cheap commercial credit, which made borrowing from official agencies that made intrusive policy demands unattractive. During this same period, McNamara's Bank was committed to expanding its own lending operations. At a time when creditors were competing to offer developing countries the most favorable terms, attaching conditions made it harder to get loans out the door.[13] As one World Bank insider subsequently commented, program loans in the 1970s were mostly about moving money and "focused on policy issues only incidentally, if at all."[14]

Over the course of the 1970s, massive spikes in oil prices created increased demand for the Bank to help borrowers weather temporary crises with quick injections of cash.[15] Nevertheless, program loans continued to be relatively rare. The Bank's articles of agreement legally precluded its involvement in nonproject lending, except under special circumstances.[16] Providing cash for balance-of-payments support was considered to be the IMF's job, not the Bank's.[17] Moreover, at a time when it was not possible to enforce tough policy conditions, program lending seems to have been considered vaguely irresponsible: in the words of a leading group of World Bank historians, such loans had only "borderline legitimacy."[18] The U.S. government, the Bank's most important shareholder, expressed reservations about expanding its activities in this area. As Assistant Treasury Secretary Charles Cooper told the House Foreign Operations Subcommittee in 1975: "There have been suggestions for a major expansion of program lending in the World Bank and even in the regional banks as a means of providing more quickly usable assistance to countries affected by higher oil prices. We do not believe an expansion of program lending for these purposes would be appropriate. It would divert the banks from their fundamental purpose of promoting long-term development."[19] To the extent that the Bank engaged in program lending in the 1970s, it was regularly challenged by its Executive Board, which eventually accepted the guideline (not a hard-and-fast rule) that only 6–10 percent of IBRD/IDA lending could be in nonproject form.[20]

The Birth of Structural Adjustment

On May 10, 1979, World Bank President Robert McNamara addressed the annual meeting of the UN Conference on Trade and Development in Manila, presenting an innovative idea. Over the previous decade, he noted, developing countries had suffered greatly from changing world economic conditions, particularly increased energy prices. This meant that poor countries were spending an increased portion of their scarce foreign currency reserves on imports, often with disastrous results—such as increased external debt, currency devaluation, and inflation. Although increased foreign aid could help alleviate these problems temporarily, the only long-term solution was for developing countries to increase their revenues from exports: "In order to benefit fully from an improved trade environment, the developing countries will need to carry out *structural adjustments* favoring their export sectors. This will require both appropriate domestic policies and adequate external help."[21]

Significantly, "structural adjustment" as McNamara proposed it in Manila was not out of line with the North-South dialogue that was in process at that time. McNamara emphasized that such a program would necessarily include generous assistance from the North in order to help developing countries make these difficult transitions. He did not propose that developing countries open their economies to the forces of free trade; instead, he suggested that Northern countries needed to open themselves to imports from the South without demanding reciprocal concessions. Over the very long haul, this would lead to a more liberal international trade system: "As additional measures are taken to protect the legitimate interests of the developing countries, and as they reach progressively higher stages of development themselves, they should, of course, be prepared to moderate their own domestic protectionist measures."[22] But it would presumably take decades for Third World countries to reach the level of development necessary for them to begin to open their economies. In the short and medium terms, structural adjustment aimed at export promotion, not free trade. Although McNamara mentioned the importance of domestic policies, he made no mention of policy leverage or conditionality.

The etymology of the term *structural adjustment* reflected its underlying purposes. These new loans were for adjustment in the sense that they helped countries repair their balance of payments. However, these loans would differ from the well-established adjustment programs of the

IMF in two major respects: first, they were supposed to provide more generous and longer-term financing, which would help alleviate the need for harsh deflationary measures; and, second, they aimed at helping countries make long-term structural changes that would increase export revenues and decrease import costs. In a sense, structural adjustment as conceived by McNamara was analogous to a job-retraining program for displaced workers, only, instead of training displaced workers to adapt to new regional economic circumstances, structural adjustment was supposed to train developing countries to adapt to changes in the international economy.

The origins of this idea could apparently be traced to Ernest Stern, McNamara's vice president for operations and the second most powerful person in the Bank. Stern had been a partisan of using program loans to encourage policies that would help governments repair their underlying balance-of-payments problems. Significantly, he had previously worked at the U.S. Agency for International Development, where he had been involved in attempts to use bilateral aid to promote policy reforms in South Asia. His senior advisor on structural adjustment loans (SALs) from 1980 to 1983 was Stanley Please, who had begun his Bank career as a fiscal economist in the Bell mission to India.[23] Early memos suggest that Stern's conception of structural adjustment placed greater emphasis on policy conditionality than did McNamara's.[24] By the time the formal proposal for the structural adjustment lending program was brought to the Bank's Board of Directors in February 1980, it had moved more in Stern's direction: SALs were conceived as quick-disbursing, nonproject loans that would provide financing over several years in support of specific policy reforms.[25] To supplement SALs, the Bank launched "sectoral adjustment loans" (SECALs) soon afterward. These were also linked to structural reforms but aimed at particular sectors of the economy.

World Bank SALs and SECALs differed from IMF loans in being longer term and in promoting changes in the underlying governance of economies (e.g., removing import restrictions) rather than short-term macroeconomic reforms (e.g., clamping down on inflation). However, as policy instruments, World Bank and IMF program loans were quite similar: both began with a quasi-contractual agreement between staff and borrowing governments concerning policy changes, including statements of measures, or "benchmarks," for gauging government compliance. These loans were divided, or "tranched," into installments and could theoretically be cut off if the government were found to be in violation of its end of the bargain.[26]

According to a group of official historians, this resemblance between IMF conditionality and the emergent variety in World Bank SALs and SECALs responded to the perceived preferences of the Bank's shareholders: "This kind of rigorous, verifiable conditioning was the type popularly associated with the International Monetary Fund, and of the two Bretton Woods sisters, the Fund was the favorite of the larger Part I [i.e., wealthy donor] governments."[27] However, until the early to mid-1980s, the size of the SAL and SECAL lending programs was limited by the convention that only 10 percent of Bank loans could go to nonproject lending.

The Debt Crisis and the Revival of the IMF

On August 18, 1982, Mexican Finance Minister Jesús Silva Herzog informed the U.S. government that Mexico would need to suspend payments on its enormous external debt. This announcement seems to have taken the Reagan administration entirely by surprise. Not only did Reagan's top Treasury officials have little experience in international finance, but they also seemed ideologically disinclined to address a problem that would require large-scale U.S. government intervention in international financial markets. According to Paul Krugman, who was on Reagan's Council of Economic Advisors at the time, the administration had ignored a Federal Reserve report issued in the spring of 1982 warning of the impending problem.[28] Even with the fact of Mexico's default staring it in the face, the Reagan Treasury seemed reluctant to act. As one former Treasury official later described the situation: "Silva Herzog kept describing the troubles to Don Regan, and Regan kept missing the message."[29] Regan's undersecretary of monetary affairs, Beryl Sprinkel, was a Chicago-trained theoretical economist whose beliefs are perhaps best described as "market fundamentalism": according to one source, when given a list of problem debtors by an outgoing Carter official (including Mexico, Argentina, and Poland), Sprinkel was dismissive, saying: "The market will take care of them."[30]

The market, however, was clearly not resolving Mexico's problem to the administration's satisfaction—and Mexico was only the tip of the iceberg. Encouraged by the low interest rates and easy credit of the 1970s, many developing countries had found themselves over their heads in debt to private banks when interest rates rose sharply at the beginning of the 1980s. As the magnitude of the debt problem in Mexico and other developing countries became increasingly apparent, it seemed possible that there might be large-scale default, perhaps in the context of a Third World "debtors' cartel." Most of the banks that were most at risk were American banks, and default could have had serious consequences for the U.S. banking system and the international economy more generally.

Miraculously, the administration was able to avert disaster. With the Federal Reserve in the lead, the U.S. government assembled a team that included the Fed, the Treasury, and the IMF.[31] The solution, for Mexico as well as for other Third World debtors, was "coordinated lending." The United States and the IMF lent their own cash to help debtor governments keep servicing their debts, but they simultaneously leaned on the banks to keep providing loans of their own, rather than each following its individual inclination to bolt. The philosophy behind this initial approach to the debt crisis was that the problem was one of illiquidity rather than insolvency.[32] Debtors were given fresh loans to help them roll over their debts, but they were, ultimately, expected to recover enough to pay their debts in full. At that time, the U.S. government viewed the debt crisis as a temporary problem to be staved off by short-term measures.[33]

The debt crisis and the U.S. response to it would have a number of important consequences for U.S. policy toward multilateral lending institutions. One consequence was that it allowed the IMF to become a significantly larger and more important organization. For the Heritage Foundation and supply-side Republicans, the IMF was an excessively interventionist organization that induced banks to make irresponsible loans to questionable debtors, with the assurance that they would be bailed out for their mistakes. In line with these ideas, the Reagan administration arrived in office committed to holding down the size of the IMF and was the only government to oppose a major increase in its resources at the IMF–World Bank meeting in Toronto in 1982.[34]

However, when faced with the growing reality of Third World default, the administration began to recognize that the IMF needed resources equal to the task at hand. In 1983, it proposed to Congress that the United States contribute $8.4 billion to a multilaterally negotiated $32 billion capital increase, a measure that would increase IMF resources by about 50 percent. Not surprisingly, Congress was difficult to convince. Many congressional Democrats were concerned that the capital increase essentially amounted to a taxpayer-financed bailout for private banks and that IMF-imposed austerity measures would make it more difficult for countries to restore economic growth. Ultimately, the Reagan administration was

forced to win over Democrats by mating the IMF funding bill to a housing bill that the administration had initially opposed. In addition to sharing some of the Democrats' concerns about bailing out the banks, congressional Republicans raised the usual right-wing criticisms of all things
multilateral. Like the World Bank, the IMF was portrayed by the Right
as another socialist multilateral institution that wasted U.S. taxpayer dollars.[35] The Republican congressional campaign committee even issued
press releases to the districts of the bill's Democratic supporters, accusing
them of supporting communism (because some IMF loans went to such
countries as Yugoslavia). As he had done two years before for the MDBs,
President Reagan intervened personally to rally his party behind the IMF
financing deal, scolding his copartisans for playing politics, and declaring
that withholding support from the IMF would be "a major disruption of
the entire world trading and financial system—an economic nightmare
that could plague generations to come."[36] Through such skillful political
maneuvering, Reagan was, ultimately, able to get the entire IMF request
appropriated by Congress.

In addition to breathing new life into the IMF, the debt crisis also
would have long-term implications for U.S. policy toward the MDBs.
Most important, the debt crisis could, if managed effectively, provide
international financial institutions (IFIs) such as the MDBs and the IMF
with enhanced leverage—the ability to persuade borrowing governments
to adopt particular policies in exchange for access to funds. During the
1970s, easy money had compromised both the MDBs' and the IMF's
ability to influence borrower policies: why submit to unwelcome outside advice when Citibank was offering money with no strings attached?
Now that Third World governments had more limited access to private
financing and were, hence, hungrier for official lending, it would be easier for the United States to move the MDBs toward using their resources
to promote changes in domestic policies. Nevertheless, the following section shows that, for the first several years after the debt crisis began, this
golden opportunity to use the MDBs to leverage policy reforms was not
fully exploited.

Putting the Treasury Assessment into Action

By the time of the Mexican crisis of August 1982, the Reagan administration had already made up its mind about what to do with the MDBs.

The United States would neither end American participation in them (as the populist Right would have liked) nor severely downsize it (as David Stockman at the Office of Management and Budget would have preferred). Rather, the February 1982 Treasury assessment outlined a policy in which the United States would use the MDBs as vehicles for spreading the magic of the marketplace to developing countries.

At the same time, however, the Reagan administration's newly minted mandate for the MDBs left considerable room for interpretation. Although all the proposals outlined in the Treasury assessment were loosely based on the ideas of Reaganomics, in reality they were quite diffuse and reflected at least four different conceptions of the best way to pursue the Reagan agenda through the banks. The first was that the U.S. government needed to be a thriftier and more cost-conscious donor—both through short-run reductions in U.S. contributions and through a long-run plan for phasing them out entirely. The second was that the banks themselves needed to become more cost-conscious donors by using their money more effectively. The third was that the banks needed to withdraw from activities better left to the private sector and increase their collaboration with private borrowers and lenders. And the fourth was that the banks needed to increase their policy leverage, thereby helping countries help themselves by adopting more market-friendly policies.

To put these policies into action, the administration had two major tools at its disposal. One tool was the power of the U.S. voting share on the banks' executive boards. However, this means of exerting U.S. influence was relatively weak. The United States did not have a majority of the votes in any of the MDBs; the only bank in which it could veto individual loans was the Fund for Special Operations (FSO) of the Inter-American Development Bank (IDB). The second tool was donor leverage: the United States could use soft loan replenishments and general capital increases as a way of winning concessions from other donors as well as from the banks. To supplement these major policy tools, the United States had other channels of influence, including its traditional power to appoint a congenial leader of the World Bank—in 1981, Robert McNamara stepped down as president and was succeeded by A. W. Clausen, the Reagan administration's chosen candidate—and its day-to-day influence on both the Bank and the IDB, which were both located in Washington.

With this ambitious list of goals and range of tools to pursue them, what did the administration actually do? In the Treasury testimonies to the congressional subcommittees from 1982 through 1985, it emphasized its success in using replenishments and capital increases to hold down the banks' overall size. It also reported back on its efforts to get the banks to become more efficient and to collaborate with the private sector. At the same time, the Treasury reported that it had been pushing for greater policy leverage through *project* loans, by opposing individual loans on the banks' executive boards. However, structural adjustment lending—the activity for which the banks would become famous—was not portrayed as a major administration initiative.

Reducing U.S. Contributions to the Banks

The reduction of U.S. contributions was the most straightforward policy goal set in the 1982 Treasury assessment since it was something the American government controlled directly. However, it was also a policy that had to be negotiated among major donors since allowing other shareholders to substantially increase their contributions (at a time of declining U.S. contributions) could mean an excessive loss of U.S. voting share.

The Reagan administration reported carrying out this policy through bargaining in general capital increases and soft loan replenishments. It appears that the administration was gambling that the recent history of failed U.S. appropriations would give the United States enough leverage over other donors to carry the day. In 1982, the Treasury official Marc Leland responded to congressional concerns that the United States would lose voting power and influence: "We are not cutting back the percentage of our voting power. We have no intention [of] doing this in the hard windows. In the soft windows nobody wants the United States to pull out. They [i.e., the other donors] want us to have a strong presence. I think there is a level at which you can see the banks have a reasonable amount of support.... If ... we went down to a $100 million IDA, and we said that we have no commitment and we are not even for it, then we [would] have a problem."[37] And as Elinor Contable, a State Department official cotestifying with Leland, added more explicitly:

> I think we have to admit that some of the figures that are coming out come as a disappointment to some of the other donors.... But I think on the other hand, the [Treasury] assessment itself came as a relief to many of the donors. I have talked to a lot of representatives of foreign governments who were very concerned about the possibility the [Treasury] assessment would explicitly diminish our commitment to the MDBs; it clearly does not, in the narrative and the

recommendations. They had hoped for a higher level of funding. But, I think, at the same time ... they understand our own budget situation, so there is a willingness to work with us on the financing side.[38]

In other words, so relieved were other donors that the United States was not pulling out of the banks altogether that they were willing to make significant concessions to avoid future problems. These concessions included allowing the United States to both reduce its own contributions and hold down the contributions of other donors.

The most celebrated moves in the direction of thriftiness occurred in the World Bank, where the contributions promised by Carter were subsequently cut through stretching them out; other donors agreed to delay their own contributions in tandem.[39] In the negotiations for a selective capital increase for the World Bank, concluded in 1984, U.S. participation was conditioned on "a conservative interpretation of the IBRD's 'sustainable level of lending.'"[40] In the negotiations for the seventh replenishment of IDA, also concluded in 1984, the United States insisted on holding down the replenishment overall to $9 billion—$3 billion less than what all the other donors had wanted and also $3 billion less than the previous replenishment.[41] Other G7 members were sufficiently dissatisfied with the trimmed-down IDA to put together a Special Facility for Sub-Saharan Africa (which was, ultimately, funded by Congress over the objections of the Reagan administration).[42]

Where the regional MDBs were concerned, the administration was committed both to holding down overall spending and to setting priorities: a higher proportion of soft loan resources would be going to the world's most impoverished regions through the African Development Fund (AfDF) and the Asian Development Fund (AsDF); a lower proportion would be going to the relatively well-off Latin America through the FSO.[43] This policy was reflected in the outcome of negotiations for the sixth capital increase of the IDB and the replenishment for its FSO as well as the third general capital increase/replenishment for the Asian Development Bank (AsDB)/AsDF and the third replenishment of the AfDF.[44] In 1985, Treasury Secretary James Baker boasted to Congress that the overall budget request being made for 1986 was 8.8 percent less than what was provided for fiscal year 1980 and that U.S. contributions to the MDB soft loan programs had been reduced by 40.5 percent, in real terms, compared to fiscal year 1981.[45]

However, the administration's aspirations went beyond reducing U.S.

appropriations and the size of the banks: the Treasury assessment had proposed the long-term goal of ending U.S. contributions to the banks altogether. This goal was soon abandoned. In 1982, Treasury Secretary Donald Regan told Congress that, in replenishment negotiations for the AsDB and the IDB, the United States was "suggesting the elimination of paid-in capital" but noted that "the reaction to total elimination from other donors has generally been negative" and that "some members of Congress also have reservations," particularly concerning the loss of influence that ending U.S. contributions would imply.[46] By 1984, the long-term goal of ending U.S. participation had been discreetly dropped from the annual Treasury testimonies. The abandonment of this plan may have resulted from the realities of the debt crisis, which made ongoing support for the banks critical to preventing Third World default. Or it may have been, as Regan's statement above implies, because the reaction of other donor nations and members of Congress was too negative. Whatever the reason or combination of reasons, U.S. participation in the banks has continued through the present day.

Promoting Cost-Effectiveness

The administration's second broad policy goal was to get the banks to use their resources more effectively. This was to be accomplished by promoting borrower maturation and graduation and by channeling resources toward the neediest countries. Unlike the goal of reducing U.S. contributions, this was not a policy the administration could implement directly: other leading shareholders would need to be convinced. However, there is no indication in the Treasury testimonies that the United States needed to bargain particularly hard to put these goals into action, and a number of successes were soon reported. In 1984, the Treasury reported to the congressional subcommittees that six countries were being "matured" from IDA to the IBRD.[47] In 1985, it testified to Congress that India's share of borrowing in IDA had dropped from 40 to 28 percent.[48] The United States also scored important gains in this area in the negotiations for the eighth replenishment of IDA, completed in 1986: sub-Saharan Africa, the region most in need, would receive between 45 and 50 percent of new IDA resources; IDA maturities would be reduced from fifty to forty years, effectively freeing more resources for immediate use.[49] During the administration of George H. W. Bush, pressures to keep more advanced developing countries from borrowing from the soft loan windows continued, and in the sixth AsDF replenishment, concluded in 1991, the United States won the concession that neither India nor China would be eligible for AsDF loans.[50]

Where the elimination of loan targetry was concerned, the administration's reported successes were, perhaps, more limited. In 1984, Treasury Secretary Regan reported that this message was being forcefully conveyed to the banks: "In our presentations of U.S. positions on policy issues in the MDBs, we have worked to discourage [the] practice [of targetry], if necessary, by limiting the growth in overall lending programs."[51] And, in 1985, Treasury Secretary Baker told Congress that World Bank lending for that year was roughly $2 billion less than originally anticipated—a consequence of the Bank's adherence to standards for loan quality.[52] However, the banks' propensity to push loans would continue to be criticized by many observers, and even today it is argued that the banks' internal and external organizational incentives tend to prioritize the moving of money over the soundness of projects.[53]

Harnessing the Power of the Private Sector

One of the major themes of the 1982 Treasury assessment was private-sector development. Beginning in 1986, *private-sector development* would be interpreted to mean using policy-based lending to get Third World governments to privatize their state-owned industries. In contrast, the first Reagan administration seems to have meant something different by the term, namely: getting the private sector to take over, at least partially, the provision of multilateral loans to governments to engage in large-scale development projects, the banks' most characteristic activity and the one that had long drawn the wrath of congressional Republicans.

One approach to the private-sector mandate was to get the banks to stop providing financing in areas in which the government ostensibly did not belong. In accordance with this thinking, the administration was quick to kill a Carter-supported proposal for an "energy affiliate" within the World Bank, which would have tapped into OPEC funds to help developing countries develop their own energy resources. The administration's view was that natural resources were best developed by the private sector alone, without the World Bank serving as an intermediary.[54]

In addition to getting the banks to stop interfering with market forces, the Reagan team thought that "[the] private sector should have a more prominent role in MDB lending programs."[55] To bring the banks and the private sector closer together, the administration encouraged bank financing of private-sector projects. The use of the banks as intermediaries for private-sector activities was an old idea: since 1959, the World Bank had possessed a lending affiliate—the International Finance Corporation (IFC)—that channeled resources to private investors. However, because of high interest rates and the debt crisis, the IFC was not doing well in the early 1980s.[56] Recognizing that the IFC was the World Bank lending affiliate most sympathetic to its policy agenda, in 1985 the Reagan administration supported a doubling of the IFC's capital resources while holding down replenishments and capital increases for the IBRD and IDA.[57]

Meanwhile, other MDBs were urged to move in a similar direction. In 1986, the Treasury announced that, in line with U.S. wishes, the AsDB was making direct loans to the private sector through its regular hard loan facility.[58] The administration also strongly supported the founding of the IDB's Inter-American Investment Corporation, which financed private firms.[59] Although there is no record in the Treasury testimonies of nudging the African Development Bank (AfDB) toward private-sector financing, the bank did create its Private Sector Development Unit in 1989.

In the 1980s, the United States made considerable strides toward getting the banks to finance private-sector activities. However, during the 1990s, it pushed too far. In another capital increase for the IFC, the George H. W. Bush administration said that it would support the request only if the World Bank and other donors would approve major changes in the Bank's articles of agreement—to remove the prohibition on IBRD lending to the private sector. The administration also wanted the Bank to agree that, by 1995, more than half of IBRD lending would go to private firms. This plan was opposed, not only by other donors, but also by Congress. The proposed measure was duly defeated, and the idea of using the biggest and oldest MDB to finance private projects was shelved.[60]

Yet another version of private-sector development was the administration's initiative to get the MDBs to cofinance projects with private financial institutions.[61] The ostensible reasons for such collaboration were that it would "offset scarce public resources" and that "[private investors] inject a greater degree of market discipline into the development process."[62] In 1983, the administration reported that the World Bank had obtained more than $3 billion in cofinancing from commercial banks; the AsDB had acquired more than $87 million.[63] However, by the second Reagan administration, it was clear that this policy initiative had not been successful. American efforts to promote MDB cofinancing with the private sector were mentioned with decreasing frequency, and examples of tangible successes in this area were no longer mentioned at all. According to World Bank annual reports, total private-sector cofinancing actually declined significantly between 1981 and 1987.[64]

Why did this initiative fail? According to one former Reagan Treasury official, some of the difficulty with the cofinancing initiative stemmed from lack of investor confidence in the wake of the debt crisis.[65] Another former Treasury official recalls that private banks were put off by the MDBs' unwieldy and private-sector-unfriendly bureaucracies.[66] In any case, this was one version of private-sector development that did not produce major results.

Promoting Policy Leverage

Of all the policy initiatives outlined in the 1982 Treasury assessment, the most ambitious and potentially difficult to implement was the plan to get the banks to promote market-friendly policies in developing countries. Unlike promoting cost-effectiveness in the banks, using them to promote policy reform was bound to be more controversial among important donors. To make matters more complicated, the administration's agenda for getting the banks to push borrowers to reform their economic policies was diffused among two different approaches, both mentioned in the 1982 Treasury assessment. One approach was to channel bank *projects* selectively toward those that emphasized "attention to market signals and incentives, to private sector development and to greater financial participation by banks, private investors, and other sources of private financing."[67] The other was getting the banks to use their *program* lending— such as the World Bank's new structural adjustment lending program—as a means of fostering borrower reforms. During the first Reagan administration, the Treasury overwhelmingly emphasized the first of these two approaches.

PROJECT CONDITIONALITY.   At the time the Reagan administration came into office, nearly 100 percent of the banks' resources were devoted to financing projects, rather than programs. Therefore, it is not surprising that changing the focus of projects was a major administration concern. In 1982, Treasury Secretary Regan stated: "If the MDBs are to use scarce budgetary resources to best effect, lending should go to countries which pursue *sound economic policies*. Thus, the United States has been reviewing project loans and policies more critically and insisting that borrowers take steps to help themselves."[68]

But how could MDB-financed projects, which mostly went to governments, be reconciled with the objective of liberating the invisible hand of the marketplace? The answers were selectivity and conditionality. *Selectivity* meant that the banks would be choosier both about the projects and about the countries they financed, with more money going to countries with market-friendly economic policies and to projects based on solid economic principles—and less to countries with illiberal policies. *Conditionality* meant conditioning project loans on sound economic policies. In this way, lending for projects could be used to send borrowers the message that, in the words of Treasury Secretary Donald Regan, "the United States will no longer passively support loans to countries pursuing ineffective economic policies."[69]

To nudge the banks toward selectivity and conditionality, the administration reported mobilizing its team of executive directors within the various banks to oppose individual project loans. In April 1982, only two months after the publication of the Treasury assessment, Secretary Regan announced that the administration had vetoed its first FSO loan for economic reasons, along with loans in other MDBs.[70] In the several years that followed, the administration regularly reported opposing project loans for economic reasons. As Treasury Secretary James Baker explained in 1985, enhancing the quality of project loans would "occasionally ... require the United States to oppose a loan based on an assessment of the economic viability of the project."[71]

Such opposition was only occasional because, as we saw in chapter 1, the fate of MDB loans was often determined before votes were actually cast: if the banks' management saw that there were not sufficient votes for a project to pass, the usual procedure was to withdraw the loan from consideration. The administration soon learned how to work effectively within this system. According to Treasury testimony to the authorizing subcommittee in the House in 1985, there was an "early warning system" in place through which the administration was notified of MDB projects that would be coming up for approval. In the words of the Treasury official Jim Conrow:

> If we look at [an MDB loan] and we think the problem is serious enough we can get into the institution and talk to them and the staff who are putting this project together to try to get changes.... [This] eliminates the need of having

to oppose a loan when it gets to the board because the loan never gets to the Board in quite the fashion that we had initially seen it. And then, finally, the ultimate is that if in fact they do bring forward a loan that we think does not make economic sense for one reason or another, that we are prepared to oppose it, and we have over the course of the last 4 years opposed a number of loans in all the Development Banks where we felt that the economic case was not made.

Now while that does not stop loans from going forward in these institutions, it does send very important signals both to the country and to the institution that here is a donor looking at these things and looking at them very carefully, and we do feel that that has a positive effect."[72]

The pattern of U.S. voting on project loans thus provides an incomplete sense of overall U.S. pressures because it excludes those loans that were never brought to a vote in the first place. Nevertheless, these voting patterns do provide a revealing record of the administration's priorities. In 1987, the Treasury provided a detailed record of U.S. negative votes and abstentions in all four MDBs and their soft loan windows since the early 1970s. Table 4.1 compares the patterns of negative votes and abstentions during the Carter administration (1977–80) and first Reagan administration (including the beginning of the second Reagan administration since the voting dates range through September 1985). All the negative votes and abstentions, with the sole exception of a 1982 loan to Ethiopia for "development finance," were project loans.

This comparison reveals some striking differences in the priorities of the two administrations. In compliance with congressional legislative mandates, both administrations opposed loans that went to recognized violators of human rights. However, while human rights concerns accounted for the vast majority of the loans opposed by the Carter administration (77.5 percent), they accounted for a relatively small percentage of the loans that the Reagan administration opposed (28.3 percent). Instead, more than half the loans opposed by the Reagan administration were opposed on the basis of economic policy—both the overall economic policies of the borrowing country (17.3 percent) and those pertaining to individual projects (34.6 percent). In contrast, the Carter administration cast only 2.8 percent of its negative votes and abstentions on the basis of country economic policies and 5.6 percent on the basis of project economic policies.

A more detailed breakdown of the rationales for opposing loans is also extremely informative. Among those loans opposed by the Reagan administration for reasons pertaining to the country's overall economic policies,

TABLE 4.1. **U.S. Negative Votes and Abstentions in the MDBs, February 1977–September 1985**

	Carter Administration (1977–80)		Reagan Administration (1981–85)	
	N	%	N	%
Reasons for vote:				
Human rights	110[a]	77.5	36[b]	28.3
Other political	20[c]	14.1	23[d]	18.1
Country economic policy	4[e]	2.8	22[f]	17.3
Project economic policy	8[g]	5.6	44[h]	34.6
Other	0	0	2[i]	1.6
Total	142	100	127	100

Source: House Appropriations Subcommittee, *Appropriations for 1987*, 737–50.
[a] 23 no, 87 abstain.
[b] 0 no, 36 abstain.
[c] 20 no, 0 abstain. Breakdown: 10 "Long Amendment," 5 "expropriation," 4 "presidential directive," 1 "commodities."
[d] 23 no, 0 abstain. Breakdown: 23 "expropriation."
[e] 1 no, 3 abstain. Breakdown: 2 "excessive tariffs," 1 "economic reasons," 1 "inappropriate strategy."
[f] 14 no, 8 abstain. Breakdown: 11 "inappropriate macroeconomic policies," 4 "economic reasons" (unspecified),
2 "inadequate sector reform conditionality," 2 "use of seriously overvalued official foreign exchange rate, inappropriate policies on agric. co-ops," 1 "poor management structure, inefficient import substitution, no govt. commit. to divestment," 1 "potentially premature due to global overcapacity and unsound sector tax pol.," 1 "added restraints on private sector."
[g] 4 no, 4 abstain. Breakdown: 2 "absorptive capacity," 2 "cost overrun," 2 "rate of return," 1 "economic viability," 1 "financial viability."
[h] 22 no, 22 abstain. Breakdown: 15 "potential displacement of foreign private capital," 9 "unjustified cost overrun," 5 "doubtful economic and/or financial viability," 3 "inadequate rate of return," 2 "poor soil and excess milling capacity," 2 "not a development priority," 1 "absorptive capacity," 1 "negative subloan interest rates," 1 "cost overrun and inadequate economic justification," 1 "inappropriate financial structure," 1 "lack of replicability," 1 "poor project design," 1 "could displace local private capital," 1 "negative real interest rates and budget subsidy."
[i] 2 no, 0 abstain. Breakdown: 1 "ineligible for concessional funds," 1 "outstanding arrearages."

the most common rationale was "potential displacement of foreign private capital," with fifteen opposing votes. Examples of projects opposed on these grounds were IBRD and IDA petroleum projects in Peru and the Ivory Coast: for the Reagan administration, energy resources were best exploited through the private sector. The second most common reason was that borrowing countries had "inappropriate macroeconomic policies."[73] By *macroeconomic*, the administration appears to have had a more expansive definition than that used by the IMF and international economists, including, not only fiscal and exchange rate policies, but also policies pertaining to government interventions in markets. For example, in 1982, Treasury Secretary Regan reported that the United States had just opposed an FSO agricultural loan "to a country where excessive governmental interference had undercut incentives to farmers," with the consequence that the borrower "raised farmgate prices and reduced subsidies."[74]

Where loans were opposed for reasons pertaining to the projects themselves, the most frequently cited reason was that the project was getting
the state into an economic area in which it did not belong, such as petroleum extraction and processing. This was the common rationale behind
the categories of "potential displacement of foreign private capital" and
"potential displacement of domestic private capital." A second common
reason was that the project cost more than it was worth, as exhibited by
the categories "unjustified cost overrun" and "not a development priority." And a third category of objections to projects was that they were
undercharging for the government services the project would provide. In
line with this general philosophy, the administration vetoed five loans on
the basis of "doubtful economic and/or financial viability" (e.g., an IDB
dam project in Ecuador), three on the basis of "inadequate rate of return"
(e.g., an AfDB highway construction project in Kenya), and another
because it had "negative sub-loan interest rates" (an AfDF agricultural
credit project in Zaire).

This latter category of U.S. objections to projects is worth elaborat-
ing on because of its importance to later controversies over "user fees."
The Reagan administration was strongly committed to raising the prices
charged by MDB-financed utilities for services such as water, electricity,
or housing. From the administration's point of view, raising user fees (otherwise known as "user charges") was not only philosophically sound (it
eliminated price distortions); it also had a practical benefit: at a time when
the administration was working hard to ensure that Third World debtors
did not fall into arrears, eliminating subsidies on public services helped
governments balance their budgets and meet their debt payments. During the first Reagan administration, such efforts were particularly evident
in the case of U.S. policy toward the IDB: in 1982, the Treasury reported
that the United States was working with the IDB "to encourage minimum
standards for realistic user charges in power and transport projects. These
user charges will be designed to cover operating and capital costs of these
services."[75] In 1983, Regan reiterated: "The MDBs must continue to insist
on sound economic criteria for their loans such as adequate financial and
economic rates of return."[76]

Overall, the Reagan team's pattern of voting on the boards of the
MDBs sent a strong message that the United States was committed to
bringing sound economics to developing countries. But how effective,
precisely, was this strategy of using the executive boards to promote reform, project loan by project loan? The evidence presented by the Trea-

sury to Congress is inconclusive. In 1985, Treasury Secretary James Baker reported that, under U.S. pressure, the IDB had implemented a significant policy change whereby it would make loans only to public utilities "that have a rate structure which enables the utility to meet full operating and maintenance costs," resulting in "a reduction in government budget subsidies."[77] Inspired by U.S. opposition to lending in areas better left to private companies, the World Bank had "issued new operating guidelines" for lending in the energy sector. Overall, Baker told Congress: "It is fair to say that there has been some improvement in the overall quality of MDB lending as a result of our continuing emphasis on this subject."[78]

However, by 1986, the U.S. Treasury was no longer testifying to Congress about its efforts to change project lending policies. By that time, the administration had, apparently, decided that project loans were not the most effective vehicle for changing the policies of borrowing governments and that a far more promising vehicle was *program* lending—an issue to which I now turn.

PROGRAM CONDITIONALITY.   As we saw in the previous section, in the early 1980s program loans were a small and little-known subset of the MDBs' activities. However, the 1982 Treasury assessment expressed a keen interest in the potential of such loans for advancing the administration's vision: "The banks should be encouraged to introduce more selectivity and policy conditionality within projects and sector programs they support. . . . The IBRD structural adjustment program and the IDB sectoral lending program should be closely monitored to assess the potential for achieving policy reform."[79] However, the sectoral adjustment program within the IDB was so obscure that it was not mentioned in the IDB's official statement of approved loans for 1981, 1982, or 1983.[80] Rather, it was the World Bank's structural adjustment program that had the greatest promise.

At the same time, the Treasury assessment also sounded a more cautious note: "The SAL program is, in some sense, still in the experimental stage and needs to be monitored closely."[81] In keeping with this mandate, in 1983 the Treasury reported to Congress: "A special group has been established in the Development Policy Office [of the Treasury] to monitor [structural and sectoral adjustment] loans and to help coordinate U.S. action on them."[82]

Although the first Reagan administration may have been closely monitoring MDB program lending, it was not overtly promoting it. In reporting

TABLE 4.2. **Program Lending as a Percentage of World Bank Lending Commitments**

	1980	1981	1982	1983	1984	1985	1986
Program, % IBRD	6.3	9	6.7	26.36	10.1	13.3	25.1
Program, % IDA	8.4	4.3	11.7	8.35	10	7	20.7
Program, % total IBRD/IDA	6.9	7.6	7.8	22.6	10.1	12.1	24.3

Source: House Appropriations Subcommittee, *Appropriations for 1987*, 688. Data shown are for calendar years.

the U.S. positions in various replenishments and general capital increases from 1982 through 1985, the Reagan Treasury had nothing to say about U.S. promotion of policy-linked program loans—instead emphasizing American victories in holding down the size of U.S. contributions and the banks' overall size. Indeed, during the four years of official testimony from 1982 through 1985, the Treasury did not even once report that it was pushing for increasing the size or efficacy of structural adjustment lending or promoting it in other MDBs besides the World Bank.

In reality, as table 4.2 shows, nonproject lending at the World Bank did grow during the period 1982–85. A particularly anomalous year was 1983, when, according to data supplied to the Treasury by the Bank and presented to Congress three years later, nonproject SALs and SECALs had grown to more than 22 percent of total lending volume.[83] The explanation for the increase appears to be the World Bank's Special Action Program of 1983, which contributed IBRD funds to the IMF-led response to the debt crisis.[84] However, IDA program lending that same year remained at 8.3 percent, and, during the two years that followed, combined IBRD/IDA lending fell to a level near—although still above—the 10 percent limit.

The First Reagan Administration in Retrospect

By 1982, all the major ingredients were, apparently, in place for Washington to mobilize the MDBs to promote a free market revolution in developing countries. The most obvious, and arguably the most effective, means for pursuing this end was structural adjustment and other program lending, in which governments committed to policy reforms in exchange for financing. Beginning in 1986, as we will see in the following chapter, the United States would promote program lending with a vengeance. But we have seen that, in the four years following the publication of the Treasury assessment, nothing of the sort was reported back to Congress.

How can we account for this? The lack of public information concerning U.S. MDB policy makes it difficult to arrive at any firm conclusion: outside researchers are privy neither to the discussions that went on in the Treasury, to the dialogues that occurred between the Treasury and the banks, nor to the negotiations that occurred among major donors. To shed light on this issue, it would be extremely helpful to examine the archival record of the donor negotiations that occurred around the seventh IDA replenishment since these might reveal the administration's positions on structural adjustment lending during the early 1980s. Unfortunately, my repeated attempts to gain access to these documents through the World Bank archive met with no success. In lieu of such hard evidence, I present the two most likely answers to this question and evaluate the likelihood of each.

Possibility 1: The Administration Did Not Want to Report on an Issue That Would Raise Congressional Ire

The first possibility is that the Reagan administration was, indeed, pushing for more policy-based program lending but did not want to raise further controversies around the MDBs in Congress. There are reasons to believe that Congress was quite suspicious of such lending during the period in question. Program lending was associated with helping governments deal with balance-of-payments problems and make their debt payments. As such, it was subject to the same kinds of political opposition as IMF loans, which were frequently lambasted by Congress as being huge taxpayer-financed bailouts for private banks. The effectiveness of program lending was also premised on tough conditionality, which Congress had little reason to believe would actually be applied, given the experience of the 1970s.

Indeed, throughout the early and mid-1980s, Treasury representatives were routinely grilled by subcommittee members wanting to know how much of the World Bank's resources were being used (by implication, irresponsibly) to finance borrowers' balance of payments and service their debts.[85] It seems significant that, in response to one such question by the New York Democrat Matt McHugh in 1984, Treasury Secretary Regan responded: "Current World Bank practice limits nonproject lending, including structural adjustment lending, to 10 percent of annual Bank commitments." The 10 percent figure was repeated by the Treasury official Jim Conrow at hearings of two subcommittees the following year.[86]

Assuming that the Treasury was informed about what the World Bank was doing, this was clearly a disingenuous answer: although it was true that the World Bank possessed a guideline capping program lending at 10 percent, we have seen that, starting in 1983, the guideline was already regularly being breached (see table 4.2 above). The Treasury's reference to this fictitious limit on program lending suggests that the administration was, indeed, concerned about congressional resistance to such lending. And, if the Reagan Treasury was reticent to tell Congress about the reality of program lending, its fears turned out to be well-founded: as we will see in the following chapter, when structural adjustment became a central element of the administration's MDB policy in 1986, it encountered sharp criticisms from both sides of the aisle.

Possibility 2: The First Reagan Administration Was an Inconsistent Advocate for Program Lending

A second possibility is that the first Reagan administration did not report on promoting structural adjustment because it was, in fact, not promoting it—or, at the very least, not promoting it consistently. As we have seen in this and other chapters, there were strong elements in the Reagan coalition that found IFIs to be distasteful on principle. Even though the 1982 Treasury assessment acknowledged that the banks could be useful tools, relations between the banks and the Reagan administration remained strained for a number of years; according to one source, in the summer of 1983 the administration even had spy software installed on World Bank computers, allowing the National Security Agency to monitor the World Bank archives.[87] It had only been in the face of the threat of a major financial meltdown that the administration was able to overcome its own distaste for expanding the size of the IMF, an organization that effectively specialized solely in program lending for supporting members' balance of payments.

It is likely that, in the immediate wake of the enormous increase of the IMF's resources, trying to push the MDBs to expand their own program lending operations was seen by some in the administration as going too far—particularly since, unlike the IMF, the World Bank did not have a well-established track record of strongly enforcing policy conditions. This was the recollection of Henry Nau, a former Reagan official who testified to Congress in 1985 on structural adjustment lending. "These loans initially drew a rather skeptical reaction from myself, as well as the [Reagan] administration," he recalled, "because we were not convinced that the Bank knew how to carry out this kind of conditionality."[88]

By 1984, it appears, resistance within the administration to structural adjustment was beginning to erode, but only slightly. As Treasury Secretary Regan explained to the congressional subcommittees in April of that year: "We frequently encounter the view that the MDBs have a prominent role to play in coping with the current debt servicing problems of some developing countries. I should like to emphasize that the MDBs are not—by design or aptitude—balance of payments lenders."[89] Yet, during the question-and-answer session in the same testimony, he gave a more ambiguous response, stating: "We believe the current project/non-project mix is appropriate." However: "If developing country demand for SALs were to increase, and assuming policy performance remained a prerequisite for SAL programs, we would be prepared to consider sympathetically with Management and other members the possibilities for an effective Bank response."[90] Two months later, this position was publicly contradicted by Beryl Sprinkel—the Reagan Treasury official who had allegedly thought that the market should take care of the debt crisis. In a World Bank–IMF meeting in June, Sprinkel stated that the United States opposed the expansion of the World Bank's structural adjustment lending program.[91] Thus, it seems that, where program lending was concerned, the first Reagan administration may have been an inconsistent advocate at best.

Conclusion

In 1984, Stanley Please—a World Bank official who helped design structural adjustment—published an essay in which he speculated on its future. "Is there a possibility," he asked, "that the SAL lending will be seen in retrospect not so much as a diversion to meet an immediate crisis but as a watershed in the role of the Bank and in the way it executes this role?"[92] Several years later, the answer would turn out to be a resounding yes. At the time Please's essay was written, however, a number of obstacles needed to be overcome for structural adjustment to be transformed into a major instrument for policy reform—and some of these obstacles were in Washington. Although it is difficult to say with certainty, the limited available evidence suggests that neither the legislative nor the executive branch of the U.S. government was ready to endorse structural adjustment as a major vehicle for bringing the market to the Third World.

Instead of forging ahead with a plan for using program lending to leverage policy reform, the first Reagan administration's greatest accomplishments with respect to the MDBs can mostly be described as disciplinary in nature: trimming the banks down to size, getting them to use their resources more efficiently, removing them from areas in which they allegedly did not belong, and blocking them from making problematic project loans. Not all these initiatives were equally successful, and some were outright failures. The administration soon discarded its plan to phase out U.S. participation in the banks as either practically or politically unrealistic. The plan to promote cofinancing with the private sector met with little success. And, although using U.S. voting share to oppose individual project loans may have been satisfying to report back to Congress, it was not the most efficient way to promote market liberalization in developing countries. After all, the United States did not possess a majority vote in any of the banks and could exercise a veto only in the soft loan window of the IDB. Even in the banks in which the United States wielded its greatest influence—the World Bank and the IDB—it did not possess enough voting share to unilaterally block loans of which it did not approve; registering opposition to loans did not guarantee changes in the banks' lending policies, much less the economic policies of borrowing governments.

In fact, the administration's first five years of policy toward the MDBs look remarkably like a government slowly learning to work with organizational tools with which it had little experience. Paradoxically, at least one of the obstacles faced by the Reagan team in formulating the most rational plan for the banks was its own radically laissez-faire ideology. On the one hand, this ideology created an opening for an influential new framing of how to use the banks to serve American interests—one that would permanently alter U.S. policy toward the banks. But, on the other hand, it predisposed at least some within the administration to believe that the magic of the marketplace would grow simply out of the MDB's downsizing and withdrawal from areas in which they did not belong. In reality, the fostering of markets in developing countries called for significant intervention, on the part of both the U.S. government and the MDBs. By Reagan's second term, the administration seems to have learned from past mistakes, as we will see in the following chapter.

CHAPTER FIVE

The Emergence of the Washington Consensus

The Washington Consensus, as John Williamson observed it in 1989, was a set of market-liberalizing economic prescriptions for indebted Latin American countries. By *Washington*, Williamson meant top decisionmakers at the International Monetary Fund (IMF), the World Bank, the Inter-American Development Bank (IDB), and the U.S. executive, as well as among "those members of Congress who take an interest in Latin America" and economic policy think tanks.[1] Although primarily developed with the Latin American debt crisis in mind, the Consensus list was soon viewed as applicable to the rest of the developing world.

Where did the Washington Consensus come from? Many commentators on this topic have focused on trends in the intellectual field—among economists and other development experts. The intellectual rejection of Third World statism grew partly out of empirical evidence of economic problems, such as the notoriously inefficient state-owned industries documented in the World Bank's 1982 report on sub-Saharan Africa.[2] At the same time, it resulted from changing intellectual fads and fashions, such as the enthusiasm for markets that accompanied the decline in Keynesian thinking.[3] The Washington Consensus reflected the general move away from the heterodoxy of postwar development economics, for as Williamson observed: "A striking fact about the list of policies on which Washington does have a collective view is that they all stem from classical mainstream economic theory.... None of the ideas spawned by the development literature—such as the big push, balanced or unbalanced growth, surplus labor, or even the two-gap model—plays any essential role in motivating the Washington Consensus."[4]

Yet, as its name implies, the Washington Consensus was not a product of scholarly ideas alone. It was not just a description of the world but a blueprint for policy—a vehicle for translating ideas into action. In exchange for financial help to meet their debt obligations, Third World governments would "fulfill their part of the proposed bargain by 'setting their houses in order,' 'undertaking policy reforms,' and 'submitting to strong conditionality.'"[5] Along with a prescription for the governments of developing countries, the Washington Consensus also contained a prescription for international financial institutions (IFIs), which were now to play a greater role than ever before in encouraging governments to implement desirable reforms through conditional policy-based lending.

Like all policy programs, the Washington Consensus had political as well as intellectual origins. In this chapter, we will see that a crucial political antecedent was the Reagan administration's move to a more pragmatic interpretation of its commitment to free market economics. From early on, the Reagan administration had expressed interest in using the multilateral development banks (MDBs) as vehicles for disseminating the magic of the marketplace to developing countries. The 1982 Treasury assessment had concluded that the World Bank's "structural adjustment program . . . should be closely monitored to assess the potential for achieving policy reform."[6] However, within the Treasury assessment, this vision coexisted with a contrasting view in which the MDBs needed to be disciplined, steadily replaced by the private sector, and eventually phased out entirely.

In this latter vision, the Treasury assessment reflected the more radical views of Republicans in Congress and the administration, conservative think tanks such as the Heritage Foundation, and some of the business press. For these critics, U.S. support for large multilateral bureaucracies represented delegating sovereignty to suspiciously statist institutions that the United States did not control directly. Policy-based lending was particularly suspect: the banks were unreliable organizations known in Republican circles for pushing loans onto socialist governments, rather than enforcing tough policy conditions.[7] In line with these views, the first Reagan administration opted to focus more heavily on disciplining the banks than on expanding policy-based lending.

It was not until James A. Baker III became Treasury secretary, under the second Reagan administration, that the idea of the MDBs as promoters of liberalizing reforms came into its own in Washington. At the October 1985 meetings of the World Bank and the IMF in Seoul, South Korea, Baker proposed a bold new plan—soon known as the Baker Plan—for addressing the Third World debt crisis. The Baker Plan marked two important turning points in U.S. policies toward the MDBs, both of which would have durable long-term effects. The first was that the United States began to actively promote policy-based lending as one of the MDBs' core activities. The second was the dawn of a new era in shareholder activism—one in which the United States would use its considerable leverage in donor negotiations to win particular kinds of policies in the banks. With the passing of time, the Baker plan would be replaced and the original Washington Consensus superseded. Yet the enhanced role of policy-based lending and U.S. shareholder activism would remain as its enduring legacies.

The Baker Plan in Brief

As it was announced in Seoul in October 1985, Baker's "Program of Sustained Growth" for addressing the Third World debt crisis was made up of three related elements. First, debtor countries needed to adopt "comprehensive macro-economic and structural policies supported by the international financial institutions, to promote growth and balance of payments adjustment, and to reduce inflation." Second, Baker called for "a continued central role for the IMF, in conjunction with increased and more effective structural adjustment lending by the multilateral development banks, both in support of the adoption by principal debtors of market-orientated policies for growth." And, third, he proposed "increased lending by the private banks in support of comprehensive economic adjustment programs."[8]

In some respects, the Baker Plan was unremarkable. In keeping with the trend set by the first Reagan administration, it had no proposal for debt reduction: developing countries would have to pay in full. It also espoused a similar practice of coordinated lending and requiring that private banks help finance the rescue plan.

Yet the Baker Plan also represented a marked departure from earlier policies. First, it contained a qualitatively new interpretation of the problem as a long-term rather than a short-term one. Third World debtors needed longer-run financing to get back on their feet and to restart economic growth. Second, unlike the administration's previous debt strategy, which had awarded a leading role to the IMF, the Baker Plan proposed a major mobilization of the MDBs. IMF loans were mostly short-term and conditioned on fiscal and monetary adjustment. The MDBs, in contrast, made their resources available over a longer period of time and, unlike the IMF, were ostensibly in the business of promoting economic growth and development. By providing fresh capital to countries with unsustainable debt burdens, in the form of nonproject, balance-of-payments loans, and by tying these loans to tough liberalizing policy conditions, the MDBs could play a central role both in addressing short-term liquidity problems and in solving the longer-term issues.[9] Most important to the Baker Plan were the two banks closest to the Latin American epicenter of the debt crisis: the World Bank and the IDB.

Third, and most important, the Baker Plan unambiguously endorsed expanding the MDBs' capacity for policy-based lending. Baker explained the reasoning behind this policy to the congressional subcommittees in the spring of 1986. Referring explicitly to the 1982 Treasury assessment, he noted: "From the outset this Administration has emphasized that a fundamental role of the MDBs should be to encourage policy reform in developing countries."[10] Renewed economic growth was the only way out of the debt crisis, but, "absent appropriate economic policies, no amount of money—whether derived from external borrowing, foreign aid, or domestic monetary expansion—will produce sustained growth."[11] In other words, if growth was the only solution to the debt crisis and liberalizing reforms the only means toward growth, then it stood to reason that IFIs needed to be fully mobilized to promote liberalizing reforms.

In line with this reasoning, both the World Bank and the IDB were expected to expand their lending through fast-disbursing structural and sectoral adjustment loans. Anticipating future appropriations requests, Baker told the congressional subcommittees in 1986: "We are ... prepared, if all the participants in the strategy do their part and there is a demonstrated increase in the demand of quality lending above these levels, to consider a general capital increase for the World Bank."[12] In the question-and-answer session, Baker elaborated: "We would expect any capital increase in the Bank to be used primarily to finance the Bank's expanded policy-based lending operations."[13]

The market-liberalizing policies that the United States wanted the World Bank to thereby promote included "growth oriented tax reform," "improvement of the environment for both domestic and foreign direct investment," "trade liberalization and the rationalization of import regimes," and "the privatization of burdensome and inefficient public enterprises."[14] This last element—the promotion of privatization—represented a significant departure from earlier U.S. policies toward the banks. During the first Reagan administration, the United States had promoted private-sector development through MDB cofinancing with the private sector or directly lending to private firms. In contrast, the Baker Plan had a much more ambitious plan: to use program lending as an incentive to get governments to divest themselves of public enterprises and, thereby, to launch a major transformation of the economic governance of developing countries.

At that time, the concept of privatization was a novel addition to the Washington policy lexicon. In the World Bank's famous 1982 report on sub-Saharan Africa (the Berg Report), there had been numerous examples of how state-owned industries contributed to economic inefficiency and stagnant growth. Yet, although the report had recommended that African economies rely more on markets and the private sector, it had refrained from calling for divestiture of state-owned industries; rather, the Berg Report focused on various ways that African governments could reform the parastate sector through better management, more market incentives, and so on.[15] The word *privatization* was not used in the *World Development Report* until 1983, when it was briefly mentioned as one of many options for reforming state-owned industries.[16] When using it for the first time in the Treasury testimonies to the congressional subcommittees in 1985, Treasury Secretary Baker found it necessary to explain the meaning of this novel term.[17]

Yet, only a year later, privatization was at the center of the U.S. agenda for the MDBs. As Baker explained: "We recognize there are honest differences of opinion regarding the role of the state in some sectors of the economy—such as utilities and telephone service. But we cannot allow these unique sectors to obscure the fact that in most industries, government ownership is disruptive, inefficient, and is not required. In our opinion, the MDBs must confront these cases head-on."[18] Also to help promote privatization (and private-sector development more generally), Baker announced that the United States was supporting the creation of the Multilateral Investment Guarantee Agency (MIGA), a multilateral insurance fund for private foreign investors in developing countries. Because MIGA advised governments on the best policies to pursue to attract foreign investment, its foundation was also an important pillar in the Baker plan.

To effectively promote policy reforms in the developing world, the banks themselves would need to undergo reforms. As Baker explained, "the expanded role for the MDBs"—"in particular, the roles of the World Bank and the IDB"—would "require important policy and procedural changes in these institutions."[19] The banks would need to be firmer about conditionality: "We want a greater resolve by the MDBs to seek strong, economic loan conditions; and an increased willingness by the MDBs to refuse funding when these conditions are not accepted, or, once accepted, not met."[20] All the banks would need "to focus more on how overall macroeconomic policies impact on projects," including variables traditionally in the purview of the IMF, such as interest rates and exchange rates.[21] Moreover, the banks needed to tailor their lending toward "country strategies," or overall plans for national economies.[22] For its part, the IMF needed to move toward considering variables traditionally considered to be within the purview of the MDBs: "We have ... asked the IMF to give more thought to growth-oriented policies and this is being done."[23]

Explaining the Shift

The first Reagan administration had downplayed program lending as an instrument for achieving U.S. policy goals and withheld financing from the World Bank. With the Baker Plan, however, policy-linked program lending became the central element for promoting U.S. objectives, and the Bank was promised resources to grow once again. The Baker Plan was immediately recognized by other donors and the international business press as an important change in U.S. policy toward the MDBs—the "abandoning [of] four years of U.S. hostility to the World Bank."[24]

A full analysis of the Reagan administration's policies toward developing countries must be left to future historians, who will have access to the internal documents and personal correspondence needed to tell the complete story. However, the available evidence points to three obvious factors behind the shift in emphasis toward the MDBs. The first was overwhelming pressure to deal with the Third World debt crisis, which the earlier policy had failed to resolve. The second was that Reagan's second Treasury Department was more flexible and pragmatic than its predecessor. And the third was that, over the course of five years of intensive interactions, the administration and the World Bank had learned to work with one another and, thereby, to arrive at a mutually beneficial plan of action.

When Baker assumed office, the state of Third World debt was extremely grave. The debt management strategy promoted by the first Reagan administration had assumed that the problem could be solved by forcing the banks to keep lending and the debtors to keep paying. But, as high interest rates compounded the debt and national growth rates stagnated, these debt burdens became increasingly unsustainable, and once again the threat of a debtor's revolt loomed on the horizon.[25] By 1985, low- and medium-income countries were a third deeper in debt than they had been at the initiation of the debt crisis in 1982.[26]

The ongoing economic crisis in the Third World caused concern in Congress, where it was noted that economic stagnation abroad was causing a reduction in demand for U.S. exports.[27] At the same time, the renewed threat of Third World default was worrisome to leaders in the U.S. financial community. In February 1984, a commission made up of representatives of twenty-six financial firms, including Goldman Sachs, First Boston, and the Bank of America, concluded that private lenders could not meet the Third World financing gap and called for increased intervention by multilateral lenders, including more structural adjustment lending.[28] American banks were heavily exposed to the risk of default, and it was imperative to find a way of shifting some of these risks to multilateral institutions. Paul Volcker, the powerful chairman of the U.S. Federal Reserve, also began to publicly advocate a new debt strategy, as did Secretary of State George Shultz and the National Security Council.[29] Thus, by the middle of 1985, the consensus among U.S. policymakers, as well as the captains of international finance, was that a new debt strategy was needed.

A second factor contributing to the new approach was the changed composition of the U.S. Treasury under the second Reagan administration. The policies of the first Reagan Treasury toward IFIs were, as we saw in the previous chapter, shaped in part by doctrinaire laissez-faire ideology. In contrast, the new Treasury secretary, James Baker, had a reputation for being pragmatic and flexible. When Baker assumed office, Undersecretary of Monetary Affairs Beryl Sprinkel, known for his view that the market would take care of the debt crisis, moved to a position on Reagan's Council of Economic Advisors, and new policymakers, such as David Mulford, were moved into top Treasury positions.[30] As the senior economist at the Morgan Guaranty Trust Company told the *New York Times* on the announcement of the Baker Plan: "The ideologues have been replaced by the pragmatists."[31]

A third factor in effecting the shift was the learning process within the Reagan administration regarding how best to work with the banks—and, reciprocally, within the World Bank regarding the best way to work with the U.S. administration. The Reagan team had originally assumed office with very little experience in international finance and a view of multilateral institutions that was heavily influenced by right-wing congressional populists, who were used to criticizing the banks from the outside. By 1985, however, the administration had experienced four years of successfully pursuing policy initiatives in the MDBs. There were occasions when it was not happy with some of the policies that the MDBs were pursuing, as the story of the IDB told below illustrates well. For the most part, however, the administration reported back to the congressional subcommittees that the banks were following the American lead, showing that they were not, as the Heritage Foundation claimed, multilateral loose cannons that were unresponsive to U.S. concerns.

More specifically, the administration's skepticism about structural adjustment lending seems to have been steadily eroded by evidence that the World Bank was willing to impose tough conditionality—and not just give away money and bail out the banks, as many had feared. Since the inauguration of the Bank's structural adjustment program in 1980, the meaning of the term *structural adjustment* had gradually been evolving. Originally, it had been used to refer to the provision of resources to developing countries suffering from external shocks; extra financing would give them time to increase the ratio of exports to imports and, thereby, restore equilibrium in their balance of payments. In the 1981 *World Development Report*, the program was described as "a new type of lending launched by the World Bank [that] will help oil importers adjust to the changing international environment." At that time, *structural adjustment* was defined as "switching resources to the production of exports and import substitutes."[32] Policy reforms were part of the package since they were presumed to help countries increase their export revenues; they were not, however, the main focus. As the original author of structural adjustment lending commented years later, there was in 1980 "no clear emergence" of what would later be recognized as structural adjustment.[33]

In contrast, by the middle of the decade, policy reform was being described as an end in itself—and not simply a means to restoring balance-of-payments equilibrium. In the *World Development Report*, this notion was first clearly articulated in 1985, when the report explained that "the focus of the Bank's structural adjustment lending . . . is to encourage governments to reduce economic distortions by cutting subsidies, sharpening incentives, and phasing out protection for inefficient producers" and that "structural adjustment loans are intended to help countries with deep-rooted balance of payments difficulties to reform their policies."[34] From that point forward, market-friendly policy reform would be the defining feature of structural adjustment.

To what extent did this redefinition respond to the demands of the Bank's most important shareholder? Because we have no records of the internal discussions among World Bank managers or between managers and the U.S. Treasury, we cannot answer this question with certainty. However, circumstantial evidence suggests that the reframing of structural adjustment was part of a very shrewd strategy on the part of the World Bank management to adapt to shareholder demands and other environmental circumstances.

The early 1980s had been very lean years for the World Bank. Under the first Reagan administration, the United States had put the Bank on a strict diet, with stretched out contributions to both the International Development Association (IDA) and the International Bank for Reconstruction and Development (IBRD) and stern reprimands against loan pushing and other undesirable practices. Meanwhile, the debt crisis was putting the Bank under a different set of environmental pressures. Weighed down during the mid-1980s by heavy debt payments, austerity programs, and high inflation, fewer governments were both willing and able to take on large World Bank project loans, and lending projections were not being met.[35] If the World Bank management was to convince major shareholders to increase the Bank's resources, it would need to come up with a plausible reason for why it needed more money at a time when the demand for its loans was decreasing. As World Bank President Tom Clausen explained to the *Washington Post* in the spring of 1985, the World Bank needed to "build a rationale": "We've got to answer [questions like] How do the shareholders want to use the institution? That's a fairly important question."[36]

By that time, the Reagan administration had begun to soften its earlier opposition to program lending. As the former administration official Henry Nau recalled in 1985: "[Structural adjustment] loans initially drew a rather skeptical reaction from myself, as well as the present administration, because we were not convinced that the Bank knew how to carry out this kind of conditionality. But today ... the administration has dropped its limitation with respect to the amount of Bank financing for these loans, and seems to be quite pleased with the emphasis in those loans on important macropolicy changes, getting prices right, reducing and rationalizing public investment programs, and unilaterally liberalizing trade."[37] That same year, Jim Baker similarly testified to the congressional subcommittees: "The World Bank is making a credible effort to ensure that a country's willingness to formulate a suitable program of structural adjustment remains a firm precondition for lending under its structural adjustment lending program and sector adjustment loans."[38]

In short, the Reagan administration had come to publicly accept the view that the World Bank was capable of imposing tough policy conditions. At least in part, this rhetorical shift must have been driven by pragmatic considerations: to advocate using World Bank program loans to address the debt crisis, the administration needed to assure Congress that the money was not being thrown away. Yet, irrespective of the sincerity of the underlying beliefs, the shift in the administration's position presented a golden opportunity to a World Bank management hoping for more generous IDA replenishments and a major new capital increase for the IBRD. Rather than advancing the implausible claim that it needed more resources for project loans, the Bank could request an increase in resources to address the blossoming debt crisis while simultaneously promoting market-friendly reforms.

This new rationale fostered a fortuitous convergence between the views of the World Bank management and the U.S. Treasury. By early 1985, the Bank was publicly reporting that it planned to be placing even more emphasis on program lending and less on projects. According to the *Washington Post*: "World Bank officials have concluded that the bank must reshape its approach to development lending following an unexpected $2 billion drop in loan commitments. . . . In particular, high officials have come to the conclusion that the economic environment in the countries receiving help may be more important than the actual projects being put in place."[39] In this, the Bank had the support of its most important shareholder: a few months later, a Treasury official told *Business Week*: "We were skeptical about the structural adjustment loans, but they have proven to be of high quality."[40] The Baker Plan, which promised the Bank more resources in exchange for an enhanced emphasis on policy reform, was announced later that year.

Policy Reform, from Baker to Brady

As a debt strategy, the Baker Plan was a failure. Third World borrowers continued to suffer from stagnant growth and unsustainable payments. By

1988, U.S. policymakers were ready for a new strategy. Baker's successor under the George H. W. Bush administration, Nicholas Brady, proposed a new plan that allowed for a measure of debt relief—something the previous strategies had lacked—and was more successful.[41]

Yet, in spite of its failures as a debt relief package, Baker's plan provided a blueprint for reforming both the MDBs and economic policies in developing countries that would endure into the subsequent administration. The Treasury testimonies to the congressional subcommittees from the Baker and Brady years show that the United States consistently pushed for all the policies outlined in the original Baker Plan in all the MDB replenishments and general capital increases negotiated through the early 1990s.

This strategy of promoting economic policy reform through the MDBs was made up of three mutually supporting elements. The first was the expansion of policy-based program lending. The second was the restructuring of the banks' lending around "country strategies." And the third was coordination among the MDBs and between the MDBs and the IMF. The remainder of this section looks at how these three elements played out in U.S. policy toward the World Bank, the Asian Development Bank (AsDB), and the African Development Bank (AfDB). The case of the IDB, which was unusually protracted and contested, will be discussed in the separate section that follows.

Policy-Based Lending

In line with the Baker Plan, by the spring of 1987 the Treasury was reporting to Congress that the World Bank had negotiated $2.9 billion in new fast-disbursing policy-based loans.[42] In return for following this agenda, the administration had promised that the United States would be more generous with the Bank. The eighth IDA replenishment, concluded in 1986, was $12.4 billion, a significant increase over the notoriously stingy $9 billion seventh IDA replenishment. The ninth replenishment, concluded in 1990, was $15 billion.[43]

Both IDA replenishments explicitly committed the Bank to more program loans. The Treasury reported that, in the eighth IDA replenishment negotiations, the administration had successfully negotiated an agreement that at least 25 percent of the new resources would go toward policy-based program lending.[44] In the ninth IDA replenishment, the United States had gotten other donors and the Bank management to agree that adjustment lending would remain at between 25 and 30 percent of IDA resources.[45] Another U.S. policy objective achieved in both replenishments was increased selectivity: previous implementation of "sound economic policies" would receive greater weight as a criterion for IDA loans.[46]

Although increased IDA replenishments brought a welcome injection of cash to the World Bank, the real prize was the general capital increase, which would lead to a permanent increase in the Bank's size and resources. Largely owing to controversies in Congress, agreement on the general capital increase was difficult to reach, and it was not until 1988 that a final $74.8 billion deal was hammered out. The final terms of the increase included explicit language committing the Bank to U.S.-led policy initiatives. These included "increased efforts to help design and implement adjustment programs and to assemble debt restructuring packages" and a "thorough review" of policy-based lending operations.[47] The new general capital increase put U.S. capital subscriptions at 18.75 percent, below the 20 percent level necessary to veto major changes to the Bank's charter. However, as part of the overall general capital increase agreement, the Board of Directors altered the constitutional majority for changing the articles of agreement from 80 to 85 percent.[48] Thus, U.S. influence was upheld in spite of its decreased share in the Bank.

Although it had not been emphasized in the original Baker Plan, the AfDB was also encouraged to move in the direction of policy-based lending. Concluded in 1986, the fourth general capital increase for the AfDB committed the bank as a whole to engage in "policy-based lending as appropriate in conjunction with the World Bank and other development institutions."[49] By 1991, the Treasury was reporting that the United States had accomplished "all its major policy objectives" in the AfDB and, consequently, agreed to a real $3.5 billion increase in resources. "The bulk of the [African Development] Fund's resources," Treasury Secretary Brady reported, "will now be allocated to countries that are providing the economic environment conducive to development and growth."[50] That replenishment also strengthened U.S. influence in a bank that had been heavily controlled by regional members, giving individual executive directors the power to return loans to the Loan Committee so that their concerns might be addressed.[51]

In contrast to the other regional banks, the AsDB's movement to structural adjustment occurred more quietly and without recourse to explicit conditions in replenishment negotiations. Neither the fourth nor the fifth replenishment of the Asian Development Fund (AsDF), completed in

1986 and 1991, respectively, formally committed the AsDB to engaging in policy-based program lending. The largest potential obstacle to U.S.-led reform in this donor-dominated bank was Japan, which controlled the same percentage voting share as the United States and appointed both the AsDB's president and most of its top management.

The Reagan administration clearly wanted the AsDB to be moving in the same direction as the other banks. In April 1987, at the bank's annual board meeting, a senior Treasury official called for a thorough external review of the AsDB's role in the region, a move seen as an implied criticism of the bank's primarily Japanese management. A major rationale for the review was that the United States, along with some other donors, wanted the bank to be moving toward structural and sectoral adjustment program lending.[52] Shortly thereafter, in November 1987, the AsDB's Board of Directors approved a new program lending facility similar to the World Bank's sectoral adjustment facility.[53]

Disagreements lingered concerning how rapidly the Asian bank would move into policy-based lending. The Reagan administration wanted the move to be rapid and the bank's professional staff to be reformed accordingly. The Japanese Treasury found these demands to be "impatient."[54] In the end, however, the U.S. view prevailed. By 1989, the bank's *Annual Report* stated that program loans aimed at such reforms as "lower[ing the] level of protection against imports," "deregulation of investment approval," and "a smaller public role in the direct provision of goods and services" accounted for more than 13 percent of total disbursements.[55]

Country Strategies

A second element in the U.S.-sponsored reform agenda was getting the MDBs to move toward a focus on overall "country strategies," rather than simply approving loans on a project-by-project basis. This approach had been pioneered at the World Bank, which, during the McNamara presidency, introduced "country program papers" to bring up larger economic policy issues with borrowing governments.[56] Country strategies would later be important for policy-based lending on two counts: first, they provided blueprints for future policy reforms; and, second, they helped ensure that traditional project loans fit into an overall policy-based strategy.

In 1987, the World Bank adopted organizational reforms that furthered its gathering focus on countries over projects.[57] By then, Tom Clausen had been replaced by Barber Conable, a former Republican congressman who

worked hard at improving World Bank–U.S. relations. Conable's 1987 reorganization led to the layoff of about 10 percent of the Bank's staff and
considerable ill feeling. Many observers at the time believed that the reorganization was directly aimed at placating congressional critics of World
Bank inefficiency and, thereby, getting a critical mass of U.S. support for
a general capital increase.[58] However, another intended effect of the reorganization was to further push the Bank into emphasizing country programming over the previous focus on projects.[59]

The AfDB and the AsDB were urged to implement similar reforms.
The AfDB general capital increase and the African Development Fund
(AfDF) replenishment, completed in 1986 and 1987, respectively, committed the bank to "more effective country programming and lending operations through development of country strategies," to "improv[ing] project
quality and ensur[ing] consistency with borrower country strategies," and
to "produc[ing] country strategy papers for most borrowers."[60] Another
AfDF replenishment completed at the end of 1991 pushed further in this
direction by requiring the "formulating of comprehensive country programs."[61] The fifth replenishment of the AsDB included a similar commitment to producing country strategy papers for most borrowers.[62]

Coordination among Donors

The third element of Baker's blueprint for the MDBs was to tighten up
coordination among IFIs, thereby making it more difficult for borrowers to
elude the conditionality of one lender by turning to another. A major innovation of the Baker years was the introduction of joint World Bank–IMF
"policy framework papers" (PFPs) in 1986. As Nicholas Brady explained
to the House and Senate subcommittees, a PFP was "a joint document
of the Fund and Bank—outlining [borrowers'] structural and macroeconomic reform efforts and containing an assessment of their financing
needs, including possible IMF and World Bank financing."[63] The IMF was
the senior partner in the preparation of these joint documents.[64] The ninth
IDA replenishment agreement, concluded in 1990, committed the Bank to
increased collaboration between IDA and the IMF on PFPs.[65]

In reality, the PFPs represented a compromise between the United
States and other leading shareholders. The United States had wanted
formal "cross-conditionality" between the World Bank and the IMF—a
policy under which failure to meet the conditions of one institution would
result in the automatic disapproval of a loan by the other.[66] According

to the IMF veteran Jacques Polak, the Baker Treasury strongly pushed for formal cross-conditionality but was so vehemently opposed by other countries that the United States was forced to accept PFPs instead.[67]

Nevertheless, the PFPs marked a significant harmonization of the two organizations' policies. The World Bank would usually wait for borrowers to arrive at a lending arrangement with the IMF before agreeing to its own program loan. The IMF, for its part, began to include World Bank–type structural reforms, such as privatization and trade liberalization, into its lending arrangements.[68] In 1986, the IMF inaugurated its Structural Adjustment Facility (SAF), designed to make longer-term loans for structural reforms, the terms of which were based on the PFPs. Market-liberalizing reforms were also included in the IMF's traditional lending vehicle, the short-term standby arrangement.[69] The Bank and the IMF were organizations with different missions and organizational cultures, and closer collaboration sometimes led to friction and conflict. Nevertheless, PFPs did, apparently, achieve their intended effect of imposing greater standardization between World Bank and IMF loans.

Just as the United States wanted the World Bank to work more closely with the IMF, so too did it want the regional banks to work more closely with the World Bank. Relations between the World Bank and its regional cousins in the 1970s had been "ragged."[70] But, if the banks were to be serious about policy-based lending, it was imperative that they not undermine one another's efforts—and it was desirable for them to follow the lead of the World Bank, which had the most experience in promoting policy reforms. The 1986 AfDB general capital increase committed the bank to "coordination with other donors and limited policy-based lending in conjunction with the World Bank."[71] In the fifth AfDF replenishment, completed in 1987, the Treasury was "successful in the negotiations in having all of [its] positions on lending and policy issues adopted," among which was the "the coordination of [AfDF] activities with major donors."[72] Beginning in 1988, between 80 and 100 percent of AfDB policy-based lending was cofinanced with the World Bank, giving the larger of the two banks considerable influence over the policies of the smaller. In the words of one observer in 1997: "It seems fair to say that the conditionality is designed by the World Bank and the [AfDB] participates by providing extra cash."[73]

In the AsDB, things played out somewhat differently. The sixth AsDF replenishment agreement, concluded in 1992, also included language committing the AsDB to heightened cooperation with other lenders in the region.[74] However, the terms of the coordination were, apparently, loose:

even by the mid-1990s, it was rare for the AsDB to engage in cofinancing with the World Bank.[75] This lack of progress suggests, once again, that the Japanese were less than enthusiastic about the move to structural adjustment lending.

The Taming of the IDB

To inject new funds and growth-stimulating reforms into the Latin American heart of the debt crisis, the Baker Plan had allotted important roles to both the World Bank and the IDB. The World Bank management seems to have been eager to engage in policies that would restore U.S. support. The IDB, in contrast, was more resistant. In 1988, the Treasury budget justification to Congress noted: "The United States believes that a number of reforms and changes are needed in the IDB before an expanded role and a significant increase in funding for the Bank can be supported. Since agreement on the reforms has not been possible, discussions about a major increase in the IDB's resources have stopped."[76]

During the eight years of the Reagan presidency, relations with the IDB had been fraught with conflict. In contrast to the World Bank, which was dominated by donor governments, the IDB had traditionally been allowed significant leeway to conduct its own activities as it saw fit. In early 1983, over the objections of the United States, the IDB approved a $30 million loan to the Soviet-tilting Sandinista government of Nicaragua for revitalizing its fishing industry.[77] Later that year, the administration successfully opposed another Nicaragua loan, this time from the Fund for Special Operations (FSO), in which the United States could exercise a veto.[78] In 1985, a third Nicaragua IDB loan was kept from coming to a vote by a personal letter from Secretary of State George Shultz to the IDB's president, Antonio Ortíz Mena, causing bitter complaints among Latin American executive directors.[79]

As in the earlier controversies over World Bank loans to Vietnam, IDB loans to Nicaragua drew fire from congressional Republicans and made it more difficult for Democrats to support the bank without appearing to be soft on communism. This time, however, the consequences were much more spectacular. Instead of merely trimming appropriations and exacting a promise to refrain from lending to the offending country, the Reagan administration harnessed congressional outrage as fuel for an ambitious agenda for reforming the bank's governance and policies.

The vehicle used for bringing this about was the negotiation over the seventh general capital increase and replenishment for the IDB and the FSO, begun in 1986. To support the IDB's role in the Baker Plan, the U.S. Treasury offered the incentive of a generous financing package. What it wanted in return was a number of reforms in the bank's policies and governing structure—most important among them being the retooling of the banks toward market-liberalizing sectoral adjustment loans and the alteration of voting rules so that the majority needed to approve IDB loans would be 65 percent, allowing the United States, in alliance with another member, such as Canada, to block them. In addition, the Baker Treasury wanted to place more North Americans in the bank's top management positions.

All the U.S. Treasury's main conditions were unacceptable to the IDB's Latin American members as well as to its independent-minded management. On initiating negotiations in the spring of 1986, IDB President Antonio Ortiz Mena stated unequivocally: "The IDB will remain a project lending institution."[80] The U.S. Treasury official in charge of negotiating with the IDB was James Conrow—the same James Conrow who had overseen the production of the 1982 Treasury assessment. Conrow acknowledged that the negotiating on policy-based lending would be tough: "Members don't want the IDB to be as reform-minded as the World Bank. I think we are going to change that, but it's got to be within the framework of cooperation with other members."[81]

Throughout the negotiations, the U.S. Treasury wielded Congress as an implicit negotiating tool. With the annoyance of congressional Republicans stirred up by the Sandinista imbroglio, the proposed replenishment and capital increase would need a strong push from the administration to get through, a circumstance that strengthened the Treasury's bargaining position. After all, it could truthfully say that there was no point in bringing an IDB financing proposal to Congress unless its proposed conditions were met. Moreover—and in contrast to previous administrations, which were fundamentally committed to keeping the IDB in business—the Reagan team was prepared to let the IDB twist in the wind. If failure to reach agreement caused the IDB to run short of funds, the United States stood ready to divert financing for Latin America through the more compliant World Bank.[82]

Recognizing the gravity of the situation, the IDB's management and Latin American members began to make concessions. By March 1987, agreement had been reached that 25 percent of the bank's resources would be earmarked for sectoral adjustment loans aimed at market-friendly reforms such as trade liberalization and privatization.[83] However, the proposal to change the bank's voting structure remained a serious sticking point with the IDB's larger Latin American members, particularly Mexico, Brazil, Argentina, and Venezuela. It also provoked resentment among the IDB management and staff. As one IDB staff member told the *Wall Street Journal*: "There are many ways to development, not just the one that's in use here in the U.S."[84] And as another IDB official angrily remarked to the *Washington Post*: "The U.S. Treasury is acting like the 20th-century equivalent of the British colonial office."[85] With negotiations stalled over the voting issue, the Reagan administration stopped asking Congress for appropriations for the IDB.[86]

On December 17, 1987, IDB President Antonio Ortiz Mena announced his resignation. Internal bank sources told the news media that the resignation was in protest over the Reagan administration's appointment of James Conrow—the Treasury official in charge of the U.S. side of negotiations with the bank—as IDB deputy vice president.[87] Later reports called this explanation into question. However, it was clear to all observers that Ortiz Mena was leaving at least in part because of his failure to negotiate a mutually acceptable agreement with the United States. It would fall to his successor, Enrique Iglesias, to guide the bank out of the impasse. Adopting a conciliatory tone, in December 1988 Iglesias proposed a modest restructuring of the bank that cut around 125 people from the staff of 1,700, a response to U.S. concerns that the IDB was overstaffed.[88] Only two months later, the recently inaugurated George H. W. Bush administration announced that it was dropping its demand for the 65 percent approval threshold, accepting instead a compromise that would give executive directors the power to delay loans of which they did not approve.[89]

With the deadlock thus broken, donors proceeded to approve a $26.5 billion increase in IDB resources. In exchange, the bank agreed to devote approximately 25 percent of its disbursements to policy-based sector lending; it pledged to strengthen its country programming to ensure that all loans would "support policy reform and self-sustaining growth"; and it reorganized its operations departments to facilitate sector lending and country programming.[90] In addition, the IDB committed to conducting its policy-based lending under the experienced supervision of the World Bank for two years.[91] From that point forward, the IDB would be much more responsive to U.S.-led policy initiatives and relations between the Treasury and the IDB management more cordial.

The Role of Other Donors

What part did other donors play in these major reform initiatives across the MDBs? What goes on in negotiations among the finance ministers of the world's wealthiest nations is a black box, about the contents of which we can only make educated guesses. However, on the basis of logic and available evidence, we can draw two conclusions. First, by the mid-1980s, the MDBs' major shareholders were far more willing to accept the view that the banks should be used to export market-liberalizing reforms than they had been at the decade's beginning. Second, the United States was the only donor that was strategically placed to push forward a major agenda for MDB reform—not only because of its size and voting share, but also because of its willingness to bargain hard and withhold resources if its demands were not met.

By the mid-1980s, there was considerably greater congruence between the U.S. vision and the views of other major shareholders than had been the case at the G7 meeting at Ottawa in 1981. At that time, the Reagan team had suggested that, instead of demanding a new international economic order, developing countries needed to be straightening out their own economies—and found this position to be unpopular. Since then, the political climate among major donors had altered considerably. The United States had, as we saw above, moved from a position of free market radicalism toward a more pragmatic stance. At the same time, other donors had moved closer to the United States. In Canada, Pierre Trudeau had been replaced by Brian Mulroney. The conservative Helmut Kohl was now chancellor of Germany; in Japan, there was the similarly conservative Yasuhiro Nakasone. And, although France's socialist government remained a thorn in the administration's side, Margaret Thatcher remained prime minister of Great Britain and the Reagan and Bush administrations' closest ally. In 1986, Baker reported to Congress that he was "encouraged by international consensus which has emerged on the critical importance of MDB support for reducing structural rigidities, strengthening incentives for the private sector, reducing the size of government, and improving the investment environment."[92]

One piece of evidence supporting Baker's claim for interdonor consensus can be found in the establishment of the Special Facility for Sub-Saharan Africa in February 1985, with contributions from France, Italy, Japan, and Germany—but not initially from the United States, which was reluctant to provide more money to the World Bank. Designed without

U.S. input, the facility was, nevertheless, set up to promote liberalizing policy reforms in sub-Saharan Africa, including producer price deregulation, interest-rate liberalization, and trade opening.[93] This suggests that the United States was not the only donor with an interest in expanding the role of the MDBs in lending for policy reform.

Of course, not all major shareholders necessarily shared America's *level* of enthusiasm for retooling the banks in this way. For example, events surrounding the reform of the AsDB suggest that the Japanese were more reluctant to prioritize policy reform over project lending; indeed, less than a decade later, the Japanese government would launch an explicit challenge to the Washington Consensus and policy-based lending, portraying them as antithetical to the "East Asian model" of economic development.[94] Moreover, we have seen that other shareholders did not all share in the U.S. zeal for cross-conditionality between the World Bank and the IMF. Nevertheless, it seems clear that, by the mid-1980s, a critical mass of major shareholders was willing to go along with Baker's plan.

Such relative interdonor consensus notwithstanding, strong U.S. leadership was essential. American willingness to withhold resources from banks that failed to comply with the U.S. policy agenda was simply unmatched among major donors. This willingness to withhold support, which was an unintended consequence of the rise of congressional activism, eroded both principled resistance to change and bureaucratic inertia, among both the banks and other shareholders. Without the U.S. executive and legislative branches first endorsing policy-based lending and later relentlessly pressing for reform, year after year, most or all of the regional development banks would, doubtless, have remained project lending institutions. The World Bank would have engaged in program lending, but such lending would have likely remained a relatively modest component of its activities. Perhaps most important, there would have been little or no harmonization among multilateral lenders to emphasize the same core set of policy reforms. The dramatic rise of structural adjustment among multilateral lenders was made possible by strong shareholder activism.

This is not to say, however, that the MDBs behaved as passive tools of their dominant shareholder. Indeed, I have argued that the World Bank appears to have taken a proactive approach to its most difficult donor by deliberately marketing itself as a vehicle for spreading market reforms while addressing the debt crisis. At the same time, shareholder preferences clearly constrained the MDBs' options, as the management of the IDB learned the hard way. In the new era of shareholder activism, a multilat-

eral bank could comply with U.S. demands, attempt to market new products to the U.S. Treasury, or even manipulate the information it provided
to shareholders as a way of securing ongoing support. However, it could
not flout American demands without suffering dire consequences.

The Role of Congress

From a broad, historical perspective, the U.S. Congress had a large role in
creating the conditions for this reform agenda. By making palpable the
threat of U.S. exit, the emergence of congressional activism around the
MDBs had the unintended consequence of enhancing U.S. leverage.

Yet, where the specific issue of policy-based lending is concerned, Congress seems mostly to have been a follower rather than a leader of the
Washington Consensus agenda; it was not the intellectual author of the
Baker Plan but was mostly happy enough to go along. Even congressional Republicans appear to have been supportive.[95] In 1986 and 1987,
the Republican-led Senate achieved large cuts in final MDB appropriations—but these cuts had nothing to do with the Baker Plan; rather, they
reflected traditional Republican concerns about bureaucratic waste, U.S.
budget pressures, and a new concern about the World Bank and the environment (discussed in chapter 7).[96]

On the other side of the aisle, congressional Democrats focused their
complaints on the Baker Plan's lack of debt relief, not on the policy-based
lending agenda. In 1986, the New Jersey Democrat Bill Bradley unveiled
an alternative plan for the debt crisis—one that included loan write-
downs and interest-rate reductions. However, like the Baker Plan, this
Democrat-led alternative proposed tying debt relief to liberalizing policy
reforms.[97] This attests to the Reagan administration's success in reframing
U.S. interests in the MDBs and convincing both sides of the congressional
aisle that the banks could be effectively used to change economic policies
in developing countries.

Conclusion

The Baker Plan cast a long shadow, although not, perhaps, in the way in
which its author intended. One long-term consequence was a qualitatively new brand of U.S. shareholder activism. It is, doubtless, true that

the United States had always negotiated quietly with MDB management, and on the banks' executive boards, to ensure that the banks were pursuing American policy goals. Yet, until the Baker Plan, U.S. leverage in the replenishments and general capital increases had been applied more or less exclusively to the issue of resource levels. From the Baker Plan until the present day, in contrast, the Treasury has regularly reported using donor leverage to promote particular policies within the banks.

The second consequence was the rise of policy-based lending as a core technology of the MDBs and a central instrument through which the United States and other donors promoted their policy objectives. This new focus on lending for policy reforms provided fertile ground for the Washington Consensus to evolve into the "augmented Washington Consensus," as we will see in the following chapter.

CHAPTER SIX

The Consensus Evolves

For decades, the multilateral development banks (MBDs) had lent almost exclusively for tangible development projects, such as roads, dams, and schools, with U.S. support. Under the Washington Consensus, in contrast, the United States expected the banks, in collaboration with the International Monetary Fund (IMF), to play a major role in reshaping the economies of developing countries, through increased program lending. In the words of the original Baker Plan, the purpose of such lending was to generate "appropriate policies" with the long-term goal of "sustained growth."[1] Program loans were designed to encourage market-liberalizing reforms, such as privatization and trade liberalization.

How durable was this new understanding of the MDBs' organizational mission in Washington? This chapter shows that, in some respects, it was quite resilient. The core of the Consensus survived a significant shift in Washington politics: the Democratic Clinton administration both endorsed policy-based lending and assumed market liberalization as the main object of reform. In other respects, however, the Washington Consensus was less resilient. During the 1990s, the list of reforms promoted under the original Baker Plan—trade liberalization, privatization, etc.—was steadily expanded to new areas, such as strengthening legal systems and alleviating poverty. Simultaneously, public disagreements began to break out among Washington-area economists and legislators—both about what developing countries needed to be doing with their economies and about what was an appropriate role for international financial institutions (IFIs). Although some observers argued that a new augmented or "post-Washington Consensus" was emerging, the reality was that the shared certainties of the late 1980s had passed: by the beginning of the twenty-first century, Washington was no longer in consensus.[2]

This chapter argues that the American political process was as central to the unraveling of the original Washington Consensus as it was to its creation. The unraveling was fostered, first, by the evolving agenda of the U.S. executive, which sought to respond to changing circumstances, such as the outbreak of financial crises in emerging economies, by adapting the tool of policy-based lending to new purposes. Second, there was the evolving agenda of Congress, responding to the same circumstances, but in ways that suited legislators' own political interests and ideas. These legislators drew on ideas coming, not only from the ivory tower, but also from think tanks, church groups, and nongovernmental organizations (NGOs).

Although such political dynamics had influenced U.S. policy toward the MDBs since the 1970s, they were particularly prone to undermining consensus in the new era of policy-based lending. Now that the IFIs were understood to be in charge of promoting appropriate policies for developing countries, there was enormous scope for debate—both about what policies were appropriate and whether the IFIs were capable of effectively promoting them. This heightened the IFIs' vulnerability to criticism, from academics, politicians, and civil society groups alike. Consequently, the U.S. executive found that it could no longer control debates on the form and content of policy-based lending, and members of Congress, allied with like-minded economists and civil society groups, increasingly developed their own policy agendas for the IMF, the World Bank, and the regional development banks.

Continuing the Reagan-Bush Legacy

In the spring of 1993, the Clinton Treasury testified for the first time to Congress on the MDBs. The Republican Doug Bereuter, of the House Committee on Banking and Finance, noted approvingly: "It appears that there is considerable continuity between the Bush administration and the Clinton administration on the particular matters that are expected to be advanced by the Secretary here today in the foreign economic policy arena."[3]

There are several plausible reasons for this continuity across administrations and political parties. Strategic political calculus undoubtedly

played a role. Both the Reagan and the Bush administrations had succeeded in selling the banks to Congress on the basis of their role in
promoting economic freedom and market-led growth; for the Clinton
administration to emulate this strategy helped ensure congressional appropriations. This approach was made even more attractive by the fall of
the Berlin Wall and the collapse of the Soviet Union, which encouraged
an emphasis on economic rather than geopolitical interests in U.S. MDB
policy.

Yet perhaps the most important reason for the continuity was the sim-
ilarity among the different administrations' underlying economic policy
programs. The Clinton administration's policy agenda differed in many
important respects from that of its predecessors—for example, its more
progressive stance toward social issues such as gays in the military, gun
control, and reproductive health. Yet, where economic issues were concerned, the Clinton team's overall plan strongly resonated with the
market-liberalizing themes of the two previous administrations and
included such initiatives as a budget plan for deficit reduction, welfare
reform, the passage of the North American Free Trade Agreement, and
the promotion of the World Trade Organization (WTO) to replace the
General Agreement on Tariffs and Trade.[4] These paradigmatic continuities were reflected in the Clinton team's policy toward the MDBs.

A survey of Treasury testimonies from the Clinton years shows three
main areas of continuity with previous administrations. First, the Clinton
Treasury advanced a similar framing of how the MDBs served U.S. interests. Second, in line with this framing, it continued and strengthened the
MDB reforms begun under the Reagan and Bush administrations. Third,
it listened to congressional concerns and actively marketed U.S. initiatives
in the banks to Congress as a way of securing appropriations.

Framing U.S. Interests

Over the course of eight years, and under three different Treasury secretaries, the Clinton administration overwhelmingly emphasized long-term
American economic objectives in the MDBs. In the words of the 1994
Treasury budget justification, the MDBs and the IMF were "the most
effective aid instruments for promoting economic policy reform in developing countries." Therefore: "The Clinton Administration believes that
the multilateral development banks are the critical element in encouraging developing countries to undertake economic and political policies
necessary to become free market–oriented democracies."[5]

The World Bank's soft loan window, the International Development Association (IDA), was portrayed as particularly important to these goals. As Secretary of Treasury Robert Rubin explained to the congressional subcommittees in 1995: "In the mid-1980s, [IDA] was given a new job: engineering economic reforms that emphasize market mechanisms and the private sector.... IDA support is essential in getting poorer countries through that transition. Those countries have no natural constituency for international capitalism and free markets. It must be built from the bottom up and against strong resistance from the status quo.... [IDA] helps remake developing countries in the image of the United States and other industrialized democracies."[6] Or as the Treasury's MDB budget justification put it in 1997: "IDA uses a carrot and stick approach to help borrowers enact the kind of fundamental, yet painful reforms that are prerequisites to growth."[7]

In addition to restarting growth in developing countries, the market-liberalizing policy agenda was portrayed as a means to other ends. First, it directly served U.S. economic interests by promoting growth and openness to U.S. exports in developing countries, which constituted the "most rapidly growing market for US goods and services."[8] This claim was continuously repeated over the Clinton years and illustrated with facts and figures. For example, the Treasury told the House Foreign Operations Subcommittee that, prior to 1991, U.S. exports to India had been nearly nonexistent but that, by 1995, they were up to $7 billion: "We believe that that would not have been possible without the World Bank pushing for the tariff reductions and ... Secretary Brown really pushing to bring U.S. companies to the development banks."[9]

Market-liberalizing reforms were also portrayed as means to humanitarian and strategic objectives. Freer markets would lead to growth and higher standards of living: "Countries that are helped to succeed economically are much more likely to become democratic, and their people are more likely to avoid debilitating disease, to learn useful skills, and to find dignified work."[10] American strategic interests were similarly served through the promotion of market-led economic growth: "Our ability to create a successful economic development strategy around the world reduces the likelihood of conflicts that we might otherwise be drawn into."[11]

Pushing for Economic Policy Reforms

Under the Clinton administration, the U.S. Treasury told Congress that it was supporting and strengthening the reform agenda established under

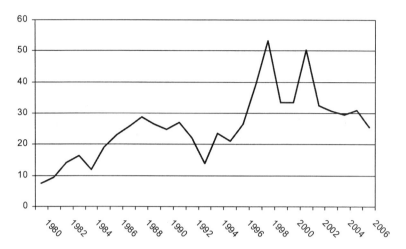

FIGURE 6.1. World Bank nonproject lending as a percentage of total loan commitments. The chart depicts total IBRD/IDA grants as well as loans. *Sources*: World Bank, "Project Database"; World Bank, *Annual Reports* (various years).

the Baker Plan and pushing for the MDBs to engage in policy reform, to collaborate with the IMF and with one another, and to emphasize country strategies over individual projects. As figure 6.1 shows, policy-based lending by the World Bank reached its highest point in the late 1990s, when it accounted for more than 50 percent of all loan commitments. During the Clinton years, market-liberalizing reforms were extended to new debt-reduction initiatives for heavily-indebted poor countries (HIPCs), discussed at greater length in chapter 7. The Clinton Treasury supported conditional debt relief: to get their debts written off, HIPC countries needed to "be successfully implementing IMF and World Bank structural adjustment and policy reform programs."[12]

Another Baker Plan theme that was continued under the Clinton administration was harmonizing the policies of IFIs. As Rubin told the Senate Foreign Operations Subcommittee in 1999: "As a general rule, the United States has strongly advocated that the MDBs have similar policies, conditions, pricing, etc., in order to ensure consistency in their treatment of individual borrowers and to prevent countries from trying to obtain better treatment in one MDB than in another."[13] For example, as part of its fourth general capital increase in the mid-1990s (discussed in the following section), the African Development Bank (AfDB) was required to use country strategies as a basis for lending decisions, to develop a formal memorandum of understanding with the World Bank, and to improve collaboration with the World Bank in a number of specific areas, including policy-based lending.[14] According to a recent analysis of the bank, by the 1990s between 80 and 100 percent of AfDB policy-based lending was cofinanced with the World Bank.[15] The Asian Development Bank (AsDB) was nudged in the same direction. As part of negotiations over its fourth general capital increase, completed in 1993, the United States "secured important changes," including more effective country programming, strengthened donor coordination, and "policy-based lending in support of needed market-oriented reforms conducted in conjunction with the World Bank and other development institutions."[16]

Playing to Congress

The Clinton administration also followed the lead of prior administrations by collaborating with Congress on MDB policy and aggressively marketing the banks as organizations that served U.S. interests and were responsive to U.S. concerns. As Treasury Secretary Bentsen put it to the House and Senate subcommittees: "Some say the development banks don't respond to U.S. policy initiatives. I think they're wrong."[17] The administration emphasized to Congress that further U.S.-led reforms were needed—but that they could be successful only if the United States continued to appropriate funds for the banks. As Bentsen put it in 1993: "Yes [the MDBs] are cost effective. Yes they are helping us meet our objectives. And yes they can be improved."[18] A year later, Bentsen reported: "We are pushing ahead on several fronts. [The MDBs] have done what we asked. Now it is time for us to respond to the changes by meeting our financial obligations."[19]

In line with this approach, the Clinton Treasury claimed to be in the lead of a number of initiatives aimed at making the MDBs leaner and more efficient. Published in 1992, the World Bank's infamous Wapenhans Report had strongly criticized the Bank's lax loan-approval procedure and its high level of project failure.[20] On entering office, the Clinton Treasury promised to "press for prompt implementation of the Wapenhans Report" and to improve the efficiency of both the World Bank and the regional MDBs.[21] Two years later it boasted that, across the MDBs, serious cost-cutting measures were being implemented and managers were being held accountable for their decisions: "These actions have been taken as a result of U.S. initiatives. They demonstrate how responsive the banks have been to our interests and concerns."[22]

The United States was also a key player in two shareholder initiatives to improve the performance of the European Bank for Reconstruction and Development (EBRD) and the AfDB. The EBRD initiative responded to a 1993 scandal in which the bank was discovered to be squandering money on such profligate items as Carrarra marble for its headquarters. With broad bipartisan support, the U.S. House and Senate cut all EBRD appropriations out of that year's budget request.[23] A year later, the Republican Mitch McConnell of the Senate Foreign Operations Subcommittee reported approvingly: "The experience with the EBRD demonstrates that cutting off resources does get the attention and results we must have if we are to continue to support the banks."[24] The bank's staff had been downsized, its spending policies reformed, and its president, Jacques Attali, replaced by Jacques de la Rosière, the former managing director of the IMF.[25]

The reforms in the AfDB were even more dramatic. The African bank had always been an anomaly among the MDBs, with regional members controlling the organization even while wealthy donor countries increased their contributions: at the beginning of the 1990s, African members of the bank still controlled 64.2 percent of the votes.[26] Yet, over the course of that decade, the bank began to accumulate bad debts, as many of its borrowers sank into arrears and economic stagnation. This situation, which donors blamed on incompetent management, led Standard and Poor's to downgrade the bank's bonds from AAA to AA+.[27]

Ultimately, major shareholder governments agreed to bail out the African bank, but conditional on a number of major changes. In 1997, the U.S. Treasury reported: "Two years of intensive efforts by the United States and others, which conditioned new funding on achieving fundamental change in the [AfDB], have culminated in the most far-reaching and comprehensive restructuring and reform ever undertaken by an MDB." The AfDB's loan portfolio was reviewed and billions of dollars in loans canceled. Questionable lending practices, such as giving soft loans to wealthier borrowers and hard loans to poorer ones, were abolished. External auditors were appointed and an information-disclosure policy instituted. The AfDB's staff was cut by 20 percent and 70 percent of management replaced.[28] Perhaps most important, nonregional members collectively raised their voting share from one-third to 40 percent, and voting rules for modifying the articles of agreement were changed to require a 70 percent majority—effectively giving wealthy shareholders a veto.[29]

In addition to publicly pushing to make the MDBs leaner and more efficient, the Clinton team used other well-known tactics to preserve them

from the legislative ax. One was to prevent India and China, the two countries most prone to sparking congressional ire, from getting loans from
the Asian Development Fund (AsDF).[30] The administration also regularly informed Congress of the opportunities the MDBs provided for U.S.
companies to acquire procurement contracts as well as its own success in
expanding these opportunities.[31] In the late 1990s, the United States successfully led an initiative for the implementation of uniform procurement
rules in the MDBs that was endorsed by both the G7 heads of state and
the World Bank Development Committee.[32]

Finally, the Clinton Treasury continually reported to Congress that the
MDBs were cost-effective organizations and were becoming even more
so. The administration wanted "to cut our costs by reducing paid-in por-
tions of upcoming capital increases and by freezing or reducing our contributions to concessional windows,"[33] and, over the course of the 1990s,
the U.S. portion of overall MDB financing continued to decline. Moreover: "U.S. leadership secured [as part of the seventh AsDF replenishment negotiation] an explicit objective to gradually reduce—and eliminate within half a generation (about 15 years)—the need for further donor
replenishments."[34] This was to be accomplished through raising interest
rates on AsDF loans.[35] Similarly, the Inter-American Development Bank
(IDB) was restructured "to lend up to $350 million per year on a sus-
tained basis without requiring additional U.S. contributions after fulfill-
ing our current obligation."[36] As this book goes to press, there have been
no donor funds provided to the IDB and the Fund for Special Operations
(FSO) since the 1994 replenishment agreement.

Washington Discovers Governance

In spite of the continuities with the past, there were also some qualitatively
new elements in American policies toward the banks in the 1990s. One of
the most significant was the promotion of "governance" reforms. Virtually
unknown in the 1980s, by the mid-1990s the term *good governance* had
become a common buzzword encompassing a range of institutional and
legal reforms, including anticorruption policies, judicial modernization,
and bankruptcy law reform. By 2000, the Treasury was proudly reporting
to Congress: "Largely due to U.S. leadership, the imperative of good governance is now firmly on the international development agenda."[37]

There were at least three factors behind this sudden interest in institutions. First, at the broadest level, the governance agenda was made possible by the rise of policy-based lending, which gave the MDBs both the tools and the mandate to reform borrower policies. Second, it was fostered by the end of the cold war, which encouraged a broader agenda of institutional reform. And, third, it was given greater impetus by international economic events that caused the U.S. administration to perceive problems with the original Washington Consensus model—and to augment it accordingly.

One of the major premises of the Baker Plan was that policy-based lending should be used to transform domestic institutions. However, the original reforms thereby promoted focused on subtracting bad institutions (i.e., excessive government intervention) and, thereby, liberating the invisible hand of the marketplace. This implicit neglect of the importance of adding good institutions was consistent with Reaganesque economic ideology, but it also reflected a much older aversion to tinkering with domestic political systems. For as Deputy Treasury Secretary Larry Summers recalled to a House subcommittee in 1993: "During the cold war period . . . it was very difficult at times to resist providing support to governments that were on our side, even if those governments were not using resources wisely."[38] Or as two top World Bank officials subsequently observed: "Until the early 1990s, the United States and its allies had refrained from scrutinizing the governance failings of proxy states, for fear of undermining what they saw as bulwarks against communist expansion."[39] The end of the cold war made it possible to contemplate a broader array of institutional reforms and opened up discussion concerning the institutions needed to transform formerly Communist countries into well-functioning capitalist democracies.

Governance reforms became more attractive as it became increasingly clear that the Baker Plan was failing to deliver its promised results. The 1980s were already widely known as Latin America's "lost decade," and even the 1990s brought only anemic economic growth to the region. Sub-Saharan Africa was an even bigger disaster, with stagnant economic growth and abysmal social indicators. In November 1989, the World Bank first introduced *governance* into the Washington policy lexicon in a report entitled "Sub-Saharan Africa: From Crisis to Sustainable Growth." The report argued not only for the "broadening and deepening" of structural adjustment reforms in Africa but also for "good governance," including "a public service that is efficient, a judicial system that is reliable, and an administration that is accountable to the public."[40]

Originally introduced by the World Bank, the good governance idea immediately resonated elsewhere in Washington. In a 1990 House sub-committee hearing on "Structural Adjustment and Economic Develop-ment in Africa," the Democrat Walter Fauntroy expressed concern about the region's poor economic performance. "Quite frankly," he said, "senti-ment here on the Hill is building for introducing non-economic criteria for qualifying for foreign assistance, criteria such as human rights and democ-racy as well as transparency, 'transparency' being the euphemism for the problems of corruption in government, and arms expenditures."[41] Ellen Johnson Sirlief, an African investment banker who would later become president of Liberia, told the subcommittee that the World Bank and other donors were "beginning to look at new and expanded approaches to adjustment which could complement existing measures which are *nec-essary but insufficient*"—some of which had previously been considered "too political."[42]

These ideas apparently appealed strongly to other major donor gov-ernments as well. The term *governance* appeared for the first time in an annual G7 communiqué in 1991, in a long passage that commended devel-oping countries for introducing radical institutional reforms, including not only "sound, market-based economic policies," but also "respect for human rights and for the law" and "democratic pluralism and open sys-tems of administration, accountable to the public." "Good governance," the communiqué asserted, "not only promotes development at home, but helps to attract external finance and investment from all sources."[43]

The idea of good governance suggested an appealing win-win situation for developing countries and their donors. Donor countries would bene-fit from sound institutional structures that protected their foreign invest-ments; developing countries would benefit from enhanced investment flows and economic growth generated by sound institutions.

However, the governance agenda also raised a new set of conceptual and legal problems. Most of the MDBs had formulated their policies dur-ing the cold war and had charters that committed them to political neu-trality. How could they ask borrowers to reform their systems of gover-nance without raising messy questions of regime type? In 1993, Treasury Secretary Lloyd Bentsen suggested that, in the case of the IDB, "although it may not be practicable to make 'democracy' an explicit goal or precon-dition of ... lending, democracy can be promoted through a pro-active pursuit of those aspects of good governance relevant to economic de-velopment, including the accountability of governments, the concepts of

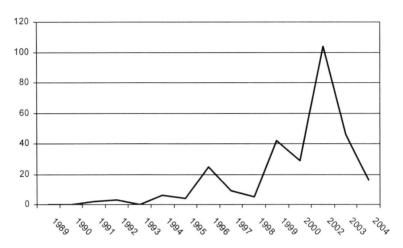

FIGURE 6.2. Frequency of the word *governance* in the *World Development Report*, 1989–2004. *Source: World Development Report,* electronic version (various years).

transparency and access to information, and predictability in decision-making and the administration of laws."[44] This "economistic" interpretation of governance was the one that was adopted at the World Bank, the IDB, the AfDB, and the AsDB. Founded in 1991, at the close of the cold war, the EBRD was able to adopt a more expansive interpretation of *governance*—one in which assistance would be provided only to countries that committed to the rule of law, human rights, and democratic institutions.[45]

During the first half of the 1990s, the Treasury reported several times that it was successfully pushing for a governance reform agenda in the MDBs. For example, in 1993, it told Congress that the tenth IDA replenishment included a commitment to "good governance, including accountability, transparency, the rule of law, and local participation."[46] In 1995, it reported that, "with U.S. approval," the World Bank had increased its "focus on institution-building to create a more favorable climate for private sector growth and foreign investment."[47] As figure 6.2 shows, discussions of governance also became a staple of the World Bank's annual *World Development Report.* The regional development banks followed suit. The Treasury reported making headway with the governance agenda in the eighth IDB replenishment and the fifth AfDB general capital increase; this latter agreement committed the African bank to allocate funds according to indicators of governance performance.[48] Among the

U.S.-led initiatives adopted by the AsDB in 1995 was a good governance policy of providing technical assistance for reforming national legal systems.[49]

However, a much more powerful U.S.-led initiative to promote good governance was launched in the wake of the Asian financial crisis of 1997–98. Encouraged by more liberal investment policies, attractive interest rates, and the removal of capital controls, foreign portfolio investors had rushed to invest in emerging Asian markets during the 1990s. In 1997, events in the industrial and financial sectors of several East Asian countries triggered a loss of investor confidence and a stampede of capital flight. In the end, investors lost billions of dollars, and Asian economies were thrown into severe economic crises, causing a global economic slowdown. As in the Third World debt crisis of the 1980s, the U.S. government assumed a central role—both providing its own resources for the bailout and taking responsibility for organizing other creditors to do the same. And, once again, both the IMF and the MDBs were called on to provide large, fast-disbursing nonproject loans to major borrowers to help alleviate the crisis.[50] One collateral result was an enormous increase in World Bank program lending, as figure 6.1 above illustrates.

The Asian financial crisis was made up of an enormously complex series of interconnected factors and events, and economists continue to disagree about its root causes. But the dominant interpretation advanced by the U.S. Treasury was that it was the result of crony capitalism and poor domestic institutions. This interpretive frame fit well with the governance ideas in vogue at the time and was easily translated into a policy agenda that could be addressed through the tools at hand: the policy-based loans of IFIs. As Treasury Secretary Robert Rubin told Congress in 1998: "The program we have supported to resolve this crisis involving the IFIs has focused first on supporting reform programs in individual nations to address the specific causes of each crisis. At their core, these programs aim to strengthen financial systems, improve transparency and supervision, eliminate the interrelationships between banks, the government, and commercial entities, open capital markets, institute appropriate monetary and fiscal policies, and liberalize trade through measures such as tariff reductions and eliminating unfair export subsidies."[51] In other words, the market-liberalizing agenda of the previous decade would be continued, but also supplemented with the institutional infrastructure needed to make markets work.

To ensure that these institutions were put in place, "the U.S. insist[ed]

that such conditions are part of loan agreements and the IFIs' policy dialogue with members. The IFIs should limit or cut off lending when governance problems are severe."[52] In answer to a congressional query concerning how this would work, the Treasury submitted for the record
Indonesia's 1997 letter of intent to the IMF in which the government committed to an extraordinary matrix of more than a hundred policy conditions, simultaneously including macroeconomic, market-liberalizing, and
governance elements. Among other things, Indonesia promised to "submit
to Parliament [a] law on bankruptcy reform for ratification" and to "prepare regulations establishing procedures for mergers, acquisitions and
exit which facilitate corporate restructuring while safeguarding against
anti-competitive behavior." The majority of the conditions, however, were
market-liberalizing ones, such as removing price controls and trade barriers and privatizing public enterprises.[53]

The Treasury also began to press the MDBs to increase their emphasis
on governance conditionality through "actively advocat[ing] MDB policies and programs to firmly establish the imperative of good governance
on the international development agenda" as well as through "day-to-day
oversight of MDB operations, close involvement in MDB policy development, and strong advocacy in resource replenishment negotiations."[54] For
example, the twelfth IDA replenishment negotiated in 1998 included a
commitment by IDA to "explicit conditionality related to good governance" and a commitment by the World Bank to strengthen the linkage
between new lending and borrower performance on governance indicators. The eighth AsDF replenishment agreement specifically included
"linkage between future lending and governance criteria as determined
by a series of monitorable indicators," and the ninth African Development Fund (AfDF) replenishment included a commitment to "limit or cut
off lending in cases in which there are serious governance problems."[55]

The MDBs and Civil Society in the 1990s

The move toward good governance was an executive-led agenda, conceived of in the World Bank, and subsequently promoted by the U.S.
administration and other donors, with the support of Congress. Yet Congress continued to have ideas of its own and to withhold appropriations
for the MDBs on a regular basis. As always, the biggest threat to the
MDBs came from the right wing of the Republican Party. Unlike the Rea-

gan and Bush administrations, the Clinton team had no means of disciplining congressional Republicans, and, when Republicans took over the House and Senate in 1995, financing for the banks was severely threatened. The House Foreign Operations Subcommittee was taken over by Sonny Callahan, an Alabama Republican who entered the position having promised his constituents in Mobile to keep foreign aid spending below $12 billion.[56] Callahan's incoming counterpart in the Senate was Mitch McConnell, a staunch conservative who advocated the abolition of the U.S. Agency for International Development. Led by Republican policymakers, Congress cut the administration's MDB appropriations request for fiscal year 1996 by 50 percent. From that point forward, the Clinton administration made noticeably smaller budget requests for the banks, and congressional cuts were more modest.[57]

The refusal of Congress to obediently follow the administration's lead on the MDBs created an opportunity for civil society groups to put pressure on the appropriations process.[58] One important source of civil society input came from NGOs (private, voluntary, citizen organizations engaging variously in advocacy, analysis, and the provision of services). Another source was think tanks—nonacademic organizations engaged in policy research. Among the most important of these civil society initiatives were campaigns to reform the MDBs' environmental practices and information-disclosure policies. These reform initiatives achieved a surprising level of bipartisan support and will be discussed at length in chapter 7.

However, other civil society initiatives generated a more partisan response. This was particularly evident in congressional discussions about policy-based lending—the policy tool that, since the Baker Plan, had served as a central justification for U.S. participation in the MDBs. During the 1990s, Democrats and Republicans drew on two distinct sets of civil society arguments to make two very different types of complaints about policy-based lending. The first complaint, made mostly by Democrats, was that structural adjustment had negative social consequences. The second complaint, made exclusively by Republicans, was that structural adjustment was ineffective and a waste of money.

The argument about the negative social consequences of structural adjustment had been a staple among progressive NGOs since the late 1980s. Catalyzing this movement was the 1987 publication by UNICEF of a two-volume report entitled *Adjustment with a Human Face*. This report used cross-national statistical data and case studies to show that a decade of balance-of-payments adjustment under the tutelage of World Bank and IMF programs had been harmful to children and the poor in developing countries.[59] One of the study's analytic problems, as was later pointed out, was that it failed to distinguish between the effects of the World Bank/ IMF programs, on the one hand, and the effects of previously existing economic problems (e.g., the debt crisis), on the other.[60] A second difficulty lay with the murky definition of the term *adjustment*. The report almost exclusively targeted *adjustment* in its original sense: old-fashioned IMF short-term recipes for adjusting troubled economies to changed international circumstances through currency devaluation as well as a cracking down on fiscal deficits and the money supply. Yet, in the years that followed, the report was frequently used to condemn *structural adjustment* of the sort endorsed by the Baker Plan—long-term economic reforms, including privatization, trade liberalization, and deregulation. As we have seen, MDB lending for such market-liberalizing reforms was extremely limited until the mid-1980s and, thus, provided little material for the 1987 UNICEF report to analyze.

Yet, although opinions differed concerning the details of the report's analysis, the validity of its central observation could not be denied: the condition of the poor in developing countries had taken a turn for the worse during the 1980s. The same year this highly influential report was published, an NGO called Bread for the World testified to the appropriations subcommittees, arguing that the World Bank needed to "raise the proportion of its assistance which directly benefits poor people."[61] Bread for the World was an ecumenical Christian NGO dedicated to fighting hunger in the United States and abroad. Over the course of the decade that followed, it and other groups concerned with the MDBs and poverty, most of them faith based, regularly brought their concerns to the House and Senate Foreign Operations subcommittees. These groups included Interfaith Action for Economic Justice, Church World Service, Catholic Relief Services, and Results (a grassroots antihunger advocacy group).

The agendas of these groups converged on a set of thematically related reforms. They opposed structural adjustment lending, which, they argued, imposed disproportionate costs on the poor. They argued instead for lending that was directly targeted toward poor people and particularly favored "microcredit." These very small loans to the poor for financing small businesses and farms were associated with the work of Muhammad Yunus, a Bangladeshi economist who had founded the Grameen Bank in the 1970s. In addition to microcredit, antipoverty NGOs advocated debt forgiveness for poor countries and argued strongly in favor of consultation with NGOs and affected populations in the designing of MDB lending activities. As the group Interfaith Action for Economic Justice put it in 1989: "The preeminent objective of the U.S. foreign aid program should be to promote self-determination and self-reliance in developing countries through a process of participatory, equitable, and sustainable development."[62]

The NGO-inspired arguments concerning the social consequences of structural adjustment were most often echoed by congressional Democrats. As Patrick Leahy of the Senate Foreign Operations Subcommittee declared to Treasury Secretary Baker in 1989: "You mention in your statement the need for economic policy reforms in developing countries. I think everyone agrees that this is important. But there is a concern, especially in Africa, about the pace of reforms and their impact on the poor."[63] Other criticisms went even further. In a 1996 hearing before a House authorizing subcommittee, the Vermont Independent Bernie Sanders argued: "For too long, the leaders and project managers within the IFIs assumed that the economic benefits of their operations would automatically trickle down. . . . History has shown and we now know better than to entrust matters of economic justice, social equity and the free exercise of fundamental worker rights to the so-called 'magic of the marketplace.'"[64] However, Sanders's views were unusual: overall, Democrats tended to express support for reform (through microcredit, consultation, etc.), rather than a revolutionary shift away from the Washington Consensus.

Whereas poverty-focused NGOs argued that structural adjustment had harsh consequences for the poor, conservative think tanks argued strenuously that structural adjustment was having no impact at all. For example, in 1994, Doug Bandow of the Cato Institute testified to the House appropriations subcommittee that the IMF "had been subsidizing the world's economic basket cases for years, without apparent effect"; neither the IMF nor the World Bank did enough to enforce their policy conditions.[65] That same year, Tom Sheehy of the Heritage Foundation argued to the same subcommittee that the structural adjustment agreements of the World Bank and the IMF were "largely jokes" that were "commonly disregarded amongst the recipient countries. The donors pretend the countries abide by them."[66]

The essence of this argument, which had been a staple of right-wing think tanks for decades, was that the MDB program was a waste of U.S. taxpayer dollars and that fast-disbursing nonproject loans were particularly wasteful. As in previous decades, these appeals to antiaid populism were most resonant among Republicans. Among the Republicans to mention the Heritage and Cato views directly on the appropriations subcommittees were Sonny Callahan, Joe Knollenberg, and Bob Livingston in the House and Mitch McConnell in the Senate. Moreover, just as before, these arguments were frequently used to justify cuts in the U.S. MDB program since they suggested that money to the MDBs was money wasted.

Washington Confronts the Social Costs of Adjustment

During the 1990s, addressing the social costs of structural adjustment became a major theme of U.S. policy toward the MDBs. In one instance, members of Congress concerned with such costs used the power of the purse strings to reduce the amount of structural adjustment lending in the IDB from 25 to 15 percent.[67] For the most part, however, the reform initiatives of the 1990s were aimed, not at reducing policy-based lending, but at containing and ameliorating its negative social impact.

One manifestation of this agenda was the revival of the World Bank's poverty theme, which can be traced to the growing alliance between antipoverty NGOs and members of Congress. Over the course of the 1990s, both the Bush and the Clinton administrations reported regularly to Congress that they were strengthening antipoverty measures—not only in the World Bank, but also in the regional development banks and HIPC debt relief initiatives. By decade's end, other initiatives related to the social costs of adjustment had emerged, including a grassroots movement to eliminate the charging of user fees for bank-financed social services and a U.S. government–led initiative to push the banks to incorporate core labor standards.

Reviving the World Bank's Poverty Agenda

Toward the end of the 1980s, after half a decade of downplaying poverty, the World Bank suddenly rediscovered the issue. The apparent impetus for this revival was a new alliance between antipoverty NGOs and sympathetic members of Congress. In September 1987, antipoverty NGOs organized a press conference and presented a letter to the World Bank carrying the signatures of 153 members of Congress and asking the World Bank to make a greater effort to fight poverty.[68]

This new political alliance caused an immediate response in the World Bank, which was in the process of attempting to convince the United States to back a major general capital increase. The Bank could not afford to lose support among Democrats, who tended to be more favorable toward IFIs than Republicans.[69] A 1987 memo from the Bank's director of external relations to World Bank President Barber Conable suggested that the Bank immediately launched a campaign of damage control:

> The Bretton Woods Committee[70] has agreed to try to develop a coalition of poverty groups who might be willing either to mute their criticisms of the Bank's structural adjustment programs, or perhaps support the [general capital increase] legislation.
>
> We will talk to UNICEF about the possibility of doing a joint briefing on the "Human Face of Adjustment." Such a briefing was suggested to us by UNICEF several months ago.
>
> Treasury must prepare regular reports for Congress on the Bank's involvement with NGOs, poverty programs, women's programs, micro-enterprises, etc. We are cooperating with them on this.[71]

The draft of a resolution for the capital increase proposed to the Executive Board in January 1988 stated: "The Bank will reassert and expand its role in the attack on poverty through a targeted program focused on eradicating the worst forms of poverty."[72]

In its annual MDB budget justifications to Congress in 1988, the Reagan Treasury also suddenly expressed concern about the poor—a group that had been conspicuously absent from the testimonies of the previous seven years. Like the World Bank management, the Treasury was concerned about controversies in Congress and the threat of withheld appropriations. That year, Treasury Secretary Baker informed Congress that, as part of the general capital increase negotiations, the United States had achieved a number of its objectives with the World Bank, including a commitment to "increased lending" that would "aim at improving the access of the poor to better food, shelter, health care and schooling, while at the same time enhancing the poor's productive potential."[73]

This new pro-poor agenda was, subsequently, reflected in the 1990 *World Development Report.* Entitled simply "Poverty," the 1990 report advocated a two-pronged approach. First, developing countries needed to foster labor-intensive patterns of growth to provide employment opportunities for the poor. Second, there needed to be "widespread provision to the poor of basic social services," both to allow the poor to take advantage of economic opportunities and to insulate vulnerable populations from the costs of adjustment. This was not a revolutionary break with the dominant paradigm. The report maintained the assumption that economic growth was the only long-term solution to poverty and that growth could be achieved only through good (market-oriented) domestic economic policies. Moreover, the report emphasized "investment in human capital"—a theoretical framing that married concern about the poor to the conceptual language of neoclassical economics.[74] The World Bank was edging away from market extremism of the early Reagan years and back toward the poverty themes of the McNamara period—but in a way that was consistent with the Washington Consensus.

The Anti-Poverty Agenda into the 1990s

Throughout the 1990s, the Treasury reported regularly on its support for pro-poor initiatives in the MDBs. One of the earliest varieties of Treasury-supported initiatives focused on performance-based allocation of resources to borrowers that were alleviating poverty more effectively. In the negotiations over the ninth IDA replenishment, the Treasury reported successfully pressing for a policy under which "the economic performance of a country, including poverty alleviation, will receive greater weight for allocation of resources; moreover, greater effort will be made to protect the poor during the adjustment process, and to involve the poor in an equitable development process."[75] Another U.S.-supported initiative accomplished in the ninth IDA replenishment was the integration of poverty reduction into country assistance strategies.[76]

Still another way in which the United States advocated tackling the issue of poverty was to get the MDBs to lend a greater percentage of their resources to social spending—as opposed to infrastructure projects or structural adjustment. In negotiations over the eleventh and twelfth IDA replenishments, it was agreed that first 30 percent and then 40 percent of IDA resources would go to social sectors—education, health, water, sanitation, and social protection. Under the twelfth replenishment, the Bank also committed to spending 50 percent of new IDA resources in sub-Saharan Africa.[77] The regional banks were encouraged to follow suit. In 1998, the Treasury reported that the AsDB had agreed to a number of U.S.-sponsored changes as part of its fourth general capital increase agreement, including devoting 40 percent of its lending to social or environmental sectors.[78] In the eighth replenishment of the AfDF and the fifth general capital increase of the AfDB, the United States reported winning a "stronger lending focus on direct poverty reduction investments" and "a comprehensive vision statement in which [the AfDB] committed to a particular focus on rural and human capital development."[79]

How much difference did these various initiatives really make for the poor in developing countries? This is a difficult question to answer because pro-poor lending is in the eye of the beholder. For example, the construction of a highway could create jobs or give poor people access to regional markets. However, critics might object that such projects primarily benefit privileged groups and only trickle down to the poor.

We can clarify the question by setting aside the controversial issue of how best to help the poor and simply asking whether more MDB lending went to benefit the poor directly in the form of financing for health, education, and social services. Yet even this question is complicated by the banks' propensity toward loosely coupling the form and substance of their activities. For example, one critic of the World Bank argues that, even during the height of the Bank's antipoverty rhetoric during the 1970s, less than 10 percent of resources went to services that benefited the poor directly. This discrepancy between rhetoric and reality was obscured by data that inflated the impression of social spending—for example, through generous definitions of what constituted a "small farmer."[80] Similarly, if one does a search on the World Bank's online project database for more recent loans categorized under *human development*, one finds loans for a variety of purposes that might or might not benefit the poor directly, such as agricultural credit or water infrastructure. Another confounding factor is that loans are rarely allocated for a single purpose; thus, one might find that only 30 percent of a loan for education actually went toward that purpose, with the remainder allocated to infrastructure.

Nevertheless, a closer examination of loan approval data from the World Bank's online project database does suggest a palpable change in the 1990s. For analytic purposes, I adopted a conservative definition of *directly benefiting the poor*, excluding all "development policy" (i.e., program) loans, and including only project loans in which at least 50 percent of the approved loan was allocated to health, education or social services. Such loans accounted for 5.8 percent of the dollar value of loans approved in 1980–81 and only about 4 percent of loans approved between 1982 and 1989. In contrast, between 1990 and 2000, such loans averaged more than 13 percent of loan commitments.[81] In short, in keeping with the

U.S. Treasury's claims, World Bank lending did shift toward more social spending in the 1990s. This suggests that similar statements regarding the other MDBs' increased social spending were also relatively accurate.

Several major elements of the Treasury's antipoverty policy agenda drew directly on the themes of NGOs testifying to Congress. For example, the Treasury supported the MDBs' involvement in microcredit lending, which was strongly supported by NGOs and was also the only form of foreign aid consistently backed by both Democrats and Republicans.[82]

The Treasury also pushed for the consultative approach to poverty alleviation favored by NGOs. The tenth IDA replenishment negotiations, completed during the last year of the George H. W. Bush administration, included a clause on "local participation."[83] In 1995, the Treasury reported that, "with U.S. approval," the World Bank had increased "lending for human resource development" and taken steps toward "expanding broad-based beneficiary participation in Bank projects, including pre-project consultations with affected people."[84] In 1999, the World Bank introduced its Comprehensive Development Framework, in which long-range development planning was conducted with "a more inclusive role for civil society." All the banks developed policies for consulting with NGOs, and, in 2000, the Treasury boasted: "As a result of strong US advocacy, MDB consultations with the public about project plans are required."[85] By decade's end, regular meetings between NGOs and the MDB management and between NGOs and the administration had been institutionalized.[86]

The consultative approach to poverty was evident in the HIPC II debt-relief initiative, approved by the G7 governments in 1999. According to the Treasury, under HIPC II, "at the insistence of the United States, the IMF and the World Bank have developed a borrower country-led comprehensive Poverty Reduction Strategy Paper (PRSP). The PRSP will be an integral part of economic and social reform programs under the Enhanced HIPC Initiative as well as all new concessional lending from the World Bank and the IMF."[87] The PRSP documents were long-term development plans to be drafted by governments in consultation with civil society groups and the private sector. They were then to be presented to the World Bank and the IMF as a precondition for HIPC debt relief and other financing.[88] Critics pointed out that PRSPs tied debt relief and antipoverty aid to market-liberalizing reforms and the IMF's traditionally austere fiscal and monetary conditions—and, therefore, represented a "new form of structural adjustment" and cross-conditionality.[89] Nevertheless, the emphasis on tackling poverty and civil society represented a considerable shift from the policies of the mid-1980s.

If these various initiatives were intended to mollify the antipoverty NGOs and their congressional allies, they apparently succeeded. By the end of the 1990s, NGOs were far more supportive of the banks than they had been at the decade's beginning. Organizations such as Catholic Relief Services and Faith Action began to testify to Congress in favor of fully funding soft loan windows such as IDA and the IDB's FSO.[90]

Other Social Initiatives

Two other noteworthy social initiatives of the 1990s emanated from distinct political sources. One was sponsored by left-of-center civil society organizations concerning the issue of user fees for public services. Another was sponsored by congressional Democrats and the Clinton administration in an attempt to involve the MDBs in the promotion of core labor standards.

User fees were charges for public services, such as water, electricity, education, or health care. As part of its mission to promote sound economic policies, the first Reagan administration had actively encouraged the MDBs to require governments to apply such fees to projects.[91] By the end of the 1990s, however, user fees for social services were drawing fire from a coalition of progressive civil society groups, including Fifty Years Is Enough and the Center for Economic and Policy Research. These critics provided many examples of how charges for health and education were keeping poor people from accessing these services.

Led by the progressive Democratic representative Jesse Jackson Jr., in 2000 Congress introduced and passed an amendment to the foreign operations appropriations bill designed to address concerns about user fees. The amendment required the Treasury to instruct the U.S. executive directors at IFIs to oppose loans that required user fees for primary health care or primary education and to notify Congress within ten days if such loans were approved. This legislation was strongly opposed by the Treasury. The following year, Congress called the Treasury to task because the World Bank was continuing to approve loans that included user fees, apparently with U.S. support and without notifying Congress.[92] This illustrates how congressional initiatives in the MDBs can be undercut by lack of executive support.

Another social initiative, promoted by Democrats in both the administration and Congress, sought to address the issue of core labor standards. Originally coined by the International Labor Organization (ILO), the *core labor standards* concept had been taken up enthusiastically by

Clinton's secretary of labor, Robert Reich. In 1994, Reich had written an editorial for the *Washington Post* arguing that the violation of certain "core labor standards" put countries "outside the community of civilized nations" and should be the basis for international sanctions. Such standards included freedom of association and organization and the proscription of prison labor, slave labor, and work by very young children. That year, a coalition led by the United States and France pushed for an investigation into incorporating labor standards into the charter of the WTO.[93] This initiative was strongly supported by a number of congressional Democrats as well as the Economic Policy Institute, a progressive Washington think tank that had support from foundations, private individuals, and organized labor.[94] However, the initiative was strongly opposed by many developing-country governments—particularly China—as well as by some G7 members. In the end, the WTO charter endorsed collaboration with the ILO, but did not allow for imposing sanctions on governments violating core labor standards.[95]

The United States also pushed for the inclusion of core labor standards in the policies of IFIs. In 1994, a legislative initiative introduced by the Independent Vermont senator Bernie Sanders and the Massachusetts Democrat Barney Frank was added to the foreign operations appropriations bill for fiscal year 1995. The amendment directed U.S. executive directors of the MDBs and the IMF to use their "voice and vote" to "encourage borrowing countries to guarantee internationally recognized worker rights and to include the status of such rights as an integral part of the institution's policy dialogue with each borrowing country."[96] It also required U.S. executive directors to screen MDB programs for any negative impact on worker rights. As Frank told the *Financial Times*: "What I've made clear to the Treasury is conscientious enforcement of this [provision] is the price they'll have to pay for continued American participation in the lending institutions."[97]

However, it was not until 1998, four years after the passage of the Frank-Sanders Amendment, that the Treasury suddenly began to testify to Congress on the MDBs' involvement in promoting core labor standards and the rights of workers. The United States had proposed a screening mechanism for incorporating core labor standards in the operations of all the IFIs.[98] "At our urging," the Treasury told Congress, "the World Bank [had] produced a policy paper on Bank steps to reduce harmful child labor." The Treasury had also "secured language in the Asian Development Fund Replenishment agreement on the importance of establishing labor standards and working conditions."[99] A year later, the Treasury reported that, as part of the twelfth IDA replenishment negotiations, it had "secured a commitment to further World Bank collaboration on core labor standards with the International Labor Organization and the explicit inclusion of a systematic analysis of core labor issues in Country Assistance Strategies."[100] U.S. participation in a general capital increase of the World Bank's Multilateral Investment Guarantee Agency was preconditioned on a commitment "to adopt contract language on core labor standards."[101] Such language was also adopted by the IDB.[102] That year, the EBRD began to include labor issues as a topic in some of its country strategies and to regularly discuss labor issues in its lending programs.[103]

It is not clear why the Treasury waited so long after the passage of the Frank-Sanders Amendment to aggressively promote labor standards in the MDBs. Possible explanations include internal administration dynamics and the need to mobilize labor supporters for the 2000 elections. But, whatever the reason, the ultimate impact appears to have been limited. Core labor standards were given a prominent place in the 2000–1 *World Development Report*, apparently largely at U.S. insistence (see below). However, the United States never insisted that workers' rights be integrated as a major element of IFI conditionality. Most important, the core labor standards initiative was temporally bounded. When the George W. Bush administration came into office in 2001, the theme of the MDBs and labor rights dwindled in importance in the annual Treasury testimonies and disappeared from the *World Development Reports*, its political backing spent.

The Meltzer Commission

While congressional leftists battled to strengthen the social conscience of the IMF and the MDBs, right-wing Republicans argued that they were pathological organizations that wasted taxpayer dollars. When the Clinton Treasury approached Congress in 1998 with a proposal for increasing the resources of the IMF, it was immediately and forcefully opposed by congressional Republicans. A protracted battle ensued. In the end, the Clinton administration won the entire $18 billion for the IMF that it had requested, but with a series of conditions imposed by Congress, including that the IMF provide more public information on its loans and operations. The final appropriations legislation also called for the establishment of a temporary bipartisan commission to consider the future of IFIs, including the IMF, the World Bank, and the regional banks.[104]

Chaired by the Republican-appointed economist Allan Meltzer, this "international financial institution advisory commission" was popularly known as the Meltzer Commission. Five other members of the commission were appointed by congressional Republicans, including the Columbia Economics Professor Charles Calomiris, Edwin Feulner of the Heritage Foundation, the central bankers Lee Hoskins and Manuel Johnson, and the Washington State representative Tom Campbell.

The commission also had five members appointed by congressional Democrats: the Harvard economist Jeffrey Sachs, the international law professor Jerome Levinson, the former Treasury official Fred Bergsten, the former Aetna head Richard Huber, and the California representative Esteban Torres.[105] It is worth noting that Bergsten and Sachs, the two most prominent economic experts appointed by Democrats, approached IFIs from very different points of view. After the dissolution of the Carter Treasury in 1981, Bergsten had become the director of the newly founded Washington think tank the Institute for International Economics (IIE). In the decades that followed, the IIE's research and publications tended to adopt positions on IFIs that were close to those of multilateral organizations and the U.S. Treasury—indeed, it was in an IIE publication that the term *Washington Consensus* was coined.[106] In contrast, Sachs was an academic economist who was already publicly criticizing the IMF and campaigning with Bono and the NGO Jubilee 2000 on behalf of Third World debt relief.

The final Meltzer Report, approved 8–3 (with Bergsten, Levinson, and Torres opposing), called for major reforms in the IMF and the MDBs. It argued for a complete write-off of the debt of HIPCs to IFIs and bilateral creditors, pending their implementation of economic and social development reforms. It also demanded that the IMF reverse its mission creep by scaling back on its steadily expanding list of conditionalities and specializing in short-term loans to countries in crisis that had met specific preconditions.

As for the MDBs, the commission recommended that they "be transformed from capital-intensive lenders to sources of technical assistance, providers of regional and global public goods, and facilitators of an increased flow of private sector resources to the emerging countries." Because capital investment needed to come from the private sector, the MDBs would provide resources only to poor countries lacking access to private capital. The MDBs would no longer serve as balance-of-payments lenders (as they had since the introduction of structural adjustment loans), and regional banks would take primary responsibility for regional development projects (with a corresponding scale-back of World Bank involvement). All the MDBs would replace project loans with grants while maintaining a category of loans for institutional reforms. They would lend only to governments that had met prior policy conditions and that had exhibited a strong policy performance record. Perhaps most surprising, given the Republican-congressional origins of the commission, was that the Meltzer Report argued for a major increase in U.S. economic development aid.[107]

The Clinton Treasury disagreed vehemently with most of the Meltzer Commission's recommendations, arguing that they "would profoundly undermine the capacity of the IMF and the multilateral development banks to perform their core functions of responding effectively to financial crises and promoting durable growth and market-oriented reforms in developing countries."[108] However, when the Meltzer Report was published in the spring of 2000, the Clinton administration's days were numbered. The emergence of George W. Bush as the victor in the bitterly contested November elections would create a new political opportunity for the ideas of the Meltzer Commission to take root and flourish.

The Role of U.S. Leadership

Throughout the 1990s, the U.S. Treasury claimed to be at the lead of major policy initiatives that were soon reflected in the MDBs' rhetoric and practice. But how important was the United States, really, to these reforms? Unfortunately, the black box of donor politics makes it impossible to say for certain: we have no access to the discussions among major shareholders and between shareholders and the management of the banks in which these matters were decided. Nevertheless, we can make educated guesses based on the tenor of congressional discussions, the timing of statements from the Treasury and the G7, and media accounts of MDB initiatives and discussions among donors.

This sequence of events suggests, for example, that the good governance agenda, like structural adjustment before it, was originally hatched within the World Bank and then successfully marketed to major donors. Augmenting the structural adjustment agenda by adding governance to the policy reform mix was very much in the Bank's interest since it expanded its role and, thereby, helped ensure its ongoing relevance. The Bank's proposal apparently generated wide support among G7 members, and good governance was, therefore, featured prominently in the 1991 summit communiqué. In contrast, the more aggressive promotion of governance-related conditionality in the wake of the Asian financial crisis appears to have been a U.S.-led project, linked to the bailout organized by the U.S. Treasury. Similarly, the core labor standards agenda looks to have been strongly led by the United States—which had also led the failed initiative to bring such standards to the WTO.

Unlike governance, the antipoverty revival of the late 1980s appears to have been initiated by donors (rather than by the World Bank), with the United States at the lead. The 1989 decision to allocate IDA resources according to borrowers' efforts to alleviate poverty was reported by Reuters as something major donors agreed on—at a time when there were major disagreements about the proportion of contributions to come from each country.[109] In contrast, the move to get the IDB to expand its social sector lending in 1993 was reported as emanating entirely from the U.S. Treasury—not surprising, given American dominance in the bank.[110]

Although leading donors mostly seem to have supported these antipoverty initiatives, U.S. leadership was central to a more contested effort to reform the AsDB. According to the *Singapore Business Times*, as part of the bank's fifth general capital increase the United States, supported by Canada and Scandinavian donors, wanted to raise the proportion of AsDB loans going to social sector investments (such as health, education, and social services) and lower the proportion going to infrastructure projects.[111] Borrowers would also need to agree to make minimum social spending commitments in order to qualify for AsDB loans. These donor demands were strongly opposed by Asian borrowers—most prominently, India and China—which saw the demand as a form of cultural imperialism.[112] Japan, the other dominant power in the AsDB, conspicuously failed to either publicly support or publicly oppose these demands—suggesting that the Japanese went along with the U.S.-led initiative reluctantly but would have preferred to maintain the focus on infrastructure. In the end, the AsDB was propelled along a trajectory similar to that of the other banks—one that put it in line with the augmented Washington consensus.

If the United States was generally in the lead of the major MDB reforms of the 1990s, it is also undoubtedly true that, without the support of

Washington, none of these reforms could have occurred. As in previous years, Washington asserted its leadership—in spite of declining contributions and mounting arrears—by being the perennially difficult shareholder. The greatest interdonor controversy of the 1990s occurred around the IDA Interim Trust Fund—a pool of financing set up by other donors without the United States because of millions of dollars of delayed American contributions. Congress, which was responsible for the delay, was outraged that American firms were not allowed to bid on projects financed by the trust fund.[113] In the end, the Treasury was able to persuade other donors to agree to set aside one-third of the fund for U.S. contractors, should they wish to bid.[114] The United States also initially opposed the general capital increase for the AsDB proposed by Japan, arguing that the bank was wasting money on unproductive projects.[115] This undoubtedly made it easier for the United States to insist on linking the capital increase to increased social spending shortly thereafter. The evolution of the Washington Consensus mattered for the MDBs—even those located outside Washington—because Washington was remarkably good at getting its way.

The End of Consensus

In the last year of the Clinton administration, the editor of *Foreign Policy*, Moisés Naím, observed that the ideas guiding thinking about economic reforms in developing countries were "as faddish as skirt lengths and tie widths." Governments that had implemented liberalizing reforms in the 1980s discovered that "the policy goals that just a few years, or even months, earlier had been specified as the final frontier of the reform process [had become] . . . a mere precondition for success. New, more complex, and more difficult goals were constantly added to the list of requirements for an acceptable performance." Naím also noted that heated debates had broken out among development experts and that "confusion among the leading lights of development thinking has even spilled over from scholarly seminars to television shows and from the pages of technical journals to those of daily newspapers."[116]

To a certain extent, these developments paralleled and reflected changes in the intellectual field, or "the marketplace of development ideas."[117] For example, within academic economics, there had been new developments in "information theory," which used the tools of neoclassical microeconomics to question one of its most important assumptions: namely, that market actors possess perfect information. Joseph Stiglitz, who served as chief economist at the World Bank between 1997 and 2000 and won the Nobel Prize for economics in 2001, was a leading representative of this approach. Stiglitz and others like him argued that markets functioned imperfectly in the absence of perfect information—and that they were particularly imperfect in developing countries, where institutions were weak. Therefore, states had to compensate by providing sound institutional frameworks—good regulations, enforcement, and so on.[118] This argument was further bolstered by the revival of institutional economics, which used a more historical approach to reach similar conclusions about the importance of strong institutions.

Another shift in the intellectual field originated in the work of Amartya Sen and other economists developing new approaches to the issue of poverty in developing countries. An Indian-born, Cambridge-trained economist, Sen argued that development economists needed to look beyond GNP growth to view economic development in terms of the expansion of the substantive freedoms that people enjoyed.[119] Sen was a leading author of the human development index, a standardized measure of national well-being that incorporated such social measures as life expectancy at birth and literacy and that became the basis of the UN Development Programme's annual publication, the *Human Development Report*. He won the Nobel Prize for economics in 1998.

With such prestigious academicians questioning some of the major assumptions of the 1980s (i.e., that liberating market forces was sufficient for restoring growth or that growth was the sole metric of economic success), it hardly seems surprising that the Washington Consensus unraveled in the 1990s. Yet the problem with attributing its unraveling to developments in the intellectual field is that it is extremely difficult to disentangle intellectual from political causes. The Consensus was not an academic theory but a policy program for IFIs, shaped by both intellectual and political forces. And as we have seen in this chapter, the rise of governance and poverty alleviation in the 1990s corresponded strongly to the policy agendas of donor governments, particularly those of the IFIs' leading shareholder, the United States. And, although these policy agendas were undoubtedly influenced by trends in academic economics, they were also strongly shaped by national politics—from the agendas of the U.S. Treasury to the concerns of social movements.

During the 1990s, such political factors helped create a favorable climate for the flourishing of innovative and sometimes contradictory ideas about the policies that developing countries should follow and the role that IFIs should assume in the international economy. For example, the fact that leading shareholders became committed to governance reforms created an opportunity for the ideas of scholars committed to an institutionalist agenda to rise to prominence. Although Joseph Stiglitz was a prolific author throughout the 1970s and 1980s and had served on the Clinton administration's Council of Economic Advisors since 1993, it was not until 1997 that one of his publications was prominently featured in the *World Development Report*. Entitled "The State in a Changing World," the report argued that "development is not just about getting the right economic and technical inputs. It is also about the underlying institutional environment."[120] The three annual reports that followed (all prepared under Stiglitz's directorship) also cited Stiglitz's work multiple times. Dissemination through World Bank publications, in turn, gave these ideas a much wider audience than they would have found if they had been confined to the pages of economics journals, and that, in turn, contributed to the strengthening of information-theoretic and institutionalist approaches to economic development within the academy.[121]

However, the outcome of these trends was not the forging of a new consensus. On the contrary, one of the most interesting trends of the 1990s was the revelation—and, perhaps, even exacerbation—of profound disagreements among experts with varying opinions, experts who had also developed alliances with distinct political sponsors. To academics, these political actors offered the opportunity to propel their scholarly ideas into the public arena. Conversely, academic economists provided political actors with the scholarly legitimacy they needed to back their policy programs. These alliances reinforced a divergence rather than a convergence of views. This dynamic was particularly evident in the case of the Meltzer Commission, for which Republicans and Democrats in Congress chose experts whose ideas resonated with their distinct political ideologies and who therefore came to very different conclusions.

With these volatile dynamics in play, the U.S. executive increasingly found that it could not control debates about the role of IFIs in Washington. This was not only because it could not control Congress but also because it could not rein in contributions to the debate emanating from the intellectual field. Academic economists proved to be a much unrulier lot than the managers of IFIs. This became particularly evident when Joseph Stigltiz, as World Bank vice president for research, began to criticize the IMF's handling of the Asian financial crisis in the late 1990s.[122] These unauthorized critiques generated a furious rebuttal from U.S. Deputy Treasury Secretary Larry Summers—an MIT-trained economist with strong scholarly credentials who had played a major role in managing the crisis. Under pressure from the Treasury, and at a time when the Bank's president, James Wolfensohn, was up for a second term, Stiglitz was forced to resign from his post as vice president.[123] Yet Stiglitz continued his critiques from his tenured position at Columbia University and shortly thereafter published an international best seller, *Globalization and Its Discontents*, that excoriated the IMF and the U.S. Treasury for adhering to an agenda of market fundamentalism.

A sequel to the IMF-Stiglitz affair occurred around the content of the 2000 *World Development Report*, "Attacking Poverty." The report was directed by Ravi Kanbur, a Cambridge-trained economist who had been teaching at Cornell University when he was appointed by Stiglitz. Under Kanbur's directorship, the *World Development Report* was prepared with an unprecedented level of consultation with NGOs around the world. For Treasury officials, the resulting report paid too little attention to economic growth, too much to income inequality, and came dangerously close to saying that economic openness was not necessarily good for reducing poverty. The Treasury put pressure on Kanbur to revise the report in line with these concerns, leading him to resign in protest in May 2000.[124] Yet the final *World Development Report*—which was not released until 2001—was remarkably faithful to the original message. According to Robert Wade, this was because Kanbur's public resignation had made it impossible for the Bank to adhere to the Treasury's revisions without being seen as "the Treasury's lackey."[125] The Bank depended on intellectual legitimacy as well as on shareholder support. The scholars that the Bank appointed to high-level economic research positions could be neither silenced nor counted on to reliably follow the agenda of the Bank's shareholders. Like Stiglitz, Kanbur returned to a tenured academic position having permanently altered the terms of Washington debates.

Conclusion

Policy programs are often partisan and ephemeral, lasting only as long as their political sponsors remain in office. Yet Peter Hall argues that some may achieve the more lasting status of policy paradigms by becoming institutionalized, thereby transcending administration and political party.[126] Was the Washington Consensus a policy paradigm? The answer, I would suggest, is that it was a policy paradigm, but also an unusually malleable and contentious one.

To the extent that it survived multiple changes in administration and transcended partisan divisions, the Washington Consensus seemed to achieve paradigmatic status. The two core tenets of the Baker Plan—that IFIs should promote policy reforms in developing countries and that markets should be at the core of their reform agenda—survived through the George H. W. Bush and Clinton administrations and never encountered any serious opposition in Congress. Nor, as we will see in chapter 8, did the George W. Bush administration stray far from these ideas. Even the Meltzer Commission, which proposed a drastic overhaul of the IFIs and a major reworking of the instruments of conditionality (i.e., grants based on preconditions rather than loans with phased disbursements) never challenged the Baker Plan's core assumptions.

Yet, beyond the bare-bones assumptions of structural conditionality and markets, the original consensus was far less durable, both evolving into an enhanced new list of reforms and devolving into contention. These developments were undoubtedly encouraged by the evolution of expert ideas, but they were also driven by political dynamics, including the shifting agenda of the U.S. executive and its interactions with an ever-troublesome Congress borrowing policy ideas variously from the academy, from social movements, and from think tanks of various political persuasions.

In the end, what unleashed all this scholarly and political contention was the core premise of the Washington Consensus itself. Had the IMF stayed in the business of imposing short-term fiscal and monetary discipline and the MDBs in the business of lending for highways and dams, there would have been much less scope for debate. Instead, the Baker Plan had put these organizations in the business of promoting a list of appropriate policies with seemingly infinite potential for modification, extension, and argumentation, subjecting them to the volatile dynamics, not only of donor politics, but also of debates among development experts. Under these circumstances, consensus was necessarily short-lived.

CHAPTER SEVEN

The Banks and Civil Society

It was a meeting to remember. On July 6, 2005, leaders of the world's wealthiest and most powerful nations converged at the Gleneagles Hotel in Perthshire, Scotland, to discuss the future of the global economy. The summit meetings of the G8 (or the G7, before Russia joined in 2002) were an annual ritual, but this year was different. Among the sober, dark-suited heads of state was a rock star, wearing jeans and his signature wraparound shades. The rock star was Bono, the lead singer of the band U2, and he represented a transnational social movement advocating debt relief for the word's poorest nations. At Gleneagles, G8 leaders agreed to cancel 100 percent of the debt owed by eighteen poor countries to the International Monetary Fund (IMF), the World Bank, and the African Development Bank (AfDB). They also opened the possibility of canceling the debts of an additional twenty countries, provided they made economic reforms.

The Gleneagles victory was the high point of a long public campaign waged by nongovernmental organizations (NGOs), religious groups, citizens, and celebrities from around the world. In Washington, the movement heavily lobbied both the executive and Congress and won over both liberal Democrats and conservative Christian Republicans, including the Bush administration. A month before the Gleneagles meeting, President George W. Bush told a group of African leaders: "We believe that by removing crippling debt burden, we'll help millions of Africans improve their lives and grow their economies."[1]

The debt-relief campaign was not the first such initiative to shape U.S. policies toward the multilateral development banks (MDBs), nor is it likely to be the last. Yet, once upon a time, social movements had little interest or influence in the banks. During the 1960s, a time when U.S. activism raged around a host of different issues, from civil rights to the Vietnam War, American social movements had nothing to say about the MDBs, and even Congress was content to leave MDB policy to the executive.

Since the 1970s, however, social movements have had a growing influence on U.S. policies toward the MDBs, as part of the growing involvement of civil society organizations in these issues. I use the term *civil society* in its broadest sense to refer to groups outside the state and political parties that seek to influence policy and are not purely representatives of vested economic interests. As we saw in the previous chapter, the evolution of the Washington Consensus in the 1990s was affected by a range of civil society groups from across the political spectrum—from think tanks such as the Heritage Foundation and the Economic Policy Institute to antipoverty NGOs such as Bread for the World. Often, these civil society groups have been linked to social movements.

The rise of civil society advocacy around the MDBs was mainly funded by two key historical developments. The first was growing congressional interest in U.S. MDB policy over the course of the 1970s and growing congressional reluctance to pony up the money that the executive requested. As a consequence, the U.S. executive learned to listen more carefully to congressional concerns about the banks and to modify its policies accordingly. This created an opening for civil society groups to influence U.S. MDB policy through sympathetic members of Congress. At the same time, the more Congress became involved, the more it wanted to know about what the banks were doing; more publicly available information, in turn, created greater space for public scrutiny and activism.

The second development was the increasing importance of NGOs. In recent decades, NGOs have both increased in number and become more weighty actors in national politics around the globe.[2] Their proliferation has created a new vehicle for social movements to become more involved in U.S.-MDB policy. Unlike grassroots social movement organizations operating on a shoestring, NGOs have permanent offices and staff. This means that they can engage in sustained campaigns, build up a body of political and technical expertise on particular topics, and learn from past mistakes. In short, NGOs allied with social movements provide them with the brain trust and the staying power they need to sustain involvement in long-term, technically complex issues such as U.S. policy toward the MDBs.

This chapter examines and compares three civil society initiatives: human rights in the 1970s, the environment in the 1980s and 1990s, and debt relief for poor countries during the past decade. Although these were not the only such initiatives to emerge around the MDBs (the anti-poverty campaign discussed in the previous chapter is another important example), they provide a useful comparison owing to their historical sequencing and contrasting properties. In all three cases, NGOs brought their concerns to interested members of Congress, who used their ability to pass laws and appropriate funds to influence U.S. MDB policies. Yet, in spite of their overall similarities, the three initiatives had varying levels of success. This chapter argues that, overall, the debt-relief initiative was the most successful and human rights the least so. These contrasting experiences offer important tactical lessons for future reform initiatives.

Human Rights

Toward the middle of the 1970s, members of Congress began to be concerned about the human rights record of MDB borrowers. Although the United States had been a strong and early supporter of the concept of international human rights at the end of World War II, the issue soon became a casualty of the cold war and the division of the world into competing blocs. Fighting Communism was the nation's first priority, and that meant supporting regimes whose human rights record was questionable, to say the least—from the shah of Iran to the Somoza dynasty in Nicaragua. These and many other dictators received large amounts of bilateral U.S. economic and military aid as well as loans from the ostensibly more neutral MDBs.

Thus, when human rights began to surface as an important congressional issue toward the end of the 1960s, it was framed around U.S. foreign aid policy. The rise of this issue in Congress was strongly related to the foreign aid rebellion discussed in chapter 2. No longer content to take the executive's word that U.S. foreign aid dollars were being spent wisely, Congress increasingly exercised its prerogative to withhold funds and exercise oversight, and formed a fragile coalition around human rights.[3] As we have seen earlier, Republicans and conservative Democrats were fundamentally upset about the fiscal profligacy of foreign aid as well as the fact that U.S. taxpayer dollars were being filtered through the MDBs to finance Communist countries, such as China and Vietnam. On the other hand, liberal Democrats such as Tom Harkin and Frank Church were most concerned about U.S. support for right-wing dictators such as Somoza and the shah.

The movement to bring human rights to U.S. foreign aid was strengthened by the rise of NGOs such as Amnesty International that helped organize concerned citizens, provide information, and initiate and lobby for specific policies. The mediation of NGOs helped propel the human rights issue from obscurity to becoming a central theme of a grassroots social movement of concerned U.S. citizens. This movement was given greater force by the U.S. defeat in Vietnam and the Watergate scandal, which put more Democrats in Congress and contributed to putting Jimmy Carter—a strong supporter of human rights—in the White House.[4] By agreeing to compromise about which kinds of countries should be targeted, congressional human rights activists scored important victories in the 1970s, such as the creation of the Office for Human Rights within the State Department, the requirement that the department prepare annual country reports on human rights, and the modification of the Foreign Assistance Act to prevent loans to human rights violators.

Although this growing concern with human rights was initially focused on bilateral aid, it spilled over into U.S. policy toward the MDBs. However, for would-be human rights reformers in Congress, the MDBs posed at least two thorny problems. First, in contrast to bilateral aid programs, Congress did not have access to the levers that could directly change the MDBs' policies: they were multilateral organizations and not subject to U.S. law. Second, throughout the 1970s, the U.S. executive jealously guarded its prerogative to make policy toward the banks as it saw fit, arguing repeatedly that the banks were nonpolitical institutions. As one analyst of U.S. policy toward the banks perceptively points out, this was a misleading argument: the banks had always been political.[5] Yet, irrespective of political party, the administrations of the 1970s, as well as other donors, clearly saw MDB policy as a matter for sovereign heads of state to hammer out among themselves—and not for the likes of Congress.

Nevertheless, human rights advocates won some important victories. Incorporated into the U.S. Foreign Assistance Act in 1976, the Harkin Amendment prohibited economic assistance "to the government of any country which engages in a consistent pattern of gross violation of human rights" (such as torture and prolonged detention without charges), "unless such assistance will directly benefit the needy people in such country."[6]

There were at least two large loopholes in the amendment—the basic human needs exemption and the fact that the administration had to acknowledge that gross violations were, in fact, occurring for the legislation to apply. Nevertheless, the legislation was viewed as a milestone for human rights. It also represented the first U.S. legislation that targeted the human rights practices of the MDBs: it applied not only to bilateral aid but also to the Inter-American Development Bank (IDB) and the African Development Fund (AfDF). In 1977, another victory was won: Section 701 of the International Financial Institutions Act extended the Harkin Amendment's human rights requirements to all the MDBs.[7]

The mechanism used in both pieces of legislation was common to most such initiatives in the MDBs: the U.S. vote on the banks' executive boards. U.S. executive directors were required to vote no or abstain when loans to human rights violators were brought up for approval. Subsequent legislation passed in the early 1980s required the administration to make regular reports to Congress on its votes in the MDBs and its reasons for these votes.[8] Both the Ford and the Carter administrations objected to using the U.S. vote in this way on the grounds that it was politicizing apolitical institutions.[9] Nevertheless, they were unable to stop the legislation from going forward, and, although the Carter administration objected to the vehicle being proposed, it wholeheartedly endorsed the principles at stake. By the end of the Carter administration, the United States had voted no or abstained on 112 loan proposals for human rights reasons.[10]

The success of this tactic was difficult to gauge. Because most MDB loans were approved by consensus rather than by votes, the voting record did not provide an accurate sense of how many loans were actually denied. As Treasury Secretary Blumenthal explained to the Senate Foreign Operations Subcommittee in 1978: "Once a loan comes up for consideration, the chances of its passing are overwhelming, so in all of these instances in which we voted 'no' or abstained the loans passed and we assumed— we knew that they would pass. What we really do in this area is try to use our influence beforehand in keeping as many of these controversial loans off the agenda, and we have succeeded in doing that in a number of instances."[11]

However, circumstantial evidence suggests that the attempt to use U.S. legislation to promote human rights through the MDBs was mostly a failure. In 1977, a Congressional Research Service report on U.S. policy toward the MDBs noted that the IDB continued to make loans to such notable human rights violators as Uruguay, Argentina, Brazil, and

Chile—in spite of the Harkin Amendment's prohibition of such lending. It also noted that another legislative initiative—the Long Amendment, which prohibited financing to nuclear proliferators—was failing to prevent ongoing MDB loans to India, which was busily acquiring and testing nuclear weapons.[12]

The fact was that legislative initiatives were an extremely indirect way of moving MDB policy because the United States lacked the formal power to unilaterally block loans in any of the banks (except within the IDB's Fund for Special Operations [FSO]). Of course, as we have seen in previous chapters, the U.S. executive also had other means to influence MDB policies, from threats to withhold financing in replenishment negotiations to behind-the-scenes conversations with management and other donors. However, during the 1970s, such levers were not yet being used to promote major programs of reform; and, in any case, Congress had no access to them.

This frustrated members of Congress who wanted to make more fundamental changes. In 1978, language was put into the appropriations bill for the following year requiring the United States to "propose and seek adoption" of charter amendments in the banks that would establish human rights standards to be taken into account with each loan. A year later, however, Treasury Secretary Blumenthal reported: "The reactions of other governments to the proposal of an amendment have been negative."[13] When asked by a subcommittee member why the other donors had opposed this, Blumenthal replied simply: "We got a unanimous reaction that such an amendment if proposed would not be adopted and that it would be argued to be contrary to certain fundamental principles in the banks." Those principles were that "the banks are to pursue economic criteria and not to stray afield from that."[14] In short, using human rights as a precondition for lending was antithetical to the banks' ostensibly apolitical nature.

In fact, there was no reason in principle why the banks could not be reformed to make political conditions on their loans. For example, the articles of agreement of the European Bank for Reconstruction and Development (EBRD), founded in 1991, were explicitly committed to lending to countries that adhered to the principles of pluralism and multiparty democracy, and the bank could deny funding on this basis.[15] Today, it is commonplace for all the MDBs to predicate their loans on a whole range of governance issues, from independent judiciaries to the transparency of legal systems.

During the 1970s, however, making such political issues part of the banks' mandates was far more problematic. At that time, in the words of a Senate Appropriations Committee report in 1976: "Authoritarian rule is and has been the way of life for much of the world. It lies beyond the power and the responsibilities of the United States to insist that all nations adopt the democratic model as their form of government."[16] Not only would the inclusion of political preconditions have drastically diminished the MDBs' client base, but it would also have violated the terms of the North-South dialogue, which was predicated on negotiating with Third World governments as sovereign representatives of their nations, irrespective of regime type. At the same time, human rights criteria would have undermined key U.S. strategic alliances. In short, political conditionality was not viable during the 1970s, and neither the United States nor other donors were willing to make it part of the MDBs' mandates.

In any case, the congressional human rights initiative died shortly thereafter, on losing its executive support. As we saw in chapter 4, the Reagan administration was hostile to the congressional human rights agenda, and, during the Reagan years, the number of U.S. abstentions in the MDBs on human rights grounds declined dramatically, and negative votes disappeared altogether.[17]

The Environment

For all practical purposes, the environment as an issue did not exist during the postwar decades. For capitalist and Communist blocs alike, these were innocent years, when economic development was defined in terms of national output and visible signs of progress, from massive dams to smoke-belching factories. By the end of the 1960s, things were beginning to change. In developed countries, a new kind of social movement had appeared—one that questioned both the means and the ends of economic progress. The United Nations became a leading international voice on environmental issues, organizing an international conference on the topic in 1972 that led to the creation of the UN Environment Program.[18]

However, this new ecological consciousness spread to the MDBs only slowly. In his annual address to the UN Economic and Social Council in 1970, Robert McNamara mentioned the potential environmental damage that accompanied economic progress. In 1972, the World Bank established a very small office of environmental affairs and then promptly seemed to forget about the issue.[19] According to Robert Wade, this was in part because Third World governments had little interest in this area and in part because of the immediate problems associated with the oil crisis—but most important because there was little pressure from leading shareholders to implement environmental reforms.[20] It was only a decade later, and under an unlikely U.S. administration, that environmental issues would rise to the fore.

The Reagan Treasury Discovers the Environment

The Reagan administration is not remembered for its high level of environmental commitment. Environmentalists will recall with a shudder that Reagan's first secretary of the interior, James Watt, pledged to "mine more, drill more, cut more timber."[21] Yet, in his testimony to the congressional subcommittees in the spring of 1985, Treasury Secretary James A. Baker III made a strong pledge to improve the MDBs' environmental performance. Baker reported that the Treasury was bringing environmentally questionable projects to the attention of senior management at the banks; he also invited members of Congress to meet with him to discuss their environmental concerns.[22] Throughout the remainder of the Reagan administration, and through the administration of George H. W. Bush and William Jefferson Clinton, the Treasury continued to pledge its commitment to making the MDBs environmentally sustainable and to using its considerable influence to leverage environmental reforms within the banks.

This remarkable shift can largely be traced to the persistent efforts of an energetic social movement working through environmental NGOs. The U.S. environmental movement had discovered the MDBs, and they did not like what they saw. As is usual with social movements, public concern was galvanized by particular events. One key event was the World Bank's loan to Brazil in the early 1980s for the Polonoroeste highway project, which cleared enormous swathes of primary rainforests and displaced many thousands of indigenous people. The Polonoroeste project caused a public outcry in the United States, drew widespread media coverage, and was covered in the 1986 Sierra Club report *Bankrolling Disasters.*[23] Although World Bank presidents claimed that this and other projects were reviewed for their environmental sustainability, in fact existing procedure was extremely weak: the Bank's environmental office was informed of projects only at the very end of the development stage, when it was virtually impossible to change or stop them. Staff members outside the environment office were not required to adhere to environmental standards or safeguards.[24]

To get these issues addressed, environmental NGOs began to bring their concerns to Congress. Such groups initially focused their attention on the Democrat-controlled House, particularly on the House Subcommittee on International Development Institutions and Finance, responsible for MDB-authorizing legislation (but not appropriations).[25] In 1984, the subcommittee hired a staff assistant to prepare a series of congressional recommendations on the MDBs, in consultation with NGOs. Among the resulting nineteen recommendations were that the United States should urge the World Bank and other MDBs to expand their environmental staffs, to consult with national environmental and health ministers in preparing projects, to solicit feedback from and share information with NGOs, and to finance more small-scale, environmentally beneficial projects.[26] In October of that year, the Democratic Congressman James Scheuer wrote to Treasury Secretary Regan, urging him to take action on the Polonoroeste project; thirty-two NGOs from eleven countries wrote to World Bank President Tom Clausen on the same subject.

However, the Bank's response was dishearteningly brief and dismissive.[27] According to the Washington environmental advocate Bruce Rich, it was at that moment that the NGOs turned "almost in desperation" to the Republican-controlled Senate and were surprised to discover that Robert Kasten, the chair of the Senate Foreign Operations Subcommittee, was sympathetic to their agenda. Senator Kasten immediately fired off strongly worded letters to Regan and Clausen. About twenty-four hours later, Rich (a lawyer at the Environmental Defense Fund) received a call from the U.S. executive director for the World Bank inviting him to a lunch that the U.S. director for the IDB would also be attending.[28]

Environmental organizations were beginning to learn the ropes of U.S. MDB policy. One important discovery was that Republicans were not necessarily foes. Another was that the appropriations subcommittees were the key pressure point, for they could threaten to withhold financing if their demands were not met. By 1986, the foreign operations subcommittees were receiving testimony from the Sierra Club along with a coalition of six national organizations that included the Natural Resources Defense Council, the National Wildlife Federation, the National Audubon Society, the Environmental Defense Fund, Friends of the Earth, and the Izaak Walton League.[29]

The Republican-controlled Senate was clearly more willing than the Democrat-controlled House to withhold financing on environmental grounds. In 1986, the Senate Appropriations Committee recommended that *no* money be earmarked for direct contributions to the World Bank, the IDB, or the AsDB; in addition to U.S. budget constrains and exorbitant World Bank salaries and benefits, the committee cited numerous environmental concerns as reasons for denying the funding. That year, the administration's initial MDB request was cut by a sizable 31 percent.[30] As Rich later recalled: "The perception that [Senator Kasten] was looking for a pretext to cut World Bank funding made the threat all the more effective. The Washington environmentalists argued that if indeed the senator was inclined to cut funds and was looking for an excuse to do so, the only solution for the World Bank was to clean up its environmental act as quickly as possible and deprive Kasten of his pretext."[31] These threats to cut funding were particularly effective at a time when the Reagan administration needed the banks to implement the Baker Plan and was hoping to get a major general capital increase through Congress.

While threatening to cut appropriations, Congress also passed legislation directing the Treasury to improve the banks' environmental record. By 1990, there were more "thirty-five separate legislative provisions encouraging [the Treasury] to promote more rapid progress toward one or another environmental objective."[32] The best known and most effective of these legislative initiatives was the Pelosi Amendment (the International Banking Environmental Protection Act of 1989), named after the California Democrat Nancy Pelosi. Written into an international financial institution (IFI) authorizations bill passed that year,[33] the amendment required that the Treasury improve public access to confidential MDB information and share this information with Congress. Most important, it prohibited U.S. executive directors from approving loans unless an environmental impact assessment had been prepared 120 days before the vote and disseminated to executive directors and the public.[34]

While Congress was exerting pressure on the administration, the administration was using its donor leverage to improve environmental performance. According to Treasury testimonies to the foreign operations subcommittees, the first bank to start reforming was the World Bank. As part of the infamous 1987 reorganization—designed to enhance the Bank's image and win U.S. support for a general capital increase—the Bank created a centralized Environmental Department, placed environmental units in each of its four regional offices, and established forty-five permanent full-time environmental positions.[35] At the same time, it began to engage NGOs in discussions about the environmental impacts of projects.[36] As part of its hard-won third general capital increase, completed in 1988, the Bank agreed to "take steps to ensure that environmental protection becomes a permanent priority in the institution," to "integrate environmental work into country development strategies, policies and programs, and to "support national and regional programs designed to improve natural resource management."[37] And, as part of the ninth International Development Association (IDA) replenishment agreement, it codified a set of environmental impact assessment procedures requiring that all loans be screened for potential harmful environmental effects.[38] It also committed to increased public access to information about projects, heightened collaboration with NGOs in borrowing countries, and increased support for debt-for-nature swaps (granting debt write-offs to countries that engaged in conservation activities).[39]

The regional development banks were also pressed to become greener and to emulate reforms already under way in the World Bank. Like the World Bank, the IDB began to consult regularly with NGOs.[40] As part of the controversial IDB replenishment discussed in the previous chapter, the bank established environmental line units "to evaluate projects early in the project cycle."[41] As part of the fifth replenishment of the Asian Development Fund, completed in 1991, the United States won a number of environment-related policy changes in the Asian Development Bank (AsDB) as a whole. These included the provision of environmental impact statements to the Board of Directors and NGOs at least 120 days before board action, the preparation of environment strategy reports for each country, and the hiring of more environmental staff experts.[42]

By 1992, the Treasury was reporting that the U.S. initiative to implement environmental impact assessments in the banks had been successful: "Systems broadly acceptable to us are now in place in the World Bank, the Inter-American Development Bank, and the Asian Development Bank."[43] However, the AfDB was more resistant: although it set up an environmental line unit and began to meet with NGOs, it resisted producing and disseminating environmental impact documents.[44] In 1991, the Treasury told Congress that it would push hard, through the sixth AfDF replenishment, to get the bank to prepare environmental impact statements for all loans and devote more of its projects to energy conservation and efficiency.[45] A year later, however, the Treasury reported "limited progress" and that the United States would "not be able to support a significant part of the [AfDB's] lending program for the foreseeable future."[46] It was not until several years later, as part of the massive donor-sponsored reorganization, that the bank put into place an information-disclosure policy, developed in partnership with NGOs.[47]

The Second Wave

Beginning in the early 1990s, there was a second wave of congressional activism around the MDBs and the environment. Whereas the outrage of the early 1980s had been galvanized by the Polonoroeste highway, the damning projects of the early and mid-1990s were both dams—one in Nepal (the Arun Dam) and the other India (Narmada, otherwise known as Sardar Sarovar). Both were World Bank–sponsored, landscape-altering behemoths that would uproot thousands of people. The Bank eventually pulled out of both projects—in the case of Arun, before it was launched, and, in the case of Narmada, after it was already under way—dramatically illustrating the heightened power of social movements to shape the banks' activities.

Yet probably the most important accomplishments of the environmental activism of the 1990s was their furthering the banks' move toward transparency and accountability. These had become major issues because activists, NGOs, and members of Congress were increasingly finding their environmental reform efforts stymied by lack of information. For example, during the Senate Foreign Operations Subcommittee hearings in 1991, Senator Kasten complained that so confidential were internal World Bank documents that even the U.S. executive director did not have access to them.[48] Senator Lautenberg expressed doubt as to whether the World Bank was complying with its own environmental impact statements—and whether the Treasury was being given sufficient information to catch the discrepancy.[49] The George H. W. Bush administration's executive director to the World Bank, Patrick Coady, was sympathetic to these criticisms.[50]

The U.S. Treasury once again used its weight as the Bank's most important donor to push for change. In 1992, Brady reported that, in the tenth IDA replenishment negotiations, the United States was pushing for more environmental reforms, including environmental action plans (national plans for sustainable economic development), more emphasis on energy efficiency, and improved public access to information.[51] A year later, he reported that the United States had been successful in getting all these reforms through.[52]

In September 1993, the World Bank created its Inspection Panel to enhance public accountability. Based on an idea originally conceived by Washington NGOs, the Inspection Panel provided a forum for people affected by projects to lodge official complaints that the Bank was not effectively following its own stated policies.[53] Although the panel had no enforcement powers, it provided NGOs, activists, and governments with a window onto the real dimensions and consequences of Bank activities.[54]

The founding of the Bank's Inspection Panel was not—unlike other environmental reforms—directly linked to replenishments or general capital increases. Rather, it appears to have been a defensive response to bad public relations that threatened to lead to future problems with congressional appropriations. In 1992, the Bank had suffered from negative publicity on the release of two internal reports: the Morse Report, which looked into the Bank's environmental record, and the Wapenhans Report, which investigated Bank lending practices more generally. Both were critical of the Bank's poor loan appraisal process and lack of adherence to its own internal standards.[55]

At the same time, NGOs were keeping up the pressure, demanding a complete review of the Bank's information policy and the creation of an appeals panel for affected populations. Their cause was taken up by Democrat Barney Frank, on the House Banking Committee.[56] In September 1993, the House Banking Committee manifested its displeasure with the World Bank's secretive procedures by cutting $1.25 billion from a three-year, $3.75 billion authorizations bill for IDA. Although the authorizations bill, as usual, never passed, the committee's report had important symbolic value: it suggested that, in lieu of a major commitment to increased transparency and accountability, future appropriations would be slashed.[57] In form and substance, the Inspection Panel was precisely what NGOs and their congressional allies had been demanding.

Although the World Bank's Inspection Panel was not directly linked to demands from the U.S. Treasury, it was direct leverage from donors that brought similar policies to the regional banks. Completed in 1993, the eighth replenishment of the IDB included an information-disclosure policy and an inspection function.[58] The fourth general capital increase of the AsDB, also completed in 1993, was similarly used to push for stronger information disclosure and an inspection function.[59]

With the changing of the guard from the Bush to the Clinton administration, the agenda for making the banks greener, more transparent, and more accountable continued. As Treasury Secretary Bentsen told the congressional subcommittees in 1993: "Many of the environmental groups tell us: 'We can't get information out of the banks.' It shouldn't be that way. The banks survive on taxpayer dollars. We want them more accountable to the taxpayers."[60] The Clinton Treasury won several reforms within the World Bank Group. As part of the twelfth replenishment of IDA, completed in 1999, all IDA country assistance strategies were made open to the public.[61] The World Bank–affiliated Multilateral Investment Guarantee Agency created its own inspection panel and adopted information-disclosure policies as part of a general capital increase.[62] The information-disclosure policies of the International Finance Corporation (IFC) were also brought closer to those of the World Bank.[63]

The Clinton administration also had some successes with the regional development banks. The administration used negotiations over an EBRD capital increase, completed in 1996, to get the bank to agree to a more open information-disclosure policy and to model its environmental standards on those used by the World Bank.[64] The AsDB implemented a reorganization intended to increase its public accountability and established a new Environment and Social Safeguards Division.[65] And, as part of a major donor-led reform initiative, the AfDB established a new Environment and Sustainable Development Unit as well as a Public Information Center.[66]

Overall, however, the environmental accomplishments of the Clinton administration were mostly small and incremental and mostly designed to get the other banks and lending windows to catch up with the pioneering reforms in the World Bank. One reason for the slowing of environmental reforms under Clinton was that the 1994 congressional elections brought to Congress Republicans who were not as environmentally friendly as Robert Kasten and who were more committed to defunding the banks no matter how much they were reformed.[67] Under these harsher circumstances, reform-minded Democrats were often forced to assume a more defensive posture, trying to rescue the MDB program from Republicans intent on gutting it. Most recently, during the George W. Bush administration, and with Republicans dominant in Congress, U.S. promotion of environmental reforms slowed even further, and environmental groups no longer bothered to testify to the foreign operations subcommittees.

Assessing the Banks' Environmental Reforms

Most analysts agree that the United States was in the lead of the movement to green the banks, although European donors and NGOs became more active over time.[68] This was partly because of the substantial U.S. formal voting share but also because the American political system provided a unique opening for environmental NGOs to intervene through sympathetic members of Congress. Because the United States played such a strong role, the banks' environmental reforms were deeply imprinted with American political values, emphasizing the virtues of civil society participation and transparency. For Paul Nelson, the environmental movement's victories, like those of other U.S.-led movements in the banks, "represent[ed] an application and even a replication of quintessentially U.S. political culture to international debates."[69]

After two decades of U.S.-led reform efforts, how green have the banks actually become? On the one hand, it is hard to ignore the movement's impressive successes—particularly with respect to the World Bank, which is universally acknowledged to have made the greatest progress toward environmental friendliness.[70] Arguably, the movement's most impressive achievement was to shift the terms of the debate. Once upon a time, the World Bank had nothing to say about the environmental limits of development. Today, in contrast, the Bank is a major promoter of the idea of sustainable development, has hundreds of environmental experts on its staff, and produces a significant volume of research and publications on the environmental dimensions of economic progress—including global warming.[71]

Yet it cannot be denied that the impact on the banks' actual lending practices has been more mixed. Environmental activists in both donor and borrowing countries still complain about inadequate consultation with affected groups and lack of access to information. This is particularly true of the regional development banks, which were less visible than the World Bank and, hence, less subject to reform initiatives.[72] The Washington-based Bank Information Center, an NGO dedicated to monitoring and publicizing information about IFIs, continues to update its list of the banks' problem projects, ranging from World Bank financing of an Uruguayan pulp mill to an IFC loan for a fuel oil terminal in Russia.[73]

It is instructive to review the overall factors that contributed both to the environmental movement's successes and to its limitations. One major factor in the movement's success was its strong compatibility with U.S. political culture—or, in the language of social movement scholarship, its frame resonance. Saving the environment was, by the 1980s, an issue with the potential to unite U.S. policymakers across party lines—to an extent that had not been true, for example, with human rights in the 1970s. This made it possible for environmental critics to wage a sustained and powerful campaign. Another facilitating factor was that the movement's demands were not at odds with the U.S. government's dominant strategy toward the banks at that time. At a time when the executive was emphasizing program loans for market reforms, the major thrust of environmental activism in the banks was about reforming *projects*, an endeavor toward which the U.S. executive could raise few principled objections. This contrasted significantly with earlier human rights activism, which went against the underlying logic of U.S. MDB policy during the cold war.

However, just as donor politics created movement opportunities, it also imposed significant constraints. American politics necessarily favored some environmental agendas over others. Reforming project lending was easy to sell to the U.S. executive when it was emphasizing program lending for structural adjustment. Yet some environmentalists argued that policy-based structural adjustment loans were also environmentally harmful since they encouraged countries to make their economies more export oriented, often through more intensive exploitation of natural resources.[74] At the beginning of the 1990s, some environmental activists and their allies in Congress wanted to include environmental conditionality as a precondition for access to debt relief under the Brady Plan.[75] However, this proposal was incompatible with the administration's priorities, and nothing of the sort was ever implemented.

Donor politics was also constraining for the environmental movement because political support could be fickle, lasting only as long as the political sponsors of reform remained in office. For example, environmental reforms during the Clinton administration were held back by changes in the profile of congressional Republicans. Such limitations became even more apparent during the George W. Bush years. As we will see in chapter 8, under the Bush administration environmental concerns largely fell off the U.S. reform agenda, and the World Bank began renewing its financing for environmentally controversial infrastructure projects, such as roads and dams.[76]

A second major constraint encountered by the environmental movement was the ubiquitous ability of bureaucratic organizations to evade shareholder attempts to change them. One reason bureaucracies are resistant to change is that organizations usually face contradictory pressures from their surrounding environment. For example, the MDBs can stay in business only to the extent that they make profitable investments but face simultaneous countervailing pressures from donors to become more environmentally friendly, which may drive away profitable projects and lead to long and undesirable delays. Some observers claimed that the World

Bank's loss of middle-income borrowers during the late 1990s was partly due to the stringency of its environmental standards, which made private borrowing more attractive.[77] One strategy for managing these contradictions is to adopt what organizational sociologists call *loose coupling*, developing green organizational subunits and programs to placate outside critics—but simultaneously buffering them from the core operations.[78] Such loose coupling of its activities allows organizations to pursue a strategy of ceremonial conformity, in which there can be considerable distance between rhetoric and reality.

The World Bank's Inspection Panel constitutes a near-textbook example of loose coupling in the interest of ceremonial conformity. The panel was created to help detect violations of the World Bank's stated policies. However, according to the Environmental Defense Fund, its establishment was accompanied by a procedural change within the Bank that reduced the number of mandatory policies to which it would hold itself accountable. Soon thereafter, the Bank implemented an institutional reform that strengthened and decentralized operations departments and made technical departments (including environmental units) more dependent on budgetary allocations from operational staff. These changes decoupled World Bank practice from the findings of the Inspection Panel and made it more difficult for environmental staff to delay projects.[79]

Another example of loose coupling in the World Bank was the addition of the Global Environment Facility (GEF) to the Bank's array of subunits. Founded in 1992, the GEF originally had joint sponsorship from the World Bank and the United Nations; it is not technically a member of the World Bank Group. In practice, however, all GEF projects are prepared and carried out by the Bank; moreover, the largest GEF projects are linked to larger Bank loan projects in areas where the Bank's environmental record is poor, such as forestry.[80] Because it carries out environmentally friendly projects, such as investing in wind or solar power, and because it is linked to World Bank projects, some critics have argued that the GEF allows the Bank to buy environmental respectability while continuing business as usual.[81]

HIPC Debt Relief

Debt relief for developing countries was an issue that took many years to gain political traction in Washington. The original Third World debt crisis—the one that broke out in 1982—mostly involved private loans to medium-income developing countries, such as Mexico and Argentina. As we saw in previous chapters, for the better part of a decade thereafter the U.S. government's attitude toward the problem was that, if more money could be pumped into the system, debtors could be made to pay in full; it was not until the Brady Plan during the George H. W. Bush administration that debt relief became part of the package.

During the darkest, most debt-ridden years of the 1980s, there were some prominent figures, such as Willy Brandt and Jimmy Carter, who called for debt relief, and some civil society organizations took up the call as well. However, in the words of one observer: "Groups had difficulty identifying legislative handles around which to mobilize grassroots membership." The political viability of a movement for debt relief was stymied by the size of the debt and the threat that default posed to the U.S. and international financial systems; this meant that "even congressional critics of the banks were reluctant to press . . . on debt reduction."[82]

It was, therefore, not until the 1990s, after the Brady Plan had removed the threat of default on private loans, that movement forces began to coalesce. By this time, a second, qualitatively different debt crisis had emerged. The new crisis involved extremely poor countries, such as Nicaragua and the Congo, that owed most of their debts to official creditors, including the MDBs, the IMF, bilateral aid agencies such as the U.S. Agency for International Development, and export credit agencies such as the Eximbank. In the mid-1990s, IFIs coined the term *heavily indebted poor country* to refer to such borrowers, and the acronym *HIPC* became widely used. Frequently, loans to HIPCs had been made for geopolitical reasons—in particular, to help prop up during the cold war friendly regimes such as Somoza's in Nicaragua or Mobutu's in Zaire. The loans also often represented pure political pork, granted so that least-developed country governments could purchase commodities from companies in lending countries. Moreover, more often than was the case with private Third World debts, the money had been siphoned off by corruption, weapons, bad projects, and capital flight.[83]

Much of the impetus for the gathering movement for canceling HIPC debts came from churches and other faith-based organizations. After several years of organizing and cross-pollination among NGOs in the United States and Europe, in 1996 the Jubilee 2000 movement was launched by British Christian aid groups. The Jubilee movement, which had more than a hundred organizational affiliates around the world, took its name from the book of Leviticus, which declared that every fiftieth year should be declared a year of jubilee in which debts were forgiven. The movement's demands were for immediate debt cancellation and for debtor governments to use the money saved to fight poverty. The movement drew strength from celebrity endorsements from figures as the dalai lama, Bono, and the pope.[84] The Jubilee USA campaign was officially launched a year later, with substantial funding from Protestant and Catholic religious organizations.[85] Increasingly, debt-relief groups in developing countries allied with their more politically influential counterparts in the North, a strategy that David Wirth has referred to as "partnership advocacy" (this strategy was also used in the environmental reform movement).[86] These Northern NGOs, in turn, engaged in a sustained campaign of grassroots mobilization and lobbying of officials in their respective governments and the management of IFIs.

Jubilee Gains Momentum

Over time, the movement for debt relief began to score important victories. One was the 1996 G7 agreement to the HIPC Debt Initiative, which provided debt relief, on a case-by-case basis, on obligations to IFIs, particularly the World Bank and IMF, to a small subset of countries that were poor, were unsustainably indebted, and had already implemented three years of sustained market-liberalizing reforms. Bilateral creditors also agreed to an up to 80 percent debt reduction. Because of the extremely modest cost of the debt relief involved, Congress appropriated the funds without comment.[87] However, the levels of debt relief were dwarfed by the magnitude of the problem: within a few years, many HIPC countries were once again swamped in debt.

To address this ongoing problem, and in response to growing pressure from NGOs, in 1999 the G7 finance ministers agreed on the Enhanced HIPC Initiative. Under the Enhanced HIPC, bilateral and multilateral creditors agreed to write off up to 45 percent of the debt of forty-one nations. As part of the agreement, each debtor needed first to design a poverty reduction strategy paper (PRSP) in consultation with the World Bank and civil society groups—a measure that was absent from the original HIPC proposal.[88] Once again, governments first had to adhere to standard World Bank/IMF structural adjustment measures.[89]

Although many NGOs argued that the debt relief proposed was still far too little and objected to the structural adjustment requirements, they nevertheless lobbied strongly on behalf of the Enhanced HIPC as a step in the right direction. Members of Jubilee 2000 USA's Legislative

Group worked tirelessly with sympathetic members of Congress, deliberately seeking bipartisan support and mobilizing constituents—particularly church groups—to contact their congressional representatives. In October 2000, President Clinton convened a White House meeting of congressional, church, and NGO leaders to discuss the upcoming debt-relief legislation.[90] Among the celebrities who met with the administration and Congress that year on behalf of Third World debt relief were Bono, the Reverend Pat Robertson, Texas Governor George W. Bush, and the pope.[91]

As part of the Enhanced HIPC Initiative, the United States was committed to contributing $1 billion over four years for the HIPC Trust Fund—designed to reimburse the World Bank and the IMF for monies lost through debt relief. Thus, unlike the original HIPC proposal, Enhanced HIPC was going to cost the U.S. government a significant sum of money. The initiative also proposed that the IMF sell off some of its gold reserves to help finance debt relief, an act that would require congressional authorization.

Both measures caused objections in the U.S. House of Representatives. House Republicans such as Dick Armey thought that revenues from any gold sales should go back to the countries that had originally contributed the gold—particularly, the United States. In return for approving the gold sales, Republicans won a commitment from the Clinton administration to further the IMF's opening of classified documents to public scrutiny.[92] Funding for the HIPC Trust Fund was also a sticking point. Democrats such as Nancy Pelosi and Nita Lowey wanted to appropriate financing for the trust fund more quickly than had originally been proposed, provoking strong opposition from Republican House Foreign Operations Subcommittee Chairman Sonny Callahan, who argued that debt relief would be siphoned off by corrupt public officials and not benefit the poor.[93] "I know," he was reported as saying, "the church groups and the people who are interested in the HIPC initiative and are lobbying Congress . . . have very noble goals in mind, [but] I don't think they totally understand the process here in Washington, nor do I think they have thought through the consequences."[94] He also argued, correctly, that trust fund money was not going directly to poor countries; rather, it was going to IFIs—with the result, as he put it, that "some bank sitting there with their marble floors and leather furniture is not going to have to write off some type of loan that they are giving to some country."[95]

In spite of this controversy, however, the HIPC Trust Fund financing was passed—albeit just barely. One winning feature of the Enhanced HIPC Initiative was its inclusion of tough policy conditionality, which was strongly supported by both Mitch McConnell and Patrick Leahy, the leading Republican and Democratic members of the Senate Foreign Operations Subcommittee.[96] Where the more skeptical House was concerned, it was clear that strong bipartisan lobbying by church groups and NGOs helped tip the vote in the trust fund's favor. Even notorious skeptics such as Sonny Callahan and Ron Packard had trouble critiquing the ethical basis of the measure, characterizing it simply as "good-hearted but unrealistic."[97] When asked by a new subcommittee member in 2001 how the Enhanced HIPC had gotten through Congress the previous year, Callahan replied with characteristic flair: "It happened because that rock singer, Bono, came over here and lobbied Congress into agreeing to anything."[98]

The Gleneagles Agreement

The debt forgiveness agreement reached at Gleneagles, known as the Multilateral Debt Relief Initiative, was preceded by an extraordinarily visible international campaign. Donor governments had been urged repeatedly by citizens, celebrities, and church leaders to support debt forgiveness. To raise awareness of the plight of the poor in Africa, a concurrent series of "Live 8" rock concerts were held in donor countries around the world in anticipation of the G8 meetings. In the United States, Jubilee had released a letter signed by two hundred religious leaders in favor of the initiative and organized a massive campaign of letters and calls to Congress, the White House, and the Treasury.[99]

The leading donor governments pushing for HIPC debt relief were the United States and Great Britain. In 2004, the British had proposed a debt-reduction scheme that borrowed some elements from the Enhanced HIPC Initiative of the late 1990s with a dash of inspiration from the new international economic order proposals of many decades before. They had proposed, first, to insulate the IFIs from the cost of debt relief through measures similar to those of the earlier initiatives. The IMF would sell some of its gold reserves to pay for its canceled debts; donors would absorb the costs to the World Bank and the AfDB. Where MDB debts were concerned, the British proposal would have donors absorb the cost of *servicing* debts until 2015, instead of actually canceling the debts.[100] Second, the British had wanted donor governments to commit to doubling foreign aid to poor countries through a new international aid agency that would require longer-term donor commitments.[101]

The administration of George W. Bush was almost entirely opposed to the British plan and made a proposal of its own. Rather than providing more generous foreign aid, the Bush team advocated converting MDB loans into selective grants, thereby ending the pretense that the money would be paid back (Bush's grant proposal will discussed at much greater length in chapter 8). The administration also wanted full debt forgiveness for all qualifying countries and the cost of the debt write-off to fall squarely on the shoulders of the IFIs—and not to be ameliorated by either gold sales or enhanced donor contributions. These organizations, it argued, were well heeled enough to afford the loss—and the loss would be minimal in any case since many countries were simply using old IFI loans to pay off new ones and both borrowers and lenders knew that the money would never be repaid.[102] In short, the British wanted more modest debt relief to be paid by the donor governments in order to shield the MDBs from potential losses; the Americans wanted more fundamental debt forgiveness to be paid for by the MDBs and the IMF.

Why was the conservative Bush administration apparently advocating a more radical debt-relief scheme than the social-democratic British? Eric Helleiner and Geoffrey Cameron argue that the Bush team had a range of political motivations. One was the administration's strong desire to get other G8 members to agree to debt relief for Iraq (which the French and Germans opposed) by getting the far more internationally popular HIPC debts out of the way. A second reason was that two strong elements in Bush's political coalition supported debt relief. The economic conservatives on the Meltzer Commission argued for 100 percent HIPC debt forgiveness: the merry-go-round of IFI loans to cover the cost of old loans needed to be stopped, and the IFIs needed to be held accountable for past mistakes. Meanwhile, religious conservatives in Congress had largely come to endorse biblical arguments for debt relief. Finally, there was the reason that debt relief provided good public relations for the Bush administration only months before an election.[103]

The larger historical context provided by this book suggests two additional reasons for the emergence of the Bush administration's leadership on the debt issue. First, it seems likely that the logic of Bush's debt relief was motivated at least as much by traditional Republican hostility toward multilateral institutions as it was by a desire to help poor countries. Second, Bush's leadership on debt relief was predicated on a proposal with the unique virtue of being cost-free to the American taxpayer, at least in the short run. What the Bush team was asking for was, thus, a quintessentially American product—one that resonated with populist desires to punish the IFIs for their past mistakes and would need no significant U.S. appropriations to be put into effect.

However, Bush's plan was unacceptable to the British, who felt that it imposed an unduly heavy burden on the World Bank and the AfDB, both of which were (unlike the IMF) highly dependent on donor contributions. The compromise that was reached was, arguably, much closer, in practice, to the American than to the British proposal. Under the final agreement, the IMF would finance its share of debt relief through the remaining proceeds of the gold reserves sold in 1999 under the Enhanced HIPC Initiative and not tap any further reserves.[104] As for the MDBs, the G8 issued a communiqué promising that donors would issue "additional contributions" to the World Bank and the AfDB "to offset dollar for dollar the foregone principal and interest of the debt cancelled."[105] In other words, the United States and other donors would not provide immediate cash to defray the cost of debt relief to the MDBs; rather, they promised to do so at some unspecified future time.

Concerned that these hypothetical future contributions would never materialize, the World Bank issued a gloomy report two months after Gleneagles, arguing that converting loans to grants, combined with writing off Third World debt without a compensating fund from donors, "could reduce IDA's financial capacity significantly"; lost revenues would mean reduced lending power in the future.[106] To calm the fears of the World Bank and other donors, the G8 finance ministers signed a letter addressed to World Bank President Paul Wolfowitz promising that future contributions would compensate for the losses incurred through debt relief.[107] Yet anyone familiar with the history of U.S. appropriations to the MDBs was right to be skeptical of this promise, and the long-run consequences of Gleneagles for the banks' financing remain to be seen.

Assessing the Progress toward Jubilee

The movement for debt relief can boast of some notable successes. In November 2006, the IDB announced that it would be following the World Bank and the AfDB's lead by pardoning between $2.1 and $3.5 billion for five poor Latin American countries.[108] According to the Jubilee USA Network, by the spring of 2008, twenty-two countries had saved more than $1 billion in debt-service payments, and many were, therefore, able to channel government revenues to needed infrastructure and social spending.[109] Nevertheless, Jubilee continues to argue that much remains to be done. It remains opposed to the requirement that recipients of debt relief submit to World Bank and IMF conditionality and wants debt relief to be expanded to include both more countries and more creditors.

As in the case of both the human rights and the environmental movements, the achievements of the debt-relief movement have always been both enabled and constrained by donor politics. They were enabled by the fact that IFIs—unlike private creditors—are not important political constituencies in donor countries. This made HIPC debts into a far more fertile terrain for movement activism than the debts of the earlier Third World crisis. Yet debt relief was constrained by donor politics as well. One price of these constraints was the inclusion of policy conditionality as part of the debt-relief package. Without conditionality, debt relief would have lost the support of both the administration and many members of Congress. It would also likely have lost the support of many other donors: for example, in the Gleneagles discussions, the Japanese and the Germans consistently argued for stronger conditionality.[110]

More generally, the form and substance of Jubilee's recent victories were strongly shaped by the politics of the United States, the IFIs' leading shareholder. Jubilee succeeded, in part, because it found a frame that resonated, not only with liberal Democrats, but also with conservative Christian Republicans in the United States. Its recent achievements could, arguably, have succeeded only with a Republican administration in office. The presidential candidate John Kerry also endorsed 100 percent debt relief in a speech in the summer of 2004.[111] Yet a Kerry-led debt-relief proposal would almost certainly have been similar in form both to the Clinton-led Enhanced HIPC Initiative and to the British proposal, with costs to the IMF and the MDBs defrayed by more gold sales and major up-front donor appropriations. Both the gold sales and the appropriations would have been difficult, if not impossible, to get through the Republican-controlled House and Senate. Just as it took a Nixon to go to China, it took a Republican administration to forgive the multilateral debts of the HIPC countries.

Conclusion

Over the past three decades, social movements working through NGOs have had a growing impact on U.S. policies toward the MDBs and, thereby, on the banks' activities. This is not a trend that draws universal approval.

Many observers, for example, are concerned that the most recent debt-relief package will cut into MDB financial resources, meaning less development financing for poor countries in the future. With respect to the environmental issue, some worry that NGOs have been allowed to run amok. NGOs do not necessarily represent the views of the populations in the countries in which they are situated—they are not, after all, elected governments.[112] The power of NGOs to cancel MDB projects could be seen as particularly problematic in cases in which the government sponsoring the project is democratically elected and, hence, formally representative of its population.

These complaints can be seen as reflecting a more fundamental underlying problem: namely, that, in spite of partnership advocacy, it is fundamentally to social movement politics in *donor* countries to which the MDBs respond. Paul Nelson observes that this situation has caused some misgiving among developing-country World Bank executive directors, some of whom feel that this is another example of the North imposing its political vision on the South.[113] Even more problematic is the dominant voice of Washington civil society, particularly in the World Bank. Because of its close ties and physical proximity to the World Bank, the U.S. Treasury monitors the Bank more closely than do the finance ministries of other governments, and, in response to perennial troubles with Congress surrounding IFI policies, the Treasury also holds regular meetings with Washington-based NGOs.[114] Overall, this means that Washington NGOs are better connected and better informed than NGOs in other countries and that the voices of Washington activists and their chosen allies in the South tend to have the greatest impact.

At the same time, it would be naive to argue that the MDBs have become excessively politicized. They have always been political organizations, supported by their donors to achieve a host of objectives from procurement contracts to defeating communism to spreading the magic of the marketplace. The past thirty years have simply seen a diversification of the political voices that are brought to bear on these institutions. No one should wax nostalgic for the days when the United States and other major shareholders made MDB policies behind closed doors.

The comparison of civil society initiatives outlined in this chapter suggests some general lessons for would-be reformers of U.S. policy toward the MDBs. The first lesson is that some reform agendas are more viable than others: movements succeed only to the extent that their goals can be made commensurate with overall U.S. goals for the banks. This is particularly clear if we compare the human rights and the debt-relief movements: whereas the former was stymied by the geopolitics of the cold war, the latter benefited from the Bush administration's relatively weak commitment to IFIs. A second lesson is that movements succeed to the extent that they can circumvent the banks' internal bureaucracy. Reform agendas involving elaborate changes in the banks' procedures are at risk of being bogged down in the quicksand of loose coupling and ceremonial conformity. This problem was particularly apparent in the environmental reform movement. In contrast, Jublilee's demand for dropping the debt has been far less subject to such problems, for the simple reason that compliance is easy to measure.

Third, some specific tactics are more effective than others. Legislation requiring U.S. executive directors to vote in particular ways seems to allow Congress to act on its own, with or without executive approval. However, we have seen that this impression is mistaken: Congress *always* needs executive collaboration to get things done in the MDBs. This is because the United States does not formally have the power to unilaterally block loans in any of the banks (with the exception of the IDB's FSO). Rather, U.S. Treasury influence in the banks and among donors occurs mostly through more informal channels that Congress cannot directly access or monitor. Consequently, if the executive is ambivalent about a legislative initiative, it has multiple means of thwarting it—from telling Congress that other donors have approved loans over U.S. objections to deliberately allowing the banks to make ceremonial rather than substantive reforms.

The most successful legislative initiative discussed in this chapter was the Pelosi Amendment, which required U.S. executive directors to oppose loans unless the banks previously disseminated environmental impact statements. Yet, had the U.S. executive opposed the Pelosi Amendment's intended result, it could have easily allowed these environmental impact statements to be ceremonial fluff, with little real substance. The Pelosi Amendment's importance was in its informational rather than its legislative content: it notified both the administration and the banks that Congress was looking for certain changes and would be willing to withhold funding in the future if these did not occur. Thus, it is only in partnership with the executive that Congress can get substantive changes through to the MDBs. The most effective way in which it can enlist such partnership is through threatening to withhold financing unless the administration takes certain agendas to the table in replenishments and general capital increases—and, most important, shows real results at the end.

The potential of this technique to promote change in the banks was apparently not widely recognized in the 1970s. For example, a 1977 Congressional Research Service study of U.S. executive and congressional influence in the banks mentioned legislative initiatives and informal U.S. influence but not donor leverage in replenishments and general capital increases.[115] Today, in contrast, getting Congress to lean on the executive, and the executive to lean on donor negotiations, is widely understood by members of Congress and savvy Washington NGOs as an important tool for changing MDB policies. A related tactic, discovered by the Jubilee movement, is to target donor politics transnationally at the end point of donor negotiations, rather than leaning on the United States alone. The experience of Jubilee shows that this can create competition among donors to assume leadership on an internationally popular issue and shame the more reluctant shareholders into going along.

Fourth, and finally, gaining bipartisan support is crucial for any movement that aims at using the congressional appropriations process to push for reforms. Although Democrats may seem to be reform movements' most natural allies, it is more often Republicans who can get things done through appropriations processes—for the simple reason that Republicans are less sympathetic toward multilateral institutions and more willing to withhold their financing. Just as willingness to exit enhances U.S. power among leading shareholders, so also does Republican willingness to exit place them in a more powerful position to move U.S. policy toward the banks.

Overall, this chapter has shown that the involvement of social movements in U.S. policy toward the MDBs has been historically cumulative: each wave of social movement involvement has paved the way for greater future activism. It is because of past social movements that members of Congress, the MDBs, and even the U.S. Treasury regularly exchange information and views with NGOs: consequently, today there is an infrastructure through which future social movements can air their concerns. It is also because of past movement activism that there is an unprecedented (albeit still insufficient) amount of information available about the banks' activities to the public and much greater public awareness about the banks than there was three decades ago. We are likely to see more NGO-sponsored reform initiatives in the years to come.

CHAPTER EIGHT

Into the New Millennium

In March 2005, Paul Wolfowitz was nominated to be president of the World Bank. It was an unusually controversial choice. Wolfowitz was U.S. deputy secretary of defense at the time of his nomination and was closely associated with the internationally unpopular invasion of Iraq. Moreover, in a major deviation from established practice, the Bush administration announced its chosen candidate without previously consulting other major shareholders. The French daily newspaper *Le Monde* called the nomination "a new manifestation of America's arrogance." The British *Financial Times* editorialized that, under Wolfowitz, the World Bank would be "no more than an instrument of U.S. power."[1] Both Wolfowitz's presidency and his scandal-ridden resignation only two years later generated controversy unprecedented in the history of the World Bank.

This concluding chapter analyzes the record of the George W. Bush years and reviews the main arguments of this book. The Bush administration's policy toward the multilateral development banks (MDBs) was colored by its famously unilateralist approach to foreign policy—an approach exemplified by Wolfowitz's appointment as World Bank president in spite of the objections of other donors. In large measure because of this uncompromising attitude, relations between the United States and other MDB donors were more strained during the Bush years than at any previous time in the banks' history.

However, although the Bush administration's policies toward the banks were unique in some ways, they also adhered to a familiar pattern. Like previous administrations, the Bush team engaged in shareholder activism, promoting reforms in the MDBs to win congressional support. The content of the Bush administration's three most major MDB policy innovations—grants, performance-based management, and debt relief—had some support among economists, but it also had strong political backing in civil society and on Capitol Hill: in this respect, too, the Bush team's policies were very much like those of its predecessors. Finally, the administration held fast to the core tenets of the Washington Consensus, in which the banks were charged with the mission of promoting market-friendly policy reforms: it was the specific instruments of conditionality, rather than the general principle of conditionality, that the Bush team sought to alter.

For more than two decades, U.S. politics and shareholder activism have shaped the banks' activities and the policy models it recommends to developing countries. Yet the U.S. commitment to these organizations remains weak, and the impulse for U.S. policymakers to promote reform initiatives therefore remains strong. The current role and visibility of shareholder politics in the banks may present reformers with enhanced opportunities for changing the banks through putting pressure on the governments that own them.

The Policy Programs of George W. Bush

Four elements of the Bush administration's overall policy program were significant in shaping its MDB agenda. The first was the administration's neoconservative foreign policy program, which, after the attacks of September 11, 2001, seemed to overshadow all other areas of administration policy. The second was a neoliberal economic policy program that differed little, in substance, from previous approaches; yet the Bush team's economic policy was unusual in its relative lack of prominence compared to other policy areas. Third, the administration's approach was shaped by a civil service reform agenda for orienting public policy toward "performance-based management." Fourth, and finally, elements of the Bush team's MDB policy were shaped by a new "compassionate conservative" approach to foreign aid increasingly supported by conservative Christian voters.

Foreign Policy

The Bush doctrine that emerged after September 11, 2001, was premised on the idea that the only way to guarantee peace and stability was for the United States to assert an aggressive, leading role in the world polity. Democratic regimes, in this view, were both necessary and sufficient to U.S. security and could be put in place through military means. The United States should be willing to pursue these ends unilaterally, if necessary, and to engage in preventive war to defend itself from external threat.[2]

The most obvious manifestation of this doctrine, and the one for which it will be most remembered, was the U.S. invasion of Iraq. However, military force was not the Bush doctrine's only tool for promoting American security: foreign aid also emerged as a major piece of this emergent foreign policy agenda. The rhetoric used to describe this new agenda was reminiscent of the cold war language of the 1960s and 1970s, when development aid had similarly been seen as crucial to American security. As Bush stated at the UN development conference held in Monterrey, Mexico, in 2002: "We fight against poverty because hope is an answer to terror."[3] During the Bush years, the U.S. Agency for International Development (USAID) was reorganized and placed under formal control of the State Department, a step that Oxfam America charged "blurred the lines traditionally separating development and humanitarian aid from political and military action."[4]

As part of its mission to spread capitalism and democracy around the world, the Bush administration oversaw an expansion of the U.S. foreign aid program to a size not seen since the Kennedy administration. However, figure 8.1 shows that the lion's share of its foreign aid financing was

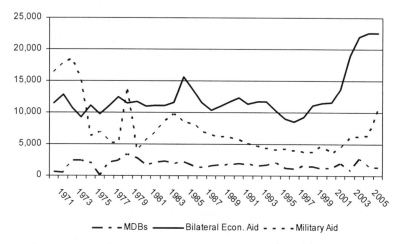

FIGURE 8.1. U.S. spending on the MDBs, military aid, and bilateral economic aid, millions of U.S. dollars (2000). *Source*: USAID, *U.S. Overseas Loans and Grants* (various years).

channeled through bilateral aid, with the MDBs playing a relatively minor role. The administration's most major foreign aid innovation was the Millennium Challenge Account (MCA), a bilateral aid initiative announced in 2002. Set up as an independent agency apart from USAID, the MCA would consume the bulk of increases in U.S. foreign aid spending in the years that followed. Its name was intended to evoke the UN Millennium Declaration of 2000, which set forth a list of development goals for the world's governments to achieve by 2015, including halving the proportion of the world's population living in poverty. The MCA's goals overlapped with those of the Millennium Declaration, but with greater emphasis on market-led economic growth and less on poverty reduction. Perhaps most important, the MCA was committed to a "results-based" or "performance-based" approach,[5] discussed at length later in this section.

Economic Policy

In many respects, the Bush administration's economic policy program resembled that of the first Reagan administration, with an emphasis on lowering taxes and removing government regulations. The Bush team also followed Reagan's lead in incurring a large budget deficit—a combined effect of lowered taxes and high spending on U.S. military interventions in the Middle East.

Yet, although George W. Bush's economic policies echoed themes from previous Republican administrations, they also seemed qualitatively different in at least two respects. First, according to many Washington policy analysts, the Bush Treasury was a significantly less powerful player than the Treasury of previous administrations.[6] As the *Washington Post* put it in 2006, the position of Treasury Secretary had become a job "more about selling policy than making it."[7] Robert Novak, a leading conservative political analyst, noted the "downgrading" of the Treasury in the Bush administration: "Treasury is not the government's economic power house that it has been traditionally." Rather than emanating from the Treasury, the administration's economic policies were generated in a weekly meeting—held every Wednesday in the Ward Room of the White House and attended by a range of administration officials—in which Vice President Cheney played a leading role.[8]

The leadership of the Bush Treasury was also seen by some analysts as evidence of its less powerful status. The new undersecretary for international affairs was John Taylor, a prominent monetary economist from Stanford University. However, at the head of the Treasury the administration initially placed a figure with less conventional qualifications: Paul O'Neill, an aluminum executive with long-standing ties to the vice president. O'Neill was viewed by many on Wall Street as a suboptimal choice, possessing neither the private financial experience of Robert Rubin or Nicholas Brady, nor the political experience of Lloyd Bentsen or James Baker, nor the economic expertise of Lawrence Summers. As Treasury secretary, O'Neill became famous for his public gaffes, and, in December 2002, the Bush administration took the highly unusual step of firing him and replacing him with John Snow, also a corporate executive, albeit one with a Ph.D. in economics. During more than three years at the head of the Treasury, Snow maintained a low profile and closely followed the lead of the White House.[9] In the spring of 2006, Snow resigned, to be replaced by Henry Paulson, a Wall Street financier with a stronger and more traditional profile but whose policies toward international financial institutions differed little from Snow's.

If the Bush administration's economic policy seemed to emanate from the White House, it also seemed that, for the Bush White House, economic matters were not an overriding concern. The administration's core policy program was its strategic agenda for fighting terrorism and promoting democracy abroad. In contrast, its economic policies seemed more idiosyncratic. The administration's expanding budget deficit was widely criticized by economists of all political persuasions, as was its inept handling of the economic crisis that began in 2008 and its inconsistent posture toward international economic affairs. Among the harshest of these critics was the prominent international economist Jeffrey Frankel, for whom Bush's economic policies exhibited a pattern of "hypocrisy and incompetence."[10] Early in the administration, Treasury Secretary O'Neill worried international currency markets by issuing contradictory statements about U.S. support for a stronger versus a weaker dollar.[11] Although the Bush administration stated that it was committed to free markets and globalization, in practice its support for these tenets was mixed: not only did the administration impose protectionist trade barriers on steel and other products, but it was also partly to blame for the collapse of the Doha round of World Trade Organization negotiations in 2003.[12] In the words of one left-wing analyst, the administration "just doesn't attach much importance to U.S. economic leadership."[13]

Performance-Based Management

Although the Bush administration will be most remembered for the national security policies that emerged after 9/11, a major element of the administration's initial policy agenda was civil service reform. The Bush team proposed to make government more transparent and accountable through performance-based management—a policy program that had become increasingly popular on Capitol Hill. Inspired by a private-sector management fashion, in 1993 Congress passed the Government Performance and Results Act (GPRA), which required all U.S. government agencies to identify indicators of progress and measure their progress toward these goals.[14]

The idea of holding the government accountable to measurable standards had support on both sides of the aisle but was particularly appealing to conservatives—many of whom liked the idea of more closely scrutinizing "wasteful" and "failing" government policy. In 2001, the Heritage Foundation argued that the incoming Bush administration should strengthen the GPRA policy agenda; this message resonated well with Bush, who campaigned as a "reformer with results." In July 2002, Bush's Office of Management and Budget (OMB) announced the development of the Program Assessment Rating Tool (PART) as "a systematic method of assessing the performance of program activities across the Federal government."[15] Bush's "No Child Left Behind" initiative, which held schools accountable for their performance through administering standardized tests and withholding federal financing to poorly performing schools, also reflected this agenda. Performance-based management was, similarly, an integral part of the administration's leading foreign-aid initiative, the MCA; it was administered according to sixteen measures of "ruling justly," "investing in people," and "economic freedom." Countries that performed well on these indexes would receive more MCA resources.[16]

Compassionate Conservatism

The Bush administration's claim that it endorsed a philosophy of compassionate conservatism was viewed by many Democrats as a cynical marketing ploy. For example, critics pointed out that the benefits of the Bush tax cuts accrued overwhelmingly to the wealthy.

Nevertheless, in the area of foreign aid, the philosophy was clearly linked to an important new trend among Republican voters. During the 1990s, conservative Christian groups, especially evangelical ones, had become increasingly supportive of foreign aid. According to one close observer, this trend grew out of the experience of missionaries in impoverished countries who shared their observations with parishioners back home.[17] This new conservative ethos made it possible for the Bush administration to launch a major increase in the U.S. bilateral aid program, to sponsor a major initiative for fighting global HIV-AIDS, and to promote the heavily indebted poor country (HIPC) debt-relief initiative discussed in chapter 7. Such policies would almost certainly have provoked major resistance among Republicans in Congress even a decade earlier; yet, now, supporting foreign aid helped Republicans secure voter support. As Jesse Helms, once a fervent foreign aid opponent, said of his newfound support for fighting HIV-AIDS: "I know that, like a Samaritan traveling from Jerusalem to Jericho, we cannot turn away when we see our fellow man in need."[18]

The Bush Team Turns to the Banks

When George W. Bush entered office in January 2001, with both houses of Congress in Republican hands, the future of the international financial institutions (IFIs) seemed uncertain. Just like the incoming Reagan team twenty years earlier, the Bush administration seemed susceptible to conservative arguments against foreign aid and multilateral organizations. These arguments had acquired considerable intellectual sophistication over two decades. Bailing out governments in crisis, conservative economists such as Allan Meltzer argued, fostered moral hazard by showing irresponsible investors and governments that they would be rescued at U.S. taxpayer expense. Drawing on such arguments as these, John Taylor had in 1998—three years prior to becoming Bush's Treasury undersecretary for international affairs—publicly called for the abolition of the International Monetary Fund (IMF).[19] At the start of Bush's first term, Paul O'Neill characterized Argentina, which was in the throes of an IMF bailout, as a country "that continues to consume the money of the plumbers and carpenters in the United States who make $50,000 a year and wonder what in the world we're doing with their money."[20]

As for the MDBs, conservatives argued that they suffered from "mission creep" and had drifted away from their core purpose of generating market-led economic growth. Early in the Bush administration's first year, Treasury Secretary Paul O'Neill alarmed World Bank officials by declaring that the Bank's activities were "too diffuse" and that it should focus on raising "productivity" and income per capita. This statement seemed to suggest that the administration would be pushing the Bank away from its mission, rediscovered in the 1990s, of alleviating poverty.[21]

In the end, however, the Bush team neither abandoned the IMF nor dismantled the MDBs' antipoverty programs. Just as had occurred with the Reagan administration, the Bush team seemed, once in office, to realize that the IMF was too useful a tool to dismantle. When the Bush Treasury supported a $30 billion IMF rescue package for Brazil in August 2002, the *Wall Street Journal* noted: "Some analysts speculate that officials finally gave in to mounting pressure from U.S. bankers." It continued: "At a time when unrest in the U.S. stock market is threatening an economic recovery, the White House seems less inclined to take the risk that turmoil in Latin America might send ripples northward."[22]

Yet, unlike the Reagan reforms, the Bush agenda was not focused on moving the banks in a more market-friendly direction. This was in large measure because the banks had already been transformed in this way, thanks to the efforts of the Reagan as well as the George H. W. Bush and Clinton administrations. Since the Baker Plan, the original Washington Consensus had been modified to acknowledge the need to compensate for the imperfections of markets and to protect the poor. This augmented agenda fit reasonably well with both the Bush team's compassionate conservative theme of helping the poor and its neoconservative theme of spreading democratic institutions around the world.

Framing U.S. Interests

In its first testimony on the MDBs in the spring of 2001, the Bush Treasury advanced a framing of U.S. interests that differed little from that of the previous three administrations. Like the Reagan, George H. W. Bush, and Clinton administrations, the George W. Bush administration emphasized the banks' role in generating economic growth through "open markets, free trade, low tax rates, and sensible regulation."[23] To this familiar list of desirables, the Bush Treasury added the new element of "productivity growth," apparently an innovation of Treasury Undersecretary for International Affairs John Taylor's, and apparently indicating a shift in focus away from equity and toward issues of economic efficiency.[24]

After the attacks of September 11, 2001, however, there was a dramatic change in the Treasury's framing of American interests in the MDBs. Virtually absent since the 1970s, security and humanitarian concerns were suddenly central rationales and remained so for the duration of the Bush presidency. In his 2002 testimony to Congress, O'Neill began by "underscoring the emphasis that President Bush places on economic development as a central commitment of American foreign policy." He then quoted President Bush: "This growing divide between wealth and poverty, between opportunity and misery, is both a challenge to our compassion and a source of instability."[25] This emergent idea of the link between poverty and global instability was further clarified in a presidential quote inserted into the Treasury MDB budget justification in 2004: "Poverty doesn't cause terrorism. Being poor doesn't make you a murderer. Most of the plotters of September 11th were raised in comfort. Yet persistent poverty and oppression can lead to hopelessness and despair. And when governments fail to meet the most basic needs of their people, these failed states can become havens for terror."[26]

The post-9/11 framing of U.S. interests in the MDBs did not abandon economic goals: "The essential goal of the MDBs is to increase economic growth and thereby reduce poverty."[27] But these economic goals were framed as means to geopolitical ends: "Creating jobs and reducing poverty throughout the world are essential to promoting stability and security."[28] Moreover, the banks also "helped pursue specific U.S. foreign policy objectives, such as supporting economic assistance to key countries in the war on terrorism [most important, Iraq and Afghanistan] and combating money-laundering and terrorist financing."[29] Thus, the Bush team's framing of U.S. interests in the banks constituted a novel amalgam of themes from the cold war, the Washington Consensus, and the neoconservative War on Terror.

Promoting Reforms

More than any presidential administration covered in this book, the Bush team's reform agenda for the MDBs is difficult to summarize. The Reagan, George H. W. Bush, and Clinton administrations' plans for the banks tended to cluster around a limited number of more or less consistent themes. In contrast, the George W. Bush agenda was a shifting collage of somewhat disparate policy elements. For the sake of convenience, we can categorize the Bush team's policy initiatives as reforms that followed previous trends, reforms that revived themes from the past, and reforms that were relatively new and unique.

FOLLOWING PREVIOUS TRENDS.   Many of the reforms for the MDBs were quite familiar. Although it used a somewhat different vocabulary, the Bush team supported policies that were broadly in line with the augmented Washington Consensus. The crown jewel of Bush's foreign aid program was the MCA, which conditioned foreign aid on "economic free-dom," "ruling justly," and "investing in people"—elements that could be translated roughly as market-friendly policies, governance, and social spending. The administration's HIPC debt-relief initiative agenda, like that of the Clinton administration, conditioned debt forgiveness on policy reforms that included fiscal and monetary, market-liberalizing, gover-nance, and poverty-alleviating elements.[30]

Although all the banks had been thoroughly retooled over the previous two decades to support market-liberalizing reforms, more work was needed in order to integrate governance and antipoverty agendas into their activi-ties. During the Bush years, the Treasury reported pressing the MDBs to make further efforts in this area. The administration took a special interest in reforming the Asian Development Bank (AsDB), which it urged to devote more resources to social spending and to "strengthen its role in good governance."[31] The administration pressed all the banks, particularly the AsDB, on issues of transparency. For example, it put pressure on the Asian bank to strengthen its inspection panel and, in 2004, reported that a new inspection mechanism had been implemented.[32] Also like the Clin-ton administration, the Bush team supported the banks' increasing involve-ment in microcredit loans, a pro-poor foreign aid agenda that was enthusi-astically endorsed by both Democrats and Republicans in Congress.

REVIVING OLDER THEMES.   In addition to promoting policies that followed the trends of the previous decades, the Bush team also revived some older themes. One of these was "private-sector development," an agenda that had played a major role in the MDB policies of the first Reagan admin-istration.

Part of the Bush team's private-sector development initiative was iden-tical to the Reagan agenda of promoting private/public partnerships. The Reagan team's efforts on this score had encountered mixed results, as we saw in chapter 3. During the Clinton administration, the United States had started once again to press the banks toward lending to private firms and cofinancing with private entities, with apparently greater success. Under Bush, the private-sector development agenda became a central focus of attention, with a special emphasis on small and medium businesses. In the fourteenth International Development Association (IDA) replenishment negotiations, the Treasury reported accomplishing heightened collabo-ration between IDA and the International Finance Corporation (IFC) and more support for micro-, small-, and medium-sized enterprises.[33] In 2004, as part of the tenth African Development Fund (AfDF) replenishment negotiations, the African Development Bank (AfDB) approved a "private-sector development strategy" and $250 million in loans to small and medium-sized enterprises, "with nearly all of this assistance provided through financial intermediaries."[34] The AsDB inaugurated its Private Sector Operations Department and, with "U.S. encouragement," "significantly expanded the scope and scale of private sector activities."[35] In the Inter-American Development Bank (IDB), a "private-sector coordinator" reporting directly to the bank's president was selected in January 2005.[36]

The Bush team also used the term *private-sector development* to refer to a broader and more ambiguous range of policies, including lending for policy reform and a new emphasis on "investment-climate surveys."[37] Under the thirteenth IDA replenishment, Bank officials agreed to collect and analyze investment-climate indicators to "help countries identify priorities for reform" and monitor their progress.[38] In 2004, the World Bank launched its Doing Business project, which analyzed and published the climate for private-sector development in 145 countries.[39]

A second revival of older themes, beginning in 2006, was the renewed emphasis on infrastructure. "Investment in physical infrastructure," the Treasury noted, "is key to faster and sustained economic growth necessary for reducing poverty."[40] During the 1990s, the banks had "significantly scaled back" on infrastructure investment, "anticipating that the private sector alone would be able to fund major infrastructure projects." This, however, had proved false. Consequently: "The MDBs have begun scaling up their activity ... with active U.S. encouragement, particularly transportation infrastructure for access to markets and infrastructure to expand access to modern energy, water and sanitation facilities." To help meet this demand, the MDBs were engaging in cofinancing with private lenders.[41]

The swing of the pendulum back to roads and dams appears to have been initiated by the World Bank, rather than by donors. In 2004, under the presidency of Jim Wolfensohn, the Bank began to make public pronouncements about the lack of infrastructure investment in East Asia and Latin America and how this deficit was hampering economic development.[42]

The Bank had a strong organizational interest in rededicating the focus on infrastructure. There had been a marked decrease in demand for World Bank loans among medium-income developing countries—the countries that could pay the hard loan terms that kept the Bank in business. With private foreign investment available, middle-income borrowers preferred to avoid the high hassle costs associated with borrowing from the MDBs—costs resulting from decades of accumulated loan conditionalities and environmental safeguards.[43] Over the long term, the loss of revenue from hard loans was making the World Bank increasingly dependent on IDA replenishments.[44] To help revive demand for infrastructure loans, the Bank began to relax some of its more stringent environmental and social safeguard standards.

Not surprisingly, environmental groups decried the infrastructure revival in the World Bank and other MDBs.[45] However, these groups seemed to acquire little political traction either with the Bush administration or with the Republican-controlled Congress: environmental protection had a low profile in the Bush Treasury's testimonies on the MDBs and was not cited as a major source of congressional concern.

TOWARD A NEW POLICY AGENDA.   The Bush administration's most novel agenda for the MDBs was the brainchild of Treasury Undersecretary for International Affairs John Taylor. A prominent monetary economist who appeared more committed to liberal internationalist principles than the rest of the administration, Taylor was criticized by the *Wall Street Journal* for not taking a more outspoken role in the administration's economic policies.[46] Nevertheless, in the specific area of the MDBs, he was able to serve as a major policy architect until his resignation in the spring of 2004.

In his memoir, *Global Financial Warriors*, Taylor wrote that he had been "morally committed" to reforming the World Bank at the outset of his tenure at the Treasury and that "the greatest motivation for our reform effort came from . . . knowing that the President of the United States was interested in it and would support it."[47] With Taylor in the lead, the Bush Treasury developed a three-pronged agenda for IDA: converting loans to grants, developing a results-measurement system, and increasing U.S. financing. Increasing financing was seen as necessary to persuade donors to implement controversial reforms; the reforms were seen as essential for securing congressional support.[48]

Both grants and results-based management were defining elements of the administration's MCA and resonated with the Bush administration's overall agenda for civil service reform and compassionate conservatism. Yet they also echoed themes for MDB reform that had been floating around in Washington for a decade or more. Starting with the Reagan administration, the United States had consistently pushed the banks to reward good behavior by providing more resources to governments that had previously adopted measurably sound policies.[49] In its last year of testimony on the MDBs, the Clinton administration told Congress: "The MDBs should rely on a smaller number of clear and measurable performance targets, set more realistically, and then more vigorously adhered to."[50]

Both performance-based management and grants were also major elements in the then recently released Meltzer Report. Under the Meltzer Plan, the MDBs and the IMF were to entirely write off their debts to heavily indebted poor countries. To prevent such countries from incurring future debts, the report argued for disbursing resources as grants rather than as low-interest loans. Grants for poverty alleviation would be channeled through outside private-sector providers (such as nongovernmental organizations [NGOs]) that would be awarded contracts on the basis of competitive bids, with performance verified by external auditors using objective measures of outcomes such as "number of children vaccinated, kilowatts of electricity delivered, cubic meters of water treated, [and] students passing literacy tests."[51] The MDBs would phase out all project lending to developing countries that enjoyed private capital market access, such as India, China, or Brazil.

Whereas the Meltzer Plan had been immediately rejected by the Clinton administration, by February 2001 Bush's chief economic adviser, Lawrence Lindsey, was publicly endorsing the Meltzer Report.[52] Treasury Undersecretary John Taylor had been a close personal friend of Allan Meltzer, a fellow conservative economist, for thirty years.[53] Some elements of the Meltzer Plan, however, were considered too radical to incorporate into the Bush administration's initial MDB reform agenda. Debt relief was discarded because, according to Taylor, it "would have encountered strong opposition at that time from Japan, Germany, and France, as well as many in our own government." "Graduating" countries like India, China, and Brazil from the MDBs was seen as too controversial among middle-income countries that needed to be enlisted to back the reform.[54] Thus, the Bush team did not end up using the Meltzer Report as a blueprint; instead, it drew selectively on these and other conservative ideas to draw up a plan for the banks that was consistent with the administration's overall policy programs.

In its first annual budget justification, the Treasury, in the person of

Secretary O'Neill, promised Congress: "The US will push for use of grant funding for HIPC countries, in order to help these countries reform and fight poverty without incurring excessive additional debt."[55] A year later, the administration reported that it was pushing for 50 percent of World Bank and other MDB funds for the poorest countries to be provided as grants, which would "help avoid the need for future HIPC debt relief."[56]

Because switching to grants posed a potential threat to its the Bank's resource base, switching from loans to grants met considerable opposition from Bank management. To thwart the grants agenda, the World Bank publicized calculations suggesting that existing debt relief was sufficient to keep the HIPC countries solvent and that switching to grants would cost multilateral lenders $100 billion over forty years. In response to these dire predictions, the U.S. Government Accountability Office issued a report of its own in the spring of 2002 showing that existing HIPC debt relief was insufficient and that introducing grants would be far less costly than the World Bank had predicted—it could be offset by only a small increase in donor contributions.[57]

Although the grant proposal was resisted by the World Bank, it was extremely popular on Capitol Hill. Grants had the strong support of anti-poverty NGOs, such as Jubilee and Bread for the World, as well as a coalition of liberal Democrats and conservative Republicans. By 2002, even such a notorious foreign aid critic as the Alabama Republican Sonny Callahan was publicly endorsing grants: "I don't know who we are trying to fool with the loans that we know will never be repaid. Why not go ahead and give them the grants up front and create, if nothing else, the public relations of the grant versus the loan?"[58] Or as Jack Kingston, a Georgia Republican put it, the grants agenda was "important for national security reasons . . . to let people know we are doing this. . . . We are interested in helping you find your way out of poverty. We want to help."[59]

In addition to the proposal's implications for promoting national security and helping the poorest of the poor, conservative skeptics were won over by the simultaneous emphasis on accountability and measurable results. The Treasury promised Congress that it would push for "increased linkages between borrower performance and lending levels" in upcoming MDB replenishment negotiations and later reported successfully moving all the banks, with the exception of the European Bank for Reconstruction and Development, in this direction.[60] By 2007, the Treasury could boast: "Over ten years ago, IDA's best performers received allocations 40% higher than the poorest performers. Today, support for IDA's best performers is 450% higher than support for the poorest performers."[61]

Perhaps the most innovative part of the plan was for the MDBs—and not just their clients—to be held accountable. The administration wanted all the banks to develop "more rigorous quantifiable measures of the impact of each aid project" and to use these measures to determine whether the banks were doing their jobs.[62] As with previous U.S. reform initiatives, the World Bank was made into a pilot case. A results-based system was set up as part of the thirteenth IDA replenishment under which the United States would grant IDA additional funds if it "produces a results measurement system, expands essential diagnostics and achieves progress toward concrete health, education and private sector goals."[63] The system was apparently quite similar to the one developed for the MCA, using metrics developed by the World Bank Institute (e.g., measuring rule of law and control of corruption), the Heritage Foundation (its index of "economic freedom"), and Freedom House (civil liberties and political rights).[64]

This plan meant that the World Bank itself—and not just World Bank borrowers—was subject to a kind of policy conditionality, with disbursements from the United States suspended if specific performance criteria were not met. The United States conditioned the first disbursement of $100 million to IDA on the initiation of a results-measurement system. The second U.S. disbursement of $200 million was conditioned on "the advancement of concrete results" in "education, health, and private sector development" in IDA countries.[65]

In the fourteenth IDA replenishment, the United States pushed for the enhancement of the measurable-results system inaugurated in the thirteenth. The replenishments' performance-measurement system included fourteen "country outcome indicators" (e.g., under-five child mortality, time for business start-up), "output indicators" (measuring IDA's contribution in such areas as health and education), "country-level institutional indicators" (number of results-based country assistance strategies prepared), and "project-level indicators" (percentage of projects with satisfactory outcome ratings).[66] The Treasury later reported to Congress that IDA had adhered to its commitments and had, therefore, secured the promised disbursements.[67] This performance-based agenda was applied beyond IDA to the World Bank as a whole. According to the Treasury, the Bank began to tie staff compensation to project outcomes, rather than lending volume.[68] The Bank also began to require its divisions to sign performance contracts laying out missions, outcomes, and measurement instruments; these documents linked "future resource availability to performance against these contracts."[69] The IFC, the World Bank's private-sector lending affiliate, set up its Development Effectiveness Unit and assembled the Development Outcome Tracking System to "define monitorable indicators for every project."[70]

As in previous bouts of reform, the U.S.-led initiative for measurable results was expanded from the World Bank outward to the regional MDBs. In the ninth AfDF replenishment, approved in 2002, management agreed to establish indicators to measure and evaluate progress and hired consultants to assist in designing its results-based management strategy.[71] In the tenth replenishment, the Board of Directors agreed that every AfDF project and strategy would have a fully operational results-based management system by 2006. The AfDB developed a "Balanced Scorecard of 6 strategic themes and 35 performance indicators to measure institutional performance."[72] In its eighth replenishment, finalized in 2001, the Asian Development Fund (AsDF) committed to improving its ability to measure results and to beginning to develop a performance-based allocation system for AsDF resources.[73] "At U.S. urging," the AsDB "made results measurement the centerpiece" of the ninth AsDF replenishment.[74] By 2007, the Treasury was reporting that, henceforth, all AsDB country strategies would be results based.[75]

In the IDB and the Fund for Special Operations, American efforts to push for measurable results assumed a somewhat different form since there were no replenishments or general capital increases for either of these windows after 1994. Nevertheless, the IDB "approved a new framework for strengthening the measurement of results and created a new oversight position that will substantially improve the Bank's efforts to focus on achieving measurable results."[76] In 2006, the IDB announced a major reorganization, which included a new performance-management framework to "create incentives for Bank staff that are linked to the development effectiveness of their work."[77] The IDB's private-sector affiliate, the Multilateral Investment Fund (MIF), finalized a replenishment in 2005 in which the Treasury reported achieving a number of U.S. objectives, including the establishment of a results-based system and an "impact evaluation program."[78]

Finally, to absolutely convince congressional skeptics that the performance-based agenda was actually being implemented, the banks were evaluated by the U.S. OMB using the PART—the same rating system that was being applied to U.S. government agencies under the Bush administration's measurable-results reform agenda. For example, in 2003, the OMB rated IDA at 100 and 71 percent in management and planning,

respectively, but only 33 percent in both program results and accountability. In 2005, the AsDF was rated at 89 percent in management but only 62
percent in planning and 25 percent in both program results and accountability.[79] These ratings were presented by the Treasury to Congress as a
basis for ongoing U.S. reform initiatives in the banks.

Donors Disagree

One of the most notable results of the Bush administration's MDB policies was a series of major public disagreements among MDB shareholders. Interdonor disagreements had emerged sporadically ever since the
1980s, mostly around the perennial problem of withheld U.S. contributions. During the Bush years, however, conflict among donors escalated
to historically unprecedented levels and increasingly responded to substantive policy differences. The common cause of these conflicts was the
administration's tendency to forcefully promote policies that did not have
widespread support among major shareholders, along with its apparent
unwillingness to compromise. As we saw in chapter 7, the administration's
debt-relief initiative was one major source of interdonor contention. Two
other significant battles fought during the Bush years concerned the issue
of grants and Paul Wolfowitz's presidency of the World Bank. In opposing the Bush team's MDB policies, other donor governments increasingly
aired their disagreements to the international media, thereby drawing
public attention to the connection between MDB policies and donor
politics.

Grants

In the summer of 2001, the Bush administration called for "compassionate
conservatism at the international level" and, at the G8 summit, proposed
that 50 percent of IDA funds be disbursed in the form of grants. Other G7
members, particularly the Europeans, were strongly opposed and argued
that a 10 percent grant component was more realistic. The British development minister, Claire Short, referred to the 50 percent grant proposal as a "crazy idea."[80] Treasury Secretary O'Neill responded irritably
to European critics: "I say to hell with it. Tell me a good reason."[81]

The reasons the Europeans gave for opposing the grant plan were
similar to their objections to the Bush team's plan for HIPC debt relief.

The World Bank and the other MDBs depended on a revenue stream from replenishments and reflows—the repayment of loans over time with interest. Both debt forgiveness and grants would, in the long term, lessen reflow income. The precise magnitude of the loss was subject to debate: supporters of grants and debt relief pointed out that the banks were concealing the magnitude of their losses incurred thus far by disbursing new loans to countries unable to pay off the old ones.[82] Nevertheless, it was clear that the loss of reflows meant lessened resources for the MDBs in the long run—unless donors compensated with more generous replenishments.[83] The Bush administration assured the international community that such future generosity would be forthcoming. Yet other donors were understandably wary, given the notorious history of failed congressional appropriations and U.S. arrears to the banks. As the Bread for the World president, David Beckmann, told the *Wall Street Journal*: "I think one reason the Europeans are so skeptical of the proposal [on grants] is they see us as so damned stingy."[84]

In spite of these misgivings, the United States was, ultimately, able to get a revised version of its grants proposal through the World Bank's Executive Board. The U.S. position on grants was strengthened by the public support of civil society organizations such as Oxfam and Bread for the World, led by public figures such as Bono, which gave the Americans the moral high ground. Moreover, as before, the United States was also placed in a strong bargaining position by its reputation for intransigence and by ample evidence that Congress would withhold funding if the conditions it wanted were not met.

With its IDA funds nearly exhausted, in May 2002 the World Bank proposed a compromise grant level of 22 percent.[85] In June, the G7 finally announced an agreement that between 18 and 21 percent of IDA disbursements would be in the form of grants. Donors also agreed to the results-based system advocated by the Bush administration as well as its proposal that U.S. contributions be conditioned on IDA reforms.[86] In the subsequent IDA replenishment (the fourteenth), the United States secured a further increase in grant financing to 31 percent of all IDA disbursements. In the tenth replenishment of the AfDF, grants were increased to 45 percent.[87] The United States also used the AsDF replenishment process to win a program under which approximately 30 percent of resources to the poorest countries would be disbursed in grant form.[88] In a replenishment of the MIF of the IDB, approved in 2005, it was agreed that roughly 75 percent of all approvals would be in the form of grants.[89]

The Wolfowitz Imbroglio

A key mechanism of U.S. influence was its prerogative to appoint top management in the banks, particularly the World Bank's managing director. Traditionally, however, the United States chose World Bank presidents whose professional profiles could generate a minimum level of interdonor consensus. In contrast, the nomination of Paul Wolfowitz caused an immediate negative reaction from other donors—not only because he was a leading architect of the Iraq War, but also because the nomination came soon after the administration's appointment of John Bolton, another notorious unilateralist, to be U.S. ambassador to the United Nations.[90]

The administration's chosen nominee went on to become the most controversial president in the half-century history of the World Bank. This was not because Wolfowitz was a tool of the Bush administration—for example, he soon broke with the Bush program on global warming and pushed back on the administration's debt-relief policy, which threatened IDA's long-term financial viability.[91] Yet his strong backing by the U.S. administration, combined with his perhaps characteristically neoconservative disregard for organizational rules, alienated World Bank management and staff as well as other major donors. Early on, World Bank staffers had complained about the appointment of close Republican loyalists with little development experience to top Bank positions and about how the new appointments violated organizational rules concerning pay scales and contracts.[92] Wolfowitz's most controversial policy was the freezing of loans to India, Bangladesh, Kenya, Chad, and Argentina, ostensibly because they were likely to be squandered on corruption, but apparently on the basis of no objective criteria to justify why these countries were being singled out.[93] At the Bank's annual meetings in September 2006, European donors lambasted Wolfowitz for the arbitrariness of his anti-corruption policies.[94]

Ultimately, Wolfowitz's overt disregard for organizational procedures was his undoing. In the spring of 2007, a scandal broke around the financial perquisites awarded to Wolfowitz's girlfriend, the World Bank staff member Shaha Riza. Riza had been sent by the Bank to work at the State Department in September 2005 and, while remaining on the Bank's payroll, had received more than $61,000 in pay raises, in apparent violation of World Bank rules. Even worse, on coming to the World Bank, Wolfowitz had not recused himself from office matters involving Riza, with whom he was already romantically involved.

For two months, the scandal festered, and a growing chorus of voices was raised—including more than forty former top Bank executives who signed an open letter published in the *Financial Times*—calling for Wolfowitz's resignation. A special internal investigative panel found that Wolfowitz had violated three separate World Bank rules. Yet European shareholders did not want to risk an open clash with the Bush administration by voting to fire him. Faced with overwhelming evidence of wrongdoing and a crisis of confidence, the Executive Board finally asked Wolfowitz to resign in mid-May 2007 but framed the resignation in exculpatory language stating that the fallen president had "assured us that he acted ethically and in good faith in what he believed were the best interests of the institution, and we accept that."[95]

On Wolfowitz's resignation, some observers speculated that the controversy might mark the end of the informal practice of allowing the United States to select the World Bank's managing director. Once again, however, other major shareholders deferred to the United States and allowed the Bush administration to nominate the former U.S. trade representative Robert Zoellick as the Bank's new managing director. Although the Executive Board invited nominations for other candidates, no other nation came forth with a rival.[96]

Implications for the Intellectual Field

Throughout this book, we have seen that the MDBs are organizations that straddle the political and the intellectual worlds—and, therefore, serve as transmission belts for ideas between the two. The banks' policies and publications help set the agenda for debates among development experts. Yet these policies and publications are not purely scholarly products: they are also shaped by donor politics. For example, the muting of the World Bank's antipoverty discourse in the early 1980s was indirectly shaped by the politics of the Reagan administration; the subsequent renewal of the its antipoverty mission was shaped by an alliance between civil society groups and members of Congress.

In contrast, the Bush administration's policies exerted a relatively subtle influence on development debates, in part because its position on the World Bank's intellectual output was comparatively passive. The Clinton Treasury had, as we saw in chapter 6, been keenly interested in managing the content of the Bank's policy prescriptions and even clashed with the Bank's research department when its experts went too far astray. In contrast, nothing like the titanic battles between Summers and Stiglitz occurred during the Bush years.

This absence of conflict seems particularly notable in light of trends in World Bank research at the time. In the fall of 2003, the French economist François Bourguignon was nominated to be the Bank's chief economist. Bourguignon, who was already well-known for arguing that reducing inequality could be good for growth, was described by a Bank official interviewed at the time of his nomination as "no neoclassical" and someone "who believes strongly in the role of the state and the public sector in playing a facilitating role and being responsible for public services."[97] Extraordinarily, Bourguignon was appointed without public comment of any kind from the Bush administration. Prepared under Bourguignon's leadership, the Bank's 2006 *World Development Report*, entitled "Equity and Development," irritated conservative economists with its arguments for ameliorating inequalities both within and between countries.

Was the World Bank's new concern with inequality part of the Bush administration's hidden neoconservative agenda—a secret weapon in its War on Terror? This seems unlikely. The tenor of the 2006 *World Development Report* had little in common with the MDB policies explicitly advanced by the Treasury in its presentations to the Republican-dominated House and Senate subcommittees. Nor was the report consistent with trends occurring elsewhere in the World Bank. During the same period, the Bank's *Doing Business* report, a new publication strongly supported by the Bush administration, was drawing criticism from progressives for the high ratings it awarded governments with the weakest labor protections and regulatory frameworks—a message that noticeably contradicted some of the arguments of the 2006 *World Development Report*.[98] Thus, circumstantial evidence strongly suggests that the leftward turn in World Bank research responded, not to an orchestrated Bush administration plan, but to dynamics internal to the Bank and to the subfield of development economics. The fact that these dynamics were allowed to unfold without interference reflected the administration's preoccupation with other matters more central to its policy agenda—such as the wars in Iraq and Afghanistan and bilateral aid programs that could be more directly linked to U.S. foreign policy.

If the Bush team had little interest in monitoring the World Bank's impact on development scholarship, this was at least in part because the Bush administration was not interested in modifying the Washington Consensus. As we have seen, the administration's ideas about appropriate development policies differed little from those of its predecessors. Instead, the policy agenda launched by Treasury Undersecretary John Taylor focused on changing the procedural assumptions of multilateral development financing by emphasizing grants, performance, and measurable results.

This implications of this agenda for development debates were complex, but undoubtedly also important. It shifted debates around the MDBs away from what poor countries should be doing with their economic policies—freeing markets versus protecting the poor etc.—and toward scrutinizing the policies of the MDBs themselves. This helped bring more radical ideas from the margins to the center of debates in and around Washington—ideas that often called the very utility of the banks into question. For example, in a 2006 article in *Foreign Affairs*, the former World Bank official Jessica Einhorn called for an "orderly, consensual dismantling" of the International Bank for Reconstruction and Development (IBRD). Echoing the Meltzer Report, Einhorn argued that private capital markets made IBRD lending for infrastructure projects obsolete and that its dismantling would leave more resources available for antipoverty grants.[99] The notion that the MDBs and other aid agencies needed to be held accountable to measurable standards also moved into the mainstream. Among the policy proposals mentioned in William Easterly's very popular 2006 development manifesto *White Man's Burden* were the following: "Fix the incentive system of collective responsibility for multiple goals. Have individual accountability for individual tasks. Let aid agencies specialize in the sectors and countries they are best at helping. Then hold the aid agencies accountable for *their* results by having truly independent evaluation of their efforts."[100]

A collection of essays published in 2006 by the Center for Global Development, a prominent Washington think tank specializing in development issues, exemplified how wide-ranging debates about the future of the MDBs had become. Entitled *Rescuing the World Bank*, the volume included a considerable variety of proposals for reform. The former Treasury official Stephen Radelet advanced a moderate reform agenda, suggesting that the Bank should do a better job of tailoring its policies to the differing characteristics of its client governments. On the more radical side, the former Meltzer Commission member Adam Lerrick argued for the complete replacement of World Bank lending with grants and the elimination of resource transfers to medium-income countries. In direct contradiction to Lerrick, the former World Bank official David de Ferranti argued that IBRD lending to medium-income countries should continue, but with minimized "hassle costs." Other suggestions included emphasizing the provision of "global public goods," such as assistance to war refugees, and subsidizing development research in developing countries.[101]

If the Bush reform agenda helped alter the zeitgeist of Washington development policy debates, it also undoubtedly had an impact on the tenor of development scholarship. The growing focus of both the MDBs and U.S. bilateral aid on measurable results created structural incentives for development research focusing on creating, deploying, and evaluating indicators of success, particularly in the area of social policy. For example, in 2003, a group of Boston-area economists founded the Poverty Action Lab at MIT, an organization that subsequently enjoyed considerable success partnering with U.S. government agencies, NGOs, private foundations, and multilateral organizations such as the World Bank. The Poverty Action Lab specializes in conducting systematic, randomized evaluations of the effectiveness of particular policies on measurable development outcomes—from the impact of girls' scholarships on exam scores in Kenya to the impact of deposit-collection services on personal savings in the Philippines.[102] The long-term impact of measurable results on development economics has not yet been analyzed systematically but will likely provide a fascinating case study of the connections between Washington policy and development scholarship.

The MDBs in Perspective

In many ways, the George W. Bush administration left a unique stamp on the MDBs. Nevertheless, this chapter has argued that, overall, the trends of the Bush years adhered to patterns that have been repeated for more than twenty years. The following sections review these historical patterns and revisit the major arguments of this book.

The Banks as Resource-Dependent Organizations

The MDBs can usefully be conceptualized as resource-dependent organizations that are roughly analogous to private corporations. Like corporations, the banks enlist external agents—donor governments—to provide them with the resources they need by awarding them control over organizational activities. The banks' shareholders, in turn, delegate authority to management—with shareholder activism varying considerably across the banks and over time.

However, even when shareholder activism is high and delegation to management low, the banks cannot be viewed as tools of their shareholders in any straightforward sense. The banks' management and staff possess their own interests separate from those of their shareholders. For example, they want their organization to grow, or at least to remain stable, to maximize their own autonomy, to acquire greater organizational autonomy, and to maximize their own individual rewards. They possess a range of means to pursue these ends in the face of countervailing shareholder demands. In some cases, management may simply say no to shareholders. At least since the inauguration of the era of shareholder activism in the 1980s, however, such overt resistance has been an inadvisable tactic, as the failed rebellion of the IDB in the late 1980s illustrates all too well.

Instead of overtly pushing back against their shareholders, resource-dependent organizations such as the MDBs may achieve better results through a range of more subtle tactics identified by organizational theorists.[103] First, they may attempt to persuade their shareholders to pursue a particular course of action by selectively screening and disseminating information to which shareholders do not have direct access. For example, when the George W. Bush administration began to campaign to replace IDA loans with grants, the World Bank responded with reports predicting catastrophic consequences for its long-term finances. Second, management may conform ceremonially to shareholder demands without making substantive changes. The banks' propensity to adopt the form but not the substance of shareholder demands is a perennial complaint of environmental NGOs. Third, we have seen that the banks can develop and market new products to their shareholders to ensure an ongoing flow of resources. This sort of entrepreneurial activity has been most characteristic of the World Bank, the banks' intellectual leader. The launching of structural adjustment loans in the 1980s was an extraordinarily successful example: it allowed the Bank to justify its request for more resources in the face of declining demand for hard project loans and persuaded the Reagan administration that the World Bank was a useful tool for pursuing U.S. economic interests.

At the same time, the analogy between the MDBs and private corporations has some notable limitations. Whereas shareholders in a corporation have a common interest in maximizing financial returns, the banks have no such clear objective. Shareholders may disagree among themselves about the ends of MDB activities as well as about the best means for pursuing these ends. Indeed, because MDB shareholders are political entities—donor governments—each shareholder may simultaneously advocate a number of distinct organizational ends. Over time, the composition of these ends tends to change, driven largely by political forces. We have seen that a particularly important shift in shareholder framing of the purpose of the MDBs occurred with the entry of the Reagan administration in 1981, which shifted the focus from the banks as diplomatic tools for fighting communism to the banks as means to long-term market-liberalizing reforms. Political factors also shape the means that a shareholder might deem appropriate for pursuing any given end. For example, the George W. Bush administration's push for grants grew out of a group of related conservative policy programs.

The Intersection of Intellectual and Political Fields

This study has argued that the banks occupy a liminal space between the world of scholarly ideas and the world of donor politics—in the language of Pierre Bourdieu, between the intellectual and the political fields. This fact has often been remarkably easy to overlook because the black box of donor politics has made it difficult for outside investigators to observe political factors in action. Moreover, because the banks' effectiveness depends on their intellectual legitimacy, and because this legitimacy is premised on professional neutrality, it is in the interest of both the banks and their shareholders to downplay the political origins of the banks' ideas and activities.

Over the past several years, however, a growing number of analysts have been paying attention to the role of donor politics in the activities of the IMF and the World Bank.[104] One reason for this heightened attention to politics is that growing shareholder activism has made it difficult to ignore. This role of donor politics was particularly hard to overlook during the George W. Bush administration, whose reform agenda and unapologetic unilateralism caused unprecedented public debates among shareholders about what the MDBs should be doing.

The analysis of the role of U.S. politics in the MDBs presented in the foregoing chapters contributes to scholarship on the complex connections between politics and scholarly ideas in the social sciences.[105] Political actors often advance policy programs that have the blessing of certified experts: by drawing on expert advice, policy programs share in the technocratic legitimacy of scholarly knowledge. Yet social science experts often disagree, and political actors usually draw selectively on their ideas to suit their own ideologies and political proclivities. For their part, scholars may choose to ally selectively with political actors, a strategy that can give them access to benefits that the ivory tower is unlikely to offer—an important job, fame, or, perhaps most important, the opportunity to see their ideas put into practice. However, the expert advice that gets implemented as policy is not necessarily the best advice but simply the advice that acquires the strongest political backing.[106]

To these observations, this study suggests a further insight concerning the role of what the sociologist Thomas Medvetz calls "interstitial fields" in transmitting ideas between the political and the intellectual worlds.[107] The banks, which occupy such a field, are famous for transmitting expert ideas, such as macroeconomic policy prescriptions, to borrowing governments—a transfer of expert ideas to the world of politics. In this book, however, I have demonstrated that the flow can also go the other way: the MDBs can transmit ideas from the political field to the world of intellectual debates. The research output of the World Bank, which has considerable scholarly legacy, plays a particularly important role in this process.

The Leading Role of the United States

The United States has a peculiar political system that has long fascinated social scientific observers. Whereas most advanced industrial democracies have parliamentary systems, the United States has a semiadversarial relationship between the executive and the legislative branches. These and other features of the American political scene have important implications for policy—and help us account for such observed phenomena as the weakness of the American welfare state.[108] This book draws our attention to another consequence of the U.S. political system: namely, its role in bolstering U.S. leadership in globalizing multilateral institutions.

Overall, the U.S. executive branch has tended to be supportive of IFIs, including the MDBs. On two occasions—that of the Reagan and the George W. Bush administrations—Republican administrations entered office with an ambivalent posture toward these organizations. In both cases, however, these initial antimultilateralist sentiments were, ultimately, tempered by the administration's realization that the banks were too useful to be abandoned.

In contrast, the U.S. Congress has been much more difficult to convince. Members of Congress, who are necessarily excluded from multilateral negotiations, have often opposed U.S. participation in the MDBs. This has been most true of right-wing Republicans, who are prone to espousing the antiaid, antimultilateralist ideas propagated by conservative think tanks. Although congressional Democrats have also been active reformers, overall their reform impulses have tended to be checked by the countervailing impulse to preserve the MDBs from their right-wing attackers. This has meant that Democrats wield a less credible threat for withholding appropriations and, hence, have less overall influence on U.S. MDB policy.

During the first several decades of the MDBs' existence, their funding constituted too small a fraction of the U.S. foreign aid program to attract much congressional attention. Yet, beginning in the 1970s, Congress began to complain about U.S. participation in the banks and to demand a greater voice in the making of MDB policies. This rise of congressional activism brought what had previously been a behind-the-scenes process into the forum of public discussions between the executive and the legislative branches. We have seen that this allowed civil society groups to participate in the forging of U.S. policies toward the banks.

Increased congressional interest in the MDBs also made the United States into the banks' leading activist shareholder—the government always striving to reform the banks in one way or another. U.S. shareholder activism in the banks grew out of both necessity and opportunity. On the one hand, the U.S. executive found that it had to perpetually sell the MDBs to Congress by perpetually reforming them—or risk having their appropriations declined. On the other hand, it had the opportunity to use Congress as an implicit threat in its negotiations with other shareholders and the banks' management. This, combined with America's demonstrated willingness to withhold financing when its policy preferences were ignored, helped enable the United States to continue to set the interdonor agenda in spite of declining contributions and voting share. According to the U.S. Treasury, by the end of the 2006 fiscal year American arrears to the MDBs totaled nearly $770 million.[109] Overall real U.S. spending on the banks was near its lowest point, as illustrated in figure 8.2, and the U.S. voting share in both IDA and the IBRD was at a historic low. Yet, in spite of meager contributions and the decline in formal voting share, other major donors have—for the most part—continued to follow the U.S. lead.

A major reason for ongoing U.S. leadership is that the small "win set"

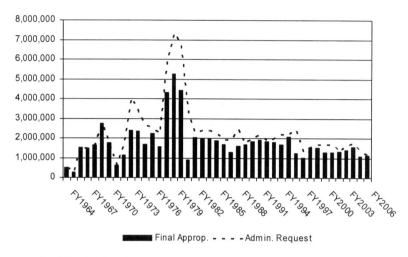

FIGURE 8.2. U.S. administration requests and final appropriations for the MDBs, thousands of U.S. dollars (2000). *Source*: *Congressional Quarterly* (various years and issues); and *Congressional Quarterly Almanac* (various years).

of the United States enhances U.S. leverage with other international negotiators with less problematic legislative branches: other negotiators know they are likely to have to adjust their own win sets to arrive at an agreement that the U.S. Congress will ratify.[110] In the case of the MDBs, the possibilities for ratification are further diminished by an additional factor— namely, that, unlike most international treaties, the MDBs are based on agreements for which funds must be regularly appropriated. This means that the issue is brought back repeatedly to the notoriously conservative appropriations subcommittees, where for decades legislators have argued that money spent on the banks is money "down a rathole."

Conclusion

This book goes to press at an uncertain time for IFIs. In recent years, after a half century of managing the fiscal problems of its borrowers, the IMF faced a fiscal crisis of its own, as it was increasingly abandoned by middle-income borrowers. The MDBs also faced decreasing demand for their hard loans. Both the IMF and the MDBs were made both less powerful and less relevant by the growth of private international capital markets— which provided medium-income developing countries with alternative sources of development and balance-of-payments financing—as well as by the erosion of their reputation as purveyors of politically neutral and technically correct advice. Meanwhile, developing countries renewed their demands for greater input into IFI policies. Faced with a crisis in legitimacy and declining demand for its loans, the IMF even implemented a modest change in its voting structure in 2008. The outbreak of the international financial crisis later that year generated renewed calls for the reform of multilateral lenders.

Is it possible that we may see the emergence of a new kind of MDB—one in which poor countries have a voice and a vote proportionate to their share in the world population? Could the future of MDB policy consensuses lie in Beijing, New Delhi, and Brasilia rather than in Washington? The history and analysis outlined in this book suggest that we should not be unduly optimistic. To secure access to needed resources, the banks were designed to respond to the demands of their shareholders. Once institutionalized, the dominance of powerful shareholders in international lending organizations is very difficult to alter: donors are naturally reluctant to use their influence to promote governance changes that will, ultimately, undermine that influence. For example, according to some analysts, the main reason for the disappointingly small 2008 IMF reform was that European governments were unwilling to sacrifice their voting shares, in spite of emerging-market governments' willingness to increase their own contributions.[111] The recent contraction of private global financial markets, which is rescuing multilateral lenders from irrelevance, is also making them more valuable to their shareholders—who may therefore be even more reluctant to relinquish control.

Perhaps most important, the unique political dynamics of the banks' most demanding shareholder are particularly uncongenial to major changes. After all, any future MDB governance reforms will have to be vetted not only by the U.S. executive but also the U.S. Congress. Given that U.S. legislators are inclined to slash the banks' financing even under the current regime, in which U.S. influence is very strong, it seems quite unlikely that they would stand for a governance reform that would significantly lessen Washington's voice and vote.

This is not to say that there is no hope for change. On the contrary, we have seen that, in recent decades, the banks changed extremely rapidly. Environmental and resettlement standards were adopted, debt forgiven, and measurable-results systems implemented. Project lending was partially supplanted by policy-based lending, and then loans were partially supplanted by grants. Organizational missions were expanded to include the promotion of appropriate policies and the provision of global public goods. The market-liberalizing wisdom of the 1980s was updated in favor of more complex development prescriptions. In these and other changes that have transformed the banks over the past quarter century, shareholder politics, and particularly American politics, has played a major role.

Through forging partnerships with politically influential intellectuals and NGOs in donor capitals, reform advocates in developing countries have become part of these changes. And the prospects for such transnational initiatives have been steadily enhanced by increases in the role and visibility of shareholder politics in the MDBs. Thirty years ago, donor governments forged the banks' policies behind closed doors. Subsequently, however, U.S. shareholder activism created new opportunities for civil society groups to influence MDB policies and increased public access to information about their practices. Most recently, the Bush administration's activism had the unintended consequence of shedding more light than ever into the black box of donor politics. At no previous time in the history of the banks has so much information about the role of shareholder governments in the MDBs been so publicly available.

This unveiling of the role of donor politics has inspired and enabled transnational networks of reformers to hold shareholder governments—rather than the IFIs they own—accountable. This tactic is exemplified by the Live 8 campaign for debt relief, explicitly named after the G8 meetings. Future reform initiatives might focus on demanding even greater public access to policy positions and discussions among donor governments, which could make it easier for transnational reformers to pressure shareholders selectively. Through an application of the principles of transparency and accountability to MDB shareholders, the banks could, ultimately, become more responsive to the publics around the world that are affected by their ideas and activities.

Notes

Preface

1. Williamson, "What Washington Means by Policy Reform," 18.

2. Naím, "Fads and Fashions in Economic Reforms," 505.

3. In theory, all foreign aid policy (including that regarding the MDBs) is supposed to go through the process just described twice: first with an authorization bill, which generally approves spending on the program in question, and then with an appropriations bill, which sets the actual amounts of funding. In practice, however, over the course of the 1960s and 1970s, delays in foreign aid legislation meant that foreign aid was often funded through "continuing resolutions" (stop-gap spending bills that usually set funding at the previous year's level) or tacked onto giant omnibus spending bills funding various programs. To remove a layer of difficulty in a complex and controversial process, it became common for Congress to waive the requirement for authorizations and move straight to the appropriations process. There has been no overall foreign aid authorization bill passed since 1985. Therefore, much of the analysis in this book focuses on the hearings of House and Senate appropriations subcommittees. See Lancaster and IIE, *Transforming Foreign Aid*, 37–38.

4. Snow, Rochford, Worden, and Benford, "Frame Alignment Processes," 464. See also Gamson and Modigliani, "Media Discourse and Public Opinion on Nuclear Power"; Goffman, *Frame Analysis*, 586; and Babb, "'True American System of Finance.'"

Introduction

1. Arndt, "Economic Development"; Rist, *History of Development*, 73.

2. Martinussen, *Society, State, and Market*, 56–64.

3. Lancaster and Van Dusen, *Organizing U.S. Foreign Aid*, 4–5; Martinussen,

Society, State, and Market, 298–303; Kapur and Webb, "Governance-Related Conditionalities."

4. Lancaster and Van Dusen, *Organizing U.S. Foreign Aid*, 5.

5. Amsden, *Asia's Next Giant*, 379; Wade, *Governing the Market*, 438.

6. Sachs, *End of Poverty*, 396; Easterly, *Elusive Quest for Growth*, 342; Easterly, *White Man's Burden*, 436.

7. Banerjee, "Inside the Machine."

8. The only regional MDB that I do not consider in this study is the European Investment Bank (EIB). The EIB was established in 1957 to serve as a source of long-term investment financing for the European Community. Since it was not designed to address the needs of poor countries, and since it is run without input from Washington, it is not relevant to the themes of this book. For an excellent discussion of the EIB and a comparison to the European Bank for Reconstruction and Development, see Gutner, *Banking on the Environment*, 269. This study does not address the issue of subregional development banks, such as the Caribbean Development Bank or the Islamic Development Bank, which are much smaller and less influential.

9. Williamson, "What Washington Means by Policy Reform."

10. See Broad, "Art of 'Paradigm Maintenance.'"

11. Ibid., 396–97.

12. Ibid., 395–96.

13. Mallaby, *World's Banker*, 71.

14. Fine, "Speculation on Social Capital," 219–20.

15. Lewis, "Development Promotion," 9; Fine, "Speculation on Social Capital."

16. Culpeper, *Multilateral Development Banks*.

17. Blyth, *Great Transformations*, 284.

18. Ibid., 139–51.

19. Campbell, *Institutional Change and Globalization*, 98.

20. Gamson and Modigliani, "Media Discourse and Public Opinion on Nuclear Power"; Snow, Rochford, Worden, and Benford, "Frame Alignment Processes."

21. Hall, "Policy Paradigms," 275.

22. Meyer, Boli, Thomas, and Ramirez, "World Society and the Nation-State"; Hafner-Burton and Tsutsui, "Human Rights in a Globalizing World." Drawing on the work of Habermas, Robin Stryker argues: "State reliance on scientific 'laws' to justify its interventions enables it to be seen as a neutral representation of societal interests discovered and served by scientific experts." Stryker, "Limits on Technocratization," 343.

23. Bourdieu, "The Forms of Capital."

24. Medvetz, "Production of Policy-Knowledge."

25. Stern, "World Bank as 'Intellectual Actor'"; Wade, "US Hegemony and the World Bank"; Broad, "Art of 'Paradigm Maintenance.'"

26. See Lancaster, *Foreign Aid*, 95.

27. Patrick, "Multilateralism and Its Discontents." See also Ostrower, *The United Nations and the United States*, 317; and Luck, *Mixed Messages*, 374.

28. Lancaster and Van Dusen, *Organizing U.S. Foreign Aid*, 37.

29. Thurber, "Presidential-Congressional Rivalry," 8–9.

30. Lancaster, *Foreign Aid*, chap. 3.

31. Foreign aid, which is distinct from military aid, is defined by Carol Lancaster as "a voluntary transfer of public resources, from a government to another independent government, to an NGO, or to an international organization (such as the World Bank or the UN Development Program) with at least a 25 percent grant element, one goal of which is to better the human condition in the country receiving the aid." Lancaster, *Foreign Aid*, 9.

32. Lancaster and IIE, *Transforming Foreign Aid*, 46, 49.

33. Tarnoff and Nowels, *Foreign Aid*.

34. Mead, *Special Providence*, 374.

35. Kapur, Lewis, and Webb, eds., *World Bank*, 1:1145.

36. Kappagoda, *Asian Development Bank*, 39.

37. Putnam, "Diplomacy and Domestic Politics"; Evans, Jacobson, and Putnam, *Double-Edged Diplomacy*, 490.

38. Lancaster, *Foreign Aid*, chap. 3.

39. See Lindsay, *Politics of U.S. Foreign Policy*, 44–47.

40. For a review of interest groups supporting foreign aid, see Lancaster, *Foreign Aid*, 100–105.

41. For an excellent treatment of the origins and role of these think tanks, see Medvetz, "Production of Policy-Knowledge."

42. Marx and Engels, "Manifesto of the Communist Party."

Chapter One

1. Bentsen in House Appropriations Subcommittee, *Appropriations for 1994*, 554.

2. For a discussion of the origins of the term *Third World* in the early 1950s, see Colburn, "Good-Bye to the 'Third World.'"

3. See Kahin, *Asian-African Conference*, 77.

4. Jolly, *UN Contributions to Development Thinking and Practice*, 387; Toye and Toye, *The UN and Global Political Economy*, 393.

5. Urquidi, "Reconstruction vs. Development."

6. Mason and Asher, *The World Bank since Bretton Woods*, 467.

7. Ibid., 178–79.

8. Jolly, *UN Contributions to Development Thinking and Practice*, 54; Kapur, Lewis, and Webb, eds., *World Bank*, 1:153.

9. Singer, "Bretton Woods Institutions."

10. Jolly, *UN Contributions to Development Thinking and Practice*, 68.

11. Ibid., 52–59; Toye and Toye, *The UN and Global Political Economy*, 30–62, 91–109.

12. Toye and Toye, *The UN and Global Political Economy*, 79–85; Ostrower, *The United Nations and the United States*, 20; Jolly, *UN Contributions to Development Thinking and Practice*, 82.

13. Mason and Asher, *The World Bank since Bretton Woods*, 347.

14. Woods quoted in ibid., 386.

15. Jolly, *UN Contributions to Development Thinking and Practice*, 54, 68, 76–83.

16. Culpeper, *Multilateral Development Banks*, 8–10.

17. For reasons more political than economic, Russia was added to the G7 list in the 1990s, thus officially making the organization into the G8. However, as a relatively resource-poor member, Russia is a weak voice on matters pertaining to international financial institutions.

18. Sanford, *U.S. Foreign Policy and Multilateral Development Banks*, 3–8; White, *Regional Development Banks*, 51.

19. Mason and Asher, *The World Bank since Bretton Woods*, 38.

20. Mikesell, *Bretton Woods Debates*, 68.

21. Mason and Asher, *The World Bank since Bretton Woods*, 30.

22. Kapur, Lewis, and Webb, eds., *World Bank*, 1:1205.

23. For the historical reasons for this, see Mason and Asher, *The World Bank since Bretton Woods*, 50; and Kapur, Lewis, and Webb, eds., *World Bank*, 1:4.

24. Woods, "Making the IMF and the World Bank More Accountable," 87.

25. Mason and Asher, *The World Bank since Bretton Woods*, 88.

26. Kapur, Lewis, and Webb, eds., *World Bank*, 1:155; Sanford and U.S. Senate Subcommittee on Foreign Assistance, *U.S. Policy and the Multilateral Banks*, 16.

27. Another affiliate, known as the Multilateral Investment Fund (MIF), was launched in 1993 to assist countries in making reforms to help foster domestic and foreign investment; the MIF provided technical assistance for policy change, a human resources facility, and an enterprise development facility. House Appropriations Subcommittee, *Appropriations for 1994*, 130–33.

28. Culpeper, *Multilateral Development Banks*, 33; Tussie, *Inter-American Development Bank*, 21, 29.

29. Tussie, *Inter-American Development Bank*, 18, 27, 30; White, *Regional Development Banks*, 165.

30. House Appropriations Subcommittee, *Appropriations for 1972*, 298.

31. Ascher, "The World Bank and U.S. Control."

32. White, *Regional Development Banks*, 154; Tussie, *Inter-American Development Bank*, 22–23, 31.

33. See Sanford, *U.S. Foreign Policy and Multilateral Development Banks*, 51.

34. Culpeper, *Multilateral Development Banks*, 36; Kappagoda, *Asian Develop-*

ment Bank, 25. In 1989, the AsDB set up the Asian Finance and Investment Corporation to make loans to private enterprise. Unlike the World Bank's IFC, however, this organization is independent and exists completely outside the AsDB's charter. See Sherk, "Emerging Markets," 47.

35. White, *Regional Development Banks*, 55–56.

36. Ibid., 63, 80; Kappagoda, *Asian Development Bank*, 38–39.

37. Culpeper, *Multilateral Development Banks*, 31.

38. Kappagoda, *Asian Development Bank*, 39.

39. White, *Regional Development Banks*, 57.

40. Kappagoda, *Asian Development Bank*, 34; Asian Development Bank, *Annual Report 2005*.

41. Kappagoda, *Asian Development Bank*, 33, 39.

42. White, *Regional Development Banks*, 106, 112–13.

43. Sanford, *U.S. Foreign Policy and Multilateral Development Banks*, 53–54; English and Mule, *African Development Bank*, 3, 21–22.

44. English and Mule, *African Development Bank*, 22, 41.

45. Ibid., 44.

46. Ibid., 47.

47. Ibid., 26.

48. Turner, "African Development Bank."

49. O'Dwyer, "African Development Bank."

50. Culpeper, *Multilateral Development Banks*, 36.

51. Weber, "Origins."

52. CEEBN, *EBRD Decision-Making Structure*; Weber, "Origins," 20.

53. Culpeper, *Multilateral Development Banks*, 32.

54. Keohane, *After Hegemony*, 290; Yarbrough and Yarbrough, *Cooperation and Governance*, 182; Koremenos, Lipson, and Snidal, "Rational Design of International Institutions"; Downs, Rocke, and Barsoom, "Managing the Evolution of Multilateralism," 397; Nielson and Tierney, "Delegation to International Organizations."

55. Payer, *World Bank*, 20.

56. Caufield, *Masters of Illusion*, 432; Goldman, *Imperial Nature*, 360; Rich, *Mortgaging the Earth*, 376; Barnett and Finnemore, *Rules for the World*, 226.

57. In this book, I borrow ideas from both the old institutionalism and the new institutionalism. For examples of the former, see Michels, *Political Parties*, 416; Gouldner, *Patterns of Industrial Bureaucracy*, 282; Selznick, *TVA and the Grass Roots*, 274; Messinger, "Organizational Transformation," 3–10; Pfeffer and Salancik, *The External Control of Organizations*, 300; Pfeffer, "Corporate Boards of Directors"; and Denton and Zald, "From Evangelism to General Service." For seminal statements of the new institutionalism, see DiMaggio and Powell, "Iron Cage Revisited"; and Meyer and Rowan, "Institutionalized Organizations."

58. Davis, "New Directions in Corporate Governance."

59. La Porta, Lopez-de-Silanes, and Shleifer, "Corporate Ownership around the World."

60. Useem, *Executive Defense*, 289; Davis and Thompson, "Social Movement Perspective," 141.

61. Meyer and Rowan, "Institutionalized Organizations"; Scott, *Organizations*, 279–80.

62. Edelman, "Legal Ambiguity and Symbolic Structures."

63. DiMaggio and Powell, "Iron Cage Revisited"; Abrahamson, "Managerial Fads and Fashions"; March and Olsen, *Ambiguity and Choice in Organizations*, 408; Fligstein, *Transformation of Corporate Control*, 391; Allison, *Essence of Decision*, 338.

64. For a clear explanation of the MDB's relationship to financial markets, see U.S. Treasury Department, *United States Participation in the Multilateral Development Banks*, 194.

65. Kapur, Lewis, and Webb, eds., *World Bank*, 1:5.

66. Michels, *Political Parties*, 416.

67. See the discussion of "normative isomorphism" in DiMaggio and Powell, "Iron Cage Revisited."

68. Lancaster, *Foreign Aid*, 12–16.

69. These are the three major policy goals identified in an important 1982 Treasury assessment of U.S. policy toward the MDBs. See U.S. Treasury Department, *United States Participation in the Multilateral Development Banks*, 194.

70. House Appropriations Subcommittee, *Appropriations for 2005*, 265.

71. Lancaster, *Foreign Aid*, 11.

72. Miller in House Appropriations Subcommittee, *Appropriations for 1981*, 26.

73. House Appropriations Subcommittee, *Appropriations for 1974*, 4.

74. House Appropriations Subcommittee, *Appropriations for 1994*, 552.

75. House Appropriations Subcommittee, *Appropriations for 1978*, 148.

76. U.S. Treasury Department, *United States Participation in the Multilateral Development Banks*, 51.

77. House Appropriations Subcommittee, *Appropriations for 1984*, 136.

78. House Appropriations Subcommittee, *Appropriations for 1978*, 148.

79. House Appropriations Subcommittee, *Appropriations for 2003*, 272.

80. Schoultz, "U.S. Participation in Multilateral Development Banks"; Ascher, "The World Bank and U.S. Control," 124.

81. Ascher, "The World Bank and U.S. Control," 124.

82. Upton, *Multilateral Development Banks*, 52.

83. Unlike general capital increases, which are major shareholder initiatives that lead to large increases in the banks' capital resources, selective capital increases are smaller increases in capital stock, the primary effect of which is to alter voting shares among member countries.

84. Mason and Asher, *The World Bank since Bretton Woods*, 408.

85. Woods, *The Globalizers*, 28–29; Kapur, "Do as I Say."

86. Kappagoda, *Asian Development Bank*, 33, 39; Woods, *The Globalizers*, 28.

87. Since 1977, World Bank donors have prorated their contributions to those of the United States. Woods, *The Globalizers*, 29. During the first Reagan administration, a time of much lower U.S. contributions to the banks, overall funding for the MDBs declined precipitously as other donors held their contributions in check. See Lancaster, *Foreign Aid*, 43.

88. Kapur, Lewis, and Webb, eds., *World Bank*, 1:1205.

89. See Gwin, "U.S. Relations with the World Bank," 249.

Chapter Two

1. Congressional Quarterly, *Congressional Quarterly Almanac 1980*, 197–203.

2. Truman, Inaugural Address; Lancaster, *Foreign Aid*, chap. 3.

3. Lancaster, *Foreign Aid*, chap. 3; Lancaster and Van Dusen, *Organizing U.S. Foreign Aid*, 10.

4. Toye and Toye, *The UN and Global Political Economy*, 176–79.

5. Lancaster, *Foreign Aid*, chap. 3; Gwin, "U.S. Relations with the World Bank," 207.

6. Toye and Toye, *The UN and Global Political Economy*, 163–82.

7. Bello, "Iron Cage," 4.

8. Galbraith, *Nature of Mass Poverty*, 31.

9. Ibid., 27–28.

10. Hirschman, "Rise and Decline," 6.

11. Kapur, Lewis, and Webb, eds., *World Bank*, 1:115–30.

12. Ibid., 17.

13. Ibid., 1193.

14. Myrdal, *An International Economy*, 21.

15. Lal, *Poverty of "Development Economics,"* 24–25; Stern, "World Bank as 'Intellectual Actor,'" 530–31.

16. Martinussen, *Society, State, and Market*, 298; Lewis, "Development Promotion," 6–7.

17. Martinussen, *Society, State, and Market*, 52.

18. Krugman, "Rise and Fall."

19. Hirschman, "Rise and Decline," 1.

20. Lancaster, *Foreign Aid*, chap. 1; Gwin, "U.S. Relations with the World Bank," 207.

21. Gwin, "U.S. Relations with the World Bank," 212–13.

22. Hellinger, Hellinger, O'Regan, and DGAP, *Aid for Just Development*, 18–22; Lancaster, *Foreign Aid*, chap. 3; Nowels, "Foreign Aid Reform."

23. Gwin, "U.S. Relations with the World Bank," 210–11.

24. Bacon, Davidson, and Keller, *Encyclopedia of the United States Congress*, 76–77.

25. "Reuss, Henry Schoellkopf."

26. Bacon, Davidson, and Keller, *Encyclopedia of the United States Congress*, 77–82.

27. Johnson, *Congress and the Cold War*, 73.

28. Ibid., xvii.

29. Gwin, "U.S. Relations with the World Bank," 243.

30. Schoultz, "U.S. Participation in Multilateral Development Banks," 570.

31. Ibid., 574.

32. Mason and Asher, *The World Bank since Bretton Woods*, 408–11.

33. Bello, "Iron Cage," 3.

34. Jolly, *UN Contributions to Development Thinking and Practice*, 121–23.

35. Upton, *Multilateral Development Banks*, 34; Sanford, *U.S. Foreign Policy and Multilateral Development Banks*, 92; Lancaster, *Foreign Aid*, 101.

36. Anonymous Treasury official quoted in Sanford, *U.S. Foreign Policy and Multilateral Development Banks*, 92.

37. Lancaster, *Foreign Aid*, 101.

38. McCormick, "Distribution of American Assistance," 100.

39. Toye and Toye, *The UN and Global Political Economy*, 244; Spanier, *American Foreign Policy*, 171.

40. House Authorizing Subcommittee, *Providing for Additional U.S. Contributions*, 4.

41. Sanford, *U.S. Foreign Policy and Multilateral Development Banks*, 58–62; Gwin, "U.S. Relations with the World Bank," 212–13.

42. White House, *Foreign Assistance for the 'Seventies*, 2.

43. Snow, Rochford, Worden, and Benford, "Frame Alignment Processes," 464.

44. House Appropriations Subcommittee, *Appropriations for 1977*, 179.

45. House Appropriations Subcommittee, *Appropriations for 1979*, 405.

46. Blumenthal in House Appropriations Subcommittee, *Appropriations for 1981*, 26.

47. House Appropriations Subcommittee, *Appropriations for 1974*, 966.

48. Butterfield, *U.S. Development Aid*, 69.

49. House Appropriations Subcommittee, *Appropriations for 1979*, 888.

50. House Appropriations Subcommittee, *Appropriations for 1973*, 179.

51. House Appropriations Subcommittee, *Appropriations for 1978*, 234.

52. House Authorizing Subcommittee, *International Development Association Sixth Replenishment*, 131–32.

53. "Long, Clarence Dickinson."

54. House Appropriations Subcommittee, *Appropriations for 1978*, 192.

55. Ibid., 332.

56. House Appropriations Subcommittee, *Appropriations for 1974*, 568.

57. House Appropriations Subcommittee, *Appropriations for 1978*, 159.

58. House Appropriations Subcommittee, *Appropriations for 1977*, 346.

59. House Appropriations Subcommittee, *Appropriations for 1974*, 343.

60. House Appropriations Subcommittee, *Appropriations for 1980*, 669.

61. House Appropriations Subcommittee, *Appropriations for 1973*, 179. Ray Sternfeld, the alternative U.S. executive director for the IDB (hence a Treasury employee), was testifying to the House Foreign Operations Subcommittee. John Connally was the Treasury Secretary.

62. House Appropriations Subcommittee, *Appropriations for 1980*, 873.

63. Gwin, "U.S. Relations with the World Bank," 220; Sanford and U.S. Senate Subcommittee on Foreign Assistance, *U.S. Policy and the Multilateral Banks*, 12–13; Schoultz, "U.S. Participation in Multilateral Development Banks," 558.

64. Schoultz, "U.S. Participation in Multilateral Development Banks," 547.

65. Sanford and U.S. Senate Subcommittee on Foreign Assistance, *U.S. Policy and the Multilateral Banks*, 30.

66. *To Amend the Foreign Assistance Act of 1961*, 2.

67. Schoultz, "U.S. Participation in Multilateral Development Banks," 566–67.

68. Ibid., 569–70.

69. Congressional Quarterly, *Congressional Quarterly Almanac 1971*, 738.

70. Congressional Quarterly, *Congressional Quarterly Almanac 1972*, 834.

71. Congressional Quarterly, *Congressional Quarterly Almanac 1974*, 517–18.

72. Congressional Quarterly, *Congressional Quarterly Almanac 1976*, 787.

73. House Appropriations Subcommittee, *Appropriations for 1980*, 185.

74. U.S. Bureau of the Census, "Statistical Abstract" (various years).

75. Kapur, Lewis, and Webb, eds., *World Bank*, 1:1144.

Chapter Three

1. Blyth, *Great Transformations*, 284.

2. Killick, *Reaction Too Far*, 77.

3. Stein, *Presidential Economics*, 246; Blyth, *Great Transformations*, 158.

4. Blyth, *Great Transformations*, 274; Krugman, *Peddling Prosperity*, 303; Medvetz, "Production of Policy-Knowledge."

5. Feulner, "The Heritage Foundation," 67.

6. See http://www.cato.org/about.php.

7. Stein, *Presidential Economics*, 236–58; Busch, *Reagan's Victory*, 25, 153.

8. For two conservative critiques of Reaganomics, see Nau, *Myth of America's Decline*, 424; and Stein, *Presidential Economics*, 414. For a more liberal critique, see Krugman, *Peddling Prosperity*, 303.

9. Stockman, *Triumph of Politics*, 116.

10. Krugman, *Peddling Prosperity*, 713.

11. Kraft, *Mexican Rescue*, 12.

12. House Appropriations Subcommittee, *Appropriations for 1983*, 175.

13. Spanier, *American Foreign Policy*, 253.

14. U.S. Treasury Department, *United States Participation in the Multilateral Development Banks*, 153.

15. Woodard, *Future of U.S. Participation*.

16. Sanford, *U.S. Foreign Policy and Multilateral Development Banks*, 74.

17. Kegley C. and Hook, "U.S. Foreign Aid and U.N. Voting."

18. ICISI, *North-South*, 285

19. Ibid., 282–91; Jolly, *UN Contributions to Development Thinking and Practice*, 124; Rist, *History of Development*, 160.

20. McCormick, "Distribution of American Assistance," 100.

21. Livingston, "International Agenda-Setting," 317–18.

22. Nau, *Myth of America's Decline*, 208. See also Kirton, "Interview with Henry Nau."

23. G7, "Declaration of the Ottawa Summit."

24. Toye and Toye, *The UN and Global Political Economy*, 256.

25. Ibid.; Nau, *Myth of America's Decline*, 210.

26. Nau, *Myth of America's Decline*, 211–16.

27. Reagan, "Remarks at the Annual Meeting."

28. Streeten, "Development Ideas in Historical Perspective," 29.

29. Edwards, "Trade Liberalization Reforms," 43.

30. Kapur, Lewis, and Webb, eds., *World Bank*, 1:226.

31. Ibid., 483, 730.

32. Hirschman, "Rise and Decline," 18.

33. See Lal, *Poverty of "Development Economics,"* 175; Bradford, "East Asian 'Models'"; Amsden, *Asia's Next Giant*, 379; and Wade, *Governing the Market*, 438.

34. Killick, *Reaction Too Far*, 13.

35. Lal, *Poverty of "Development Economics,"* 7; Dasgupta, *New Political Economy of Development*, 19–24.

36. Stern, "World Bank as 'Intellectual Actor,'" 528.

37. Kapur, Lewis, and Webb, eds., *World Bank*, 1:511.

38. Ibid., 1198. According to Catherine Caufield, Clausen was "too hard-line and politically inept" to lead the Bank. See Caufield, *Masters of Illusion*, 178. For Susan George and Fabrizio Sabelli, the reason was the opposite—namely, that the Reagan administration thought that Clausen was not tough enough with the Third World. See George and Sabelli, *Faith and Credit*, 54. My own suspicion is that Clausen was simply a casualty of the anti-IFI hostility of the early Reagan administration.

39. Kapur, Lewis, and Webb, eds., *World Bank*, 1:511.

40. Ibid., 1193.

41. Stern, "World Bank as 'Intellectual Actor,'" 537.

42. Helleiner, "Policy-Based Program Lending," 62.

43. Stern, "World Bank as 'Intellectual Actor,'" 539.

44. Kapur, Lewis, and Webb, eds., *World Bank*, 1:331, 340.

45. Annis, "Shifting Grounds," 103.

46. Birdsall and de la Torre, *Washington Contentious*.

47. Stern, "World Bank as 'Intellectual Actor,'" 523–609.

48. Kapur, Lewis, and Webb, eds., *World Bank*, 1:506–8.

49. Livingston, "International Agenda-Setting," 321.

50. Stockman, *Triumph of Politics*, 118–19.

51. Conrow, interview with author; U.S. Treasury Department, *United States Participation in the Multilateral Development Banks*, 194.

52. Sanford, *U.S. Foreign Policy and Multilateral Development Banks*, 77.

53. U.S. Treasury Department, *United States Participation in the Multilateral Development Banks*, 58.

54. Ibid., 59.

55. Ibid., 62.

56. Ibid., 3–4.

57. Ibid., 4.

58. Ibid., 77.

59. Ibid., 67 (emphasis added).

60. Ibid., 7.

61. Ibid., 66.

62. Ibid., 7.

63. Ibid., 7–8.

64. House Authorizing Subcommittee, *Future of the Multilateral Development Banks*, 321.

65. House Appropriations Subcommittee, *Appropriations for 1981*, 26.

66. House Appropriations Subcommittee, *Appropriations for 1985*, 459.

67. House Appropriations Subcommittee, *Appropriations for 1977*, 171, 164.

68. House Authorizing Subcommittee, *To Provide for Increased Participation . . . 1971*, 89 (emphasis added).

69. House Appropriations Subcommittee, *Appropriations for 1981*, 26.

70. House Appropriations Subcommittee, *Appropriations for 1978*, 149.

71. Lebovic, "National Interests"; Butterfield, *U.S. Development Aid*, 200.

72. House Appropriations Subcommittee, *Appropriations for 1982*, 195.

73. Ibid.

74. Ibid., 199.

75. Ibid., 563.

76. Ibid.

77. Congressional Quarterly, *Congressional Quarterly Almanac 1981*.

78. Ibid., 339.

79. Ibid., 339–47.

80. House Appropriations Subcommittee, *Appropriations for 1984*, 32; Kapur, Lewis, and Webb, eds., *World Bank*, 1:1143.

81. Congressional Quarterly, *Congressional Quarterly Almanac* (various years).

82. House Authorizing Subcommittee, *Future of the Multilateral Development Banks*, 18, 8.

83. Congressional Quarterly, *Congressional Quarterly Almanac 1988*, 695; Congressional Quarterly, *Congressional Quarterly Almanac 1987*, 468.

84. Congressional Quarterly, *Congressional Quarterly Almanac 1983*, 525; Congressional Quarterly, *Congressional Quarterly Almanac 1984*, 390; Congressional Quarterly, *Congressional Quarterly Almanac 1985*, 367.

85. House Appropriations Subcommittee, *Appropriations for 1986*, 115; Congressional Quarterly, *Congressional Quarterly Almanac 1986*, 165, 369.

86. Congressional Quarterly, *Congressional Quarterly Almanac 1988*, 676, 679.

Chapter Four

1. U.S. Treasury Department, *United States Participation in the Multilateral Development Banks*, 7.

2. House Appropriations Subcommittee, *Appropriations for 1984*, 7.

3. Although the IMF refers to *lending arrangements*, not *loans*, I have chosen to use the term *loan* for purposes of simplification.

4. Dell, *On Being Grandmotherly*; De Vries and IMF, *Balance of Payments Adjustment*, 336; Babb, "Embeddedness, Inflation, and International Regimes."

5. Babb and Buira, "Mission Creep, Mission Push."

6. Boughton, *Silent Revolution*, 588–89.

7. Mosley, Harrigan, and Toye, *Aid and Power*, 27.

8. According to Kapur, Lewis, and Webb, the abandonment of policy-linked project loans occurred partly because they were seen as ineffective and partly because policy conditionality was inconsistent with the 1970s goal of increasing the volume of World Bank lending operations. See Kapur, Lewis, and Webb, eds., *World Bank*, 1:463.

9. Mason and Asher, *The World Bank since Bretton Woods*, 265.

10. Ibid., 264.

11. Kapur, Lewis, and Webb, eds., *World Bank*, 1:487–88.

12. Ibid., 465–66.

13. Ibid.; Cox and Jacobson, "Power, Polities and Politics."

14. Please, "The World Bank," 85.

15. Mosley, Harrigan, and Toye, *Aid and Power*, 31.

16. Please, "The World Bank," 85.

17. Mason and Asher, *The World Bank since Bretton Woods*, 287.

18. Kapur, Lewis, and Webb, eds., *World Bank*, 1:487.

19. House Authorizing Subcommittee, *To Provide for Increased Participation . . . 1975*, 103.

20. Kapur, Lewis, and Webb, eds., *World Bank*, 1:487.

21. McNamara and World Bank, *McNamara Years at the World Bank*, 549 (emphasis added).

22. Ibid., 549.

23. Mosley, Harrigan, and Toye, *Aid and Power*, 29.

24. Kapur, Lewis, and Webb, eds., *World Bank*, 1:507–9.

25. Ibid., 509–10.

26. Please, "The World Bank," 87.

27. Kapur, Lewis, and Webb, eds., *World Bank*, 1:24.

28. Krugman, "LDC Debt Policy," 693.

29. Kraft, *Mexican Rescue*, 5.

30. Ibid., 12.

31. Krugman, "LDC Debt Policy," 711.

32. Cline, *International Debt Reexamined*, 92.

33. Krugman, "LDC Debt Policy," 694–95.

34. Cline, *International Debt Reexamined*, 205; Krugman, "LDC Debt Policy," 693. Krugman points out that, extraordinarily, the administration maintained this position even though the Toronto meetings were held in September, a month *after* the Mexican bailout.

35. Congressional Quarterly, *Congressional Quarterly Almanac 1983*, 241–48, 536–39.

36. Silk, "The Infighting over the IMF."

37. House Appropriations Subcommittee, *Appropriations for 1983*, 34.

38. Ibid.

39. Ibid., 33.

40. House Appropriations Subcommittee, *Appropriations for 1986*, 125.

41. Stephens, "UK to Help Top Up."

42. Kapur, Lewis, and Webb, eds., *World Bank*, 1:1144–45.

43. House Appropriations Subcommittee, *Appropriations for 1984*, 139.

44. In 1981, the United States officially joined the AfDB; negotiations for initial U.S. contributions had been carried out during the Carter administration, as had negotiations for the third general capital increase for the IBRD and the notoriously controversial sixth IDA replenishment. The United States had been a member of the AfDF (but not the AfDB) since 1976.

45. House Appropriations Subcommittee, *Appropriations for 1986*, 120.

46. House Appropriations Subcommittee, *Appropriations for 1983*, 11.

47. House Appropriations Subcommittee, *Appropriations for 1985*, 460.

48. House Appropriations Subcommittee, *Appropriations for 1986*, 121.

49. House Appropriations Subcommittee, *Appropriations for 1987*, 651.

50. House Appropriations Subcommittee, *Appropriations for 1993*, 448.

51. House Appropriations Subcommittee, *Appropriations for 1985*, 460.

52. House Appropriations Subcommittee, *Appropriations for 1986*, 122.

53. For an analysis of the relative organizational incentives for the staff of the World Bank and the IMF to push loans, see Willett, "Upping the Ante." For a broad critique of the propensity of official donors to lend irresponsibly, see Easterly, *Elusive Quest for Growth*, 342.

54. Kapur, Lewis, and Webb, eds., *World Bank*, 1:1086; House Appropriations Subcommittee, *Appropriations for 1986*, 122.

55. House Appropriations Subcommittee, *Appropriations for 1983*, 8.

56. Kapur, Lewis, and Webb, eds., *World Bank*, 1:864.

57. Ibid., 869.

58. House Appropriations Subcommittee, *Appropriations for 1987*, 597. According to one experienced former U.S. Treasury official, this policy change occurred in two stages: in 1983, the bank modified its lending policies to allow it to make equity investments in private companies; in 1985, the AsDB's Board of Directors allowed the bank to undertake a modest amount of direct lending without government guarantees to private enterprises. See Sherk, "Emerging Markets," 47.

59. House Appropriations Subcommittee, *Appropriations for 1985*, 463.

60. Gwin, "U.S. Relations with the World Bank," 241, 252; Sanford, "Change and Continuity."

61. House Appropriations Subcommittee, *Appropriations for 1983*, 9.

62. House Appropriations Subcommittee, *Appropriations for 1984*, 134.

63. Ibid., 135.

64. World Bank, *Annual Report 1987*, 60; World Bank, *Annual Report 1983*, 19.

65. Conrow, interview with author.

66. Leland, interview with author.

67. House Appropriations Subcommittee, *Appropriations for 1983*, 7.

68. Ibid.

69. Ibid., 73.

70. Ibid.

71. House Appropriations Subcommittee, *Appropriations for 1986*, 122.

72. House Authorizing Subcommittee, *To Provide for Increased Participation . . . 1985*, 27.

73. It is not clear whether *macroeconomic* in this context referred exclusively to the usual variables used by international economists (e.g., the exchange rate, inflation, GDP) or to a broader set of issues pertaining to overall economic regime (e.g., the role of the state in the economy).

74. House Appropriations Subcommittee, *Appropriations for 1983*, 7.

75. Ibid., 73.

76. House Appropriations Subcommittee, *Appropriations for 1984*, 134.

77. House Appropriations Subcommittee, *Appropriations for 1986*, 123.

78. Ibid., 122.

79. U.S. Treasury Department, *United States Participation in the Multilateral Development Banks*, 7.

80. IDB, *Annual Report* (various years).

81. U.S. Treasury Department, *United States Participation in the Multilateral Development Banks*, 177.

82. House Appropriations Subcommittee, *Appropriations for 1984*, 66.

83. These data match up with the summary statistics presented in Kapur, Lewis, and Webb, eds., *World Bank*, 1:520.

84. Ibid., 613.

85. House Appropriations Subcommittee, *Appropriations for 1982*, 577; Senate Appropriations Subcommittee, *Appropriations for Fiscal Year 1982*, 347; House Appropriations Subcommittee, *Appropriations for 1982*, 347.

86. House Appropriations Subcommittee, *Appropriations for 1985*, 496; House Appropriations Subcommittee, *Appropriations for 1986*, 29; House Authorizing Subcommittee, *To Provide for Increased Participation . . . 1985*, 29.

87. Caufield, *Masters of Illusion*, 201.

88. House Authorizing Subcommittee, *U.S. Role in Development Banks*, 5.

89. House Appropriations Subcommittee, *Appropriations for 1985*, 461.

90. Ibid., 496.

91. Fleming, "Time 'Not Ripe.'"

92. Please, "The World Bank," 87.

Chapter Five

1. The policies included fiscal discipline, shifting priorities for public expenditure to areas (such as health and education) where the private sector was least effective, tax reform, market-determined interest rates, competitive exchange rates, trade liberalization, the encouragement of foreign direct investment, deregulation, secure property rights, and the privatization of state-owned industries. See Williamson, introduction to *Latin American Adjustment*, 1, 8–17.

2. World Bank, *Accelerated Development*, 198.

3. Naím, "Fads and Fashions in Economic Reforms"; Killick, *Reaction Too Far*, 77.

4. Williamson, "What Washington Means by Policy Reform," 19.

5. Ibid., 7.

6. U.S. Treasury Department, *United States Participation in the Multilateral Development Banks*, 7.

7. See ibid., 175.

8. Montagnon, "Baker's Third World Debt Plan."

9. Cline, *International Debt Reexamined*, 208–9.

10. House Appropriations Subcommittee, *Appropriations for 1987*, 596.

11. Ibid., 595.

12. Ibid., 596.

13. Ibid., 664.

14. Ibid., 595.

15. World Bank, *Accelerated Development*, 38.

16. World Bank, *World Development Report 1983*, 24, 85–86.

17. House Appropriations Subcommittee, *Appropriations for 1986*, 123.

18. House Appropriations Subcommittee, *Appropriations for 1987*, 597.

19. Ibid., 595.

20. Ibid., 596.

21. Ibid.

22. Ibid., 597.

23. Ibid., 595.

24. Fleming, "Budget Ghost."

25. Riemer, "Washington's Gambit."

26. IMF international financial statistics summarized in Cline, *International Debt Reexamined*, 44.

27. Gwin, "U.S. Relations with the World Bank," 234.

28. "Group of Leading US Decision-Makers."

29. Fleming, "Budget Ghost," 16.

30. Krugman, "LDC Debt Policy," 713.

31. Kilborn, "Assertive Economic Stance."

32. World Bank, *World Development Report 1981*, 55, 66.

33. Stern, "World Bank as 'Intellectual Actor,'" 539.

34. World Bank, *World Development Report 1985*, 66.

35. Rowen, "World Bank to Rethink Policy Loans."

36. Rowen, "Clausen Sees Bigger World Bank Role."

37. House Authorizing Subcommittee, *U.S. Role in Development Banks*, 5.

38. House Appropriations Subcommittee, *Appropriations for 1986*, 137.

39. Rowen, "World Bank to Rethink Policy Loans."

40. Riemer, "Jim Baker's Plan."

41. Cline, *International Debt Reexamined*, 218–22.

42. House Appropriations Subcommittee, *Appropriations for 1988*, 649.

43. Ibid., 1481.

44. Ibid., 1049.

45. House Appropriations Subcommittee, *Appropriations for 1991*, 710.

46. Ibid., 709–10; House Appropriations Subcommittee, *Appropriations for 1988*, 651.

47. House Appropriations Subcommittee, *Appropriations for 1989*, 1043.

48. Kapur, Lewis, and Webb, eds., *World Bank*, 1:1205; House Appropriations Subcommittee, *Appropriations for 1990*, 739.

49. House Appropriations Subcommittee, *Appropriations for 1989*, 1086.

50. House Appropriations Subcommittee, *Appropriations for 1992*, 341.

51. Ibid.

52. "Senior US Treasury Secretary"; Gourlay, "US Calls for Review."

53. Asian Development Bank, *Annual Report 1987*.

54. Tenorio, "Asian Development Bank."

55. Asian Development Bank, *Annual Report 1987*, 35–46, 41.

56. Kapur, Lewis, and Webb, eds., *World Bank*, 1:244.

57. George and Sabelli, *Faith and Credit*, 126.

58. "Reform at the World Bank."

59. Kapur, Lewis, and Webb, eds., *World Bank*, 1:1200.

60. House Appropriations Subcommittee, *Appropriations for 1989*, 1075.

61. House Appropriations Subcommittee, *Appropriations for 1992*, 448.

62. House Appropriations Subcommittee, *Appropriations for 1988*, 652.

63. House Appropriations Subcommittee, *Appropriations for 1990*, 822.

64. Kapur, Lewis, and Webb, eds., *World Bank*, 1:764.

65. House Appropriations Subcommittee, *Appropriations for 1993*, 417–18.

66. Dell, "Question of Cross-Conditionality," 557.

67. Polak, "The World Bank and the IMF," 501; Woods, *The Globalizers*, 49.

68. Dell, "Question of Cross-Conditionality," 557; Polak, "The World Bank and the IMF," 473–521; Feinberg, "Changing Relationship," 555.

69. Babb and Buira, "Mission Creep, Mission Push."

70. Kapur, Lewis, and Webb, eds., *World Bank*, 1:1189.

71. House Appropriations Subcommittee, *Appropriations for 1989*, 1086.

72. House Appropriations Subcommittee, *Appropriations for 1990*, 1090.

73. Culpeper, *Multilateral Development Banks*, 42.

74. House Appropriations Subcommittee, *Appropriations for 1993*, 448.

75. Culpeper, *Multilateral Development Banks*, 42.

76. House Appropriations Subcommittee, *Appropriations for 1989*, 1063.

77. "Loan to Nicaragua Gets Backing."

78. Farnsworth, "U.S. Blocks Bank Loan."

79. De Young, "Shultz Intervenes on Loan."

80. Friedland, "Dispute Expected over Lending."

81. Ibid.

82. On the collapse of negotiations in March 1987, Treasury Secretary Baker told the press that the United States would prepare for increasing World Bank lending to Latin American countries. See "Baker Withdraws Compromise."

83. Pine, "U.S. Faces Showdown."

84. Ibid.

85. Rowen, "U.S. and Canada Seeking Veto Power."

86. House Appropriations Subcommittee, *Appropriations for 1989*, 1062.

87. Kilborn, "Chief of Latin Lender."

88. Farnsworth, "Restructuring Planned by Latin Aid Bank."

89. "U.S. Drops Demand."

90. House Appropriations Subcommittee, *Appropriations for 1990*, 826.

91. House Appropriations Subcommittee, *Appropriations for 1991*, 723.

92. House Appropriations Subcommittee, *Appropriations for 1987*, 665.

93. See McNamara's testimony in House Authorizing Subcommittee, *Mandate for Development*, 12.

94. Wade, "Art of Paradigm Maintenance."

95. After delivering his testimony on the Baker Plan to the Senate Foreign Operations Subcommittee in the spring of 1986, Baker received expressions of strong support from both Alfonse D'Amato and Robert Kasten. See Senate Appropriations Subcommittee, *Appropriations for Fiscal Year 1987*, 25, 26.

96. Congressional Quarterly, *Congressional Quarterly Almanac 1986*, 162–71; Congressional Quarterly, *Congressional Quarterly Almanac 1987*, 466–74.

97. Rowe, "Fed Casts Doubt on Bradley Plan."

Chapter Six

1. House Appropriations Subcommittee, *Appropriations for 1987*, 595.

2. Kuczynski and Williamson, eds., *After the Washington Consensus*; Naím, "Fads and Fashions in Economic Reforms"; Rodrik, "Goodbye Washington Consensus."

3. House Authorizing Subcommittee, *Authorizing Contributions to IDA, GEF, and ADF*, 3.

4. See Pollin, *Contours of Descent*, 238; Baker, *The United States since 1980*; and Meeropol, *Surrender*, 377.

5. House Appropriations Subcommittee, *Appropriations for 1995*, 1266.

6. House Appropriations Subcommittee, *Appropriations for 1996*, 90.

7. House Appropriations Subcommittee, *Appropriations for 1998*, 119.

8. House Appropriations Subcommittee, *Appropriations for 1994*, 552.

9. House Authorizing Subcommittee, *Administration's Plan for Authorization of FY 96 Funding*, 9.

10. House Appropriations Subcommittee, *Appropriations for 2001*, 248.

11. Ibid.

12. House Appropriations Subcommittee, *Appropriations for 2000*, 55.

13. Senate Appropriations Subcommittee, *Appropriations for Fiscal Year 1999*, 168.

14. House Appropriations Subcommittee, *Appropriations for 2000*, 249.

15. Culpeper, *Multilateral Development Banks*, 42.

16. House Appropriations Subcommittee, *Appropriations for 1996*, 202.

17. House Appropriations Subcommittee, *Appropriations for 1995*, 195.

18. House Appropriations Subcommittee, *Appropriations for 1994*, 551.

19. Senate Appropriations Subcommittee, *Appropriations for Fiscal Year 1994*, 533.

20. Udall, "The World Bank and Public Accountability," 395.

21. House Appropriations Subcommittee, *Appropriations for 1994*, 555.

22. House Appropriations Subcommittee, *Appropriations for 1996*, 92.

23. Congressional Quarterly, *Congressional Quarterly Almanac 1993*, 603.

24. House Appropriations Subcommittee, *Appropriations for 1995*, 529.

25. Ibid., 195.

26. English and Mule, *African Development Bank*, 48.

27. Turner, "African Development Bank."

28. House Appropriations Subcommittee, *Appropriations for 1998*, 141.

29. House Appropriations Subcommittee, *Appropriations for 2000*, 196.

30. House Appropriations Subcommittee, *Appropriations for 1997*, 138.

31. House Appropriations Subcommittee, *Appropriations for 1994*, 557.

32. House Appropriations Subcommittee, *Appropriations for 1999*, 193.

33. House Appropriations Subcommittee, *Appropriations for 1996*, 198.

34. House Appropriations Subcommittee, *Appropriations for 1998*, 138.

35. House Appropriations Subcommittee, *Appropriations for 2000*, 246.

36. House Appropriations Subcommittee, *Appropriations for 1998*, 129.

37. House Appropriations Subcommittee, *Appropriations for 2000*, 186.

38. House Authorizing Subcommittee, *Authorizing Contributions to IDA, GEF, and ADF*, 14–15.

39. Wolfensohn and Bourguignon, "Development and Poverty Reduction."

40. "World Bank Report."

41. House Authorizing Subcommittee, *Structural Adjustment and Economic Development*, 14.

42. Ibid., 55 (emphasis added).

43. G7, "Economic Declaration: Building World Partnership."

44. House Appropriations Subcommittee, *Appropriations for 1994*, 396.

45. Weber, "Origins," 11.

46. House Appropriations Subcommittee, *Appropriations for 1994*, 100.

47. House Appropriations Subcommittee, *Appropriations for 1996*, 146.

48. House Appropriations Subcommittee, *Appropriations for 1995*, 1310; House Appropriations Subcommittee, *Appropriations for 2000*, 249–53.

49. House Appropriations Subcommittee, *Appropriations for 1996*, 192; House Appropriations Subcommittee, *Appropriations for 1998*, 133.

50. Rich, *World Bank under James Wolfensohn*, 51.

51. House Appropriations Subcommittee, *Appropriations for 1999*, 15.

52. Ibid., 143.

53. Ibid., 80–85.

54. House Appropriations Subcommittee, *Appropriations for 2002*, 119.

55. Ibid., 159, 163, 119.

56. Congressional Quarterly, *Congressional Quarterly Almanac 1995*, 11–40.

57. Congressional Quarterly, *Congressional Quarterly Almanac* (various years).

58. In using the term *civil society*, I do not intend to take a position in the intellectual debates that rage around this concept; instead, I use it as a convenient shorthand referring to organizations outside the state and conventional political parties that are not merely representative of organized economic interest groups.

59. Cornia, Jolly, and Stewart, *Adjustment with a Human Face*.

60. See Kapur, Lewis, and Webb, eds., *World Bank*, 352; and Mosley, Harrigan, and Toye, *Aid and Power*, xxi.

61. House Appropriations Subcommittee, *Appropriations for 1988*, 152.

62. House Appropriations Subcommittee, *Appropriations for 1990*, 179.

63. Ibid., 932–42.

64. House Authorizing Subcommittee, *Administration's Authorization Requests for International Financial Institutions*, 42.

65. House Appropriations Subcommittee, *Appropriations for 1995*, 265.

66. Ibid., 553.

67. Ibid., 234, 246.

68. Kapur, Lewis, and Webb, eds., *World Bank*, 1:367.

69. Nelson, *The World Bank and Non-Governmental Organizations*, 62.

70. The Bretton Woods Committee was founded in 1985 as a bipartisan group of former government officials committed to mobilizing grassroots U.S. political support for the World Bank and the IMF. It explicitly aimed at ameliorating the harmful impact of congressional controversies and cuts in appropriations. See Auerbach, "Group Formed to Promote IMF, World Bank."

71. Kapur, Lewis, and Webb, eds., *World Bank*, 1:368.

72. Kapur, Lewis, and Webb, eds., *World Bank*, 1:368.

73. House Appropriations Subcommittee, *Appropriations for 1989*, 1043.

74. Kapur, Lewis, and Webb, eds., *World Bank*, 1:370; World Bank, *World Development Report 1990*, iii, 79.

75. House Appropriations Subcommittee, *Appropriations for 1992*, 407–8.

76. House Appropriations Subcommittee, *Appropriations for 1994*, 100.

77. House Appropriations Subcommittee, *Appropriations for 1999*, 200; House Appropriations Subcommittee, *Appropriations for 2000*, 196.

78. House Appropriations Subcommittee, *Appropriations for 1999*, 215.

79. House Appropriations Subcommittee, *Appropriations for 2000*, 196, 249.

80. Caufield, *Masters of Illusion*, 106–21.

81. The source for total loan commitments is World Bank, *Annual Report* (various years); that for social sector loans is World Bank, "Project Database."

82. See House Appropriations Subcommittee, *Appropriations for 2002*, 213, 222. For a discussion of congressional support for microcredit, see the text of HR 1143: U.S. Congress, *Microenterprise for Self-Reliance and International Anti-Corruption Act of 2000*.

83. House Appropriations Subcommittee, *Appropriations for 1994*, 100.

84. House Appropriations Subcommittee, *Appropriations for 1996*, 147.

85. House Appropriations Subcommittee, *Appropriations for 2001*, 253.

86. Nelson, *The World Bank and Non-Governmental Organizations*, 235.

87. House Appropriations Subcommittee, *Appropriations for 2001*, 127.

88. Cheru, "Building and Supporting PRSPs."

89. Raghavan, "Speed Debt Relief."

90. House Appropriations Subcommittee, *Appropriations for 1997*, 17; House Appropriations Subcommittee, *Appropriations for 1999*, 22.

91. See House Appropriations Subcommittee, *Appropriations for 1983*, 8.

92. Weissman, "Phasing Out User Fees"; House Authorizing Subcommittee, *FY 2002 Authorization Requests for International Programs*, 44.

93. Reich, "Escape from the Global Sweatshop."

94. Dunne, "Seeking."

95. Urakami, "G-8 Agree to Reinforce ILO."

96. House Appropriations Subcommittee, *Appropriations for 2000*, 26.

97. Dunne, "US Pushes Workers' Rights."

98. House Appropriations Subcommittee, *Appropriations for 1999*, 151.

99. Ibid., 152.

100. House Appropriations Subcommittee, *Appropriations for 2000*, 190.

101. Ibid.

102. Ibid., 26.

103. House Appropriations Subcommittee, *Appropriations for 2002*, 227.

104. Congressional Quarterly, *Congressional Quarterly Almanac 1998*, 2–54.

105. Morris Goldstein, "Strengthening the International Financial Architecture."

106. Balassa, *Toward Renewed Economic Growth*, 205; Williamson, ed., *Latin American Adjustment*.

107. IFIAC, *Report of the International Financial Institution Advisory Commission*.

108. U.S. Treasury Department, "Response to the Report of the International Financial Institution Advisory Commission."

109. "IDA Deputies Make Little Progress."

110. "Latin America: U.S. to Press Regional Bank."

111. Rowley, "Bank Gets Mandate."

112. Rowley, "Developing Nations Baulk."

113. "World Bank/IDA-2."

114. House Appropriations Subcommittee, *Appropriations for 1998*, 140.

115. "Japan, U.S. Split."

116. Naím, "Fads and Fashions in Economic Reforms," 506.

117. Wolfensohn and Bourguignon, "Development and Poverty Reduction." 3.

118. Fine, Lapavitsas, and Pincus, "Development Policy in the Twenty-First

Century"; Fine, "Economics Imperialism"; Deraniyagala, "From Washington to Post-Washington."

119. Sen, *Development as Freedom.*

120. World Bank, *World Development Report 1997*, iii.

121. For a discussion of this trend, see Rodrik, "Goodbye Washington Consensus," 973–87. For a prominent example, see Acemoglu, Johnson, and Robinson, "The Colonial Origins of Comparative Development."

122. These arguments are summarized and elaborated in Stiglitz, *Globalization and Its Discontents*, 282.

123. Gopinath, "Wolfensohn Agonistes"; Wade, "US Hegemony and the World Bank."

124. Gopinath, "Wolfensohn Agonistes."

125. Wade, "US Hegemony and the World Bank," 232.

126. Hall, "Policy Paradigms," 275.

Chapter Seven

1. Tomkins, "Bush Lauds African Move."

2. Sikkink and Smith, "Infrastructures for Change."

3. Johnson, *Congress and the Cold War*, 94–95; Arnson, *Crossroads*, 3–9; Sikkink, *Mixed Signals*, 39–52.

4. Sikkink, *Mixed Signals*, 52–56; Arnson, *Crossroads*, 9.

5. Schoultz, "U.S. Participation in Multilateral Development Banks," 537–74.

6. Apodaca, "U.S. Human Rights Policy," 67.

7. CIP, *Multilateral Aid Law*, 5.

8. Ibid., 6.

9. Schoultz, "U.S. Participation in Multilateral Development Banks," 559–62.

10. House Appropriations Subcommittee, *Appropriations for 1988*, 737–50.

11. Senate Appropriations Subcommittee, *Appropriations for Fiscal Year 1979*, 195.

12. Sanford and U.S. Senate Subcommittee on Foreign Assistance, *U.S. Policy and the Multilateral Banks*, 17.

13. House Appropriations Subcommittee, *Appropriations for 1980*, 70–71.

14. Ibid., 660.

15. U.S. Treasury Department, *Treasury International Programs — Budget Request, FY 2006.*

16. Congressional Quarterly, *Congressional Quarterly Almanac 1976*, 787.

17. House Appropriations Subcommittee, *Appropriations for 1988*, 737–50.

18. Jolly, *UN Contributions to Development Thinking and Practice*, 286.

19. Wade, "Greening the Bank," 618, 628.

20. Ibid., 618–25.

21. Helvarg, "The Three Horsemen."

22. House Appropriations Subcommittee, *Appropriations for 1986*, 123.

23. Wade, "Greening the Bank," 638.

24. Rich, *Mortgaging the Earth*, 112.

25. Ibid., 113.

26. Ibid., 119.

27. Ibid., 122–23.

28. Ibid.

29. House Appropriations Subcommittee, *Appropriations for 1987*.

30. Congressional Quarterly, *Congressional Quarterly Almanac 1986*, 162–71.

31. Rich, *Mortgaging the Earth*, 125.

32. House Appropriations Subcommittee, *Appropriations for 1991*, 313.

33. The passing of this authorizations bill was an unusual event. Since the 1980s, authorizing legislation for the MDBs has generally been written into appropriations bills as a way of streamlining the process.

34. Wirth, "Partnership Advocacy," 66.

35. House Appropriations Subcommittee, *Appropriations for 1989*, 523.

36. Rich, *Mortgaging the Earth*, 146.

37. House Appropriations Subcommittee, *Appropriations for 1989*, 1043.

38. House Appropriations Subcommittee, *Appropriations for 1991*, 314.

39. Ibid.

40. Ibid., 314–15.

41. House Appropriations Subcommittee, *Appropriations for 1990*, 815.

42. House Appropriations Subcommittee, *Appropriations for 1993*, 449.

43. Ibid., 24.

44. House Appropriations Subcommittee, *Appropriations for 1989*, 523–24; House Appropriations Subcommittee, *Appropriations for 1991*, 314–15.

45. House Appropriations Subcommittee, *Appropriations for 1992*, 450.

46. House Appropriations Subcommittee, *Appropriations for 1993*.

47. House Appropriations Subcommittee, *Appropriations for 1999*, 219.

48. Senate Appropriations Subcommittee, *Appropriations for Fiscal Year 1992*, 83.

49. Ibid., 68.

50. Udall, "The World Bank and Public Accountability," 400–401.

51. Senate Appropriations Subcommittee, *Appropriations for Fiscal Year 1993*, 22.

52. House Appropriations Subcommittee, *Appropriations for 1994*, 101.

53. Udall, "The World Bank and Public Accountability," 413.

54. Fox, "World Bank Inspection Panel," 131.

55. Udall, "The World Bank and Public Accountability," 413.

56. Ibid., 402; "World Bank: Got a Light?" 81.

57. Taylor, "House Panel Cuts Contribution."

58. House Appropriations Subcommittee, *Appropriations for 1996*, 173.

59. Ibid., 192.

60. Senate Appropriations Subcommittee, *Appropriations for Fiscal Year 1994*, 555.

61. House Appropriations Subcommittee, *Appropriations for 2001*, 253.

62. House Appropriations Subcommittee, *Appropriations for 2000*, 229.

63. U.S. Treasury Department, *Treasury International Programs — Budget Request, FY 2006*, 73.

64. House Appropriations Subcommittee, *Appropriations for 1998*, 145.

65. House Appropriations Subcommittee, *Appropriations for 2001*, 207.

66. Ibid.

67. Wirth, "Partnership Advocacy," 67.

68. Nelson, "Agendas, Accountability, and Legitimacy"; Gutner, *Banking on the Environment*, 9; Fox and Brown, introduction; Wade, "Greening the Bank," 611–734.

69. Nelson, "Agendas, Accountability, and Legitimacy," 136.

70. Gutner, *Banking on the Environment*, 3, 94.

71. As Robert Wade points out, the Bank portrays these changes as responding to an internal process of learning when, in fact, the greening of the World Bank was overwhelmingly driven by external pressures: "The 'logic of discovery' of new facts has played only a minor role." Wade, "Greening the Bank," 731.

72. Ibid., 731.

73. See the Bank Information Center's Web site: http://www.bicusa.org.

74. Fifty Years Is Enough, "How Structural Adjustment Destroys the Environment."

75. Senate Appropriations Subcommittee, *Appropriations for Fiscal Year 1991*, 194.

76. Rowley, "World Bank to Step Up Infrastructure Role."

77. Gutner, *Banking on the Environment*, 3; Mallaby, *World's Banker*, 339.

78. Meyer and Rowan, "Institutionalized Organizations"; Scott, *Organizations*, 279–80.

79. Environmental Defense Fund, Friends of the Earth, and International Rivers Network, *Gambling with People's Lives*.

80. Rich, *Mortgaging the Earth*, 176.

81. Gutner, "World Bank Environmental Reform," 777.

82. Donnelly, "Proclaiming Jubilee," 159.

83. Roodman, Peterson, and Worldwatch Institute, *Still Waiting for the Jubilee*, 6–7, 42–44.

84. Ibid., 55.

85. Donnelly, "Proclaiming Jubilee," 162.

86. Wirth, "Partnership Advocacy."

87. House Appropriations Subcommittee, *Appropriations for 1998*; Congressional Quarterly, *Congressional Quarterly Almanac 1997*, 9-37–9-43.

88. Roodman, Peterson, and Worldwatch Institute, *Still Waiting for the Jubilee*, 58; House Appropriations Subcommittee, *Appropriations for 1998*, 140.

89. House Appropriations Subcommittee, *Appropriations for 2000*, 55; House Appropriations Subcommittee, *Appropriations for 2001*, 251.

90. Donnelly, "Proclaiming Jubilee," 165–67.

91. Kahn, "Relief for the Poorest."

92. Congressional Quarterly, *Congressional Quarterly Almanac 1999*, 2-62–2-80.

93. Congressional Quarterly, *Congressional Quarterly Almanac 2000*, 2075.

94. House Appropriations Subcommittee, *Appropriations for 2001*, 242.

95. Ibid., 259. David Roodman of the Worldwatch Institute argued against the HIPC Trust Fund because it insulated multilateral lenders from their past mistakes; it was unnecessary, given the considerable capital reserves of the World Bank and the IMF; and it created an asymmetry between the treatment of borrowing governments (who had to go through an elaborate process to prove their creditworthiness) and the treatment of IFIs (who were given money without strings attached). See Roodman, Peterson, and Worldwatch Institute, *Still Waiting for the Jubilee*, 71.

96. Senate Appropriations Subcommittee, *Appropriations for Fiscal Year 2001*, 141–42.

97. House Appropriations Subcommittee, *Appropriations for 2001*, 287.

98. House Appropriations Subcommittee, *Appropriations for 2002*, 106.

99. Helleiner and Cameron, "Another World Order?" 133.

100. Ibid., 127.

101. Frankel, "G-7 Backs Debt Plan."

102. Ibid.; Helleiner and Cameron, "Another World Order?" 128.

103. Cameron, "Another World Order?"

104. Weiss, *Debt Relief*.

105. Blustein, "Debt Cut Is Set."

106. Ibid.

107. The Netherlands was the donor government specifically concerned about the defunding of the, IDA. See Blustein, "IMF, World Bank Advance."

108. Bachelet, "IDB OK's Massive Debt Relief Package."

109. Jubilee USA Network, "Background Briefing and Frequently Asked Questions."

110. Helleiner and Cameron, "Another World Order?" 128, 129.

111. Ibid., 134.

112. Mallaby, "NGOs."

113. Nelson, Nelson, "Agendas, Accountability, and Legitimacy," 151.

114. Ibid., 138, 148, 151. Jonathan Sanford mentions a monthly joint conference of the Bank Information Center (a Washington NGO) and USAID's Office of Donor Coordination as a particularly important venue for NGOs to raise their concerns to the Treasury. See Sanford, "U.S. Policy towards the MDBs."

115. Sanford and U.S. Senate Subcommittee on Foreign Assistance, *U.S. Policy and the Multilateral Banks*, 33.

Chapter Eight

1. *Le Monde* and the *Financial Times* cited in Mallaby, "Blinkered by His Big Ideas."
2. Jervis, "Understanding the Bush Doctrine."
3. White House, "President Outlines U.S. Plan."
4. Engler, "Abandoning the World Bank," 58.
5. Ibid., 59; Lancaster, *Foreign Aid*, 91; Soederberg, "American Empire and 'Excluded States.'"
6. Novak, "Who Is Behind Bush Economic Policy?" 8.
7. Baker and Blustein, "Treasury Secretary to Step Down."
8. Novak, "Who Is Behind Bush Economic Policy?"
9. Baker and Blustein, "Treasury Secretary to Step Down."
10. Frankel, "Bush's Spectacular Failure," 27.
11. Ibid., 25.
12. Ibid., 24; Engler, "Abandoning the World Bank," 57.
13. Steinberger, "Neo-Economics," 42.
14. Dull, "Why PART?"
15. Ibid.; OMB, "Program Assessment Rating Tool (PART)."
16. Engler, "Abandoning the World Bank," 59; Lancaster, *Foreign Aid*, 91; Soederberg, "American Empire and 'Excluded States.'"
17. Lancaster, *Foreign Aid*, 92–93.
18. Helms quoted in ibid., 93.
19. Taylor, *Global Financial Warriors*, 101–2.
20. Catan and Alden, "IMF's Delay."
21. Blustein, "O'Neill Again Criticizes World Bank."
22. Phillips, Karp, and King, "IMF Approves $30 Billion Loan."
23. House Appropriations Subcommittee, *Appropriations for 2002*, 87.
24. Taylor mentions "raising productivity growth" in his autobiography. See Taylor, *Global Financial Warriors*, 304. The productivity rhetoric disappeared from the Treasury budget justifications after Taylor's departure in 2005.
25. House Appropriations Subcommittee, *Appropriations for 2003*, 271.
26. House Appropriations Subcommittee, *Appropriations for 2005*, 115.
27. Ibid., 265.
28. U.S. Treasury Department, *Treasury International Programs — Budget Request, FY 2007*.
29. House Appropriations Subcommittee, *Appropriations for 2004*, 258.
30. See U.S. Treasury Department, *Treasury International Programs — Budget Request, FY 2007*, 28–29; and Tan, *Debt and Conditionality*, 10–12.

31. House Appropriations Subcommittee, *Appropriations for 2003*, 207, 212. Whereas the Treasury later reported success getting the AsDB to adopt more governance-related policies, the social spending agenda was soon dropped.

32. House Appropriations Subcommittee, *Appropriations for 2005*, 121.

33. U.S. Treasury Department, *Treasury International Programs — Budget Request, FY 2006*.

34. Ibid., 50.

35. U.S. Treasury Department, *Treasury International Programs — Budget Request, FY 2007*, 114.

36. Ibid.

37. U.S. Treasury Department, *Treasury International Programs — Budget Request, FY 2006*, 55.

38. Ibid.

39. House Appropriations Subcommittee, *Appropriations for 2005*, 157.

40. U.S. Treasury Department, *Treasury International Programs — Budget Request, FY 2007*, 18.

41. U.S. Treasury Department, *Treasury International Programs — Budget Request, FY 2008*.

42. "World Bank: E Asia Developing Nations Need Infrastructure"; "World Bank: Latin America Needs Infrastructure Investment."

43. For a discussion of vested bureaucratic interests in the continuation of the IBRD, see Einhorn, "Reforming the World Bank."

44. Mallaby, *World's Banker*, 339.

45. "World Bank Degradation."

46. Evidently, Taylor's influence was also undercut by Summers's doubling of the permanent international economics staff before departing the Treasury, which forced Taylor to work with a team not of his own choosing. See "John Taylor's Woes."

47. Taylor, *Global Financial Warriors*, 138–39.

48. Ibid., 142.

49. House Appropriations Subcommittee, *Appropriations for 1984*, 140.

50. House Appropriations Subcommittee, *Appropriations for 2001*, 225. Getting the MDBs to evaluate results was also a recommendation of a 1998 report published by the Center for Strategic and International Studies. See CSIS, *The United States and the Multilateral Development Banks*.

51. IFIAC, *Report of the International Financial Institution Advisory Commission*.

52. Baker and Wolffe, "'Kinder, Gentler' Deal."

53. Taylor, *Global Financial Warriors*, 135.

54. Ibid., 142.

55. House Appropriations Subcommittee, *Appropriations for 2002*, 121.

56. House Appropriations Subcommittee, *Appropriations for 2003*, 273.

57. USGAO, *Developing Countries*, 36.

58. House Appropriations Subcommittee, *Appropriations for 2003*, 290.

59. Ibid., 296.

60. Ibid., 271; House Appropriations Subcommittee, *Appropriations for 2002*, 121; House Appropriations Subcommittee, *Appropriations for 2003*, 214; House Appropriations Subcommittee, *Appropriations for 2004*, 104.

61. U.S. Treasury Department, *Treasury International Programs — Budget Request, FY 2008*, 17.

62. House Appropriations Subcommittee, *Appropriations for 2003*, 107.

63. House Appropriations Subcommittee, *Appropriations for 2004*, 260.

64. U.S. Treasury Department, "Treasury Under Secretary John B. Taylor."

65. House Appropriations Subcommittee, *Appropriations for 2004*, 102, 103.

66. U.S. Treasury Department, *Treasury International Programs — Budget Request, FY 2006*, 46.

67. Ibid.

68. U.S. Treasury Department, *Treasury International Programs — Budget Request, FY 2007*, 10.

69. U.S. Treasury Department, *Treasury International Programs — Budget Request, FY 2008*, 13.

70. U.S. Treasury Department, *Treasury International Programs — Budget Request, FY 2007*, 45.

71. House Appropriations Subcommittee, *Appropriations for 2003*, 199, 168.

72. U.S. Treasury Department, *Treasury International Programs — Budget Request, FY 2006*, 28, 10, 62.

73. House Appropriations Subcommittee, *Appropriations for 2004*, 194.

74. U.S. Treasury Department, *Treasury International Programs — Budget Request, FY 2006*, 112.

75. U.S. Treasury Department, *Treasury International Programs — Budget Request, FY 2008*, 51.

76. House Appropriations Subcommittee, *Appropriations for 2004*, 103.

77. U.S. Treasury Department, *Treasury International Programs — Budget Request, FY 2008*, 46.

78. U.S. Treasury Department, *Treasury International Programs — Budget Request, FY 2007*, 41; U.S. Treasury Department, *Treasury International Programs — Budget Request, FY 2008*, 47.

79. U.S. Treasury Department, *Treasury International Programs — Budget Request, FY 2008*, 36, 54.

80. Willard, "Rich Countries at Loggerheads."

81. Phillips, "Treasury Secretary O'Neill Pushes Plan."

82. Roodman, Peterson, and Worldwatch Institute, *Still Waiting for the Jubilee*, 86.

83. Mallaby, "Saving the World Bank"; Sanford, "IDA Grants and HIPC Debt Cancellation."

84. Phillips, "Treasury Secretary O'Neill Pushes Plan."

85. Rebello, "World Bank Favors Big Increase."

86. Crutsinger, "Administration Hails Agreement."

87. U.S. Treasury Department, *Treasury International Programs — Budget Request, FY 2006*, 47, 101.

88. House Appropriations Subcommittee, *Appropriations for 2005*, 265.

89. U.S. Treasury Department, *Treasury International Programs — Budget Request, FY 2007*, 51.

90. Alden, Dinmore, and Swann, "Wolfowitz Nomination a Shock."

91. Mallaby, "Blinkered by His Big Ideas," 2.

92. Blustein, "World Bank Staffers Protest Appointments"; Blustein, "Muttering at the World Bank"; Balls, "Wolfowitz Aides Spark World Bank Dispute."

93. House Appropriations Subcommittee, *Appropriations for 2005*, 112; U.S. Treasury Department, *Treasury International Programs — Budget Request, FY 2006*.

94. "European Critics Inflict Defeat on Wolfowitz."

95. Anderson, Ward, and Goodman, "Europeans Wince, Wait"; Goodman, "Ending Battle, Wolfowitz Resigns."

96. Guha, "World Bank Confirms Zoellick."

97. Beattie, "World Bank Appoints New Chief Economist."

98. Bakvis, "Giving Workers the Business."

99. Einhorn, "Reforming the World Bank."

100. Easterly, *White Man's Burden*, 369–70.

101. Radelet, "Role of the Bank"; Lerrick, "Has the World Bank Lost Control?" De Ferranti, "The World Bank and the Middle-Income Countries." See also Kapur, "The 'Knowledge' Bank"; and Kremer, "The Missing Mandate."

102. "Abdul Latif Jameel Poverty Action Lab."

103. Meyer and Rowan, "Institutionalized Organizations"; Scott, *Organizations*, 279–80; Edelman, "Legal Ambiguity and Symbolic Structures."

104. A few leading examples are Stiglitz, *Globalization and Its Discontents*; Woods, *The Globalizers*, 253; Mallaby, *World's Banker*, 462; and Birdsall and CGD, *Rescuing the World Bank*, 201.

105. Stryker, "Limits on Technocratization"; Babb, *Managing Mexico*, 295; Blyth, *Great Transformations*, 284; Hall, "Policy Paradigms," 275; Campbell, *Institutional Change and Globalization*, 247.

106. Stryker, "Limits on Technocratization."

107. Medvetz, "Production of Policy-Knowledge."

108. See Huber, Ragin, and Stephens, "Social Democracy, Christian Democracy"; and Crepaz, "Inclusion versus Exclusion."

109. U.S. Treasury Department, *Treasury International Programs — Budget Request, FY 2008*, 69.

110. Putnam, "Diplomacy and Domestic Politics."

111. Chowla, "IMF Makes Only Marginal Changes."

Bibliography

House Appropriations Subcommittee, House Authorizing Subcommittee, and Senate Appropriations Subcommittee documents are collected in three separate sections at the end, with all items listed chronologically. It should be noted that the name of the House Appropriations Subcommittee changed several times, as did the name of the House Authorizing Subcommittee. The name of the Senate Appropriations Subcommittee changed after 1987. In the notes I use *House Appropriations Subcommittee, House Authorizing Subcommittee,* and *Senate Appropriations Subcommittee* as shorthand for the "authors" of the documents in question.

"Abdul Latif Jameel Poverty Action Lab." Abdul Latif Jameel Poverty Action Lab, Massachusetts Institute of Technology, Cambridge, MA. http://www.poverty actionlab.com/ (accessed July 7, 2007).

Abrahamson, Eric. "Managerial Fads and Fashions: The Diffusion and Rejections of Innovation." *Academy of Management Review* 16, no. 3 (1991): 586–612.

Acemoglu, Daron, Simon Johnson, and James A. Robinson. "The Colonial Origins of Comparative Development: An Empirical Investigation." *American Economic Review* 91, no. 5 (December 2001): 1369–1401.

Alden, Edward, Guy Dinmore, and Christopher Swann. "Wolfowitz Nomination a Shock for Europe." *Financial Times*, March 17, 2005.

Allison, Graham T. *Essence of Decision: Explaining the Cuban Missile Crisis.* Boston: Little, Brown, 1971.

Amsden, Alice H. *Asia's Next Giant: South Korea and Late Industrialization.* New York: Oxford University Press, 1989.

Anderson, John Ward, and Peter S. Goodman. "Europeans Wince, Wait for Wolfowitz Saga to End." *Washington Post*, May 10, 2007, sec. D.

Annis, Sheldon. "The Shifting Grounds of Poverty Lending at the World Bank." In *Between Two Worlds: The World Bank's Next Decade*, ed. Richard E. Feinberg et al. New Brunswick, NJ: Transaction, 1986.

Apodaca, Clair. "U.S. Human Rights Policy and Foreign Assistance: A Short History." *Ritsumeikan International Affairs* 3 (2005): 63–80.

Arndt, H. W. "Economic Development: A Semantic History." *Economic Development and Cultural Change* 29, no. 3 (April 1981): 457–66.

Arnson, Cynthia. *Crossroads: Congress, the President, and Central America, 1976–1993*. 2nd ed. University Park: Pennsylvania State University Press, 1993.

Ascher, William. "The World Bank and U.S. Control." In *The United States and Multilateral Institutions: Patterns of Changing Instrumentality and Influence*, ed. Margaret P. Karns and Karen A. Mingst. Boston: Unwin Hyman, 1990.

Asian Development Bank. *Annual Report*. Manila: Asian Development Bank, 1987.

———. *Annual Report*. Manila: Asian Development Bank, 2005.

Auerbach, Stuart. "Group Formed to Promote IMF, World Bank." *Washington Post*, January 18, 1985, sec. B.

Babb, Sarah. "'A True American System of Finance': Frame Resonance in the U.S. Labor Movement, 1866 to 1886." *American Sociological Review* 61, no. 6 (December 1996): 1033–52.

———. *Managing Mexico: Economists from Nationalism to Neoliberalism*. Princeton, NJ: Princeton University Press, 2001.

———. "Embeddedness, Inflation, and International Regimes: The IMF in the Early Postwar Period." *American Journal of Sociology* 113, no. 1 (July 2007): 128–64.

Babb, Sarah, and Ariel Buira. "Mission Creep, Mission Push and Discretion: The Case of IMF Conditionality." In *The IMF and the World Bank at Sixty*, ed. Ariel Buira. London: Anthem, 2005.

Bachelet, Pablo. "IDB OK's Massive Debt Relief Package for Five Nations." *Miami Herald*, November 18, 2006.

Bacon, Donald C., Roger H. Davidson, and Morton Keller. *The Encyclopedia of the United States Congress*. New York: Simon & Schuster, 1995.

Baker, Dean. *The United States since 1980*. New York: Cambridge University Press, 2007.

Baker, Gerard, and Richard Wolffe. "A 'Kinder, Gentler' Deal for US Allies." *Financial Times*, February 14, 2001.

Baker, Peter, and Paul Blustein. "Treasury Secretary to Step Down." *Washington Post*, May 26, 2006, final edition, sec. A.

"Baker Withdraws Compromise on IADB Voting Changes." *Dow Jones News Service*, March 23, 1987.

Bakvis, Peter. "Giving Workers the Business: World Bank Support for Labor Deregulation." *Multinational Monitor*, July/August 2006, 22–27.

Balassa, Bela A., ed. *Toward Renewed Economic Growth in Latin America*. Mexico City: Colegio de Mexico; Washington, DC: Institute for International Economics, 1986.

Balls, Andrew. "Wolfowitz Aides Spark World Bank Dispute." *Financial Times*, January 31, 2006.

Banerjee, Abhijit Vinayak. "Inside the Machine: Toward a New Development Economics." *Boston Review*, March/April 2007. http://bostonreview.net/BR32.2/banerjee.html (accessed August 15, 2007).

Barnett, Michael N., and Martha Finnemore. *Rules for the World: International Organizations in Global Politics*. Ithaca, NY: Cornell University Press, 2004.

Beattie, Alan. "World Bank Appoints New Chief Economist." *Financial Times*, September 18, 2003.

Bello, Walden. "The Iron Cage: The WTO, the Bretton Woods Institutions, and the South." In *The Future in Balance: Essays on Globalization and Resistance*, ed. Walden Bello. Oakland, CA: Food First, 2001.

Birdsall, Nancy, and Center for Global Development (CGD), eds. *Rescuing the World Bank: A CGD Working Group Report and Selected Essays*. Washington, DC: CGD, 2006. http://www.cgdev.org/content/publications/detail/9957.

Birdsall, Nancy, and Augusto de la Torre. *Washington Contentious: Economic Policies for Social Equity in Latin America*. Washington, DC: Carnegie Endowment for International Peace and Inter-American Dialogue, 2001. http://www.cgdev.org/files/2923_file_WashCont.pdf (accessed July 18, 2006).

Blustein, Paul. "O'Neill Again Criticizes World Bank." *Washington Post*, June 28, 2001, sec. E.

———. "Debt Cut Is Set for Poorest Nations." *Washington Post*, June 12, 2005, sec. A.

———. "IMF, World Bank Advance Debt Relief Pact." *Washington Post*, September 25, 2005, sec. A.

———. "Muttering at the World Bank; Wolfowitz's Appointment of Loyalists Disturbs Some Staffers." *Washington Post*, February 8, 2006, sec. D.

———. "World Bank Staffers Protest Appointments: Wolfowitz Defends Naming of Republican Loyalists, Says He's Trying to Bolster Ethics." *Washington Post*, January 24, 2006, sec. D.

Blyth, Mark. *Great Transformations: Economic Ideas and Institutional Change in the Twentieth Century*. New York: Cambridge University Press, 2002.

Boughton, James M. *Silent Revolution: The International Monetary Fund, 1979–1989*. Washington, DC: International Monetary Fund, 2001.

Bourdieu, Pierre. "The Forms of Capital." In *The Sociology of Economic Life*, ed. Mark Granovetter and Richard Swedberg. 2nd ed. Boulder, CO: Westview, 2001.

Bradford, Colin I. "East Asian 'Models': Myths and Lessons." In *Development Strategies Reconsidered*, ed. John P. Lewis and Vallerina Kallab. New Brunswick, NH: Transaction, 1986.

Broad, Robin. "Research, Knowledge, and the Art of 'Paradigm Maintenance': The World Bank's Development Economics Vice-Presidency (DEC)." *Review of International Political Economy* 13, no. 3 (August 2006): 387–419.

Busch, Andrew. *Reagan's Victory: The Presidential Election of 1980 and the Rise of the Right*. American Presidential Elections Series. Lawrence: University Press of Kansas, 2005.

Butterfield, Samuel Hale. *U.S. Development Aid—an Historic First: Achievements and Failures in the Twentieth Century*. Contributions to the Study of World History, vol. 108. Westport, CT: Praeger, 2004.

Campbell, John L. *Institutional Change and Globalization*. Princeton, NJ: Princeton University Press, 2004.

Catan, Thomas, and Edward Alden. "IMF's Delay on Argentina Hits Bonds." *Financial Times*, August 17, 2001.

Caufield, Catherine. *Masters of Illusion: The World Bank and the Poverty of Nations*. New York: Henry Holt, 1996.

Center for Global Development (CGD) Working Group. *The Hardest Job in the*

World: Five Crucial Tasks for the New President of the World Bank. Washington, DC: CGD, 2005. http://www.cgdev.org/files/2868_file_WBWG_Report.pdf (accessed July 18, 2006).

Center for International Policy (CIP). *Multilateral Aid Law: A Guide to U.S. Human Rights Law Affecting Multilateral Aid Section 701 of the International Financial Institutions Act.* Washington, DC: CIP, 1991.

Center for Strategic and International Studies (CSIS). *The United States and the Multilateral Development Banks: A Report of the CSIS Task Force on Multilateral Development Banks.* Washington, DC: CSIS, 1998.

Central and Eastern Europe Bankwatch Network (CEEBN). *EBRD Decision-Making Structure.* Prague: CEEBN, 2002. http://www.bankwatch.org/guide/ebrd/cgebrd-structure.pdf (accessed July 18, 2006).

Cheru, Fantu. "Building and Supporting PRSPs in Africa: What Has Worked Well So Far? What Needs Changing?" *Third World Quarterly* 27, no. 2 (2006): 355–76.

Chowla, Peter. "IMF Makes Only Marginal Changes in Its Governance Reform." Penang: Third World Network, 2008. http://www.twnside.org.sg/title2/finance/twninfofinance20080402.htm (accessed May 23, 2008).

Cline, William R. *International Debt Reexamined.* Washington, DC: Institute for International Economics, 1995.

Colburn, Forrest D. "Good-Bye to the 'Third World.'" *Dissent*, Spring 2006, 38–41.

Congressional Quarterly. *Congressional Quarterly Almanac.* Washington, DC: Congressional Quarterly News Features, various years.

Conrow, James. Interview with the author. Alexandria, VA, May 4, 2006.

Cornia, Giovanni Andrea, Richard Jolly, and Frances Stewart. *Adjustment with a Human Face.* Oxford: Oxford University Press, 1987.

Cox, Robert W., and Harold K. Jacobson. "Power, Polities and Politics: The Environment." In *The Anatomy of Influence: Decision Making in International Organization*, ed. Robert W. Cox and Harold Karan Jacobson. New Haven, CT: Yale University Press, 1973.

Crepaz, Markus M. L. "Inclusion versus Exclusion: Political Institutions and Welfare Expenditures." *Comparative Politics* 31, no. 1 (October 1998): 61.

Crutsinger, Martin. "Administration Hails Agreement on World Bank Loans, Grants to Poor Countries." *Associated Press Newswires*, July 2, 2002.

Culpeper, Roy. *The Multilateral Development Banks: Titans or Behemoths?* Boulder, CO: Lynne Rienner, 1997.

Dasgupta, Biplab. *Structural Adjustment, Global Trade, and the New Political Economy of Development.* New Delhi: Vistaar, 1998.

Davis, Gerald F. "New Directions in Corporate Governance." *Annual Review of Sociology* 31 (2005): 127–41.

Davis, Gerald F., and Tracy A. Thompson. "A Social Movement Perspective on Corporate Control." *Administrative Science Quarterly* 39, no. 1 (March 1994): 141.

De Ferranti, David. "The World Bank and the Middle-Income Countries." In *Rescuing the World Bank: A CGD Working Group Report and Selected Essays*, ed. Nancy Birdsall and Center for Global Development. Washington, DC: Center for Global Development, 2006.

De Vries, Margaret Garritsen, and International Monetary Fund (IMF). *Balance of Payments Adjustment, 1945 to 1986: The IMF Experience.* Washington, DC: International Monetary Fund, 1987.

De Young, Karen. "Shultz Intervenes on Loan." *Washington Post,* March 8, 1985.

Dell, Sydney. *On Being Grandmotherly: The Evolution of IMF Conditionality.* Essays in International Finance. Princeton, NJ: International Finance Section, Department of Economics, Princeton University, 1981.

———. "The Question of Cross-Conditionality." *World Development* 16, no. 5 (1988): 557–68.

Denton, Patricia, and Mayer N. Zald. "From Evangelism to General Service: The Transformation of the YMCA." *Administrative Science Quarterly* 8 (September 1963): 214–34.

Deraniyagala, Sonali. "From Washington to Post-Washington, DC: Does It Matter for Industrial Policy?" In *Development Policy in the Twenty-first Century: Beyond the Post-Washington Consensus* (Studies in Development Economics, vol. 17), ed. Ben Fine, Costas Lapavitsas, and Jonathan Pincus. 2001; reprint, London: Routledge, 2003.

DiMaggio, Paul J., and Walter W. Powell. "The Iron Cage Revisited: Institutional Isomorphism and Collective Rationality in Organizational Fields." *American Sociological Review* 48, no. 2 (April 1983): 147–60.

Djiraibe, Delphine, Korinna Horta, and Samuel Nguiffo. *Access to Justice from Local Village to Local Boardroom: An Experience in International Accountability.* Washington, DC: Environmental Defense, USA, 2004. http://www.envi ronmentaldefense.org/documents/4065_AccessToJustice.pdf (accessed July 19, 2007).

Donnelly, Elizabeth. "Proclaiming Jubilee: The Debt and Structural Adjustment Network." In *Restructuring World Politics: Transnational Social Movements, Networks, and Norms,* ed. Sanjeev Khagram, James V. Riker, and Kathryn Sikkink. Minneapolis: University of Minnesota Press, 2002.

Downs, George W., David M. Rocke, and Peter N. Barsoom. "Managing the Evolution of Multilateralism." *International Organization* 52, no. 2 (Spring 1998): 397–419.

Dull, Matthew. "Why PART? The Institutional Politics of Presidential Budget Reform." *Journal of Public Administration Research and Theory* 16, no. 2 (April 2006): 187–216.

Dunne, Nancy. "Seeking." *Financial Times,* September 16, 1994.

———. "US Pushes Workers' Rights." *Financial Times,* August 16, 1994.

Easterly, William Russell. *The Elusive Quest for Growth: Economists' Adventures and Misadventures in the Tropics.* Cambridge, MA: MIT Press, 2001.

———. *The White Man's Burden: Why the West's Efforts to Aid the Rest Have Done So Much Ill and So Little Good.* New York: Penguin, 2006.

Edelman, Lauren B. "Legal Ambiguity and Symbolic Structures: Organizational Mediation of Civil Rights Law." *American Journal of Sociology* 97, no. 6 (1992): 1531–76.

Edwards, Sebastian. "Trade Liberalization Reforms and the World Bank." *AEA Papers and Proceedings* 87, no. 2 (1997): 43–48.

Einhorn, Jessica. "Reforming the World Bank: Creative Destruction." *Foreign Affairs* 85, no. 1 (January–February 2006): 17–22. http://www.foreignaffairs.org/.

Engler, Mark. "Abandoning the World Bank: Pitfalls When Right and Left Agree." *Dissent* 53, no. 4 (2006): 57–73.

English, E. Philip, and Harris M. Mule. *The African Development Bank*. Boulder, CO: Lynne Rienner, 1996.

Environmental Defense Fund, Friends of the Earth, and International Rivers Network. *Gambling with People's Lives: What the World Bank's New "High Risk–High Reward" Strategy Means for the Poor and the Environment*. Washington, DC: Environmental Defense Fund, 2003.

"European Critics Inflict Defeat on Wolfowitz." *Financial Times*, September 25, 2006.

Evans, Peter B., Harold Karan Jacobson, and Robert D. Putnam. *Double-Edged Diplomacy: International Bargaining and Domestic Politics*. Studies in International Political Economy, vol. 25. Berkeley and Los Angeles: University of California Press, 1993.

Farnsworth, Clyde H. "U.S. Blocks Bank Loan for Nicaragua Roads." *New York Times*, June 30, 1983.

———. "Restructuring Planned by Latin Aid Bank." *New York Times*, December 20, 1988, sec. D.

Feinberg, Richard E. "The Changing Relationship between the World Bank and the International Monetary Fund." *International Organization* 42, no. 3 (1988): 545–60.

Feulner, Edwin. "The Heritage Foundation." In *Think Tanks and Civil Societies: Catalysts for Ideas and Action*, ed. James G. McGann and R. Kent Weaver. New Brunswick, NJ: Transaction, 2000.

Fifty Years Is Enough. "How Structural Adjustment Destroys the Environment." Washington, DC: Fifty Years Is Enough, September 26, 2000. http://www.50years .org/action/s26/factsjeet4/html (accessed November 26, 2006).

Fine, Ben. "Economics Imperialism and the New Development Economics as Kuhnian Paradigm Shift?" *World Development* 30, no. 12 (December 2002): 2057–70.

———. "The World Bank's Speculation on Social Capital." In *Reinventing the World Bank*, ed. Jonathan R. Pincus and Jeffrey A. Winters. Ithaca, NY: Cornell University Press, 2002.

Fine, Ben, Costas Lapavitsas, and Jonathan Pincus. "Development Policy in the Twenty-first Century: Beyond the Post-Washington Consensus: Preface." In *Development Policy in the Twenty-first Century: Beyond the Post-Washington Consensus* (Studies in Development Economics, vol. 17), ed. Ben Fine, Costas Lapavitsas, and Jonathan Pincus. 2001; reprint, London: Routledge, 2003.

Fleming, Stewart Art. "Time 'Not Ripe' for World Bank Funds Boost." *Financial Times*, June 26, 1984, sec. 1.

———. "The Budget Ghost at Mr. Baker's Feast." *Financial Times*, October 9, 1985, sec. I.

Fligstein, Neil. *The Transformation of Corporate Control*. Cambridge, MA: Harvard University Press, 1990.

Fox, Jonathan A. "The World Bank Inspection Panel and the Limits of Accountability." In *Reinventing the World Bank*, ed. Jonathan R. Pincus and Jeffrey A. Winters. Ithaca, NY: Cornell University Press, 2002.

Fox, Jonathan A., and L. David Brown. "Assessing the Impact of NGO Advocacy Campaigns on World Bank Projects and Policies." In *The Struggle for Accountability: The World Bank, NGOs, and Grassroots Movements* (Global Environmental Accord: Strategies for Sustainability and Institutional Innovation series), ed. Jonathan A. Fox and L. David Brown. Cambridge, MA: MIT Press, 1998.

———. Introduction to *The Struggle for Accountability: The World Bank, NGOs, and Grassroots Movements* (Global Environmental Accord: Strategies for Sustainability and Institutional Innovation series), ed. Jonathan A. Fox and L. David Brown. Cambridge, MA: MIT Press, 1998.

Frankel, Glen. "G-7 Backs Debt Plan for Poor Countries." *Washington Post*, February 6, 2005, sec. A.

Frankel, Jeffrey. "Bush's Spectacular Failure." *International Economy* 18, no. 2 (Spring 2004): 22–27, 71. http://www.abe.pl/html/english/detailsj.php?id=0898 -4336.

Friedland, Jonathan. "Dispute Expected over Lending at Inter-American Bank Meeting." *American Banker*, March 24, 1986.

Galbraith, John Kenneth. *The Nature of Mass Poverty*. Cambridge, MA: Harvard University Press, 1979.

Gamson, William A., and Andre Modigliani. "Media Discourse and Public Opinion on Nuclear Power: A Constructionist Approach." *American Journal of Sociology* 95 (July 1989): 1–37.

George, Susan, and Fabrizio Sabelli. *Faith and Credit: The World Bank's Secular Empire*. Boulder: Westview, 1994.

Goffman, Erving. *Frame Analysis: An Essay on the Organization of Experience*. Cambridge, MA: Harvard University Press, 1974.

Goldman, Michael. *Imperial Nature: The World Bank and Struggles for Social Justice in the Age of Globalization*. Yale Agrarian Studies Series. New Haven, CT: Yale University Press, 2005.

Goldstein, Morris. "Strengthening the International Financial Architecture: Where Do We Stand?" Washington, DC: Peterson Institute for International Economics, 2000. http://www.petersoninstitute.org/publications/wp/00–8.pdf (accessed May 14, 2007).

Goodman, Peter S. "Ending Battle, Wolfowitz Resigns from World Bank." *Washington Post*, May 18, 2007, sec. A.

Gopinath, Deepak. "Wolfensohn Agonistes." *Institutional Investor* 34, no. 9 (2000): 9.

Gouldner, Alvin Ward. *Patterns of Industrial Bureaucracy*. Glencoe, IL: Free Press, 1954.

Gourlay, Richard. "US Calls for Review of Asian Development Bank." *Financial Times*, April 29, 1987, sec. 1.

"Group of Leading US Decision-Makers on Latin American Banking and Business...." *Latin American Weekly Report*, February 17, 1984.

Group of Seven (G7). "Declaration of the Ottawa Summit." July 21, 1981. Available (through University of Toronto, G8 Centre) at http://www.g8.utoronto.ca/ summit/1981ottawa/communique/index.html (accessed September 12, 2006).

———. "Economic Declaration: Building World Partnership." Declaration of the

London Summit, July 17, 1991. Available (through University of Toronto, G8 Centre) at http://www.g8.utoronto.ca/summit/1991london/communique/index .html (accessed September 12, 2006).

Guha, Krishna. "World Bank Confirms Zoellick as President." *Financial Times*, June 27, 2007.

Gutner, Tamar L. *Banking on the Environment: Multilateral Development Banks and Their Environmental Performance in Central and Eastern Europe.* Cambridge, MA: MIT Press, 2002.

———. "World Bank Environmental Reform: Revisiting Lessons from Agency Theory." *International Organization* 59, no. 3 (Summer 2005): 773–83.

Gwin, Catherine. "U.S. Relations with the World Bank, 1945–1992." In *Perspectives*, vol. 2 of *The World Bank: Its First Half Century*, ed. Devesh Kapur, John P. Lewis, and Richard Webb. Washington, DC: Brookings Institution Press, 1997.

Hafner-Burton, Emilie M., and Kiyoteru Tsutsui. "Human Rights in a Globalizing World: The Paradox of Empty Promises." *American Journal of Sociology* 110, no. 5 (March 2005): 1373–1411.

Hall, Peter A. "Policy Paradigms, Social Learning, and the State: The Case of Economic Policymaking in Britain." *Comparative Politics* 25, no. 3 (April 1993): 275.

Helleiner, Eric, and Jeffrey Cameron. "Another World Order? The Bush Administration and HIPC Debt Cancellation." *New Political Economy* 11, no. 1 (March 2006): 125–40.

Helleiner, Gerald K. "Policy-Based Program Lending: A Look at the Bank's New Role." In *Between Two Worlds: The World Bank's Next Decade*, ed. Richard E. Feinberg et al. New Brunswick, NJ: Transaction, 1986.

Hellinger, Steve, Doug Hellinger, Fred O'Regan, and Development Group for Alternative Policies (DGAP). *Aid for Just Development: Report on the Future of Foreign Assistance.* Boulder, CO: Lynne Rienner, 1988.

Helvarg, David. "The Three Horsemen." *The Nation*, January 29, 2001. http://www .thenation.com/doc/20010129/helvarg (accessed November 22, 2006).

Hirschman, Albert O. "The Rise and Decline of Development Economics." In *Essays in Trespassing: Economics to Politics and Beyond*, ed. Albert O. Hirschman. Cambridge: Cambridge University Press, 1981.

Huber, E., C. Ragin, and J. D. Stephens. "Social Democracy, Christian Democracy, Constitutional Structure, and the Welfare State." *American Journal of Sociology* 99, no. 3 (1993): 711–49.

"IDA Deputies Make Little Progress on Main Issues." *Reuters*, September 22, 1989.

Independent Commission on International Development Issues (ICIDI). *North-South, a Programme for Survival: Report of the Independent Commission on International Development Issues.* 1980; reprint, Cambridge, MA: MIT Press, 1980.

Inter-American Development Bank (IDB). *Annual Report.* Washington, DC: IDB, various years.

International Financial Institution Advisory Commission (IFIAC). *Report of the International Financial Institution Advisory Commission.* Washington, DC:

IFIAC, March 2000. http://www.house.gov/jec/imf/meltzer.pdf (accessed July 6, 2007).

"Japan, U.S. Split over ADB Capital Increase." *Jiji Press Ticker Service*, May 5, 1993.

Jervis, Robert. "Understanding the Bush Doctrine." *Political Science Quarterly* 118, no. 3 (Fall 2003): 365–88.

"John Taylor's Woes." *International Economy*, Spring 2003, 4.

Johnson, Robert David. *Congress and the Cold War*. New York: Cambridge University Press, 2006.

Jolly, Richard. *UN Contributions to Development Thinking and Practice*. UN Intellectual History Project. Bloomington: Indiana University Press, 2004.

Jubilee USA Network. "Background Briefing and Frequently Asked Questions: Debt Cancellation and the Jubilee Act for Responsible Lending and Expanded Debt Cancellation." Washington, DC: Jubilee USA Network, 2008. http://www.jubileeusa.org/fileadmin/user_upload/Resources/JUBILEE_Act/408_hearing/042408JubileeUSA_BackgroundMemo.pdf (accessed May 27, 2008).

Kahin, George McTurnan. *The Asian-African Conference, Bandung, Indonesia, April 1955*. Port Washington, NY: Kennikat, 1972.

Kahn, Joseph. "Relief for the Poorest." *New York Times*, October 22, 2000, sec. 4.

Kappagoda, Nihal. *The Asian Development Bank*. Vol. 2 of *The Multilateral Development Banks*. Boulder, CO: Lynne Rienner, 1995.

Kapur, Devesh. "Do as I Say and Not as I Do: A Critique of G-7 Proposals on Reforming the MDBs." Discussion Paper 16. Washington, DC: Center for Global Development, 2002.

———. "The 'Knowledge' Bank." In *Rescuing the World Bank: A CGD Working Group Report and Selected Essays*, ed. Nancy Birdsall and Center for Global Development. Washington, DC: Center for Global Development, 2006.

Kapur, Devesh, John Prior Lewis, and Richard Charles Webb, eds. *The World Bank: Its First Half Century*. 2 vols. Washington, DC: Brookings Institution Press, 1997.

Kapur, Devesh, and Richard Webb. "Governance-Related Conditionalities of the International Financial Institutions." Discussion Paper 6. Washington, DC: G24, 2000.

Kegley C., J. R., and S. Hook. "U.S. Foreign Aid and U.N. Voting: Did Reagan's Linkage Strategy Buy Deference or Defiance?" *International Studies Quarterly* 35, no. 3 (September 1991): 295–312.

Keohane, Robert O. *After Hegemony: Cooperation and Discord in the World Political Economy*. Princeton, NJ: Princeton University Press, 1984.

Kilborn, Peter T. "Administration Is Adopting Assertive Economic Stance." *New York Times*, September 7, 1985, sec. A.

———. "Chief of Latin Lender May Quit in Protest." *New York Times*, December 18, 1987, sec. D.

Killick, Tony. *A Reaction Too Far: Economic Theory and the Role of the State in Developing Countries*. ODI Development Policy Studies. London: Overseas Development Institute, 1989.

Kirton, John. "Interview with Henry Nau, George Washington University, Senior

Staff Member of the National Security Council in the White House Responsible for International Economic Affairs from 1981 to 1983." Toronto: G8 Information Centre, University of Toronto, 2004. http://www.g7.utoronto.ca/oral history/nau040507.html (accessed September 12, 2006).

Koremenos, Barbara, Charles Lipson, and Duncan Snidal. "The Rational Design of International Institutions." *International Organization* 55, no. 4 (Autumn 2001): 761–99.

Kraft, Joseph. *The Mexican Rescue.* New York: Group of Thirty, 1984.

Kremer, Michael. "The Missing Mandate: Global Public Goods." In *Rescuing the World Bank: A CGD Working Group Report and Selected Essays,* ed. Nancy Birdsall and Center for Global Development. Washington, DC: Center for Global Development, 2006.

Krugman, Paul R. "LDC Debt Policy." In *American Economic Policy in the 1980s,* ed. Martin Feldstein. Chicago: University of Chicago Press, 1994.

———. *Peddling Prosperity: Economic Sense and Nonsense in the Age of Diminished Expectations.* New York: Norton, 1994.

———. "The Fall and Rise of Development Economics." In *Development, Geography, and Economic Theory,* Ed. Paul Krugman. Cambridge, MA: MIT Press, 1995.

Kuczynski, Pedro-Pablo, and John Williamson, eds. *After the Washington Consensus: Restarting Growth and Reform in Latin America.* Washington, DC: Institute for International Economics, 2003.

La Porta, Rafael, Florencio Lopez-de-Silanes, and Andrei Shleifer. "Corporate Ownership around the World." *Journal of Finance* 54, no. 2 (April 1999): 471–517.

Lal, Deepak. *The Poverty of "Development Economics."* 2nd rev. and expanded U.S. ed. Cambridge, MA: MIT Press, 2000.

Lancaster, Carol. *Foreign Aid: Diplomacy, Development, Domestic Politics.* Chicago: University of Chicago Press, 2007.

Lancaster, Carol, and Institute for International Economics (IIE). *Transforming Foreign Aid: United States Assistance in the 21st Century.* Washington, DC: IIE, 2000.

Lancaster, Carol, and Ann Van Dusen. *Organizing U.S. Foreign Aid: Confronting Challenges of the Twenty-first Century.* Global Economy and Development. Washington, DC: Brookings Institution Press, 2005.

"Latin America: U.S. to Press Regional Bank on Social Spending." *IPS–Inter Press Service,* November 3, 1993.

Lebovic, James H. "National Interests and US Foreign Aid: The Carter and Reagan Years." *Journal of Peace Research* 25 (June 1988): 115–35.

Leland, Marc. Interview with the author. Arlington, VA, March 2, 2006.

Lerrick, Adam. "Has the World Bank Lost Control?' In *Rescuing the World Bank: A CGD Working Group Report and Selected Essays,* ed. Nancy Birdsall and Center for Global Development. Washington, DC: Center for Global Development, 2006.

Lewis, John P. "Development Promotion: A Time for Regrouping." In *Development Strategies Reconsidered,* ed. John P. Lewis and Valeriana Kallab. New Brunswick, NJ: Transaction, 1986.

Lewis, John P., and Valeriana Kallab, eds. *Development Strategies Reconsidered.* New Brunswick, NJ: Transaction, 1986.

Lindsay, James M. *Congress and the Politics of U.S. Foreign Policy.* Baltimore: Johns Hopkins University Press, 1994.

Livingston, Steven G. "The Politics of International Agenda-Setting: Reagan and North-South Relations." *International Studies Quarterly* 36, no. 3 (September 1992): 313.

"Loan to Nicaragua Gets Backing." *Reuters,* February 4, 1983.

"Long, Clarence Dickinson (1908–1994)." *Biographical Directory of the United States Congress.* http://bioguide.congress.gov/scripts/biodisplay.pl?index=L000413 (accessed August 22, 2006).

Luck, Edward C. *Mixed Messages: American Politics and International Organization, 1919–1999.* Washington, DC: Brookings Institution Press, 1999.

Mallaby, Sebastian. "NGOs: Fighting Poverty, Hurting the Poor." *Foreign Policy,* no. 144 (September/October 2004): 50–58.

———. *The World's Banker: A Story of Failed States, Financial Crises, and the Wealth and Poverty of Nations.* New York: Penguin, 2004.

———. "Saving the World Bank." *Foreign Affairs* 84, no. 3 (May–June 2005): 75–85.

———. "Blinkered by His Big Ideas." *Washington Post,* April 23, 2006, sec. B.

March, James G., and Johan P. Olsen. *Ambiguity and Choice in Organizations.* Bergen: Universitetsforlaget, 1979.

Martinussen, John. *Society, State, and Market: A Guide to Competing Theories of Development.* London: Zed, 1997.

Marx, Karl, and Fredrick Engels. "Manifesto of the Communist Party." Marxists Internet Archive. http://www.marxists.org/archive/marx/works/1848/communist-manifesto/cho1.htm (accessed February 1, 2008).

Mason, Edward Sagendorph, and Robert E. Asher. *The World Bank since Bretton Woods: The Origins, Policies, Operations, and Impact of the International Bank for Reconstruction and Development and the Other Members of the World Bank Group: The International Finance Corporation, the International Development Association [and] the International Centre for Settlement of Investment Disputes.* Washington, DC: Brookings Institution, 1973.

McCormick, James M. "The NIEO and the Distribution of American Assistance." *Western Political Quarterly* 37, no. 1 (March 1984): 100.

McNamara, Robert S., and World Bank. *The McNamara Years at the World Bank: Major Policy Addresses of Robert S. McNamara, 1968–1981.* Baltimore: Johns Hopkins University Press, 1981.

Mead, Walter Russell. *Special Providence: American Foreign Policy and How It Changed the World.* New York: Knopf, 2001.

Medvetz, Thomas. "Think Tanks and the Production of Policy-Knowledge in America." Ph.D. diss., University of California, Berkeley, 2007.

Meeropol, Michael. *Surrender: How the Clinton Administration Completed the Reagan Revolution.* Ann Arbor: University of Michigan Press, 1998.

Messinger, Sheldon N. "Organizational Transformation: A Case Study of a Declining Social Movement." *American Sociological Review* 20 (1955): 3–10.

Meyer, John W., John Boli, George M. Thomas, and Francisco O. Ramirez. "World

Society and the Nation-State." *American Journal of Sociology* 103, no. 1 (July 1997): 144–81.

Meyer, John W., and Brian Rowan. "Institutionalized Organizations: Formal Structure as Myth and Ceremony." *American Journal of Sociology* 83, no. 2 (1977): 340–63.

Michels, Robert. *Political Parties: A Sociological Study of the Oligarchical Tendencies of Modern Democracy*. New York: Dover, 1959.

Mikesell, Raymond. *The Bretton Woods Debates: A Memoir*. Essays in International Finance, vol. 192. Princeton, NJ: International Finance Section, Department of Economics, Princeton University, 1994.

Miller-Adams, Michelle. *The World Bank: New Agendas in a Changing World*. Studies in Development Economics. London: Routledge, 1999.

Montagnon, Peter. "Baker's Third World Debt Plan." *Financial Times*, October 9, 1985, sec. I.

Mosley, Paul, Jane Harrigan, and J. F. J. Toye. *Aid and Power: The World Bank and Policy-Based Lending*. 2nd ed. London: Routledge, 1995.

Myrdal, Gunnar. *An International Economy: Problems and Prospects*. New York: Harper, 1956.

Naím, Moisés. "Fads and Fashions in Economic Reforms: Washington Consensus or Washington Confusion?" *Third World Quarterly* 21, no. 3 (2000): 505–28.

Nau, Henry R. *The Myth of America's Decline: Leading the World Economy into the 1990s*. New York: Oxford University Press, 1990.

Nelson, Paul J. *The World Bank and Non-Governmental Organizations: The Limits of Apolitical Development*. International Political Economy Series. New York: St. Martin's, 1995.

———. "Agendas, Accountability, and Legitimacy among Transnational Networks Lobbying the World Bank." In *Restructuring World Politics: Transnational Social Movements, Networks, and Norms*, ed. Sanjeev Khagram, James V. Riker, and Kathryn Sikkink. Minneapolis: University of Minnesota Press, 2002.

Nielson, Daniel L., and Michael J. Tierney. "Delegation to International Organizations: Agency Theory and World Bank Environmental Reform." *International Organization* 57, no. 2 (Spring 2003): 241–76.

Novak, Robert D. "Who Is Behind Bush Economic Policy? Check Out the Ward Room of the White House." *International Economy*, Spring 2005, 6–9.

Nowels, Larry. "Foreign Aid Reform: Commissions, Tasks Forces, and Initiatives: From Kennedy to the Present." In *Security by Other Means: Foreign Assistance, Global Poverty, and American Leadership*, ed. Lael Brainard. Washington, DC: Brookings Institution Press, 2006.

O'Dwyer, Mark. "The African Development Bank: A New Lease on Life." *Financial Times*, June 2, 1998.

Office of Management and Budget (OMB). "Program Assessment Rating Tool (PART)." http://www.whitehouse.gov/omb/part/ (accessed July 10, 2007).

Ostrower, Gary B. *The United Nations and the United States*. International History series. New York: Twayne/Simon & Schuster Macmillan, 1998.

Patrick, Stewart. "Multilateralism and Its Discontents: The Causes and Consequences of U.S. Ambivalence." In *Multilateralism and U.S. Foreign Policy: Am-*

bivalent Engagement, ed. Stewart Patrick and Shepard Forman. Boulder, CO: Lynne Rienner, 2002.

Payer, Cheryl. *The World Bank: A Critical Analysis.* New York: Monthly Review Press, 1982.

Pfeffer, Jeffrey. "Size and Composition of Corporate Boards of Directors: The Organization and Its Environment." *Administrative Science Quarterly* 17, no. 2 (June 1972): 218–28.

Pfeffer, Jeffrey, and Gerald R. Salancik. *The External Control of Organizations: A Resource Dependence Perspective.* New York: Harper & Row, 1978.

Phillips, Michael M. "Treasury Secretary O'Neill Pushes Plan to Make Grants Part of Aid to Poor Nations." *Wall Street Journal,* February 12, 2002, sec. A.

Phillips, Michael M., Jonathan Karp, and Neil King Jr. "IMF Approves $30 Billion Loan to Stabilize Brazil—Bush Team Reverses Course amid Pressure from Banks." *Wall Street Journal,* August 8, 2002, sec. A.

Pincus, Jonathan, and Jeffrey A. Winters, eds. *Reinventing the World Bank.* Ithaca, NY: Cornell University Press, 2002.

Pine, Art. "U.S. Faces Showdown over Bid to Gain Power to Override Loans at the IADB." *Wall Street Journal,* March 20, 1987.

Please, Stanley. "The World Bank: Lending for Structural Adjustment." In *Adjustment Crisis in the Third World* (Overseas Development Council, U.S.–Third World Policy Perspectives series, no. 1), ed. Richard E. Feinberg and Valeriana Kallab. New Brunswick, NJ: Transaction, 1984.

Polak, Jacques. "The World Bank and the IMF: A Changing Relationship." In *Perspectives,* vol. 2 of *The World Bank: Its First Half Century,* ed. Devesh Kapur, John P. Lewis, and Richard Webb. Washington, DC: Brookings Institution Press, 1997.

Pollin, Robert. *Contours of Descent: U.S. Economic Fractures and the Landscape of Global Austerity.* London: Verso, 2003.

Putnam, Robert D. "Diplomacy and Domestic Politics: The Logic of Two-Level Games." *International Organization* 42, no. 3 (Summer 1988): 427–60.

Radelet, Stephen. "The Role of the Bank in Low-Income Countries." In *Rescuing the World Bank: A CGD Working Group Report and Selected Essays,* ed. Nancy Birdsall and Center for Global Development. Washington, DC: Center for Global Development, 2006.

Raghavan, Chakravarthi. "Speed Debt Relief, Delink HIPC and PRSP." Penang: Third World Network, 2001. http://www.twnside.org.sg/title/delink.htm (accessed May 16, 2007).

Reagan, Ronald. "Remarks at the Annual Meeting of the Boards of Governors of the World Bank Group and International Monetary Fund." Washington, DC, September 29, 1981.

Rebello, Joseph. "World Bank Favors Big Increase in Grants to Poor Nations." *Dow Jones International News,* May 8, 2002.

"Reform at the World Bank." *Financial Times,* May 8, 1987, sec. I.

Reich, Robert B. "Escape from the Global Sweatshop: Capitalism's Stake in Uniting the Workers of the World." *Washington Post,* May 22, 1994, sec. C.

"Reuss, Henry Schoellkopf (1912–2002)." *Biographical Directory of the United States*

Congress. http://bioguide.congress.gov/scripts/biodisplay.pl?index=r000165 (accessed August 22, 2006).

Rich, Bruce. *Mortgaging the Earth: The World Bank, Environmental Impoverishment, and the Crisis of Development.* Boston: Beacon, 1994.

———. "The World Bank under James Wolfensohn." In *Reinventing the World Bank,* ed. Jonathan R. Pincus and Jeffrey A. Winters. Ithaca, NY: Cornell University Press, 2002.

Riemer, Blanca. "Jim Baker's Plan to Stave off a New Debt Crisis." *Business Week,* April 22, 1985, 39.

———. "Washington's Gambit to Head off a Debtor Revolt." *Business Week,* September 23, 1985, 39.

Rist, Gilbert. *The History of Development: From Western Origins to Global Faith.* London: Zed, 1997.

Rodrik, Dani. "Goodbye Washington Consensus, Hello Washington Confusion?" *Journal of Economic Literature* 44 (December 2006): 973–87.

Roodman, David Malin, Jane A. Peterson, and Worldwatch Institute. *Still Waiting for the Jubilee: Pragmatic Solutions for the Third World Debt Crisis.* Worldwatch Papers, vol. 155. Washington, DC: Worldwatch Institute, 2001.

Rowe, James L., Jr. "Fed Casts Doubt on Bradley Plan." *Washington Post,* January 20, 1987, sec. C.

Rowen, Hobart. "Clausen Sees Bigger World Bank Role." *Washington Post,* March 31, 1985.

———. "U.S. and Canada Seeking Veto Power on IDB Loans." *Washington Post,* March 18, 1987.

———. "World Bank to Rethink Policy: Loans May Be Tied to Nations' Economic Environments." *Washington Post,* February 21, 1985.

Rowley, Anthony. "Bank Gets Mandate to Double Capital Injection." *Business Times* (Singapore), May 6, 1994.

———. "Developing Nations Baulk at ADB's Lending Rigidity." *Business Times* (Singapore), March 28, 1994.

———. "World Bank to Step Up Infrastructure Role." *Business Times* (Singapore), May 30, 2006.

Sachs, Jeffrey. *The End of Poverty: Economic Possibilities for Our Time.* New York: Penguin, 2005.

Sanford, Jonathan E. "Change and Continuity: U.S. Policy towards the MDBs." Typescript, Congressional Research Service/FTD, Library of Congress, Washington, DC, 2005.

———. "IDA Grants and HIPC Debt Cancellation: Their Effectiveness and Impact on IDA Resources." *World Development* 32, no. 9 (2004): 1579–1607.

———. "Making and Executing U.S. Policy towards the MDBs." Typescript, Congressional Research Service/FTD, Library of Congress, Washington, DC, 2005.

———. *U.S. Foreign Policy and Multilateral Development Banks.* Special Studies in International Relations. Boulder, CO: Westview, 1982.

Sanford, Jonathan E., and U.S. Senate Subcommittee on Foreign Assistance. *U.S. Policy and the Multilateral Banks: Politicization and Effectiveness: Staff Report to the Subcommittee on Foreign Assistance of the Committee on Foreign Rela-*

tions, United States Senate. Washington, DC: U.S. Government Printing Office, 1977.

Schoultz, Lars. "Politics, Economics, and U.S. Participation in Multilateral Development Banks." *International Organization* 36 (Summer 1982): 537–74.

Scott, W. Richard. *Organizations: Rational, Natural, and Open Systems*. 3rd ed. Englewood Cliffs, NJ: Prentice-Hall, 1992.

Selznick, Philip. *TVA and the Grass Roots: A Study in the Sociology of Formal Organization*. Berkeley: University of California Press, 1949.

Sen, Amartya Kumar. *Development as Freedom*. New York: Oxford University Press, 1999.

"Senior US Treasury Secretary, Mr Charles Hallara, Has Called for a Thorough External Review of the Asian Development Bank's Future Lending Policies." *Financial Times*, April 29, 1987, sec. 1.

Sherk, Donald R. "Emerging Markets and the Multilateral Development Banks." *Columbia Journal of World Business* 29, no. 2 (Summer 1994): 44–52.

Sikkink, Kathryn. *Mixed Signals: U.S. Human Rights Policy and Latin America*. Ithaca, NY: Cornell University Press, 2004.

Sikkink, Kathryn, and Jackie Smith. "Infrastructures for Change: Transnational Organizations." In *Restructuring World Politics: Transnational Social Movements, Networks, and Norms*, ed. Sanjeev Khagram, James V. Riker, and Kathryn Sikkink. Minneapolis: University of Minnesota Press, 2002.

Silk, Leonard. "The Infighting over the IMF." *New York Times*, September 28, 1983, sec. D.

Singer, Hans W. "The Bretton Woods Institutions and the UN." *Briefing Notes in Economics*, no. 8 (January 1994).

Snow, David A., E. Burke Rochford, Steven K. Worden, and Robert D. Benford. "Frame Alignment Processes, Micromobilization, and Movement Participation." *American Sociological Review* 51, no. 4 (1986): 464–81.

Soederberg, Suzanne. "American Empire and 'Excluded States': The Millennium Challenge Account and the Shift to Pre-Emptive Development." *Third World Quarterly* 25, no. 2 (2004): 279–302.

Spanier, John W. *American Foreign Policy since World War II*. 10th ed. New York: Holt, Rinehart & Winston, 1985.

Stein, Herbert. *Presidential Economics: The Making of Economic Policy from Roosevelt to Reagan and Beyond*. New York: Simon & Schuster, 1984.

Steinberger, Michael. "Neo-Economics." *American Prospect* 16, no. 3 (March 2005): 42–45.

Stephens, Phillip. "UK to Help Top Up World Bank Loan Fund for Poorer Countries." *Financial Times*, January 30, 1984, sec. 1.

Stern, Nicholas. "The World Bank as 'Intellectual Actor.'" In *Perspectives*, vol. 2 of *The World Bank: Its First Half Century*, ed. Devesh Kapur, John P. Lewis, and Richard Webb. Washington, DC: Brookings Institution Press, 1997.

Stiglitz, Joseph E. *Globalization and Its Discontents*. New York: Norton, 2002.

Stockman, David Alan. *The Triumph of Politics: How the Reagan Revolution Failed*. New York: Harper & Row, 1986.

Streeten, Paul. "Development Ideas in Historical Perspective." In *Toward a New Strategy for Development*, ed. Kim Q. Hill. New York: Pergamon, 1979.

Stryker, Robin. "Limits on Technocratization of the Law: The Elimination of the National Labor Relations Board's Division of Economic Research." *American Sociological Review* 54, no. 3 (June 1989): 341–58.

Tan, Celine. *Debt and Conditionality: Multilateral Debt Relief Initiative and Opportunities for Expanding Policy Space.* TWN Global Economy Series, no. 9. Penang: Third World Network, 2007.

Tarnoff, Curt, and Larry Nowels. *Foreign Aid: An Introductory Overview of U.S. Programs and Policy.* Washington, DC: Congressional Research Service, 2005.

Taylor, Andrew. "House Panel Cuts Contribution to Put Heat on World Bank." *Congressional Quarterly Weekly,* September 25, 1993, 2530.

Taylor, John B. *Global Financial Warriors: The Untold Story of International Finance in the Post-9/11 World.* New York: Norton, 2007.

Tenorio, Vyvyan. "Asian Development Bank Faces Declining Relevance as a Lender." *Toronto Globe and Mail,* May 4, 1988, sec. B.

Thurber, James A. "An Introduction to Presidential-Congressional Rivalry." In *Rivals for Power: Presidential-Congressional Relations* (2nd ed.), ed. James A. Thurber. Lanham, MD: Rowman & Littlefield, 2002.

To Amend the Foreign Assistance Act of 1961, and for Other Purposes. Public Law 93-189. Washington, DC: U.S. Government Printing Office, 1973.

Tomkins, Richard. "Bush Lauds African Move to Democracy." *UPI,* June 13, 2005.

Toye, J. F. J., and Richard Toye. *The UN and Global Political Economy: Trade, Finance, and Development.* UN Intellectual History Project. Bloomington: Indiana University Press, 2004.

Truman, Harry S. Inaugural Address, January 20, 1949. Available online at http://www.trumanlibrary.org/whistlestop/50yr_archive/inagura120jan1949.htm (accessed August 21, 2006).

Turner, Mark. "The African Development Bank." *Financial Times,* May 21, 1999.

Tussie, Diana. *The Inter-American Development Bank.* Multilateral Development Banks, vol. 4. Boulder, CO: Lynne Rienner, 1995.

Udall, Lori. "The World Bank and Public Accountability: Has Anything Changed?" In *The Struggle for Accountability: The World Bank, NGOs, and Grassroots Movements* (Global Environmental Accord: Strategies for Sustainability and Institutional Innovation series), ed. Jonathan A. Fox and L. David Brown. Cambridge, MA: MIT Press, 1998.

U.S. Agency for International Development (USAID). *U.S. Overseas Loans and Grants.* Washington, DC: USAID, various years. http://dec.usaid.gov/.

U.S. Bureau of the Census. Data User Services Division. "Statistical Abstract of the United States." Various years. http://www.census.gov/compendia/statab/ (accessed April 19, 2006).

"U.S. Drops Demand to Veto Loans by Inter-American Bank." *Financial Times,* February 13, 1989, sec. D.

U.S. General Accounting Office (USGAO). *Developing Countries: Switching Some Multilateral Loans to Grants Lessens Poor Country Debt Burdens: Report to Congressional Requesters.* Washington, DC: U.S. General Accounting Office, 2002.

U.S. Treasury Department. *United States Participation in the Multilateral Development Banks in the 1980s.* Washington, DC: U.S. Treasury Department, 1982.

———. "Response to the Report of the International Financial Institution Advisory Commission." News release, June 8, 2000. http://www.ustreas.gov/press/releases/docs/response.pdf (accessed May 15, 2007).

———. "Treasury Under Secretary John B. Taylor: Testimony Before the House Committee on International Relations: Edited by House Committee on International Relations." News release, March 6, 2003. http://www.treas.gov/press/releases/js89.htm.

———. *Treasury International Programs — Budget Request, FY 2006.* Washington, DC: U.S. Treasury Department, 2005. http://www.treasury.gov/offices/international-affairs/intl/ (accessed August 23, 2006).

———. *Treasury International Programs — Budget Request, FY 2007.* Washington, DC: U.S. Treasury Department, 2006. http://www.treasury.gov/offices/international-affairs/intl/ (accessed August 23, 2006).

———. *Treasury International Programs — Budget Request, FY 2008.* Washington, DC: U.S. Treasury Department, 2007. http://www.treasury.gov/offices/international-affairs/intl/ (accessed July 5, 2007).

Upton, Barbara. *The Multilateral Development Banks: Improving U.S. Leadership.* The Washington Papers, vol. 178. Westport, CT: Praeger, 2000.

Urakami, Keiji. "G-8 Agree to Reinforce ILO, Reject U.S. Proposal." *Japan Economic Newswire,* February 26, 1999.

Urquidi, Victor L. "Reconstruction vs. Development: The IMF and the World Bank." In *The Bretton Woods–GATT System: Retrospect and Prospect After Fifty Years,* ed. Orin Kirshner. Armonk, NY: Sharpe, 1996.

U.S. Congress. House. *Microenterprise for Self-Reliance and International Anti-Corruption Act of 2000.* HR 1143. 106th Cong., 2nd sess. Available online at http://www.govtrack.us/congress/billtext.xpd?bill=h106-1143 (accessed September 26, 2008).

Useem, Michael. *Executive Defense: Shareholder Power and Corporate Reorganization.* Cambridge, MA: Harvard University Press, 1993.

Wade, Robert. *Governing the Market: Economic Theory and the Role of Government in East Asian Industrialization.* Princeton, NJ: Princeton University Press, 1990.

———. "Japan, the World Bank, and the Art of Paradigm Maintenance: The East Asian Miracle in Political Perspective." *New Left Review,* no. 217 (May–June 1996): 3–36.

———. "Greening the Bank: The Struggle Over the Environment, 1970–1995." In *Perspectives,* vol. 2 of *The World Bank: Its First Half Century,* ed. Devesh Kapur, John P. Lewis, and Richard Webb. Washington, DC: Brookings Institution Press, 1997.

———. "US Hegemony and the World Bank: The Fight Over People and Ideas." *Review of International Political Economy* 9, no. 2 (2002): 215–43.

Weber, Steven. "Origins of the European Bank for Reconstruction and Development." *International Organization* 48, no. 1 (Winter 1994): 1–38.

Weiss, Martin A. *Debt Relief for Heavily Indebted Poor Countries: Issues for Congress.* Washington, DC: Congressional Research Service, 2006.

Weissman, Robert. "Phasing Out User Fees." *Multinational Monitor* 21, no. 12 (December 2000). http://multinationalmonitor.org/mm2000/00december/phasing.html (accessed May 12, 2007).

White, John Alexander. *Regional Development Banks: The Asian, African, and Inter-American Development Banks*. Praeger Special Studies in International Economics and Development. New York: Praeger, 1972.

White House. *Foreign Assistance for the 'Seventies: Message from the President of the United States Proposing a Transformation of Foreign Assistance Programs*. 91st Cong., 2nd sess., H. Doc. 91-385. Washington, DC: U.S. Government Printing Office, 1970.

———. "President Outlines U.S. Plan to Help World's Poor: Remarks by the President at United Nations Financing for Development Conference, Cintermex Convention Center, Monterrey, Mexico." News release, March 22, 2002. http://www.whitehouse.gov/news/releases/2002/03/20020322–1.html.

Willard, Anna. "Rich Countries at Loggerheads over Cash for Poor." *Reuters News*, November 18, 2001.

Willett, Thomas D. "Upping the Ante for Political Economy Analysis of the International Financial Institutions." *World Economy* 24, no. 3 (March 2001): 317–32.

Williamson, John. Introduction to *Latin American Adjustment: How Much Has Happened?* ed. John Williamson. Washington, DC: Institute for International Economics, 1990.

———, ed. *Latin American Adjustment: How Much Has Happened?* Washington, DC: Institute for International Economics, 1990.

———. "What Washington Means by Policy Reform." In *Latin American Adjustment: How Much Has Happened?* ed. John Williamson. Washington, DC: Institute for International Economics, 1990.

Wirth, David A. "Partnership Advocacy in World Bank Environmental Reform." In *The Struggle for Accountability: The World Bank, NGOs, and Grassroots Movements* (Global Environmental Accord: Strategies for Sustainability and Institutional Innovation series), ed. Jonathan A. Fox and L. David Brown. Cambridge, MA: MIT Press, 1998.

Wolfensohn, James D., and Francois Bourguignon. "Development and Poverty Reduction: Looking Back, Looking Ahead." Washington, DC: World Bank, 2004. http://www.worldbank.org/ambc/lookingbacklookingahead.pdf.

Woodard, Susan P. *The World Bank and the Future of U.S. Participation*. Washington, DC: Heritage Foundation, 1979. http://www.heritage.org/Research/InternationalOrganizations/bg107.cfm (accessed September 6, 2006).

Woods, Ngaire. "Making the IMF and the World Bank More Accountable." *International Affairs* (London) 77, no. 1 (January 2001): 83–100.

———. *The Globalizers: The IMF, the World Bank, and Their Borrowers*. Cornell Studies in Money. Ithaca, NY: Cornell University Press, 2006.

World Bank. *Accelerated Development in Sub-Saharan Africa: An Agenda for Action*. Washington, DC: World Bank, 1982.

———. *Annual Report*. Washington, DC: World Bank, various years.

———. "Chronology." Washington, DC: World Bank, n.d. http://web.worldbank.org/WBSITE/EXTERNAL/EXTABOUTUS/EXTARCHIVES/0,,contentMDK:20035653~menuPK:56305~pagePK:36726~piPK:36092~theSitePK:29506,00.html (accessed September 26, 2008).

———. "Project Database." World Bank, n.d. http://web.worldbank.org/WBSITE/
  EXTERNAL/PROJECTS/0,,menuPK:41389~pagePK:95863~piPK:95983~tar
  getDetMenuPK:228424~targetProjDetPK:73230~targetProjResPK:95917~tar
  getResMenuPK:232168~theSitePK:40941,00.html (accessed September 6, 2008).
———. *World Development Report*. Washington, DC: World Bank, various years.
"World Bank: E Asia Developing Nations Need Infrastructure." *Dow Jones International News*, January 23, 2004.
"World Bank: Got a Light?" *The Economist*, June 26, 1993, 81.
"World Bank: Latin America Needs Infrastructure Investment." *Dow Jones International News*, April 14, 2004.
"World Bank Degradation." *Multinational Monitor*, May/June 2004, 4.
"World Bank Report: A Way Out for 'Marginalised' Africa Sought." *Financial Times*, November 22, 1989.
"World Bank/IDA-2: Rubin Noted 'Enormous Resentment.'" *Dow Jones International News*, October 3, 1996.
Yarbrough, Beth V., and Robert M. Yarbrough. *Cooperation and Governance in International Trade: The Strategic Organizational Approach*. Princeton, NJ: Princeton University Press, 1992.

House Appropriations Subcommittee Documents

"Author" cited in notes as *House Appropriations Subcommittee*.

U.S. Congress. House. Committee on Appropriations. Subcommittee on Foreign Operations and Related Agencies. *Foreign Assistance and Related Agencies Appropriations for 1972: Hearings Before a Subcommittee of the Committee on Appropriations, House of Representatives, Ninety-second Congress, First Session*. Washington, DC: U.S. Government Printing Office, 1971.
———. *Foreign Assistance and Related Agencies Appropriations for 1973: Hearings Before a Subcommittee of the Committee on Appropriations, House of Representatives, Ninety-second Congress, Second Session*. Washington, DC: U.S. Government Printing Office, 1972.
———. *Foreign Assistance and Related Agencies Appropriations for 1974: Hearings Before a Subcommittee of the Committee on Appropriations, House of Representatives, Ninety-third Congress, First Session*. Washington, DC: U.S. Government Printing Office, 1973.
———. *Foreign Assistance and Related Agencies Appropriations for 1977: Hearings Before a Subcommittee of the Committee on Appropriations, House of Representatives, Ninety-fourth Congress, Second Session*. Washington, DC: U.S. Government Printing Office, 1976.
———. *Foreign Assistance and Related Agencies Appropriations for 1978: Hearings Before a Subcommittee of the Committee on Appropriations, House of Representatives, Ninety-fifth Congress, First Session*. Washington, DC: U.S. Government Printing Office, 1977.
———. *Foreign Assistance and Related Agencies Appropriations for 1979: Hearings*

Before a Subcommittee of the Committee on Appropriations, House of Representatives, Ninety-fifth Congress, Second Session. Washington, DC: U.S. Government Printing Office, 1978.

U.S. Congress. House. Committee on Appropriations. Subcommittee on Foreign Operations and Related Programs. *Foreign Assistance and Related Programs Appropriations for 1980: Hearings Before a Subcommittee of the Committee on Appropriations, House of Representatives, Ninety-sixth Congress, First Session.* Washington, DC: U.S. Government Printing Office, 1979.

———. *Foreign Assistance and Related Programs Appropriations for 1981: Hearings Before a Subcommittee of the Committee on Appropriations, House of Representatives, Ninety-sixth Congress, Second Session.* Washington, DC: U.S. Government Printing Office, 1980.

U.S. Congress. House. Committee on Appropriations. Subcommittee on Foreign Operations and Related Agencies. *Foreign Assistance and Related Programs Appropriations for 1982: Hearings Before a Subcommittee of the Committee on Appropriations, House of Representatives, Ninety-seventh Congress, First Session.* Washington, DC: U.S. Government Printing Office, 1981.

———. *Foreign Assistance and Related Programs Appropriations for 1983: Hearings Before a Subcommittee of the Committee on Appropriations, House of Representatives, Ninety-seventh Congress, Second Session.* Washington, DC: U.S. Government Printing Office, 1982.

———. *Foreign Assistance and Related Programs Appropriations for 1984: Hearings Before a Subcommittee of the Committee on Appropriations, House of Representatives, Ninety-eighth Congress, First Session.* Washington, DC: U.S. Government Printing Office, 1983.

———. *Foreign Assistance and Related Programs Appropriations for 1985: Hearings Before a Subcommittee of the Committee on Appropriations, House of Representatives, Ninety-eighth Congress, Second Session.* Washington, DC: U.S. Government Printing Office, 1984.

———. *Foreign Assistance and Related Programs Appropriations for 1986: Hearings Before a Subcommittee of the Committee on Appropriations, House of Representatives, Ninety-ninth Congress, First Session.* Washington, DC: U.S. Government Printing Office, 1985.

———. *Foreign Assistance and Related Programs Appropriations for 1987: Hearings Before a Subcommittee of the Committee on Appropriations, House of Representatives, Ninety-ninth Congress, Second Session.* Washington, DC: U.S. Government Printing Office, 1986.

———. *Foreign Assistance and Related Programs Appropriations for 1988: Hearings Before a Subcommittee of the Committee on Appropriations, House of Representatives, One Hundredth Congress, First Session.* Washington, DC: U.S. Government Printing Office, 1987.

U.S. Congress. House. Committee on Appropriations. Subcommittee on Foreign Operations, Export Financing, and Related Programs. *Foreign Operations, Export Financing, and Related Programs Appropriations for 1989: Hearings Before a Subcommittee of the Committee on Appropriations, House of Representatives, One Hundredth Congress, Second Session.* Washington, DC: U.S. Government Printing Office, 1988.

———. *Foreign Operations, Export Financing, and Related Programs Appropriations for 1990: Hearings Before a Subcommittee of the Committee on Appropriations, House of Representatives, One Hundred First Congress, First Session.* Washington, DC: U.S. Government Printing Office, 1989.

———. *Foreign Operations, Export Financing, and Related Programs Appropriations for 1991: Hearings Before a Subcommittee of the Committee on Appropriations, House of Representatives, One Hundred First Congress, Second Session.* Washington, DC: U.S. Government Printing Office, 1990.

———. *Foreign Operations, Export Financing, and Related Programs Appropriations for 1992: Hearings Before a Subcommittee of the Committee on Appropriations, House of Representatives, One Hundred Second Congress, First Session.* Washington, DC: U.S. Government Printing Office, 1991.

———. *Foreign Operations, Export Financing, and Related Programs Appropriations for 1993: Hearings Before a Subcommittee of the Committee on Appropriations, House of Representatives, One Hundred Second Congress, Second Session.* Washington, DC: U.S. Government Printing Office, 1992.

———. *Foreign Operations, Export Financing, and Related Programs Appropriations for 1994: Hearings Before a Subcommittee of the Committee on Appropriations, House of Representatives, One Hundred Third Congress, First Session.* Washington, DC: U.S. Government Printing Office, 1993.

———. *Foreign Operations, Export Financing, and Related Programs Appropriations for 1995: Hearings Before a Subcommittee of the Committee on Appropriations, House of Representatives, One Hundred Third Congress, Second Session.* Washington, DC: U.S. Government Printing Office, 1994.

———. *Foreign Operations, Export Financing, and Related Programs Appropriations for 1996: Hearings Before a Subcommittee of the Committee on Appropriations, House of Representatives, One Hundred Fourth Congress, First Session.* Washington, DC: U.S. Government Printing Office, 1995.

———. *Foreign Operations, Export Financing, and Related Programs Appropriations for 1997 and Supplemental for 1996: Hearings Before a Subcommittee of the Committee on Appropriations, House of Representatives, One Hundred Fourth Congress, Second Session.* Washington, DC: U.S. Government Printing Office, 1996.

———. *Foreign Operations, Export Financing, and Related Programs Appropriations for 1998: Hearings Before a Subcommittee of the Committee on Appropriations, House of Representatives, One Hundred Fifth Congress, First Session.* Washington, DC: U.S. Government Printing Office, 1997.

———. *Foreign Operations, Export Financing, and Related Programs Appropriations for 1999: Hearings Before a Subcommittee of the Committee on Appropriations, House of Representatives, One Hundred Fifth Congress, Second Session.* Washington, DC: U.S. Government Printing Office, 1998.

———. *Foreign Operations, Export Financing, and Related Programs Appropriations for 2000: Hearings Before a Subcommittee of the Committee on Appropriations, House of Representatives, One Hundred Sixth Congress, First Session.* Washington, DC: U.S. Government Printing Office, 1999.

———. *Foreign Operations, Export Financing, and Related Programs Appropriations for 2001: Hearings Before a Subcommittee of the Committee on Appro-*

priations, House of Representatives, One Hundred Sixth Congress, Second Session. Washington, DC: U.S. Government Printing Office, 2000.

———. *Foreign Operations, Export Financing, and Related Programs Appropriations for 2002: Hearings Before a Subcommittee of the Committee on Appropriations, House of Representatives, One Hundred Seventh Congress, First Session.* Washington, DC: U.S. Government Printing Office, 2001.

———. *Foreign Operations, Export Financing, and Related Programs Appropriations for 2003: Hearings Before a Subcommittee of the Committee on Appropriations, House of Representatives, One Hundred Seventh Congress, Second Session.* Washington, DC: U.S. Government Printing Office, 2002.

———. *Foreign Operations, Export Financing, and Related Programs Appropriations for 2004: Hearings Before a Subcommittee of the Committee on Appropriations, House of Representatives, One Hundred Eighth Congress, First Session.* Washington, DC: U.S. Government Printing Office, 2003.

———. *Foreign Operations, Export Financing, and Related Programs Appropriations for 2005: Hearing Before a Subcommittee of the Committee on Appropriations, House of Representatives, One Hundred Eighth Congress, Second Session, 2004.* Washington, DC: U.S. Government Printing Office, 2004.

House Authorizing Subcommittee Documents

"Author" cited in notes as *House Authorizing Subcommittee.*

U.S. Congress. House. Committee on Banking and Currency. Subcommittee on International Finance. *To Provide for Increased Participation by the United States in the International Development Association: Hearing, Ninety-second Congress, First Session, on H.R. 8750, July 6, 1971.* Washington, DC: U.S. Government Printing Office, 1971.

———. *Providing for Additional U.S. Contributions to the Asian Development Bank and the International Development Association: Hearings, Ninety-third Congress, First Session.* Washington, DC: U.S. Government Printing Office, 1973.

U.S. Congress. House. Committee on Banking, Currency and Housing. Subcommittee on International Development Institutions and Finance. *To Provide for Increased Participation by the United States in the Inter-American Development Bank: Hearing Before the Subcommittee on International Development Institutions and Finance of the Committee on Banking, Currency and Housing, House of Representatives, Ninety-fourth Congress, First Session, on H.R. 8905 . . . July 29, 1975.* Washington, DC: U.S. Government Printing Office, 1975.

U.S. Congress. House. Committee on Banking, Finance, and Urban Affairs. Subcommittee on International Development Institutions and Finance. *International Development Association Sixth Replenishment and African Development Bank Membership.* Washington, DC: U.S. Government Printing Office, 1980.

———. *The Future of the Multilateral Development Banks: Report of the Subcommittee on International Development Institutions and Finance of the Committee* on Banking, Finance, and Urban Affairs, House of Representatives, 97th Congress, Second Session. Washington, DC: U.S. Government Printing Office, 1982.

———. To Provide for Increased Participation by the United States in the International Bank for Reconstruction and Development, the International Finance Corporation, and the African Development Fund: Hearing Before the Subcommittee on International Development Institutions and Finance of the Committee on Banking, Finance, and Urban Affairs, House of Representatives, Ninety-ninth Congress, First Session on H.R. 1948 . . . April 16, 1985. Washington, DC: U.S. Government Printing Office, 1985.

———. The U.S. Role in Development Banks: Hearing Before the Subcommittee on International Development Institutions and Finance of the Committee on Banking, Finance, and Urban Affairs, House of Representatives, Ninety-ninth Congress, First Session, July 18, 1985. Washington, DC: U.S. Government Printing Office, 1985.

———. A Mandate for Development: The Future of the World Bank: Hearing Before the Subcommittee on International Development Institutions and Finance of the Committee on Banking, Finance, and Urban Affairs, House of Representatives, Ninety-ninth Congress, First Session, September 5, 1985. Washington, DC: U.S. Government Printing Office, 1986.

U.S. Congress. House. Committee on Banking, Finance, and Urban Affairs. Subcommittee on International Development, Finance, Trade, and Monetary Policy. Structural Adjustment and Economic Development in Africa: Hearing Before the Subcommittee on International Development, Finance, Trade, and Monetary Policy of the Committee on Banking, Finance, and Urban Affairs, House of Representatives, One Hundred First Congress, Second Session, April 24, 1990. Washington, DC: U.S. Government Printing Office, 1990.

———. Authorizing Contributions to IDA, GEF, and ADF: Hearing Before the Subcommittee on International Development, Finance, Trade, and Monetary Policy of the Committee on Banking, Finance, and Urban Affairs, House of Representatives, One Hundred Third Congress, First Session, May 5, 1993. Washington, DC: U.S. Government Printing Office, 1994.

U.S. Congress. House. Committee on Banking and Financial Services. Subcommittee on Domestic and International Monetary Policy. Administration's Plan for Authorization of FY 96 Funding for the International Financial Institutions: Hearing Before the Subcommittee on Domestic and International Monetary Policy of the Committee on Banking and Financial Services, House of Representatives, One Hundred Fourth Congress, First Session, May 2, 1995. Washington, DC: U.S. Government Printing Office, 1995.

———. The Administration's Authorization Requests for International Financial Institutions: Hearing Before the Subcommittee on Domestic and International Monetary Policy of the Committee on Banking and Financial Services, House of Representatives, One Hundred Fourth Congress, Second Session, April 25, 1996. Washington, DC: U.S. Government Printing Office, 1996.

U.S. Congress. House. Committee on Financial Services. Subcommittee on International Monetary Policy and Trade. FY 2002 Authorization Requests for International Programs: Hearing Before the Subcommittee on International Monetary

Policy and Trade of the Committee on Financial Services, U.S. House of Representatives, One Hundred Seventh Congress, First Session, June 12, 2001. Washington, DC: U.S. Government Printing Office, 2001.

Senate Appropriations Subcommittee Documents

"Author" cited in notes as *Senate Appropriations Subcommittee.*

U.S. Congress. Senate. Committee on Appropriations. Subcommittee on Foreign Operations. *Foreign Assistance and Related Programs Appropriations for Fiscal Year 1979: Hearings Before a Subcommittee of the Committee on Appropriations, United States Senate, Ninety-fifth Congress, Second Session, on H.R. 12931....* Washington, DC: U.S. Government Printing Office, 1978.

———. *Foreign Assistance and Related Programs Appropriations for Fiscal Year 1982: Hearings Before a Subcommittee of the Committee on Appropriations, United States Senate, Ninety-seventh Congress, First Session.* Washington, DC: U.S. Government Printing Office, 1981.

———. *Foreign Assistance and Related Programs Appropriations for Fiscal Year 1987: Hearings Before a Subcommittee of the Committee on Appropriations, United States Senate, Ninety-ninth Congress, Second Session on H.R. 5339/ S. 2824.* S. Hrg., vol. 99-872. Washington, DC: U.S. Government Printing Office, 1987.

U.S. Congress. Senate. Committee on Appropriations. Subcommittee on Foreign Operations, Export Financing, and Related Programs. *Foreign Operations, Export Financing, and Related Programs Appropriations for Fiscal Year 1991: Hearings Before a Subcommittee of the Committee on Appropriations, United States Senate, One Hundred First Congress, Second Session, on H.R. 5114.* S. Hrg., vol. 101-1093. Washington, DC: U.S. Government Printing Office, 1990.

———. *Foreign Operations, Export Financing, and Related Programs Appropriations for Fiscal Year 1992: Hearings Before a Subcommittee of the Committee on Appropriations, United States Senate, One Hundred Second Congress, First Session, on H.R. 262.* S. Hrg., vol. 102-295. Washington, DC: U.S. Government Printing Office, 1991.

———. *Foreign Operations, Export Financing, and Related Programs Appropriations for Fiscal Year 1993: Hearings Before a Subcommittee of the Committee on Appropriations, United States Senate, One Hundred Second Congress, Second Session, on H.R. 5368.* S. Hrg., vol. 102-947. Washington, DC: U.S. Government Printing Office, 1992.

———. *Foreign Operations, Export Financing, and Related Programs Appropriations for Fiscal Year 1994: Hearings Before a Subcommittee of the Committee on Appropriations, United States Senate, One Hundred Third Congress, First Session, on H.R. 2295.* S. Hrg., vol. 103-430. Washington, DC: U.S. Government Printing Office, 1994.

———. *Foreign Operations, Export Financing, and Related Programs Appropriations for Fiscal Year 1999: Hearings Before a Subcommittee of the Committee on*

Appropriations, United States Senate, One Hundred Fifth Congress, Second Session, on H.R. 4569/S. 2334. S. Hrg., vol. 105-809. Washington, DC: U.S. Government Printing Office, 1999.

———. *Foreign Operations, Export Financing, and Related Programs Appropriations for Fiscal Year 2001: Hearings Before a Subcommittee of the Committee on Appropriations, United States Senate, One Hundred Sixth Congress, Second Session, on H.R. 4811 and 5526/S. 2522.* S. Hrg., vol. 106-821. Washington, DC: U.S. Government Printing Office, 2001.

Index